Here are your
1995 SCIENCE YEAR
Cross-Reference Tabs

For insertion in your WORLD BOOK

Each year, SCIENCE YEAR, THE WORLD BOOK ANNUAL SCIENCE SUPPLEMENT, adds a valuable dimension to your WORLD BOOK set. The Cross-Reference Tab System is designed especially to help you link SCIENCE YEAR's major articles to the related WORLD BOOK articles that they update.

How to use these Tabs:

First, remove this page from SCIENCE YEAR.

Begin with the first Tab, **BLACK HOLE**. Take the B volume of your WORLD BOOK set and find the **Black hole** article. Moisten the **BLACK HOLE** Tab and affix it to that page.

Glue all the other Tabs in the appropriate WORLD BOOK volumes. Your set's V volume may not have an article on **Virtual reality**. Put the **VIRTUAL REALITY** Tab in its correct alphabetical location in that volume—near the **Virus** article.

SCIENCE Year

1 9 9 5

The World Book Annual Science Supplement

A review of Science and Technology
During the 1994 School Year

World Book, Inc.

a Scott Fetzer company
Chicago London Sydney Toronto

The Year's Major Science Stories

From the successful mission to fix the Hubble Space Telescope to the discovery of a vast ancient city under Mexican cropland, it was an eventful year in science and technology. On these two pages are the stories that *Science Year* editors picked as the most memorable, exciting, or important of the year, along with details about where you will find information about them in the book.   *The Editors*

Tracking the top quark
Physicists announced in April 1994 that they had found evidence of the top quark, one of the basic building blocks of matter and the last undiscovered quark of the six predicted by theory. In the Special Reports section, see CONVERSATION WITH A PARTICLE SMASHER. In the Science News Update section, see PHYSICS.

Buried archaeological treasure ▲
In February 1994, an archaeologist reported the discovery of a vast city that flourished about 1,500 years ago near present-day Veracruz, Mexico. In the Science News Update section, see ARCHAEOLOGY.

Swollen rivers ▲
Unusual weather conditions led to record flooding in the Midwestern United States in summer 1993. In the Special Reports section, see THE COST OF TAMING A RIVER. In the Science News Update section, see ATMOSPHERIC SCIENCE.

World Book, Inc.
525 W. Monroe
Chicago, IL 60661

ISBN: 0-7166-0595-3
ISSN: 0080-7621
Library of Congress Catalog Number: 65-21776
Printed in the United States of America.

"Lucy" era skull
Anthropologists announced in March 1994 the discovery of the first nearly complete skull of *Australopithecus afarensis*, the earliest known humanlike species. In the Science News Update section, see ANTHROPOLOGY.

California quake
Movement along a previously unknown blind thrust fault on Jan. 17, 1994, caused southern California's costliest earthquake to date. In the Science News Update section, see GEOLOGY [Close-Up]. ▼

Radiation revelations ▲
United States officials acknowledged in 1993 and 1994 that secret, government-sponsored experiments during the 1940's to 1970's had intentionally exposed some citizens to radiation. In the Science News Update section, see SCIENCE AND SOCIETY [Close-Up].

Human embryo cloning
Scientists in October 1993 reported that they had cloned cells from human embryos, sparking a debate over the ethics of such experiments. In the Special Reports section, see CLONING RESEARCH ON THE MARCH.

◄ **Repaired Hubble Telescope finds black hole**
During a record-setting five spacewalks in December 1993, astronauts successfully repaired the Space Telescope, and astronomers soon used the device to provide conclusive evidence of the existence of black holes. In the Special Report section, see THE SEARCH FOR BLACK HOLES. In the Science News Update section, see SPACE TECHNOLOGY [Close-Up].

Contents

Page 76

Science News Update 204

Twenty-eight articles, arranged alphabetically, report on the year's major developments in all areas of science and technology, from "Agriculture" and "Archaeology" to "Science and Society" and "Space Technology." In addition, six Close-Up articles focus on especially noteworthy developments:

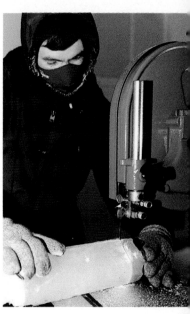

Page 232

Page 306

Science You Can Use 309

Five articles present various aspects of science and technology as they apply to the consumer.

World Book Supplement 329

Twelve new or revised articles from the 1994 edition of *The World Book Encyclopedia*: "Laser," "Magnetism," "Computer chip," "Materials," "Transplant," plus seven new articles about dinosaurs.

Page 330

Index 353

A cumulative index of topics covered in the 1995, 1994, and 1993 editions of *Science Year*.

Cross-Reference Tabs

A tear-out page of cross-reference tabs for insertion in *The World Book Encyclopedia* appears before page 1.

Staff

■ **Editorial**

Managing Editor
Darlene R. Stille

Associate Editor
Jinger Hoop

Senior Editors
Meira Ben-Gad
John Burnson
Mary Carvlin
David L. Dreier
Mark Dunbar
Lori Fagan
Carol L. Hanson

Contributing Editors
Karin C. Rosenberg
Rod Such

Editorial Assistant
Ethel Matthews

Cartographic Services
H. George Stoll, Head
Wayne K. Pichler

Index Services
Beatrice Bertucci, Head
David Pofelski

■ **Art**

Executive Director
Roberta Dimmer

Senior Designer,
Science Year
Cari L. Biamonte

Senior Designers
Melanie J. Lawson
Brenda Tropinski

Art Production Assistant
Stephanie K. Tunney

Photography Director
John S. Marshall

Senior Photographs Editor
Sandra M. Dyrlund

Photographs Editor
Julie Laffin

■ **Research Services**

Director
Mary Norton

Library Services
Mary Ann Urbashich, Head

■ **Production**
Daniel N. Bach, Vice President
of Production and
Technology

Manufacturing/Pre-Press
Sandra Van den Broucke,
Director
Barbara Podczerwinski
Joann Seastrom
Julie Tscherney

Proofreaders
Anne Dillon
Daniel Marotta

Text Processing
Curley Hunter
Gwendolyn Johnson

Permissions Editor
Janet Peterson

Publisher Emeritus
William H. Nault

Editorial Advisory Board

Contributors

Andrews, Peter J., B.A., M.S.
Free-Lance Writer and Biochemist.
[Science You Can Use: *Preserving Your Family's Keepsakes*]

Asker, James R., B.A.
Space Technology Editor,
Aviation Week & Space Technology Magazine.
[*Space Technology*]

Bakker, Robert T., B.S., Ph.D.
Adjunct Curator,
University of Colorado Museum, Boulder.
[Special Report, *Unearthing the Jurassic*]

Bartusiak, Marcia, B.A., M.S.
Free-Lance Science Writer.
[Special Report, *The Search for Black Holes*]

Baskin, Yvonne, B.A.
Free-Lance Science Writer.
[Special Report, *A New Look at the Endangered Cheetah*]

Bolen, Eric G., B.S, M.S., Ph.D.
Dean, Graduate School,
University of North Carolina, Wilmington.
[*Conservation*]

Brett, Carlton E., M.A., Ph.D.
Professor,
Department of Earth and Environmental Sciences,
University of Rochester.
[*Fossil Studies*]

Brody, Herb, B.S.
Senior Editor,
Technology Review Magazine.
[Special Report, *Gearing Up for the Information Superhighway*]

Cain, Steve, B.S.
News Coordinator,
Purdue University School of Agriculture.
[*Agriculture*]

Chiras, Dan, B.A., Ph.D.
Adjunct Professor of Environmental Policy and Management,
University of Denver.
[*Environment*]

Coffin, John M., B.A., Ph.D.
American Cancer Society Research Professor of Molecular Biology and Microbiology,
Tufts University.
[Special Report, *Exploring the Mysteries of the Retrovirus*]

Coleman, Ellen J., M.A., M.P.H., R.D.
Sports Nutritionist,
The Sport Clinic.
[Science You Can Use: *A Scientific Look at Sports Drinks*]

Cosgrove, Daniel J., Ph.D.
Professor of Biology,
Pennsylvania State University.
[*Biology*]

Ferrell, Keith
Editor,
Omni Magazine.
[Special Report, *Welcome to the Virtual World; Computers and Electronics*]

Fisher, Arthur, B.A., M.A.
Science and Technology Editor,
Popular Science Magazine.
[Science Studies: *The Promise of Renewable Energy*]

Freidel, David A., B.A., Ph.D.
Professor of Anthropology,
Southern Methodist University.
[*Archaeology* (Close-Up)]

Goodman, Richard A., M.D., M.P.H.
Adjunct Professor, Division of Epidemiology,
Emory University.
[*Public Health*]

Graff, Gordon, Ph.D.
Technical Editor,
McGraw-Hill Incorporated, and Free-Lance Science Writer.
[*Chemistry*; Science You Can Use: *Choosing the Right Gasoline*]

Gregory, Stanley V., B.S., M.S., Ph.D.
Professor of Fisheries and Wildlife,
Oregon State University.
[Special Report, *The Cost of Taming a River*]

Hay, William W., Ph.D.
Professor of Geology,
University of Colorado, Boulder.
[*Geology*; *Geology* (CloseUp)]

Haymer, David S., Ph.D.
Associate Professor,
Department of Genetics,
University of Hawaii.
[*Genetics*]

Hester, Thomas R., B.A., Ph.D.
Professor of Anthropology and Director,
Texas Archeological Research Laboratory,
University of Texas, Austin.
[*Archaeology*]

Jones, William Goodrich, A.M.L.S.
Assistant University Librarian,
University of Illinois at Chicago.
[*Books of Science*]

King, Lauriston R., Ph.D.
Assistant Professor of Political Science,
Texas A&M University;
Member, Ocean Governance Study Group.
[*Oceanography*]

Klein, Richard G., Ph.D.
Professor of Anthropology,
Stanford University.
[*Anthropology*]

Kowal, Deborah, M.A.
Adjunct Professor,
Division of International Health,
Emory University.
[*Public Health*]

Lapidus, Leah Blumberg, B.A., M.A., Ph.D.
Professor and Clinical Psychologist,
Columbia University.
[*Psychology*]

Latter, John H., B.A., D.I.C., Ph.D.
Volcanologist,
Institute of Geological & Nuclear Sciences.
[Special Report, *The Biggest Eruptions on Earth*]

Lechtenberg, Victor L., B.S., Ph.D.
Interim Dean of Agriculture,
Purdue University.
[*Agriculture*]

Limburg, Peter R., B.A., M.A.
Free-Lance Science Writer.
[Science You Can Use: *Paper or Plastic: Which Bag Is Better for the Environment?*]

Lunine, Jonathan I., B.S., M.S., Ph.D.
Associate Professor of Planetary Sciences,
University of Arizona.
[*Astronomy* (Solar System)]

March, Robert H., Ph.D.
Professor of Physics,
University of Wisconsin.
[*Physics*]

McKinnell, Robert Gilmore, Ph.D.
Professor of Genetics and Cell Biology,
University of Minnesota.
[Special Report, *Cloning Research on the March*]

Meyer, B. Robert, M.D.
Director,
Department of Medicine,
Bronx Municipal Hospital.
[*Drugs*]

Moser-Veillon, Phylis B., Ph.D.
Professor,
Department of Nutrition and Food Science,
University of Maryland.
[*Nutrition*]

Radetsky, Peter, B.A., M.A., Ph.D.
Lecturer,
Science Communication Program,
University of California, Santa Cruz.
[Science You Can Use: *Snuffing Out the Sniffles*]

Sforza, Pasquale M., B.Ae.E., M.S., Ph.D.
Professor and Head of Aerospace Engineering,
Polytechnic University.
[*Energy*]

Snow, John T., Ph.D.
Dean,
College of Geosciences,
University of Oklahoma.
[*Atmospheric Sciences*]

Snow, Theodore P., B.A., M.S., Ph.D.
Director, Center for Astrophysics and Space Astronomy,
Professor of Astrophysics,
University of Colorado, Boulder.
[*Astronomy; Astronomy* (Close-Up)]

Stephenson, Joan, B.S., Ph.D.
Chief, Chicago Bureau,
International Medical News Group.
[*Medical Research*]

Tamarin, Robert H., B.S.,Ph.D.
Professor and Chairman,
Department of Biology,
Boston University.
[*Ecology*]

Teich, Albert H., B.S., Ph.D.
Director,
Science and Policy Programs,
American Association for the Advancement of Science.
[*Science and Society; Science and Society* (Close-Up)]

Terr, Lenore C., M.D.
Child and Adolescent Psychiatrist and Author.
[*Psychology* (Close-Up)]

Truxal, John G., Sc.D., D.Eng.
Distinguished Teaching Professor Emeritus,
State University of New York, Stony Brook.
[Special Report, *Is It Worth the Risk?*]

Woods, Michael, B.S.
Science Editor
The (Toledo, Ohio) *Blade*.
[*Engineering*]

Page 12

Page 28

Page 60

Page 44

The Search for Black Holes

Astronomers believe they have found proof of the existence of black holes, objects so dense that not even light can escape them.

BY MARCIA BARTUSIAK

In the celestial zoo, there is no stranger creature than a black hole. It is the astronomical equivalent of the kraken, an enormous sea monster that coils its long tentacles around unwary ships and pulls them down to their doom. But the kraken exists only in legend. Black holes, more incredible and fearsome than any terror of the deep, are real—or so astronomers are now convinced.

The name *black hole* is an apt one for these monsters of the depths of space. They are objects with such powerful gravity that nothing, not even light, can escape from them. A black hole is an utterly dark abyss—one that draws matter and energy to itself and holds them in an iron grip.

The proof that black holes exist is accumulating rapidly. Astronomers have been reporting evidence of probable black holes for several years, and in May 1994 astronomers using the recently repaired Hubble Space Telescope announced the most conclusive observation yet. They said a swirling concentration of matter at the center of a galaxy known as M87 could be explained only by the presence of a huge black hole with the *mass* (quantity of matter) of up to 3 billion suns.

Black holes come in various sizes, theorists believe. Many are formed from the collapsed remnants of very large stars. Others, like the near-certain black hole in M87, are supermassive objects lurking at the heart of some galaxies. There may even be mini black holes, far smaller than an atom, that originated in the *big bang*, the huge explosion of matter and energy that scientists think gave birth to the universe some 15 billion years ago.

Because black holes have such strange characteristics, physicists and astronomers thought for years that they existed only on paper, as a mysterious solution to a set of mathematical equations. That black holes might actually exist seemed beyond the bounds of possibility. Since the late 1960's, however, most doubts about the reality of black holes have been dispelled, and astronomers have been searching the heavens for them.

Early ideas about "dark stars"

Although the search for black holes began fairly recently, the idea of black holes can actually be traced back more than two centuries, to early speculations about the nature of gravity. The first person to theorize the existence of anything like a black hole was an English scientist and church rector named John Michell. In 1783, Michell suggested that if a star were as dense as the sun but had a diameter 500 times larger, the star's gravity would be so powerful that no light could escape from it. The star would appear as a black void in space.

The author:
Marcia Bartusiak is a free-lance writer specializing in astronomy and physics.

Today, scientists know that the kind of star Michell was imagining can't exist in nature. Still, Michell's work explored a concept that is vital to our present-day understanding of black holes, the notion of escape velocity. Escape velocity is the speed that something—a cannonball, space shuttle, or anything else—must attain to break free of another object's gravitational pull. The stronger the gravitational pull, the greater the speed necessary. Michell calculated that the escape velocity for his gargantuan star would be greater than the speed of light (which is now known to be 299,792 kilometers [186,282 miles] per second). Like a stone thrown into the air, a ray of light moving outward from the giant star would curve back downward.

The concept of escape velocity is based on fundamental discoveries about gravity made in the 1600's by the English physicist and mathematician Isaac Newton. Newton had found that the gravitational attraction between two objects is related to the distance between them. If the distance between two bodies is halved, the gravitational force between them becomes four times as great. If the distance doubles, the attraction decreases to one-fourth what it had been. The distance measurement in these calculations is the distance from one object's center of mass to that of the other object. The center of mass is the point around which an object's mass is evenly distributed.

If two objects are touching, the distance between their centers of mass could be made shorter if one or both of the objects could be squeezed into a smaller volume. Consider the example of the Earth and a space shuttle. If the Earth could somehow be compressed to half its normal diameter, a space shuttle on a launching pad would be half as far from Earth's center of mass as before. As a result, Earth's gravitational pull on the shuttle would be four times stronger, and the escape velocity would increase by 1.414 (the square root of 2—escape velocity increases by a different amount than gravitational attraction).

Newton's formula shows that Michell's scenario is not the only way to imagine a star whose gravity prevents light from escaping. The same result would occur if an ordinary star were somehow compressed into a small enough volume. As the star shrank, its surface would get closer and closer to its center of mass, and the escape velocity at the surface would climb. At some point, the star would be so compact and dense that the escape velocity would exceed the speed of light.

Einstein enters the picture

Until the 1900's, speculations about such "dark stars"—no one had yet called them black holes—were considered interesting but of no practical concern. But then the work of the German-American physicist Albert Einstein in 1916 provided a new theory of gravity that led to our present understanding of black holes.

The key to understanding Einstein's view of gravity is his notion that three-dimensional space is intimately linked with a fourth dimension, time, to form what he called space-time. According to Einstein's general theory of relativity, gravity is a distortion of the four dimensions of space-time—rather than invisible tendrils of attraction between objects, as Newton had assumed. We can envision this by thinking of space-time as a boundless rubber sheet. Large masses, such as a star, indent the flexible mat of space-time much the way a bowling ball would create a depression in a soft mattress. Any rocket, planet, or light beam skimming by the star would follow the natural depression

The physics of a black hole

The first black holes were discovered on paper, when physicists calculated the gravitational pull of very massive and dense stars. Scientists knew that an object at the surface of such a star would have to accelerate to tremendously high speeds to break free of the star's intense gravity. If the star's matter were packed densely enough, nothing, not even the star's own light, could travel fast enough to escape.

Scientists can calculate the gravitational pull of a star in terms of the *escape velocity* associated with it—the speed an object must attain to break free of the star's gravity. The escape velocity for a spaceship or any other object on the sun, for example, is 624 kilometers per second (388 miles per second). A spaceship moving at a lower speed would eventually fall back to the sun.

The laws of physics say that the gravitational attraction between two objects increases as the centers of the objects get closer together. If two objects are already in contact with each other, this increase could occur only if the matter in one or both of the objects were compressed into a smaller volume. For example, if the sun could somehow be squeezed to half its diameter, the escape velocity for a spaceship at its surface would rise to 882 kilometers per second (548 miles per second).

Escape velocity less than speed of light

Physicists imagined what would happen if a star became smaller and smaller without losing any of its mass. Because the star's outer edge would get ever closer to the center of the star, the escape velocity would get increasingly higher.

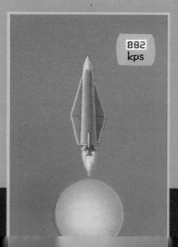

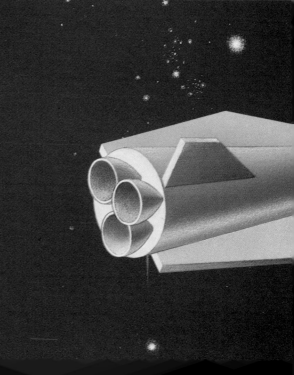

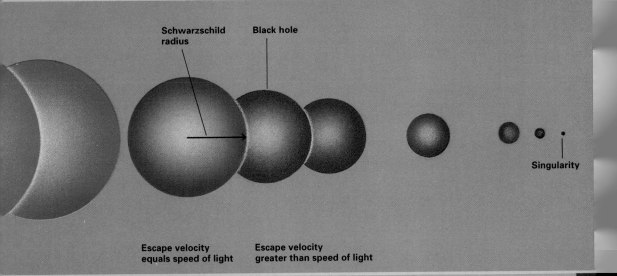

Schwarzschild radius

Black hole

Singularity

Escape velocity equals speed of light

Escape velocity greater than speed of light

When the star is squeezed down to a certain size, the escape velocity equals the speed of light—299,792 kilometers (186,282 miles) per second. The distance from the center of such a star to its outer edge is called the *Schwarzschild radius*. The Schwarzschild radius varies according to a star's mass—the more massive the star is, the longer the radius. Once a star shrinks within the Schwarzschild radius, not even light can escape from it. It has become a black hole.

According to scientists' calculations, any object that is squeezed within its Schwarzschild radius will continue to contract by gravity. Within a moment, it contracts to a point of infinite density called a *singularity*.

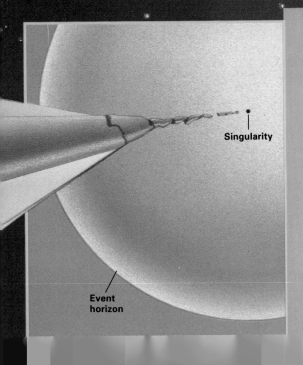

Singularity

Event horizon

A black hole consists of both the singularity and a spherical region of empty space traced out by the Schwarzschild radius. The surface of that sphere is an invisible boundary known as the *event horizon*. An unwary spaceship that crossed that point of no return would be drawn helplessly toward the singularity. In its final moments, the ship would be stretched like taffy by the enormous gravitational field of the singularity and then torn to pieces before being crushed out of existence. But the fate of the doomed spaceship would be unseen by anyone watching from outside the event horizon, to whom the black hole would look like an utterly dark and featureless disk. That is why the boundary of a black hole is called the event horizon—because no event that occurs within it can be observed from outside the black hole.

How black holes are born

Astronomers and physicists think the heavens are populated by three kinds of black holes, each of which formed in a different manner. "Ordinary" black holes were created by the collapse of large stars. Supermassive black holes formed at the heart of many galaxies. And mini black holes may have been created during the explosive birth of the universe.

From burned-out stars

Two types of stars can turn into black holes when they run out of the fuel that keeps them burning.

An extremely large star—one about 8 to 25 times as massive as the sun—usually dies violently as a *supernova* (exploding star). If the core of the star that remains after the explosion contains at least three times the mass of the sun, it will collapse from the weight of its own gravity, shrinking past the Schwarzschild radius and becoming a black hole.

The core of a star that is more than 25 times as massive as the sun may collapse without creating an explosion. If the core is at least three times as massive as the sun, it will shrink past the Schwarzschild radius to form a black hole.

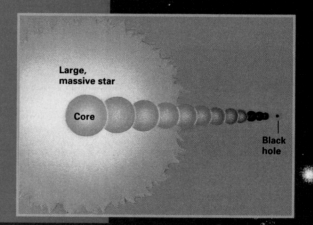

in space-time carved out by the star. If the object veered too close, it might fall into the star.

As soon as Einstein published his equations, researchers began trying to discover their implications, seeing with pen and paper how the new and improved view of gravity operated in certain situations. In 1916, a paper written by the German astronomer Karl Schwarzschild explored what would happen if all the mass of an object such as the sun were squeezed down to a very small size. It was during this theoretical tinkering that Schwarzschild revealed the strange and astounding properties of what we now call black holes.

Schwarzschild determined that a mass compressed to a small enough size would be surrounded by a spherical region of empty space-time

From matter in the center of galaxies

Scientists believe that supermassive black holes formed at the center of many galaxies in the early days of the universe. In a young galaxy, huge gas clouds and swarms of stars rotate in a swirling mass. At the center of the galaxy, stars and gas clouds may become so closely packed that they are drawn together by gravity, eventually forming a single large mass. Continued gravitational contraction produces a black hole with the mass of millions or billions of suns.

Merging stars and gas

Stars and gas clouds at center of young galaxy

Supermassive black hole

From the violent birth of the universe

Countless mini black holes may have formed in a fraction of a second during the *big bang,* the titanic explosion of matter and energy that gave birth to the universe. The tremendous pressures within the big bang could have squeezed pockets of subatomic particles to incredibly high densities, converting them to mini black holes far smaller than an atom.

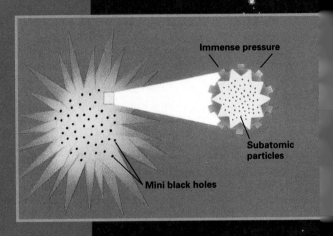

Immense pressure

Subatomic particles

Mini black holes

from which nothing—not a particle of matter nor a glimmer of light—could escape. The radius of this sphere, called the *Schwarzschild radius,* is the point where the escape velocity from the object is exactly equal to the speed of light, the ultimate speed limit in the universe. The radius varies according to the amount of mass. The greater the mass, the larger the Schwarzschild radius.

The outer edge of the spherical region of empty space-time is a crucial element of a black hole. It marks a gravitational point of no return. This boundary is known as the *event horizon,* because no event that occurs within it—where the escape velocity is even higher than the speed of light—can be observed from the outside. Once you crossed that invisible border, there would be no way out, only a sure plummet into the pit in space-time dug out by the black hole. Neither would there be any way of communicating with those you left behind, because any radio signal directed to the outside world would be trapped by the intense gravitational field. Completely cut off from the rest of the universe, you would be on a one-way trip to oblivion. Your bizarre journey would end only when the black hole's tremendous gravity stretched you like a rubber band, tore you to pieces, and finally crushed you out of existence.

General relativity showed that any quantity of matter—a million stars or a handful of sand—could become a black hole if it could be squeezed into a small enough sphere. The Schwarzschild radius for the sun, for example, is about 3 kilometers (2 miles). If the sun could be forced into a sphere with that radius, no light could escape from it, and it would be a black hole. Its light extinguished, the sun would then continue to contract under its own gravity. Within a tiny fraction of a second, it would shrink to a point called a *singularity*. All the sun's mass would be contained in that one point. The event horizon would remain at a distance of 3 kilometers from the singularity.

From neutron stars to black holes

Schwarzschild's calculations were essentially an academic exercise. After all, how could any mass be compressed within its Schwarzschild radius? In the late 1930's, however, theoretical work directed by the American physicist J. Robert Oppenheimer (who later headed the development of the first atomic bomb) indicated that our universe might actually be churning out black holes as the end point in the lives of very massive stars.

Oppenheimer contemplated a star that has exhausted its store of hydrogen. Hydrogen fuels the nuclear reactions in the *core* (central region) that produce a star's tremendous heat and light. The outward pressure of the hot gases provides a counterbalance to the inward pull of the star's gravity. When the nuclear reactions cease, the core of the star is no longer able to support itself, and gravity causes it to contract. For a star as massive as our sun, the core shrinks to about the size of the Earth and continues to glow as a star called a white dwarf. The white dwarf's gravity cannot jam the star's atoms any closer. For a star a bit heavier than the sun, however, the core collapses even further to form a tiny *neutron star,* a ball about 30 kilometers (18.6 miles) wide consisting purely of subatomic particles called neutrons. Here the mass of a million Earths is packed into a sphere the size of a city. A teaspoonful of a neutron star would weigh about a billion tons.

But what if the star is even more massive? Oppenheimer and his collaborators showed that there is a maximum mass for a neutron star, now believed to be about three times that of the sun. Above that mass, not even tightly packed neutrons can withstand the force of gravity. Collapse to a black hole is inevitable.

While Oppenheimer's findings were certainly fascinating, most astronomers regarded them as no more than a mathematical speculation. It was still somewhat radical to believe that a star could even be scrunched into a neutron star. A Swiss-American astronomer, Fritz Zwicky, had suggested in 1934 that *supernovae* (exploding stars) were associated with the formation of neutron stars, but no one took the idea very seriously. A star shrinking to a black hole seemed more unlikely still.

Astronomers' indifference to the subject of collapsed stars didn't change much until the 1960's. Credit for finally arousing their interest goes to the noted theorist John A. Wheeler of Princeton University in New Jersey. Wheeler felt certain that stars undergoing the ultimate collapse had a reality beyond the equations in Oppenheimer's dust-covered journal articles. Perhaps Wheeler's greatest contribution was in finally naming these bizarre objects. In 1967, he dubbed them *black holes*, a name that caught on at once.

Wheeler's certainty that black holes must exist was further advanced by recent developments in astronomy. Earlier in 1967, astronomers had finally detected their first neutron star, and by the end of 1968 at least two dozen more had been identified. Today, astronomers know of hundreds of neutron stars. As Zwicky had predicted, many of them were found to be the remnants of supernovae. Once it was confirmed that neutron stars truly inhabit the heavens, the thought of black holes became easier to contemplate.

With black holes finally a respectable subject for study, theorists began to imagine the various forms black holes can take. Schwarzschild's calculations dealt with nonrotating black holes, but most black holes probably rotate. That is because black holes—at least ones of any appreciable size—are formed from stars. And stars, like just about everything else in the universe, from planets to galaxies, rotate. In a rotating black hole, Einstein's equations revealed, the singularity would be a ring rather than a point. Space travelers venturing into a large, rotating black hole could conceivably pass through the ring without harm—if they had enough energy and technological know-how to keep the passage open. But where would that lead? Some theorists have speculated that a black hole punches through space-time and ends up in a separate universe or in another part of our universe. If true, a ring singularity could be a tunnel to those otherworldly destinations. But such ideas cannot be verified for now. Indeed, recent calculations suggest that stray radiation from space falling into a black hole would pinch off the tunnel. So, cosmic portholes of this sort may be closer to science fiction than science fact.

Black holes from single stars—or billions of them

What does seem to be a fact is that black holes exist, and that becoming a black hole is the inevitable end point of the most massive stars. Although just one star in millions is massive enough to end its life as a black hole, the typical galaxy contains at least 100 billion stars, so black holes resulting from collapsed stars would hardly be rarities. The Milky Way alone probably contains hundreds of them.

How to find a black hole

Although black holes do not emit light, astronomers know how to search for them—by looking for their effects on nearby stars and gas clouds.

A black hole in a *binary* (two-star) system should be fairly easy to spot, because the black hole's strong gravity tears gases away from the visible star. The gas swirls around the event horizon in a flattened cloud called an *accretion disk* before being swallowed up. Friction and pressure in the disk cause the gases to become exceedingly hot and to emit X rays, which could be detected from Earth.

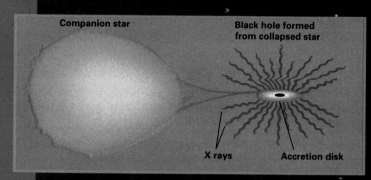

Companion star

Black hole formed from collapsed star

X rays

Accretion disk

A supermassive black hole in another galaxy may make its presence known even more dramatically. The accretion disk of such a huge black hole could be so big that it would be visible in astronomers' telescopes. Other visible signs of a supermassive black hole would be jets of *plasma* (hot, electrically charged gases) shot far into space by the disk's magnetic lines of force.

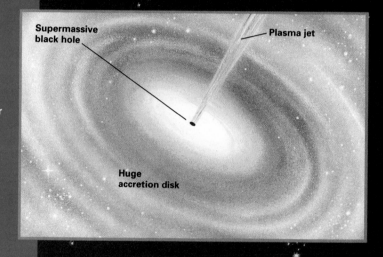

Supermassive black hole

Plasma jet

Huge accretion disk

Since the 1960's, research on very massive stars has clarified how they can become black holes. A star with a mass more than about eight times that of the sun usually ends its life as a supernova when its core runs out of fuel, collapses under its own weight, and forms a neutron star. Additional matter falling onto the rigid surface of the neutron star rebounds in a shattering explosion that rips apart the outer layers of the original star. A neutron star is often the surviving remnant of a supernova. But a neutron star that gains extra mass during the explosion may become massive enough to collapse further into a black hole.

Astronomers think that in very massive stars—those with a total mass more than about 25 times that of the sun—the core may already have enough mass to become a black hole. When such a star's nuclear reac-

Mini black holes should be detectable because of a phenomenon called *Hawking radiation,* a type of radiation emitted just outside the event horizon. According to physicists' calculations, Hawking radiation causes black holes to lose tiny amounts of mass over time. The loss is insignificant for large black holes, but many mini black holes created during the big bang should now be running out of matter. Physicists think that in its final hours, a mini black hole becomes tremendously hot and then explodes, producing a detectable burst of high-energy radiation called gamma rays.

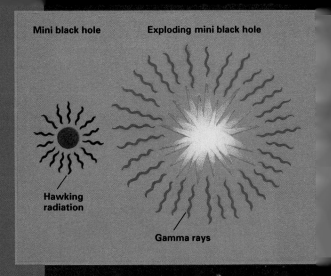

Mini black hole

Exploding mini black hole

Hawking radiation

Gamma rays

The collision and merger of two black holes should produce *gravity waves,* "spacequakes" that travel at the speed of light from the site of violent celestial events. Researchers are now trying to detect these waves with highly sensitive instruments.

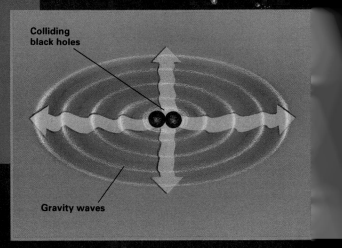

Colliding black holes

Gravity waves

ions cease, no supernova occurs. The star's core just quietly shrinks and becomes a black hole.

Even more awesome than black holes resulting from collapsed stars are the supermassive black holes that astronomers suspect lie at the center of the Milky Way and many other large galaxies. These enormous black holes are thought to have formed when galaxies were first taking shape, as huge gas clouds and dense herds of stars were drawn together by their mutual gravity. Galactic black holes may be so massive that they have an event horizon hundreds of millions of kilometers across, making some of them comparable in size to the Earth's orbit about the sun.

Well before reporting the almost certain presence of a supermassive black hole in the M87 galaxy in 1994, astronomers had found indirect evidence for these gigantic black holes. They did so by observing the motions of stars in nearby galaxies, including our closest large neighbor, the Andromeda galaxy. In 1987, for example, astronomers Alan Dressler of the Observatories of the Carnegie Institution of Washington, in Pasadena, Calif., and Douglas O. Richstone of the University of Michigan in Ann Arbor studied stars in the central part of Andromeda. They found that the stars in that region of the galaxy are crowded together and move unusually fast, suggesting that the stars are racing around a dark central object containing the mass of up to 70 million suns.

Supermassive black holes are thought to explain the tremendous fountains of energy spewing from the celestial objects known as quasars. These dazzling objects, situated billions of light-years away from us at the edge of the visible universe, were first sighted in the 1960's. (A light-year is the distance light travels in one year, about 9.5 trillion kilometers [5.9 trillion miles].) Astronomers theorize that quasars are galaxies in an early stage of life. In each quasar, they believe, a supermassive black hole at the center of the developing galaxy is consuming nearby stars and gas, in the process emitting as much energy as a trillion suns.

That energy, according to the theory, is produced when matter being drawn toward the black hole orbits the hole in a tightening spiral called an *accretion disk,* as if it were water flowing down a space-time drain. As the matter gets ever closer to the hole, it accelerates to nearly the speed of light. Compression and friction cause the matter to become progressively hotter, until its temperature is in the tens of millions of degrees. The hot gases emit enormous amounts of radiation and high-energy particles.

Astronomers don't think there are many quasars around today, because the quasars we now see at the edge of the visible universe were emitting their stupendous energies when the universe was young. We are just now seeing them because it took billions of years for their light to reach us across the vast expanse of space. Many nearby galaxies were undoubtedly also quasars long ago, until their central black holes ran out of nearby matter to consume.

Mini black holes and their disappearing act

At the opposite extreme from supermassive black holes are mini black holes. The possible existence of these objects was first suggested in 1971 by British physicist Stephen Hawking of Cambridge University. Hawking suggested that the incredible densities that existed in the turbulent first moments of the big bang could have compressed pockets of matter into countless tiny black holes.

At about the same time, Hawking surprised the scientific community by announcing that "black holes ain't so black." They emit radiation, though in very tiny amounts. Hawking realized this after studying the effects of *quantum mechanics*—the physical laws governing the world of

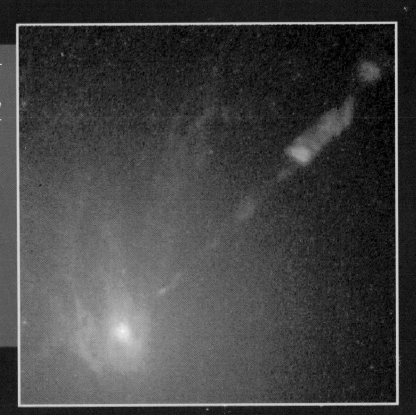

A bright disk of hot gases glows at the heart of a galaxy named M87, shown in a 1994 Hubble Space Telescope image. Calculations indicate that the disk of gases is rotating so fast that it must be swirling around a huge black hole with the mass—and gravity—of up to 3 billion suns. A jet of matter streams away from the disk toward the upper right. In May 1994, astronomers reported that the Hubble data on M87 provided conclusive evidence that black holes exist.

elementary particles—in the vicinity of black holes. According to quantum mechanics, even the vacuum of space isn't really empty. It is filled with pairs of *virtual particles*—subatomic particles, created from energy "borrowed" from the vacuum, that blink into fleeting existence. Ordinarily, virtual particles exist for the briefest of moments before vanishing again. At the event horizon of a black hole, however, things can work out a bit differently. The black hole's strong gravity can draw one virtual particle over the event horizon. At the same time, the other member of the pair extracts enough energy from the black hole's gravitational field to become a real particle that moves away from the hole. Because matter and energy are equivalent—that is, one can be transformed into the other—the black hole loses a bit of mass whenever this phenomenon occurs.

For a massive black hole, this quantum-mechanical process, known as *Hawking radiation*, is insignificant. A black hole with the mass of a few suns would need more than 10 million trillion trillion trillion trillion trillion years to shrink away to nothingness in this manner. But for a mini black hole, these mass losses are very significant. The tiniest black holes would have disappeared long ago, but ones with the mass of a mountain would be shedding the last of their mass right about now. At the end, according to this theory, a mini black hole dies in a final and violent burst of pure energy. Astronomers have not yet detected any unusual bursts of radiation from space that would indicate minihole explosions, but they are keeping their sensors tuned for the distinctive pop, just in case.

Looking for black holes

Although astronomers may never be able to detect a mini black hole, the search for larger black holes is heating up. But how do you see something that by definition cannot be seen? By looking for telltale celestial footprints. Even though a black hole itself is invisible, its incredibly powerful gravitational field would wreak havoc on surrounding matter, and those effects can be detected. If a black hole is a member of a *binary* (two-star) system, for example, it would tear gases away from its partner and gobble them up. X rays emitted by the accretion disk could be detected by astronomers' instruments.

Astronomers suspect that such a process is generating the powerful X rays being emitted from a source in the Milky Way known as Cygnus X-1 (because of its location in the constellation Cygnus the Swan). Cygnus X-1 was first spotted in the 1960's, when pioneering rocket flights lofted sensitive X-ray detectors far above Earth's atmosphere. Follow-up observations with ground-based optical and radio telescopes determined that Cygnus X-1's X rays come from a binary system in which a giant bluish star orbits an invisible companion once every 5½ days. The orbital motion of the visible star tells astronomers that the unseen object must have a mass 6 to 15 times that of our sun. The dark companion is unlikely to be a normal star because a star so massive would almost certainly be visible. And it cannot be a neutron star because a neutron star cannot have a mass more than three times that of the sun. That leaves one other suspect: a black hole.

Cygnus X-1 was astronomy's first prime candidate for a black hole, and only a handful of other possible black holes formed from dead stars have been found so far. Among them are V404 Cygni, another suspicious object in Cygnus; LMC X-3, an erratic X-ray source in a nearby galaxy called the Large Magellanic Cloud; and A0620-00, an orange sunlike star whipping around a dark companion in the Monoceros constellation.

While astronomers must rely on circumstantial evidence to deduce the presence of these black holes, they are finding that they can often observe the accretion disks around suspected supermassive black holes directly. Many of the largest black holes, including ones that once powered quasars, are apparently now sitting quietly at the centers of galaxies, having devoured all the matter in their vicinity. But some have evidently flared up again, forming a new accretion disk. That could happen when a black hole has been provided with more stars and gas to feed on—as occurs, for example, when galaxies occasionally collide.

The accretion disk around a supermassive black hole that is swallowing large amounts of matter can be so enormous, stretching across much of the core of a galaxy, that it can be visible in telescopes. The acccretion disk of the apparent black hole in M87 is an estimated 500 light-years in diameter. Some of the matter in an accretion disk, in the form of a *plasma* (hot, electrically charged particles), is deflected upward or downward along magnetic lines of force generated by the disk. A jet of matter is visible in M87, and astronomers have observed such jets streaming out of certain other galaxies.

The search for black holes should be aided by a form of astronomical observation that researchers began working on in the 1960's: gravity-wave detection. According to Einstein's theory of general relativity, gravity waves radiate outward in all directions at the speed of light whenever space-time is fiercely disrupted—as would happen when a star collapses into a black hole. Unlike light waves, gravity waves do not travel *through* space. They are "spacequakes," agitations of the fabric of space-time itself. Anyone in the path of the waves would experience space-time contracting and expanding, though these gravitational quivers would be very subtle and hard to detect once they had expanded across vast stretches of space. Gravity waves from a star that had exploded in a distant corner of the Milky Way would change the dimensions of the page you are reading, but by no more than one-thousandth the width of a proton, one of the particles in an atomic nucleus.

Around the world in 1994, physicists were operating finely tuned instruments to detect these incredibly tiny swells in space-time. These gravity-wave "telescopes" function like extremely sensitive versions of a seismometer, the instrument that geologists use to amplify and record the motion of earthquakes. Some gravity-wave detectors use automobile-size cylindrical bars that would "ring" like bells whenever a sizable gravity wave passed through them. Others employ a set of suspended weights that would sway ever so slightly as a series of gravity waves alternately squeezed and stretched the space between them.

The strongest gravity waves we could detect would be generated by the collision and merger of two nearby black holes. That could occur in a binary system in which both stars had become black holes. It might also be possible to discern supermassive black holes in far-off galaxies as they devour their celestial victims. Whatever a black hole was up to, it would give itself away by the distinctive ripples it transmits through space-time. If scientists are able to detect those unmistakable signatures, they will have added to the mounting visible evidence of black holes. Such findings ensure that the black hole, far from being a mythological beast, is a full-fledged member of the celestial zoo.

For further reading:

Gribbin, John. *Unveiling the Edge of Time.* Harmony Books, 1992.

Rees, Martin J. "Black Holes in Galactic Centers." *Scientific American,* November 1990, pp. 56-66.

Thorne, Kip. *From Black Holes to Time Warps: Einstein's Outrageous Legacy.* W. W. Norton Company, 1994.

Wald, Robert M. *Space, Time, and Gravity: The Theory of the Big Bang and Black Holes.* University of Chicago Press, 1992.

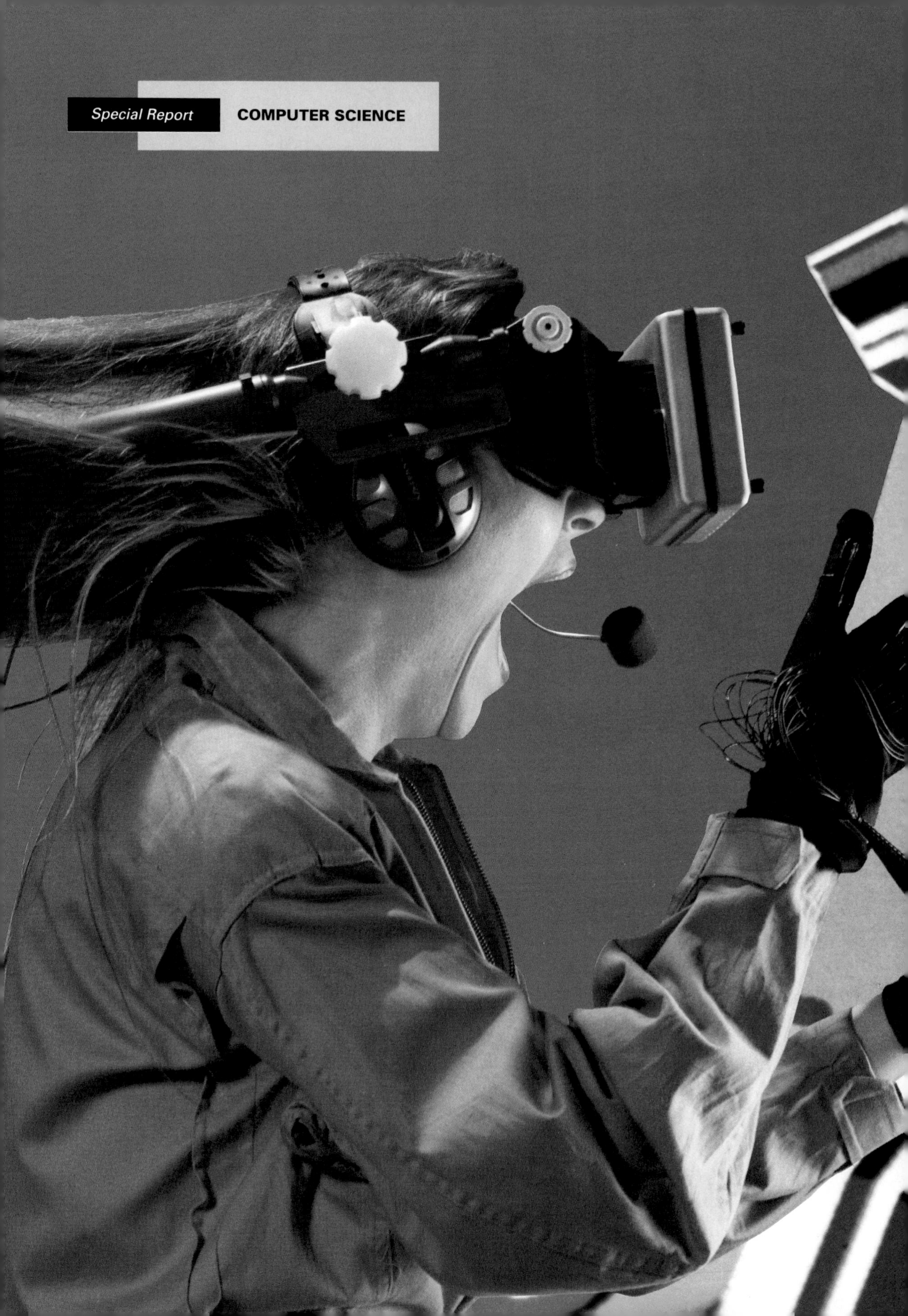

Welcome to the Virtual World

BY KEITH FERRELL

Virtual reality technology will allow computer users to experience sights, sounds, and sensations that mimic those of the real world.

Imagine, many years down the road, taking a tour around your dream home under construction. You have worked hard for this house, and you want it to be perfect. You walk slowly through each room, looking left and right. Almost everything seems satisfactory, but you notice a few small problems. The doors leading onto the patio are too far to the right to afford a good view of the gardens. And the upper cabinets in the kitchen are so high you cannot reach into them easily.

You leave the house to discuss these problems with your architect. But instead of walking out through the front door, you remove gloves laced with wires, step down from a motorized platform, and take off a heavy set of goggles. Immediately, your house vanishes, and you find yourself in your architect's office.

Your dream home exists not in the real world but in the memory of a computer. The computer turned the architect's blueprint of your house into a three-dimensional (3-D) computer model, the goggles displayed video images of the model on tiny television screens, the gloves gave you the illusion of touching and moving objects in the model, and the platform let you walk around it. The computer model of the house was convincing but not real. You've just experienced virtual reality.

Since the early 1990's, the term *virtual reality* (VR) has become a catch phrase used to describe almost any vividly rendered computer graphic. Programmers and computer engineers use the term more strictly, to refer to computer-created environments that users not only look at but also move through and interact with. The environment can be completely imaginary, such as a city populated by giant robots, or it can be a mock-up of a real-world environment, such as the cockpit of an airplane or the surface of Mars.

Complete VR systems are expensive and complicated setups that require powerful computers, elaborate software, and high-tech goggles and other electronic devices. But because the field is fairly new, even today's most sophisticated VR systems are not advanced enough to create completely realistic environments. Experts nevertheless believe that the technology is beginning to come of age and now holds promise for a range of fields—from training and scientific research to entertainment and telecommunications.

Using computers to simulate the real world

Virtual reality can be thought of as a very advanced form of *computer simulation,* the creation of computer models of the real world. In a typical simulation, a researcher feeds data into a computer that has been programmed to estimate how conditions in a physical system change over time. For example, scientists can create a simulation to calculate how populations of fish in a lake respond to fluctuating food levels. Or an engineer might create a simulation to calculate how air currents flow over the surface of a car.

Simulations have been around for decades, and over time they have grown steadily more realistic. In the simplest simulations, the comput-

The author:
Keith Ferrell is editor of *Omni* magazine.

Bringing "reality" to computer models

Virtual reality systems can be thought of as sophisticated *computer simulations,* models of real or imaginary environments. The simplest simulations run on personal computers. More advanced types give users the feeling of actually being in the virtual environment.

A simple flight simulator runs on a personal computer. The screen shows an instrument display and a view of the computerized landscape. A computer user "flies" the plane by moving a joystick or pressing keys on a keyboard.

A more sophisticated simulator for training fighter pilots has a cockpit with controls that respond to the pilot's touch. A wraparound display screen provides a view of the simulated landscape in every direction, enhancing the illusion of flying a real plane.

A virtual reality system enables an astronaut to practice maneuvering the space shuttle's robotic arm. Special equipment blocks out sensations from the real world, allows the astronaut to see the computer environment, and enables him to manipulate objects in the environment by moving his hands.

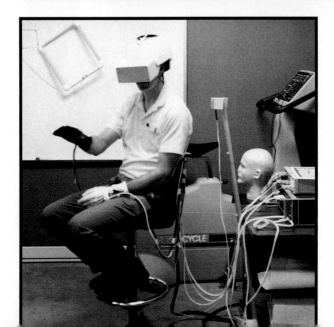

Virtual-reality gear

A user "enters" a virtual environment by wearing devices that project images and stereo sounds and that detect the user's movements. The devices are controlled by a computer, which contains in its memory the characteristics of all the items in the virtual world.

A headset is fitted with two tiny image-display screens—one for each eye—that convey pictures of the virtual landscape. The computer may send slightly different images to the two screens to create the illusion of depth. The headset also contains a pair of speakers for projecting the sound of objects in the virtual world. Finally, sensors in the headset note the movement of the user's head. That information is relayed to the computer, which adjusts the images accordingly.

A bodysuit conveys the user's movement to the computer. For example, the suit may contain electrical wires in which currents arise when the user moves through a magnetic field. The computer detects the pattern of currents to determine what parts of the user's body are moving and how. It then accommodates the changes in the images sent to the headset.

A computer collects data from the headset, gloves, and bodysuit. Using this information, it rapidly calculates the user's position and action in the virtual world; determines what the user should see, hear, and sense through touch; and sends the appropriate data to the headset and gloves.

Special gloves give the user the illusion of interacting with objects in the virtual environment. In some instances, the gloves contain *optical fibers* (thin glass tubes that carry light). The computer monitors the light waves, interprets any changes as hand or finger movements, and adjusts the position of virtual objects that have been "touched" or "grasped." More sophisticated gloves also contain mechanical devices that press against the user's fingertips to give the sensation of touch.

er simply displays columns of numbers that correspond to various features of the model, such as the size of a fish population or the speed of an air current. As computers became more powerful, they could be programmed to display images or diagrams of the simulated model on a monitor. Many programs offering this type of simulation are available today for personal computers (PC's). Such a program may use animation to show the mixing of chemicals in a test tube, for example, or the workings of certain systems in the human body.

Flight simulators are another type of simulation controlled by a computer. In addition to the computer and software, these systems also contain machinery that gives the user the ability to participate in the simulation as if it were the real thing. A pilot interacts with the software by manipulating realistic controls, and he or she feels the cockpit moving appropriately as the simulation proceeds.

Immersion in the computerized world

The goal of virtual reality systems is to allow users to experience the computer simulation even more fully. To increase the realism, VR systems immerse users in the computer's world, providing all the sights, sounds, and sensations of the simulation and also the ability to move through it and interact with it.

To perform this task, a VR system requires several components. The most important is a computer that coordinates the interaction between the user and the virtual world. Sophisticated VR programs require a machine of considerable computing speed. One popular VR computer is the Reality Engine, manufactured by Silicon Graphics, a computer-design firm in Mountain View, Calif. A typical Reality Engine has eight *central processors* (the silicon "chips" inside a computer that carry out instructions), instead of the single central processor found in PC's.

Whatever its speed, a computer can do nothing without the proper software. For VR, programmers must first decide on the boundaries of the virtual world and the objects that can be found within it. Then, experts tell the computer the shape of each object, its location, and what its surface is like. The program is designed to automatically calculate what each object would look like from any angle and under various lighting conditions.

The best computer pictures are as sharp as photographs. Changing the display of such pictures on a computer monitor may require a great deal of time, however, so programmers often compromise by using less realistic images the computer can handle more easily. For this reason, many of the graphics in today's VR programs look unnaturally blocky.

The time required to design a virtual world depends on its complexity. A simple virtual environment could be created by one person on a PC during about 100 working hours. Such a world might consist of only a flat landscape containing a few simple geometric shapes, such as cubes, spheres, and pyramids. At the other end of the extreme is a complex world—for example, a realistic mock-up of part of the surface of another planet. Creating such a complicated design would require

Virtual recreation

A virtual reality arcade game, *above,* allows players to compete in an imaginary environment. Video displays show the players as animated figures, *right.* Another system for recreation allows users to "walk" through a room in which a quartet plays music, *below.* The volume of the music changes depending on where the user stands.

hundreds of times more labor than creating the flat landscape.

A second essential component of a VR system is a monitor that displays images of the virtual world. Most systems use a head-mounted display (HMD) in the form of a helmet or goggles. The HMD contains two tiny color screens, one for each eye. A VR program provides 3-D images by sending slightly different views to the left-eye and right-eye screens. In a program showing the architecture of a house, for example, the computer calculates the angle of view for each eye of a person standing in any part of the building.

To enhance the realism of VR, most HMD's also contain speakers to relay sounds likely to occur in the virtual world. The computer adjusts the volume and timing of the sounds to help create the illusion of a 3-D world. Noises from distant virtual objects sound fainter than noises from closer virtual objects. A virtual car suddenly becomes quieter as it passes behind a virtual building. In addition, HMD's equipped for sound use two earphones or speakers to provide stereo sound. The computer calculates the slight difference in the time each ear would hear a sound and engages each speaker at the proper time. The audio thus reinforces a user's impression of a world with depth.

The computer can adjust the pictures and sounds sent to the user's HMD because special tracking devices tell the computer how the user has moved and which direction his or her head is turned. When the user looks up, for example, the computer sends a picture of the virtual world's sky to the HMD. When the person steps forward, the sound of a rocket or other object in the background grows slightly louder.

In the most widespread tracking system for the position of the user's head, the device is a sensor that consists of three coils of wire oriented in different directions. An identical sensor is placed outside the HMD along with a device that constantly emits radio waves. When the radio waves strike the sensors, they generate magnetic fields. Interactions between the two fields cause weak electric currents to flow through each of the three coiled wires in the sensors. The strength of each current changes as the sensor in the HMD changes its distance or orientation from the fixed sensor. By analyzing the currents, the computer determines the location and position of the HMD.

Simpler devices may allow the computer to monitor the position of the rest of the user's body as it "moves" through the virtual world. For example, the person may stand on a platform that contains a set of movable handle bars. To go forward in the virtual world, the user pushes the handle bars. To stop, the user pulls back on the handle bars, and to change direction, he or she turns them. All those movements cause the platform to send signals to the computer. The computer calculates the user's new position in the virtual world and sends new pictures to the screens in the HMD.

This mechanical type of tracking system is relatively easy to create, but it does not give users the freedom to move naturally. A more sophisticated setup tracks movement using the same technique as HMD tracking systems. The user wears a bodysuit threaded with insulated wires that are connected to the VR computer. Strong magnets in the ceiling create a magnetic field around the user. When the user moves, currents arise in the bodysuit wires that cross the magnetic field. The strength of each current varies according to its distance from the magnet. Using a *voltmeter* (an instrument for measuring the strength of an electric current) attached to each wire, the VR computer can determine which part of the user's body is moving and how.

With any tracking system, the computer must continuously update the sights and sounds of the virtual world. The update rate depends on the speed of the computer. VR programs running on fast PC's can update their images at a rate of only a few pictures per second, much slower than the 24 frames per second motion pictures use to provide the illusion of seamless action. The slow rate in VR systems makes movement through the virtual world seem jerky, with a small but noticeable lag between a user's movement and the corresponding change in the view.

The thorny problem of virtual touch

The final component of a VR system is a device that allows people to manipulate and feel objects in the virtual world. Currently, most virtual reality systems have *tactile* (touch) devices for input—that is, equipment that lets a person adjust the position of virtual objects. One of the first tactile input units was the Dataglove, designed in 1984 by engineer Jaron Lanier. The Dataglove is lined with *optical fibers*—hair-thin glass tubes that conduct light. When a user moves the glove, the fibers bend and twist, and the properties of the light flowing through them changes in subtle ways. The VR computer can analyze these changes, which are detected with the aid of a *photometer* (an instrument for

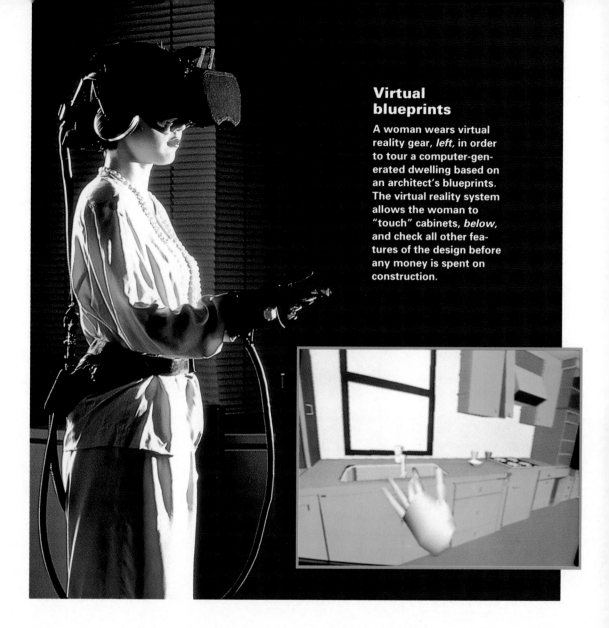

measuring light), to discover how the glove moved. The computer combines this information with the location of the user in the virtual world to determine whether and how the user has manipulated a virtual object. If, for example, the user reaches out to open a virtual door, the computer sends images to the HMD showing the door swinging open.

Manipulating objects is only half the story of virtual touch. True VR systems must provide *tactile output*, the sensation of virtual objects touching the user's skin. Unfortunately, realistic tactile output has been much harder to achieve than input. Researchers have not yet found an effective way to turn contact with a virtual object into real pressure on a user's body. Some devices that have been tried include a bodysuit laced with tiny balloons that inflate along a user's body and a glove with metal strips that press back against a user's fingertips. But no VR system has yet come close to providing realistic touch sensations.

Virtual medicine

Researchers study the bones and muscles in a computerized image of a leg, *right,* in a test of a virtual reality system for medical training. Using special equipment, the researchers can also "dissect" the leg. Another experimental virtual reality program could help people conquer their fear of heights, *below.* In this system, the patient gradually becomes accustomed to heights by riding up and down in a computer-created glass elevator above a courtyard.

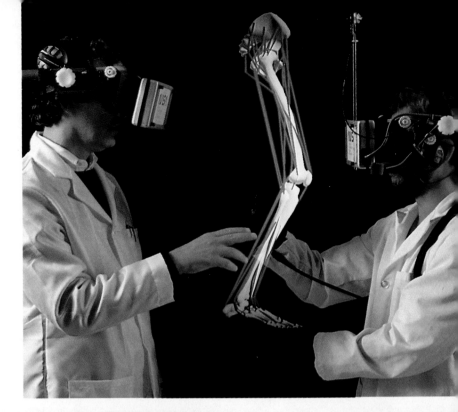

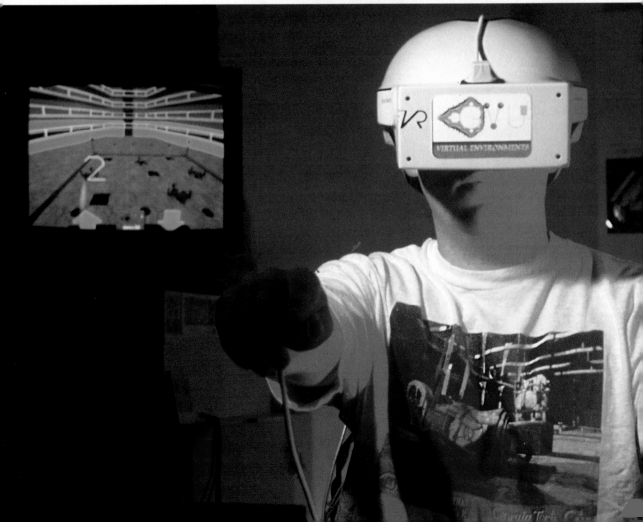

Real-world uses for virtual reality systems

Engineers at several institutions in the United States are investigating practical uses for virtual reality. The technology appeals to researchers for several reasons. First, it can reduce the time and expense involved in engineering and design. For example, architects can use virtual reality to bring their blueprints to life and examine them in detail before any money is spent on construction.

Virtual reality could also be an ideal training tool, especially for dangerous tasks, such as bomb dismantling, or those in hard-to-reach environments. Such training programs may eventually be more practical than traditional methods. Because virtual worlds do not exist physically, VR systems do not require much room to operate. Also, the computer software that controls a virtual world can usually be altered or reprogrammed fairly easily. In fact, the same VR equipment can be used to create any number of distinct worlds.

The National Aeronautics and Space Administration (NASA) has already used virtual reality systems to help prepare astronauts for the challenges of working in space. Astronauts prepared for the 1993 space shuttle mission to repair the Hubble Space Telescope using sophisticated virtual reality models of the tasks they needed to perform. The models mimicked the experience of handling telescope equipment in a weightlessness environment.

Virtual reality could be used to help physicians prepare for complex or high-risk surgical procedures. Imaging techniques such as computerized tomography (CT) and magnetic resonance imaging (MRI) are already available to provide 3-D pictures of patients' anatomy. Virtual reality could let doctors manipulate those images and observe the effect. Thus, a surgeon could rehearse a tricky operation using a virtual patient created from the real patient's CT or MRI scans.

One surgical training system under development in 1994 was designed by Exos, Incorporated, an engineering company located in Woburn, Mass. The Exos system includes a mechanical clamp inside a small box connected to a computer. Also connected to the computer is a large television screen that displays a 3-D image of a patient. To perform virtual surgery, the physician first inserts a scalpel into an opening in the box. The clamp inside the box grabs the instrument and holds it. When the doctor moves the scalpel as if cutting tissue, the clamp relays information to the computer, which determines what the scalpel motions would do to the patient and displays updated images of the patient on the TV screen. The clamp also provides tactile output by mimicking the sensation of cutting a body. If the doctor slices thick tissue in the virtual patient, the clamp slows the movement of the scalpel. If the physician hits bone, the clamp stops the scalpel.

Researchers at the Georgia Institute of Technology in Atlanta in 1994 were testing a virtual reality system designed to give a different group of users the opportunity to practice a procedure they considered dangerous. Researchers there studied the effectiveness of virtual reality as an aid in the treatment of *acrophobia* (the fear of heights). Traditional acrophobia treatment involves training patients to be more

Controlling virtual air traffic

In a virtual reality program for air-traffic control being developed in 1994, a controller would see a three-dimensional display of an airport, showing the altitude, location, and direction of nearby planes. To get information about a flight or to establish communication with a pilot, the controller would simply touch a plane's image.

comfortable with heights by encouraging them to repeatedly imagine being in a high place or by actually taking them to the upper floors of tall buildings or to other heights. The experimental Georgia Tech system was designed to improve this process by saving time and increasing patients' sense of control. In the comfort of a doctor's office, the patient would wear an HMD that presents the view from inside a glass elevator. Using a handheld device with two buttons that control the up-and-down movement of the elevator, the patient would gradually get used to the sensations of traveling to greater and greater heights. As with any VR session, if the situation ever became too difficult or tense, the patient could simply take off the HMD and stop the procedure.

Another major application for VR is telecommunications, primarily for VR's ability to bring together people who are geographically far apart. *Teleconferences*—meetings in which a group of workers are linked by telephone or video hookups—were by 1994 a growing replacement for expensive travel. With virtual reality, the two-dimensional video screens would be replaced by 3-D virtual conference rooms. Workers could see and communicate with other participants, all of whom would appear to be seated at the same virtual table. They could even distribute and handle virtual documents or product models.

NEC Corporation of Japan in 1994 was developing such a "virtual workbench," in which up to five people could work in the same virtual environment. A central computer collects the movement and tactile input of all five users and constantly updates the shared virtual world. With the NEC system, workers could refine the design of a 3-D model together. When one member made a change to the design, all other participants would immediately see the alteration. The five users could be located on different floors of the same office building or different continents. In the latter case, information would be transmitted to and from the central computer via satellite.

Finally, VR holds great potential for its sheer entertainment value. Game manufacturers are particularly excited by the increased degree of realism in VR compared with video games played on TV screens. Several VR games have already hit arcades. One of the most advanced is an arcade game system called Virtuality from W Industries in the United Kingdom. Virtuality players wear an HMD that has two TV screens and four-channel sound. Some Virtuality programs allow multiple players to move through the same virtual environment, depicted as blocky human shapes, and interact with each other. Virtuality machines are located in arcades in about 60 cities in the United States.

Virtual reality has entered the home entertainment market as well, though in a more limited fashion. In the late 1980's, Nintendo Corporation of Japan introduced a version of the Dataglove called the

Virtual engineering

In a virtual reality program at the National Aeronautics and Space Administration (NASA), an engineer studies how air flows across an aircraft under development. Some such programs allow engineers to adjust their designs while in the virtual environment and instantly see the results of their changes.

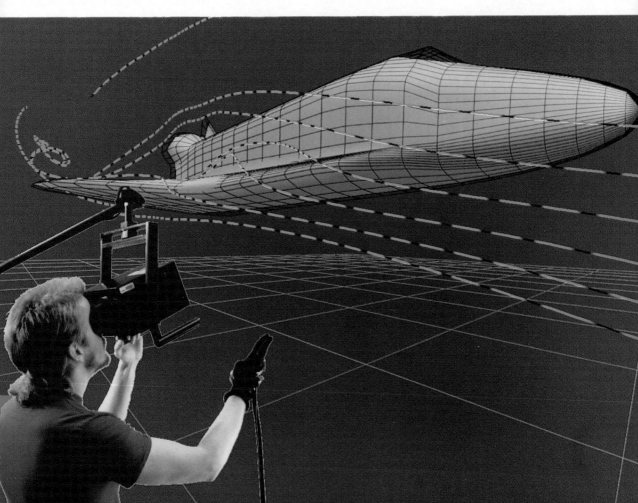

Exploring virtual planets

A NASA researcher works on a virtual reality system for exploring other planets, *left*. The computer uses images from space probes to create a simulation of Mars's surface, *above*. Virtual reality simulations of Mars could be used to train astronauts to guide future Martian surface probes.

Powerglove for use with its video game systems. And in 1994, Sega Corporation of Japan, which also makes video game systems, was set to unveil an HMD in the form of wraparound goggles. The HMD would serve as a replacement for a TV screen and would allow the user to see different parts of the game's landscape by turning his or her head.

Hard realities: Jerky images, less-than-convincing sound

Since the late 1980's, game developers and engineers have made great strides toward creating computer environments that seem to possess the concreteness of real ones. VR gear is becoming more lightweight and flexible every year, thanks to advances in the miniaturization of electronic components and the transmission of data without wires via radio waves. But many obstacles still lie in the path of wholly convincing and affordable VR systems.

Realism of movement is one of the biggest challenges. Our acceptance of an environment as "real" rests not only on the presence of lifelike 3-D images but also on the ability to move among those images at a reasonable speed. One of the great limitations of current VR systems is the jerkiness of the images of the virtual world. The jerkiness is so severe in slow VR systems that some users may feel nauseated. Only the fastest and most expensive computers are powerful enough to collect information from the user's gear, process the information, and update the images and sounds of the virtual world quickly enough to provide the illusion of smooth motion. As computer chips become cheaper and more powerful, experts say, convincing virtual reality will become feasible on smaller and more affordable machines.

Engineers also need to improve the sharpness of virtual images. Virtual worlds lack convincing detail because even the best HMD's offer a resolution less than one-fiftieth the sharpness that the human eye can perceive.

Sound poses another major problem. Current VR software is very good at determining how a person hears sound coming directly from a source. But the programs are not so good at calculating how virtual walls, ceilings, and furniture absorb and reflect sound. In the real world, the objects and surfaces in a room play an important role in creating the final sound. Without those adjustments, sound in a virtual world is less authentic.

Finally, position-tracking and tactile output systems lack both sensitivity and responsiveness. Until the arrival of virtual reality, there was little call for electronic devices capable of tracking a human being's body movements or able to mimic the sensation of objects touching the skin. Experts say that researchers have a lot of work to do before they can build equipment that adequately performs these functions.

If these hurdles can be overcome, however, virtual reality has the potential to become one of the great products of the computer revolution. When that day arrives, the techniques will move out of the computer lab and arcade and into our everyday lives. Instead of going to work in the morning, we may put on a VR outfit and enter a virtual office, where we "meet" co-workers and clients who live around the globe. After work, we may relax by browsing through virtual libraries or exploring virtual museums. Such notions are little more than dreams today, but tomorrow they may well be virtual reality.

For further reading:

Kalawsky, Roy. *The Science of Virtual Reality and Virtual Environments.* Addison-Wesley, 1993.

Sheridan, Thomas B., and Zeltzer, David. "Virtual Reality Check." *Technology Review,* October 1993, pp. 20-28.

A New Look at the Endangered Cheetah

For years, scientists thought genetic problems in the cheetah were helping doom the swift cat to extinction. But new research is casting doubt on that view.

BY YVONNE BASKIN

Glossary

Genes: Components of living cells that are responsible for the transmission of inherited characteristics.

Genetic variation: The degree to which members of a population carry differing forms of the same genes.

Inbreeding: Mating between siblings, cousins, and other close relatives for many generations.

Population bottleneck: A drastic population crash in which most members of a species die.

Savanna: Grassland with scattered trees. The cheetah's native habitat.

A plaintive meow rises from the deep grass inside a large enclosure at the San Diego Wild Animal Park. Suddenly, the grass rustles and a black-spotted golden cat, the size of a large dog, stalks into view. This sleek, powerful animal with amber eyes and the voice of a tiny tomcat is Punchow, a magnificent male cheetah.

Punchow and his kind are the fastest sprinters on Earth, and human beings have admired, captured, and even hunted with them for thousands of years. But now, as humanity carves up the cat's native habitat in Africa, the survival of the cheetah is at stake. So for decades, researchers at zoos and cheetah breeding centers have been trying to boost the cheetah population by encouraging captive cats like Punchow to breed.

Scientists' limited understanding of cheetah biology has made this task extremely difficult, and Punchow himself symbolizes the puzzle biologists face as they work to save these animals from extinction. Punchow may be genetically almost identical to all other members of his species, a possibility that some experts believe accounts for the health problems they have observed in captive cheetahs—for example, poor breeding success and a high susceptibility to disease. Indeed, a researcher armed only with Punchow's lab tests might conclude that the cat is sterile. What is puzzling is that Punchow managed to father nine cubs by two different females the first two times he was bred.

Punchow's reproductive success—and that of other cheetahs in the 1990's—has sparked a debate over how the cheetah's genetic makeup affects the species' chances for survival. Researchers looking at the cats in the wild point out that free-living cheetahs are endangered primarily because their habitat is shrinking and because cheetah behavior prevents the animals from thriving in game reserves. For cheetahs in captivity, changing the way zoos manage the cats appears to boost the success of breeding programs. These developments have led many researchers to look anew at the cheetah—and to conclude that, at least for captive cheetahs, the outlook may not be as gloomy as they had thought.

Portrait of a sprinter

Cheetahs have long been famed as the fastest, and among the most fascinating, short-distance runners in existence. Scientists believe cheetahs can accelerate from walking speed to about 65 kilometers (40 miles) an hour in less than two seconds and briefly explode to top speeds of 110 kilometers (70 miles) an hour. The cheetah arches and bends its flexible spine as it gathers its long front and hind legs beneath its body, then leaps as far as 7 meters (23 feet)—about five times the length of its body—in a single stride. The cat can sustain its full-speed pursuit for only 200 to 300 meters (220 to 330 yards), a distance equal to about two or three football fields. But that can be far enough to allow the cheetah to overtake swift prey, typically a Thomson's gazelle or other small antelope. The cheetah then knocks the

The author:
Yvonne Baskin is a free-lance science writer.

animal to the ground with a forepaw and strangles it with a crushing bite to the throat.

For thousands of years, cheetahs have been prized in royal menageries for their spectacular hunting style, as well as their regal grace and soulful faces, marked by distinctive black lines that curve like a trail of tears from the eyes to the mouth. The structure of cheetahs' windpipes prevents these gentle-looking cats from roaring like lions. Instead, they make sounds described as chirps, stutters, moans, and purrs. Cheetahs can be tamed, and beginning at least 3,000 years ago with the ancient Egyptians, aristocrats commonly trained the cats to hunt just as they trained falcons. A royal chronicle tells how Akbar the Great, who ruled India's Mogul Empire in the A.D. 1500's, captured at least 9,000 cheetahs during his 49-year reign to aid him in hunting deer.

Cheetah conservationists would give a great deal to have Akbar's 9,000 cheetahs back today. Conservationists estimate that around the year 1900, hundreds of thousands of cheetahs lived throughout most of Africa, western Asia, and India. That is no longer the case. The cheetah disappeared from India in the 1940's, and by the 1970's, fewer than 200 survived in Iran, probably the cat's last Asian stronghold. Today, only scattered pockets of cheetahs remain, chiefly in southern and eastern Africa and in the semiarid Sahel region south of the Sahara. Estimates of cheetah numbers are imprecise, because cheetahs, like nearly all wild cats, are shy, stealthy, solitary, and therefore difficult to count. Estimates of the current African cheetah population range from a low of 5,000 to highs of 15,000 to 25,000. Another 1,000 cheetahs live in captivity around the world, some 300 of them in North America.

Wild cheetahs: A struggle to survive

The cheetah is endangered today largely because human beings have taken over much of the cat's habitat and killed off the small antelope the cheetah hunts for food. People have also killed many cheetahs directly. By the early 1970's, the fur trade had become a major threat to large cats such as tigers and cheetahs. At the time, the United States alone was importing 25,000 large-cat skins each year for fur coats, rugs, and other fashion items. Passage of the United States Endangered Species Act in 1973 and the Convention on International Trade in Endangered Species, an international treaty administered by the United Nations, in 1975 gave the cats protected status and reduced the trade in cheetah fur. Nevertheless, cheetahs are still routinely shot by African farmers and ranchers who view the cats as a threat to livestock, just as American ranchers view wolves and mountain lions.

Africa's animal parks and game reserves protect many animals from human beings. However, cheetahs are poorly suited to life in these reserves. Within the borders of a typical game reserve, herd animals such as zebras, wildebeest, and antelope are protected from

An animal built for speed

Cheetahs are the fastest sprinters on Earth, able to reach speeds of 110 kilometers (70 miles) an hour for short distances. A running cheetah can leap five times the length of its body in a single stride, *right*. Special physical features enable the cheetah to perform its high-speed feats, *below*.

Small, aerodynamic head

Extra-wide nasal passages supply oxygen to lungs and heart

Small canine (cuspid) teeth have shallow roots to leave room for broad nasal passages

Flexible spine enables the cheetah to use many muscle groups while running

Sliding shoulder joint lengthens the stride

Light bones

Enlarged lungs, heart, and arteries keep powerful running muscles supplied with oxygen

Muscular tail provides stability

Long legs

Unretractable claws provide traction

human hunters and so thrive in numbers not normally seen on the open *savanna* (grassland with scattered trees). As a result, populations of the large or powerful predators that feed on herd animals—predators such as lions, hyenas, and leopards—also are high. But middle-sized predators such as cheetahs and wild dogs suffer when they are forced to compete in this crowded and confined landscape, according to Timothy M. Caro of the University of California at Davis, who has studied wild cheetahs in Tanzania's Serengeti Plain since 1980.

Cheetahs are handicapped, for example, by the very fact that they can perform spectacular high-speed chases. To catch its breath after making a kill, a cheetah may need to lie panting for up to 30 minutes before it can even begin to eat. During this resting period, hyenas, lions, leopards, and even flocks of vultures may steal the winded cat's kill. According to Caro, 1 in 10 cheetah kills is lost this way. Moreover, unlike most of their competitors, cheetahs will not eat *carrion* (rotting meat). If they lose a kill, they must hunt again to get fresh meat.

Because the cheetah is built for speed and not for fighting, the animal has little chance of fending off lions or hyenas even when it is rested. Its bones are light and its body is thin and elongated, making the cat a poor match for a heavier adversary. And cheetahs are the only cats whose claws are always bared, like those of a dog, rather than being pulled back into protective sheaths. This feature gives cheetahs extra traction for running, but it also dulls the claws and makes them relatively useless for fighting. In addition, the cat's unusually broad nasal passages, which help the cheetah take in a large supply of oxygen while running, leave less room in the skull for the roots of long *canines* (tearing teeth), which are characteristic of lions and other wild cats. As a result, the cheetah's fangs are too short to take on fierce competitors.

Cheetahs face another threat from their larger relatives, Caro discovered. Beginning in 1987, Caro and his student Karen Laurenson attached radio collars to the necks of 20 free-ranging female cheetahs. For the next few years they tracked the cheetahs' movements, and whenever a cheetah had a litter, the researchers periodically examined the cubs. Caro and Laurenson concluded that 95 percent of cheetah cubs born in the Serengeti die before adulthood, most of them while still helpless in their dens, and that 75 percent of these cubs were killed by marauding lions. In protected areas across Africa, the researchers found, a high lion population correlates with a low cheetah population.

Captive cheetahs: A puzzling failure to breed

As cheetah populations have dwindled in the wild, biologists have felt mounting pressure to try to breed cheetahs in captivity. Their task has seemed monumental. Indeed, Akbar the Great unwittingly set a record that was to last 400 years when one of his cheetahs gave birth to a litter of three cubs in the 1500's. Even with thousands of the cats to work with, Akbar's cheetah keepers never recorded producing a second litter. And no other captive births are on record until 1956, when a female in the Philadelphia Zoo also produced a litter of three, all of which died in infancy. A handful of other cheetah births were reported during the 1960's at zoos in Europe and the United States, but not until the early 1970's did a captive-born cub survive to maturity and give birth to a second generation of captive-born cubs. Zoos still had to purchase wild-caught animals to restock their exhibits.

During the 1970's, zoos began to realize the urgency of establishing a self-sustaining population of captive cheetahs, both to avoid taking any more animals from the wild and to build up a pool of cheetahs that might one day be used to restock Africa's remaining savannas. The zoos redoubled their efforts, and the number of captive births rose steadily. Most of these births, however, were at only a few institutions, including the San Diego Wild Animal Park, the Columbus Zoo in Ohio, and Wildlife Safari in Winston, Ore. By the end of the decade, researchers at other zoos began to wonder whether their efforts were being foiled by biological problems in the cheetahs themselves.

A surprising discovery about cheetah biology

In the late 1970's, the National Zoo in Washington, D.C., asked David E. Wildt, then a biomedical researcher working with domestic cats, for help with the cheetah. Wildt collected sperm samples from captive cheetahs belonging to several American zoos. By looking at the samples under a microscope, he found to his surprise that about 70 percent of the sperm were abnormal. The abnormal sperm appeared damaged, with strangely bent or coiled tails or other deformities that would prevent them from penetrating and fertilizing a female's egg.

At first, Wildt thought the abnormalities in the cheetahs' sperm must be a result of the stressful conditions under which most zoo cheetahs were kept. Then, in 1981, Wildt went to South Africa to perform similar studies on male cheetahs at the DeWildt Cheetah Breeding and Research Center, near Pretoria. The South African cats, most of them bred in captivity but including some caught in the wild, showed the same level of sperm abnormalities as cheetahs in U.S. zoos.

To help determine why the cheetah had such high rates of abnormal sperm, Wildt sent blood samples from each male cat to Stephen J. O'Brien, a researcher at the U.S. National Cancer Institute in Bethesda, Md. O'Brien wondered whether the cheetah's reproductive problems were due to a genetic problem, possibly a lack of genetic variation among individual cats. Genes are components of living cells that contain the blueprint for the organism's characteristics and functions. In human beings, for example, genes control the color of

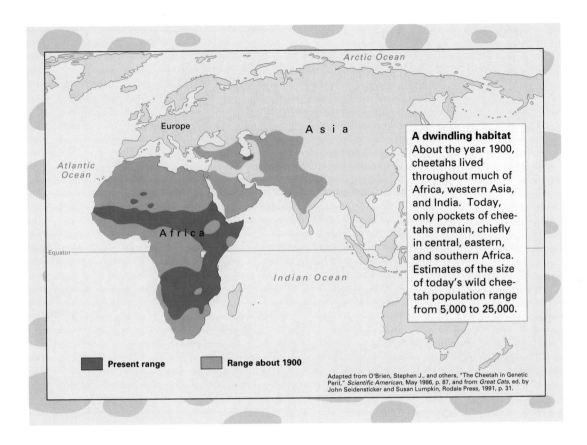

A dwindling habitat About the year 1900, cheetahs lived throughout much of Africa, western Asia, and India. Today, only pockets of cheetahs remain, chiefly in central, eastern, and southern Africa. Estimates of the size of today's wild cheetah population range from 5,000 to 25,000.

Present range Range about 1900

Adapted from O'Brien, Stephen J., and others, "The Cheetah in Genetic Peril," *Scientific American*, May 1986, p. 87, and from *Great Cats*, ed. by John Seidensticker and Susan Lumpkin, Rodale Press, 1991, p. 31.

a person's skin, eyes, and hair, his or her blood type, and all other inherited characteristics. The genes for our species come in many versions, and that genetic variety explains why human beings are not all as alike as identical twins.

Why genetic variation matters

Scientists think genetic variation may be a natural safeguard for a species, because such variation increases the likelihood that individuals will respond differently to most threats that arise. For example, a disease may be deadly to most members of a population, but if a few individuals are genetically different enough to survive it, the species will live on.

Genetic variation may also help guard against the disorders caused by inheriting flawed genes. Generally speaking, organisms inherit two copies of each gene, one from each parent. In human beings and other animal species, most inherited diseases occur only if an individual inherits a flawed version of the same gene from both parents. In a population with a great deal of genetic variation among its members, the odds of both parents having the same flawed gene are low. But in a population without much variation, it may be highly likely

A look at cheetah genetics

Some scientists believe the cheetah is endangered in part because of its genetic makeup. Genes are components of cells that serve as the blueprint for the organism's characteristics and functions. Laboratory studies suggest that all cheetahs are genetically extremely alike, almost as though they were all members of the same family. Some, but not all, scientists believe that such genetic uniformity makes the cheetah susceptible to breeding problems and disease. Other experts say there is no evidence that cheetahs suffer health or reproductive problems as a result of their genetic makeup.

Genetic variation and heredity

All individuals carry two copies of every gene, one inherited from each parent. These two copies can occur in different forms that differ in their effects. For example, one form of a gene that helps determine the texture of an animal's coat may produce soft fur, while another form may produce coarse fur.

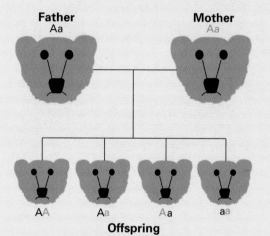

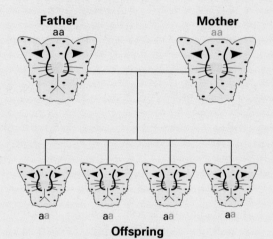

High genetic variation
In a species with high genetic variation, the various forms of genes are likely to be widely distributed throughout the population. This is so because parents are likely to have differing forms of any given gene, and their offspring can inherit either copy of each gene from each parent. Suppose a male and a female each carried one gene for soft fur, *A,* and one gene for coarse fur, *a.* If the two adults mated and produced four cubs, one cub, on average, would carry two *A* genes and one would carry two *a* genes. Two cubs would be likely to carry one *A* and one *a* gene.

Low genetic variation
In a species with low genetic variation, most members of the population are likely to carry two copies of the same form of each gene. If a male and a female each carried two copies of the gene for coarse fur, for example, all of their cubs would inherit that characteristic. Scientists believe such genetic uniformity can result from severe *inbreeding*—in which mating occurs between siblings, cousins, and other close relatives—over many generations.

Uncertain effects of low genetic variation

Problems related to low genetic variation	But do they harm the cheetah?
Because of genetic uniformity, most cheetahs may carry two copies of one or more genes that make the males produce large numbers of abnormal or deformed sperm. Male cheetahs exhibit high levels of sperm abnormalities.	Studies on captive cheetahs have shown that males who have high levels of abnormal sperm may father numerous offspring despite the defect. Other studies have found no evidence that cheetahs are poor breeders in the wild.
Cheetahs may be more likely than most other species to inherit two copies of *mutated* (altered) genes that cause birth defects or other physical problems. Such problems could make newborns unable to survive for long.	Before 1986, 37 percent of newborn cheetahs in North American zoos died, and some scientists assumed the species' genetic similarity was to blame. However, zoos were able to reduce cub mortality to 28 percent, primarily by limiting matings between closely related adults. In the wild, cub mortality may be as high as 95 percent—but most of the cubs are killed by lions, not illness or diseases linked to low genetic variation.
Genetic variation makes some members of a population better able to resist certain diseases than others. Cheetahs' immune systems may be so genetically similar that any disease-causing agent can hit all the animals equally hard.	Scientists cannot say with certainty whether the cheetah population has suffered severe epidemics related to immune problems.

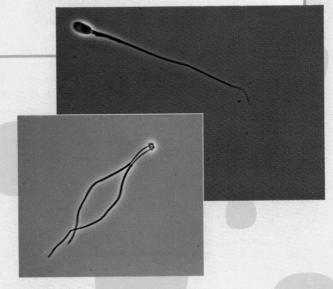

Researchers who examined the sperm of captive and wild-born cheetahs under a microscope found that only some 30 percent of the sperm were normal, *top right*. The remainder, *bottom right,* had deformities that would prevent them from penetrating and fertilizing a female's egg.

that both parents will have the same versions of genes. In such a group, many offspring may be born with inherited disorders.

Genetic variation in the cheetah

To find out if cheetahs showed a lack of genetic variation, O'Brien tested blood samples from 55 of the cats, comparing 52 different proteins found in the blood of each animal. Genes carry the instructions for building proteins, and any slight variation in the makeup of a protein reflects a corresponding variation in a gene. O'Brien found that for nearly all the proteins he tested, the cheetahs in his study had virtually the same genetic makeup. His tests showed that cheetahs may be as similar genetically as mice that scientists have deliberately *inbred*—by mating cousins, siblings, and other close relatives for many generations—to create uniform strains of mice for use in laboratory experiments.

But most of the cheetahs in O'Brien's study had been out of the wild only a generation or two at most, so their genetic uniformity was not the result of in-

Although the cheetah's speed makes it a good hunter, a cheetah must rest for as long as 30 minutes after making a kill before it can begin to eat, *above*. While the cheetah is catching its breath, a lion or other predator may steal the kill, forcing the cheetah to hunt again. Some researchers believe this fact makes the cheetah poorly suited to life in game reserves, where lions and other powerful meat-eaters thrive.

breeding by zoos. How, then, did cheetahs become so similar?

O'Brien speculated that in the distant past, the cheetah population experienced one or more *bottlenecks*—drastic population crashes in which a large proportion of the species died, leaving, perhaps, only a handful of survivors. Using the cheetah's current degree of variability as a guide, O'Brien calculated that the cheetah probably fell to the brink of extinction beginning 12,000 to 10,000 years ago, at the end of the Pleistocene Ice Age, a period in which many other mammals, such as mammoths and saber-toothed cats, became extinct. According to this view, each of the cheetah's population bottlenecks was followed by extreme inbreeding among the few survivors, which in a drastic case may have numbered only a few litters. This inbreeding, continued over many generations, would have eventually produced a population in which nearly all individuals shared the same limited pool of genes.

Not all experts accept the bottleneck theory. A more likely scenario, some say, is that the cheetah population remained abundant but was fragmented into numerous small, isolated subpopulations. Such fragmentation could have taken place toward the end of the Ice Age, as climate fluctuations caused the advance and retreat of ecosystems such as forest and savanna. As a forest extended into a savanna, cutting off one portion from another, the animals on either side of the forest could have been separated and remained so for thousands of years. According to this theory, when one such group died out because of disease, overhunting, or some other reason, its territory was eventually recolonized by a few individuals from a nearby subpopulation. Repeated over and over, this process would eventually lead to a loss of genetic variation.

Population geneticist Philip W. Hedrick of Arizona State University in Tempe is one expert who agrees that the cheetah could have achieved its low genetic variation without its population dropping to the verge of extinction. But Hedrick also points out that several animal species—including beavers in Sweden and northern elephant seals living off the California coast—have low genetic variation, yet their large populations appear to suffer no health or reproductive problems as a result. "We don't really know how much variation is required for a species to be fit and healthy," Hedrick says.

Cheetah genetics: The debate over disease

Thus, a more important question for the cheetah than how it got its low genetic diversity is whether the cat's survival has been compromised by it. Scientists ask, for instance, whether the cheetah's genetic uniformity has indeed made it overly susceptible to disease. To answer that question, they consider a disaster that began in May 1982, when a female cheetah that had been recently brought to Oregon's Wildlife Safari became ill and died from *feline infectious peritonitis* (FIP), a viral disease that strikes domestic cats but is rarely fatal to them. Within the next year, 18 of the 42 cheetahs at the park died of FIP-related illnesses.

O'Brien suggested that the "catastrophic sensitivity" the cheetahs displayed to the virus was a consequence of their lack of genetic variation. In other words, the genes that code for certain defenses in the cheetah's disease-fighting immune system were so similar among the cats that if FIP could evade the defenses of one cat, the same virus could hit all the cheetahs equally hard.

In research published in 1985, O'Brien and his colleagues tested the amount of genetic variation in the cheetah's immune system by grafting patches of skin between pairs of unrelated cheetahs. Normally, when skin or other tissue is transplanted from one individual to another, the recipient's immune system rejects the foreign tissue, attacking and trying to destroy it. Strong drugs are necessary to prevent this rejection response in human transplant patients, and biologists have found that a house cat usually rejects a skin graft from an unrelated cat within 14 days. In contrast, of the 14 cheetahs that received skin grafts in O'Brien's study, only 3 appeared to reject the grafts, and these rejections took 40 days or more. Thus, the investigators concluded, the cheetahs' immune systems must have been genetically very similar.

Signs of hope for the cheetah

Conservationists are working to promote the survival of free-ranging cheetahs in areas where the animals come into conflict with human beings. In addition, biologists and zoo managers are seeking to breed a pool of captive cheetahs that could serve as a reservoir for declining cheetah populations in the wild.

Farmers in southern Africa once routinely shot cheetahs, which they viewed as a threat to their livestock. Today, conservationists have persuaded many farmers not to kill the cheetahs but simply to capture them, *right,* so the animals can be moved to other areas.

Nevertheless, other scientists question whether the cheetahs' vulnerability to FIP resulted from genetic uniformity or simply from the fact that the cats had never before been exposed to the virus. Now that cheetahs have been exposed to FIP, these researchers note, the cats seem to be developing resistance to the disease. Only three captive cheetahs died of FIP between 1987 and 1991, and by 1991 two-thirds of the captive cats in the United States carried *antibodies* (protective proteins) to FIP in their blood, showing that their immune systems had learned to ward off the virus.

A new look at breeding problems

By the early 1990's, scientists were also questioning the link, first suggested by O'Brien and Wildt, between the cheetah's lack of genetic diversity and the cat's poor breeding history in zoos. Caro and his team, for instance, pointed out in 1992 that cheetahs in the wild have the same sperm defects as captive cheetahs, yet they seem to have no breeding problems. Then, in January 1993, researchers working with the Cheetah Species Survival Plan (Cheetah SSP) of the American Zoo and Aquarium Association, based in Bethesda, Md., published the results of nearly five years of exhaustive studies on the North American captive cheetah population. The reports included a detailed study by Wildt of reproduction among 128 cheetahs in American zoos. The males showed the same high levels of abnormal

Some farmers in Africa have also begun to use aggressive animals such as donkeys to guard their herds, *left,* so that shooting cheetahs is not necessary. Cheetahs are easily frightened and are less likely to attack livestock with a donkey as guardian.

sperm Wildt had seen before. But surprisingly, these abnormalities seemed to bear no relation to the animals' fertility. Successful sires like Punchow had lab reports that looked just as bad as those of males that had failed to father cubs.

Other SSP researchers pointed out that even as scientists debated the genetics-fertility link, the tide of opinion in the zoo community was turning away from genetic factors as the chief cause of the cheetah's breeding problems. These researchers noted that as zoos changed how they managed cheetahs, the number of captive births in North America had risen to 201 cubs in 58 litters during the five years between 1987 and 1991. That was nearly half the number of cubs born in these institutions during the previous 30 years. These results convinced most cheetah specialists that the main reason for captive cheetahs' failure to breed lay not with the cheetahs' genes, but with how the cats' keepers have managed them.

A cheetah and her cubs rest in natural surroundings at the Fossil Rim Wildlife Center in Glen Rose, Tex., *above.* Many zoos have begun housing and handling cheetahs to more closely mimic the way these shy cats live in the wild. The result has been a steady increase in births in a species that has traditionally been a poor breeder in captivity.

How successful breeding programs work

Unfortunately, no simple lab tests can help identify just what successful zoos are doing right, though a few strategies are suggested by studies of cheetahs in the wild. For instance, cheetahs seem to breed more readily when they are not housed with other wild cats, where they are intimidated by lions in nearby cages. Another strategy entails keeping female cheetahs alone except for their cubs to mimic their solitary existence on the savanna.

To find out what else goes on in successful breeding programs, SSP researcher Nadja Wielebnowski, another of Caro's students, has spent much time observing the cats in zoos, rather than on the savanna. One thing some successful programs do, she found, is keep the cats in relatively large areas generally secluded from visitors, rather than on exhibit. A second strategy involves keeping a large number of cheetahs on hand so that animals can be introduced to several possible mates. Researchers at the San Diego Wild Animal Park, as well as at other zoos, also have noticed that some females seem to prefer certain males and tend to reject advances by others.

Some of the most successful breeding facilities have set up two separate living areas so that cheetahs can be moved around periodically and be stimulated by seeing and, especially, smelling unfamiliar cheetah neighbors. Zoologists note that because cheetahs are solitary, wide-ranging mammals, their sense of smell is an important means of communication and "courtship" between potential mates. Wielebnowski agrees, adding that a female in the Serengeti may range over 800 square kilometers (300 square miles). Wielebnowski also notes that cheetahs, like other intelligent animals, "seem to get bored and lose interest in their surroundings" if they are deprived of stimulation for prolonged periods. Since 1990, several zoos have tried to combat cheetah boredom by setting up coursing tracks, such as those used for training greyhounds, to encourage cheetahs to do what they do best: run.

Looking toward the future

Despite the evidence that behavioral explanations for the cheetah's low reproductive rates are at least as important as genetic ones, few scientists are complacent about the cat's potential for future genetic problems. For this reason, researchers working with the Cheetah SSP are seeking to preserve whatever genetic variation the cheetah does have. Their plan is to avoid inbreeding by reducing zoos' reliance on cheetahs that have already produced many young and attempting to get offspring from cheetahs that have never bred. In November 1993, the Cheetah SSP management group met to pore over the cheetah studbook, a record of all the cheetahs in North America, which includes family trees for the captive-born animals. The group set out a master plan for the coming year's breeding efforts, choosing 20 male and 20 female cheetahs that are not closely related to most of the cats in the North American population. Because a number of cats chosen for the program are past the normal breeding age, the group plans to use techniques such as artificial insemination to help some of them reproduce.

Zoo breeding successes are extremely heartening, according to zoologist Jack Grisham of the Oklahoma City Zoo, who directs the Cheetah SSP. Grisham has even begun to believe that if zoos don't manage the size of the captive population, they'll eventually run out of room for cheetahs. Still, the captive breeding is just "icing on the cake" for the cheetah species, according to Caro. In his view, boosting populations in this way provides only a temporary stopgap to the loss of cheetahs in the wild.

Unfortunately, few conservation efforts are directed at free-living cheetahs. The most well-known was launched in 1990 by a husband-wife team, conservationists Daniel Kraus and Laurie Marker-Kraus of the National Zoo, who now live in Namibia. This nation on the southwest coast of Africa hosts the world's largest concentration of surviving cheetahs, perhaps as many as 2,500. However, 95 percent of the cats live outside Namibia's reserves and thus come into direct conflict with human beings. The Krauses try to persuade skeptical farmers to ward off cheetahs rather than shoot them when the cats attack their livestock. The conservationists suggest, for instance, that farmers keep cows with vulnerable calves in corrals, or that they use aggressive animals such as horned steers, hard-kicking donkeys, guard dogs, or even baboons to guard their herds against the easily frightened cheetah.

These efforts may buy the cheetah a little more time. It is too early, though, to tell whether biologists will win for wild cheetahs the kind of security that captive cheetahs seem finally to have grasped.

For further reading:

Caro, Timothy M. *Cheetahs of the Serengeti Plains.* University of Chicago Press, 1994.

O'Brien, Stephen J.; Wildt, David E.; and Bush, Mitchell. "The Cheetah in Genetic Peril." *Scientific American,* May 1986, pp. 84-92.

Zoo Biology, January 1993. A special issue devoted to research conducted under the Cheetah Species Survival Plan of the American Association of Zoological Parks and Aquariums.

The severe floods of 1993 and 1994 highlighted the potential drawbacks of altering rivers—increased flood damage and disrupted ecosystems.

The Cost of Taming a River

BY STANLEY V. GREGORY

In summer 1993, unusually heavy rainfall turned the Mississippi River into a powerful, sprawling force. As the river level rose higher and higher, riverside communities scrambled to maintain their levees, wide walls of earth built to contain the river when it rises to flood stage. But by August, the Mississippi had broken through nearly 70 percent of the more than 1,500 levees, carving soil from the land and sweeping across forests and farmlands. In all, 93,000 square kilometers (36,000 square miles) of land were submerged. The damage was immense, with 50 people killed, tens of thousands left homeless, and billions of dollars in property destroyed.

In late 1993, Europeans also suffered from rivers on the rampage. Flooding of the Niers River in the Netherlands and the Aisne River in

France forced thousands of people to abandon their homes for higher ground. The Rhine River, which flows through France, Germany, the Netherlands, and Switzerland, overflowed its banks in what was called that river's worst flooding in 100 years. In the German city of Cologne, for example, the floodwaters drove an estimated 50,000 people from their homes.

Afterward, Americans and Europeans alike considered the role humanity may have played in the tragedies. Community leaders in the United States in particular questioned the wisdom of founding towns and cities so close to riverbanks. Some experts claimed that levees and other "river improvement" projects had actually increased the damage caused by major floods.

Glossary

Dredge: To scrape out sediment from a river or lake.

Ecosystem: Communities of plants, animals, and microbes along with the nonliving features of their environment.

Erode: Wear away.

Meander: A wide curve in the channel of a natural river.

Point bar: A ridge of sand and gravel built up on the inside curve of a river bend.

Pool: An area of deep water at the outside curve of a river bend.

Riffle: An area of shallow water in a river downstream from a pool.

Sediment: Sand, gravel, and organic material that has settled to the bottom of a river or other body of water.

Silt: Fine particles of soil carried by water.

The author:
Stanley V. Gregory is professor of fisheries and wildlife at Oregon State University in Corvallis.

Such ideas have been known to scientists since the 1970's. Before that time, research was very sparse on whether river management had unintended consequences. But since the mid-1970's, studies have shown that rivers are varied and changeable and that attempting to control them may cause unexpected problems—not just for people living in the area, but also for the animals and plants that make the river their home. That research has prompted new ideas about how rivers should be managed and has encouraged attempts to restore selected rivers to a more natural state.

River settlement and civilization

Rivers have long been important to humanity, because they can provide us with water, food, and transportation. For these reasons, human history is in many ways a history of rivers. The great river valleys of Asia, Egypt, and the Middle East, where civilizations first arose, show evidence of thousands of years of human settlement. People in early civilizations must have quickly discovered that the banks of rivers were ideal places to live. There, the soil is fertile and the ready supply of water can be used for agriculture as well as for drinking.

Eventually, people learned to modify rivers to suit their needs—for instance, by damming a river to create a reservoir for use during dry seasons, when less water flowed through the channel. By draining the marshy land alongside rivers, communities created enough dry land to accommodate towns and farms. By constructing levees, they were able to keep the rivers in their channels, at least during mild floods.

In the United States, such projects are older than the nation itself. When periodic floods interrupted the early settlement of a flood-prone area, authorities responded by building levees, dams, or other structures to control the river. Those measures kept the river in its channel and attracted more settlers to the region. As towns grew up, the flood-control structures became more elaborate. The first levee along the Mississippi River was constructed in 1717. By 1858, the river was lined with more than 3,200 kilometers (2,000 miles) of levees. Since then, municipal, state, and federal agencies in the United States have spent hundreds of billions of dollars altering the natural flow of rivers and modifying river channels.

The nature of a natural river

Research into the nature of rivers has helped scientists understand how these changes affect river *ecosystems* (communities of plants, animals, and microbes along with the nonliving features of their environment). On the simplest level, rivers are products of gravity, which forces water to run downhill, following the shortest available route. Beginning as tiny rivulets on a slope, water creates narrow channels that join to form streams and then rivers. Stream ecosystems spread out like ribbons across the landscape, continually merging to form increasingly larger rivers as they flow down to a lake or the sea.

River ecosystems differ widely—according to the type of landscape they pass through, the climate, and a host of other factors. Even a single river is not the same ecosystem throughout its length. A small stream may support less than 10 fish species, for example, while the larger river it becomes downstream may contain 50 to 100 species.

Nevertheless, river ecosystems share several characteristics. All rivers *erode* (wear away) their channels and carry the eroded material downstream. All have natural cycles of high flow, normal flow, and low flow, depending upon the amount of rainfall and ground water that enters the river. Every natural river overflows its banks at one time or another, though only some rivers flood regularly—typically in the spring, when rainfall is heavy and snow is melting.

Life in a river ecosystem

Animal life in almost all natural streams and rivers is richly varied. A single ecosystem is likely to contain many different species of fish, some of which may be important to people as sources of food or for sport fishing. Freshwater clams inhabit the river bottom, and snails cling to plants rooted in the streambed. Amphibians, such as salamanders and frogs, are equally at home in the water and on nearby land, as are certain reptiles such as water-loving snakes and turtles.

Many species of insects abound in and near rivers. Some species hover over the water, some float on the surface, others swim through it, and still others crawl along or burrow under sediment on the bottom. Insects are a major source of food for larger aquatic animals and even for other insects, such as the diving beetle and common water strider.

Aquatic animals also feed on plants growing in the water. The most common and widespread types are microscopic algae, which may consist of single cells, multicellular filaments, or colonies. Often, these films of algae are barely visible to the naked eye. Mosses and liverworts are somewhat higher forms of plants found in most streams and rivers. Larger, rooted plants common to many river ecosystems include water lilies, cattails, and water milfoil. The array of species of plants provides food and shelter for a variety of animals.

Alternating patterns of deep and shallow water along the length of the river also give animals and plants varied habitat. Areas of deep water are called *pools*, and places where the water is shallow are called *riffles*. Fish seek out the tranquil waters in pools during times of high flow, when currents are swift and turbulent. Because water in a pool is deeper than in other parts of the channel, pools enable some aquatic animals to survive when water levels drop dangerously. Water over a riffle, on the other hand, is relatively shallow, and currents there are more rapid and turbulent. Certain plant and insect species have adapted to life in this fast lane. The larvae of caddis flies, for example, spin cone-shaped nets to capture food particles swept along in the swift currents. The disklike body of a water penny (the larva of a riffle beetle) forms a suction so strong that it can cling to rocks in the most rapid rivers.

Elements of a river ecosystem

The centerpiece of a river ecosystem is the river itself, a ribbon of water pulled by gravity from relatively high ground down to the shores of a lake or ocean. Along its length, a river cuts through a variety of landscapes, each of which affect life in the river. The river's width also changes, according to natural cycles of high and low flow that create lakes and marshes that periodically fill and dry out. Species of plants and animals on land and in the water have adapted to all these fluctuations, making a river ecosystem a complex mosaic of life.

Animal species have adapted to the river's unique environment. Animals that live on the riverbank include beavers, muskrat, and otters, as well as birds such as herons. In addition to fish, animals such as crayfish, clams, eels, snails, and insects inhabit the water at different depths. Frogs and salamanders are at home in the water and on land, as are many turtles and snakes.

Vegetation that falls into the water, such as leaves, needles, and twigs, supplement the diet of some fish. Dead tree branches that settle to the river bottom and wads of roots that grow into the water provide hiding places for small fish seeking to avoid predators.

The river channel is not a straight-sided chute but a winding stream with deep and shallow places. Areas of deep water, called *pools*, are found on the outside curve of bends, where swift currents erode soil and rocks from the riverbed. On inside curves, gravel suspended in the water drops to the bottom, forming a ridge called a *point bar*. Downstream from a pool, more gravel drops out of suspension and creates a shallow area called a *riffle*.

Trees and other vegetation along the river keep the riverbank from *eroding* (wearing away). Plants also shade the water during hot summer months, keeping daily and seasonal temperature variations within a range that sustains a variety of aquatic animals and plants.

Large branches or entire trees that fall into the river may alter the waterway dramatically, as the blockage forces the river to form a new channel.

The flood plain is the low-lying land alongside a river. Some flood plains are only narrow strips, but others extend for miles on both sides of the river. When the river floods, water flows out onto the flood plain, where it stays temporarily rather than rushing downstream. As the river falls to normal levels, the water in the flood plain slowly returns to the channel, leaving nutrient-rich sediment behind. Over thousands of years, such flooding cycles give the flood plain its flat surface and rich soil.

— Flood plain —

Shore and river intertwined

More than any other ecosystem, rivers are characterized by their edges. Plants all along the riverbank affect life in the stream. Needles, leaves, and twigs that fall into the water provide food for insects, snails, worms, and fish. Dead trees that fall into rivers can change the shape of the channel or form dams that force the water to seek a new path.

The shade cast across the water by plants on land limits the types of species found in the river. A small stream passing through a dense forest may receive so little sun that only aquatic plants that do not require direct sunlight, such as mosses and liverworts, can survive. For wider streams and rivers, land plants cast shade primarily along the river edges. Sunlight streaming into the center of the channel encourages the growth of algae.

Even the plants on land well away from the riverbanks can be an important part of a river ecosystem. Ground water flowing toward the river channel passes below trees and other plants, and their roots take up more than half the nutrients, such as nitrogen and phosphorus, in the water. This filtering greatly improves the purity of the river water.

Life on land and in the river are perhaps most closely linked in flood plains—wide, flat regions that extend on either side of a river. Rivers form flood plains over thousands of years. The process begins where a river flows into a low valley and a single channel may braid into multiple channels. During a flood, the multiple channels overflow their banks. As the water spreads out across the land, it slows, and any soil or gravel being carried along drops out as sediment. Over time, the build-up of sediment levels the landscape, creating the extensive flat surface of a flood plain. In just this way, the Brahmaputra, Ganges, and Meghna rivers, which flood every rainy season, have created the broad plains that nearly cover what is now Bangladesh in south Asia.

Many flood plains are underwater at least once every year. There, the only plants that thrive may be grasses or shrubs. But some flood plains are rarely flooded at intervals of less than hundreds of years. Flooding that infrequent permits the growth of forests that cover large areas and contain large, old trees.

The importance of flooding

Floods are important natural processes that do more than create flood plains, however. Most stream channels were first carved out during floods, for example, and the turbulence and swift currents of a flood scour out pools and drop sediment to create riffles.

Where flooding occurs with seasonal regularity, aquatic life may require floods to thrive. Many fish species reproduce toward the end of flood seasons, when submerged land plants provide a plentiful source of food for hatchlings. Even in areas where flooding occurs more rarely, fish seem to benefit from floodwaters. River ecologists reported in 1989 that more fish appear in major world rivers in years following floods than in years with relatively constant low flows, particularly in tropical rivers.

Plants growing alongside the river also benefit from flooding. River sediments commonly contain organic material rich in nutrients essential for plant growth, and when floodwaters deposit this sediment, they enrich the soil. After the 1993 Mississippi flood, for example, biologists noted an explosion in the growth of grasses and other plants alongside the river.

Major floods that extend far beyond the banks of the normal stream channel can benefit ecosystems for miles on either side of a river. The Mississippi flood carried fish to ponds and streams where they had not previously been seen. Researchers found increases not only in the numbers of fish in those areas but in the populations of eagles and hawks, which eat fish.

Altering rivers to prevent floods

Flood cycles and the other dynamic characteristics of rivers make these ecosystems among the most complex on Earth. Unfortunately, that changeability almost always causes problems for people living near the water's edge.

Most river management projects—all of which have drawbacks as well as benefits—try to avoid those problems by placing rivers under human control. One aim is to hold back river waters in order to prevent, or at least reduce, the damage caused by floods. Another is to modify the river channel so that the land drains more rapidly after floods or during storms. A third goal is to capture and store water to ensure a reliable supply the year around.

A common method of holding back river waters is to construct levees, which are also called *dikes*. These structures are usually made of earth piled higher than the water level would rise during a typical flood. Another way of constraining floodwater is by covering the riverbank with concrete or another material to prevent the river from eroding its banks. Such structures are called revetments or armored banks.

Levees, dikes, and revetments all constrict the flow of water to a central channel. That keeps floodwaters out of property flanking the river, but it causes other problems because it increases the speed of the current. The effect is similar to running the water through a narrow pipe instead of letting it flow over a broad stretch of land. The force of water at the end of the pipe will be much greater than it is at any point along the wide sheet of water. The increased power of the water in a river altered in this way causes the riverbank downstream to erode more rapidly than before the levees were built. Downstream communities may end up requiring levees along their waterfronts to combat erosion caused by levees upstream.

The system of levees on the Mississippi increased the damage to downstream communities during the 1993 floods. The levees forced water downstream with unnatural speed and power, so that when high waters broke through downstream levees, waves flowed farther across the flood plain than ever before. Then, when the waters began to re-

Controlling the flow of a river

People alter rivers by straightening them, damming them, raising their banks, or deepening and widening their channels. Such changes are primarily designed to reduce the damage caused by floods and heavy storms or to store water to ensure a reliable, year-round supply.

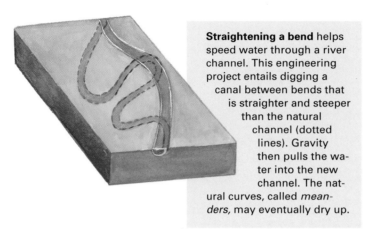

Straightening a bend helps speed water through a river channel. This engineering project entails digging a canal between bends that is straighter and steeper than the natural channel (dotted lines). Gravity then pulls the water into the new channel. The natural curves, called *meanders,* may eventually dry up.

Widening and deepening a channel is designed to prevent flooding so that the flood plain is suitable for agriculture or other uses. A wider and deeper canal holds more water than the original channel (light blue), so the river is able to handle larger volumes of water flowing downstream during seasonal floods or heavy storms.

Building a levee or dike can help prevent a river from overflowing its banks and flooding adjacent buildings or farmlands. Most levees are made of earth piled higher than the typical water level during floods.

Constructing a diversion channel allows water from a river to be drawn off to irrigate cropland. The new channel (left) is made narrower and straighter than the natural river.

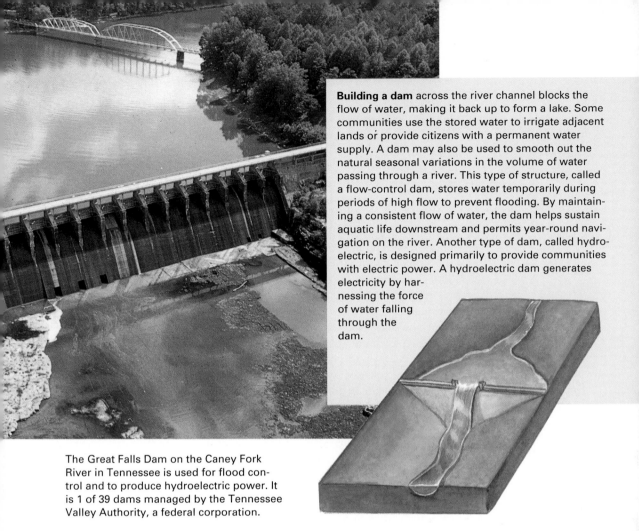

Building a dam across the river channel blocks the flow of water, making it back up to form a lake. Some communities use the stored water to irrigate adjacent lands or provide citizens with a permanent water supply. A dam may also be used to smooth out the natural seasonal variations in the volume of water passing through a river. This type of structure, called a flow-control dam, stores water temporarily during periods of high flow to prevent flooding. By maintaining a consistent flow of water, the dam helps sustain aquatic life downstream and permits year-round navigation on the river. Another type of dam, called hydroelectric, is designed primarily to provide communities with electric power. A hydroelectric dam generates electricity by harnessing the force of water falling through the dam.

The Great Falls Dam on the Caney Fork River in Tennessee is used for flood control and to produce hydroelectric power. It is 1 of 39 dams managed by the Tennessee Valley Authority, a federal corporation.

cede, the levees prevented the river's immediate return to the channel, making flood conditions last longer than they would have if the river had been unaltered.

Levees also cause trouble upstream. Water in a natural channel must pick up speed as it nears an altered section, where the water flows more swiftly. The force of the accelerating water causes erosion in the riverbed directly upstream from the altered site. That erosion steadily advances upstream. As it does so, a heavier and heavier load of sediment is gouged from the riverbed and carried downstream. All that sediment eventually makes the river shallower and wider, conditions that tend to increase the summertime water temperature. Many forms of aquatic life cannot tolerate the changes.

This destructive chain of events has occurred in the Mississippi River since levee building began in the 1800's. So that sediment would not deposit at the mouth of the river and make it too shallow for navigation, engineers in the late 1800's built leveelike structures called jetties out into the Gulf of Mexico. Ecologists are now worried that funneling the heavy sediment into the Gulf is affecting fish populations there.

Benefits and drawbacks of other river alterations

Another type of river-alteration project is designed to drain adjacent land during floods or storms. Landowners bury ceramic pipes below the surface in such a way that gravity pulls ground water through the pipes and down to the stream or river. Pumps can hasten the drainage. The system of pipes allows lowlands flanking a river to be planted with crops, often very near the riverbank. The remaining fringe of stream-side habitat is generally too small to support enough plants and insects to sustain many species of amphibians and reptiles, however, and so the river ecosystem is changed. Water that runs off the fields is also likely to contain pesticides and animal wastes, which will directly enter the stream without the benefit of being filtered through plant roots. The pollution can greatly alter river life and even kill off some species.

Any method of forcing a river to flow more quickly can also help drain adjacent land and make it suitable for agriculture or construction. The simplest technique is to remove obstructions in the water. Almost every municipal water-management plan in the United States calls for removing wood from urban streams. Most large rivers in the nation are "snagged" regularly to remove logs and jams. Doing so removes important sources of food for aquatic animals, however. And because snagging increases the speed of water through the channel, it can cause erosion problems similar to those caused by levees.

Straightening projects are another technique for routing water out of an area quickly. Straightening projects involve digging a channel between two bends. The new channel is made straighter and steeper than the natural river, so that gravity pulls the water into the new channel, leaving the curves, called *meanders*, to become marshy lakes that may eventually fill in and disappear.

Obviously, as meanders dry out, life there is reduced to creatures that can live in marshy habitats. Straightening projects can also have other, less-predictable consequences. Various studies have shown, for example, that the altered section is likely to contain fewer fish species than lived in the meanders. Among the species that remain, the average weight of the fish generally falls.

Straightening projects usually involve clearing vegetation to construct the new channel, and the loss of plants can also cause ecological problems. More sunlight penetrates the water, and the temperature of the water rises beyond the level tolerated by some aquatic creatures. Amphibians, reptiles, and other small animals lose their streamside hiding places from hungry predators such as otters and minks. Without the sheltering effect of trees and other plants, daily and seasonal variations in temperature become more extreme and also occur more rapidly than in the untouched river. Some forms of aquatic life can no longer exist under these new conditions.

Deepening a river channel by *dredging* (scraping) out sediment can also speed the routing of water. Some dredging projects break up a riverbed and remove debris. Engineers also dredge to form one steeper channel where there were several braided channels. Sometimes that process is hastened by filling in the unwanted channels.

Dredging can disrupt a river ecosystem in several ways. The procedure removes the river's natural pools and riffles, eliminating the variety of habitat that helps support a range of creatures. Dredging can also remove the aquatic plants, roots and all, that sustain fish. Finally, if dredging removes *silt* (fine soil particles carried by water) from the riverbed, the environment for plant life changes. As some plants die off, so do the aquatic animals that feed off them.

Probably the most dramatic way people alter river systems is by constructing dams. There are several types of dams, all of which slow or stop the flow of a stream or river. The water backs up behind the dam, forming a reservoir that provides a reliable source of water for irrigating fields and for supplying towns and communities nearby.

Some dams are used to generate electricity. Water falling through the dam spins a turbine, which turns a generator, a device that converts mechanical energy into electricity. Many dams are used as a supplement to a community's power supply, rather than as the primary source of electricity. In this case, engineers hold water back during daylight hours and then release it at night, when demand for electricity tends to be greater. Because those fluctuations from low to high flow are more rapid than in natural cycles, they can prove extremely harmful to aquatic organisms downstream. Species of small fish, very young fish, and species of insects normally found in waters along the banks are frequently missing altogether.

Flow-control dams are designed to smooth out variations in the volume of water passing through a river from season to season. Maintaining a consistent flow downstream ensures an adequate supply to sustain aquatic life and permits year-round navigation on the river. The dam stores water during periods of high flow to prevent flooding downstream, and dam authorities release water during periods of lower flow.

Flow-control dams, levees, and other river projects can reduce the effect of small floods—generally ones that recur at intervals of several decades. But no existing river control project is designed to eliminate the effects of floods that are so large they would occur only once in several centuries. In fact, major floods such as those of the 1990's may cause so much damage in some areas that the costs of the flood outweigh the benefits of developing the land in the first place. The very presence of levees, dams, and other flood controls may indirectly increase the damage toll of extremely large floods, because the structures encourage more people to settle on the flood plain than would risk it otherwise.

Balancing people's needs with those of the river

It's important to remember that almost every member of U.S. society benefits directly from the changes made to streams and rivers. They help provide drinking water, waste treatment, and food, and they are useful to the production of many manufactured goods. But humanity has also paid a price for altering rivers to suit human needs. The U.S. Congress appropriated $5.7 billion to pay for damages for the 1993

The ecological price of river alteration

Major engineering projects such as dam building can drastically alter the character of the landscape. But even small river alterations may cause unexpected changes in a natural river ecosystem.

Frequently, shoreline vegetation is removed to construct a new channel, robbing many amphibians such as frogs and turtles of their favorite habitat. Without trees and other plants to shade the water during the summer, water temperatures rise higher than many forms of aquatic life can tolerate. The lack of vegetation on the shore also makes the riverbank unstable and susceptible to erosion.

Water flows through a straightened channel more quickly than through a natural, meandering river. Many species of plants cannot tolerate the steady high speed of the water, and they die off. Fish may die off or simply move to an unaltered section of the river.

A river channel that has been straightened to speed the flow of water typically has a uniform depth and unvaried riverbed. But aquatic ecosystems evolved and are maintained by a variety of habitat. Caddis fly larvae need the fast-moving, shallow water over a riffle, and trout need accumulations of gravel on which to lay their eggs. The lack of pools, riffles, and point bars means that far fewer aquatic species can live in a reconstructed channel than in a natural river.

After a river is deepened and widened to drain the land for agricultural use, rain may wash pesticides, fertilizer, topsoil, and animal waste into the river from the adjacent fields. Fertilizers and animal waste can disrupt the ecological balance of the river by encouraging the growth of some species to the detriment of others. Pesticides can kill plants and animals directly. Particles of topsoil suspended in the water reduce the amount of sunlight reaching the riverbed. With less sunlight, fewer aquatic plants survive, forcing fish and other animals to seek food elsewhere or die.

If rivers are altered to keep floodwaters off the floodplain, the land may dry out, *right,* drastically changing the ecosystem. Building cities on such a floodplain may lead to property damage during unusually severe flooding. When France's Marne River overflowed its banks in December 1993, nearby towns were flooded, *below.*

Restoring a river
A pilot project on a section of the straightened Kissimmee River in Florida shows that a *weir* (gate) in the altered channel forces water into old, natural bends, *top*. In 1994, the U.S. Army Corps of Engineers was working to restore 35 kilometers (22 miles) of the straight channel into 69 kilometers (43 miles) of natural meanders. Studies using a scale model at the University of California, Berkeley, *above*, indicate that the project will be successful.

Midwestern floods, for example, and thousands of citizens suffered emotional turmoil beyond any dollar figure.

Scientists have no simple way to resolve the conflict between our need to use rivers and our desire to avoid the problems river alteration projects cause. It is impossible to move New Orleans and St. Louis, Mo., for example, even though those communities were founded perilously close to a river prone to flooding.

We can make a difference, however, in the decisions made today. An increasing number of experts say that programs that provide flood insurance, such as the National Flood Insurance Program, should be revised so that they discourage, rather than encourage, development on flood plains. And ecologists urge government officials to create programs that recognize the dynamic nature of rivers and prompt wise use of their resources.

Similarly, scientists see no quick fixes for river ecosystems that have been extensively altered. Unfortunately, most of the rivers of North America fall into this category, according to a 1982 project conducted by the U.S. National Park Service. The project, the Nationwide Rivers Inventory, sought to identify high-quality, free-flowing streams longer than 200 kilometers (124 miles) that could be protected from development. In the lower 48 states, only 42 rivers—2 percent of the total—met the criteria, according to Arthur Benke, a stream ecologist at the

University of Alabama in Tuscaloosa who reviewed the data in 1988.

On the other hand, it is possible to restore a river, or at least sections of it, to a more natural condition. In one such project underway in 1994, 35 kilometers (22 miles) of Florida's Kissimmee River were being changed from an artificially straight channel to a 69-kilometer (43-mile) reach of meandering river.

One of the most effective restoration approaches may be to avoid "correcting the damage" caused by certain floods. A major flood—one that happens once in 100 years—can obliterate artificial structures and carve out new channels, full of riffles and pools. The floodwaters can move a tremendous volume of sediment, enough to remake the land-scape. In 1993, for example, the Mississippi dropped sediment up to 1.8 meters (6 feet) deep in some places. For rivers earmarked for restoration, such a flood could correct more mistakes and restore more ecological function than any government project. Experts thus say the challenge is to develop sound after-the-flood policies that will identify the benefits of a flood—and other natural features of the eco-system—before we rush in to try to force the river under our control.

For further reading:

"The Mississippi River Under Siege," *Water: The Power, Promise, and Turmoil of North America's Fresh Water.* National Geographic Special Edition, January 1994.
Clark, C. *Flood.* Time-Life Books, 1982.
Frank, A. D. *The Development of the Federal Program of Flood Control on the Mississippi River.* Ames Press, 1968.
Mairson, A. "Great Flood," *National Geographic,* January 1994.
Mitsch, W. J., and Gosselink, J. G. *Wetlands.* Van Nostrand Reinhold, 1993.
Scarpino, P. V. *Great River. An Environmental History of the Upper Mississippi 1890-1950.* University of Missouri Press, 1985.

■ ■ ■

Questions for thought and discussion

Imagine that you are the mayor of an old riverside town. A group of city offi-cials has proposed a way to bring much-needed revenue into the city—a proj-ect to turn some historical riverfront buildings into a tourist attraction. Past floods washed some of the buildings away, but those that remain are in fair condition, needing only cleaning and minor repairs. The plan calls for the construction of a few other buildings that will resemble the originals and round out the impression of a thriving mid-1800's town.

Before any work starts, the officials agree that levees must be constructed, as has been done upstream, to prevent future flood damage. As mayor, it is your responsibility to present the levee proposal to the county river management au-thorities. Friends warn you that farmers who cultivate land downstream from your town are planning to raise strong objections at the meeting.

Questions: What arguments could you use to support the plan to build the levees? Why do you think the farmers object to it? What compromises could be proposed?

The story of the prehistoric world of the
Jurassic Period has been assembled piece
by piece by fossil hunters past and present.

Unearthing
the Jurassic

BY ROBERT T. BAKKER

"**M**y dear Dr. Grant. Welcome to Jurassic Park."
With those words, filmgoers were introduced to the dinosaur
zoo in 1993's summer blockbuster, the movie version of
Michael Crichton's novel *Jurassic Park.* Many fossil hunters would
say Crichton chose wisely when he selected that title. Even though
the story's fearsome *Tyrannosaurus rex* and raptors lived later, in the
Cretaceous Period, the word *Jurassic* evokes the spirit of the dinosaurs,
and of ancient days on Earth. The Jurassic was the heart of the Age of
Dinosaurs.

The Jurassic has special meaning for scientists, because it was rocks
of Jurassic age that taught us how to study fossils and unravel the rid-
dles of geological time. But the story of the scientific pioneers who explored the Jurassic world is not a tale of stuffy professors in laboratory
coats. Jurassic fossil hunters were a colorful troop of characters that included beachcombers, clergy, university professors, self-taught amateurs, and even dinosaur rustlers. Their quests uncovered the evidence
that, piece by piece, created for us a picture of the Jurassic environment and the plants and animals that inhabited it.

Our knowledge of the Age of Dinosaurs had small beginnings in the
1790's on the coast of southern England. There, the constant waves of
the English Channel washed beautiful fossil shells, coiled like snails,
out of the rocks. At a resort town called Lyme Regis, natives made
pocket money by finding the fossils and selling them to tourists in curiosity shops clustered along narrow streets. Storefront displays showed

The author:
Robert T. Bakker, a paleontologist, is adjunct curator at the University of Colorado Museum in Boulder and the author of *The Dinosaur Heresies* (1986).

the lovely fossil shells, which had a bewildering variety of surface textures. Some shells had cross-ridges, some had knobs and bumps, and some had glassy, smooth surfaces. Looking at specimens cut open by rock saws, shoppers would see that the interiors of the coiled shells were divided into compartments.

Natural history buffs named these coiled shells *ammonites,* after the ancient Egyptian god Amon, who was sometimes portrayed as a ram with tightly coiled horns. The scientific names for different varieties of ammonites usually end in *-ceras,* which means *ram's horn.* For example, *Zigzagiceras* ("Zig-zag horn") is an ammonite with zigzag folds in the shell partitions.

The amazing variety of the ammonites pricked the curiosity of nature lovers in the 1700's. An old legend claimed that the coiled shells were evil serpents killed by Saint Hilda, founder of an abbey at the North Sea coastal town of Whitby in the 600's. According to the tale, thousands of snakes had plagued the ancient town of Yorkshire, frightening the inhabitants and stampeding livestock. The abbess allegedly laid a curse on the snakes, and their heads fell off. The shells found in the rocks were the supposed remains of the snakes' bodies, tightly coiled in a final, headless convulsion. *Paleontologists* (scientists who study prehistoric life) in 1880 honored the abbess by naming one famous Yorkshire ammonite *Hildoceras* ("St. Hilda's horn").

Timekeepers of the Jurassic

The truth about the ammonites is even more colorful, at least in a scientific sense. Observant fossil hunters in the 1840's saw that ammonites must not have been the remains of snakes or snails. In fact, ammonites are related to the present-day nautilus, a member of the squid and octopus clan whose tightly coiled shell is subdivided by cross-partitions. The nautilus's body plan matches the ammonite fossils found at Lyme Regis, with some exceptions. The nautilus surface texture is smoother, and its cross-partitions are not bent into the folds that are ammonite trademarks.

The Lyme Regis fossils showed that the ancient ammonites grew to tremendous abundance. The crinkled partitions of the shells made them quite strong, for the same reason that corrugated cardboard, which is pressed in wavy ridges, is stronger than smooth cardboard. Those strong shells would have allowed ammonites to descend to great ocean depths, protected from the intense water pressure that would otherwise crush them. Equipped with dozens of nautilus-style tentacles, each with tiny hooks for grabbing prey, ammonites cruised about the ocean, hunting for small fish and other animals to feed upon. And when an ammonite died, its remains settled into the sediment at the bottom of the sea. Millions of years later, that bottom silt had become the sedimentary rock, such as shale and limestone, where the fossils were found.

Fossil ammonites weren't merely pretty souvenirs, however. They became the timekeepers of the Jurassic Period, used to date the age of the layers, or *strata*, of rock in which they were discovered.

The idea that the remains of creatures like ammonites could mark the passage of geological time was worked out as a scientific principle by a self-taught country boy, William "Strata" Smith. Growing up on a farm in Oxfordshire, England, in the 1770's and 1780's, Smith amused himself by examining the fossil sea urchins, oysters, and ammonites brought to the surface during spring plowing. His boyish curiosity grew into a lifelong quest to understand fossil history.

As an adult, Smith worked as a civil engineer, mapping roadways and canals all over southern England. At the time, industry needed precise surveys of the underground rock layers that might contain coal, lime, or other useful minerals, but no one knew how to map such strata. Smith solved the problem. His keen eye for telling fossil shells apart enabled him to see that different strata contained different ammonite species. Armed with this insight, Smith drew up

Early fossil hunters used prehistoric mollusks called ammonites, *right,* to date the different layers of rock visible on eroded cliffs on the coast of England, *above,* and at other sites. Different ammonite species lived at different times, so finding one of the mollusks enabled fossil hunters to estimate the age of the layer of rock in which it was discovered.

Placing the Jurassic in time

The Jurassic was a geological period that began 205 million years ago, *below.* In the 1800's, amateur fossil hunters used Jurassic fossils, *bottom,* to develop the first estimates of the ages of various layers of earth.

Period or epoch and its length			Beginning (years ago)
Cenozoic Era	Quaternary Period	Holocene Epoch 10 thousand years	10 thousand
		Pleistocene Epoch 2 million years	2 million
	Tertiary Period	Pliocene Epoch 3 million years	5 million
		Miocene Epoch 19 million years	24 million
		Oligocene Epoch 14 million years	38 million
		Eocene Epoch 17 million years	55 million
		Paleocene Epoch 8 million years	63 million
Mesozoic Era	Cretaceous Period 75 million years		138 million
	Jurassic Period 67 million years		205 million
	Triassic Period 35 million years		240 million
Paleozoic Era	Permian Period 50 million years		290 million
	Carboniferous Period	Pennsylvanian Period 40 million years	330 million
		Mississippian Period 30 million years	360 million
	Devonian Period 50 million years		410 million
	Silurian Period 25 million years		435 million
	Ordovician Period 65 million years		500 million
	Cambrian Period 70 million years (?)		570 million (?)
	Precambrian Time Almost 4 billion years (?)		4½ billion (?)

Learning about Jurassic plant life

Discoveries of plant fossils in the mid-1800's provided people with the first glimpse of the Jurassic environment.

Fossils of Jurassic Period ferns, *above,* were found in England in the 1800's. Along with other finds, those discoveries indicated that the Jurassic was one of the warmest episodes of Earth's history, and that there were no flowers or trees such as oaks, birches, and elms. The fossil evidence enabled an artist in 1851 to depict the Jurassic plant world in some detail, *above right.*

tables showing that each species existed for a brief geological instant and then went extinct. Geologists of the 1900's would find that the average ammonite species lasted only about 1 million years. A new ammonite species appeared to replace the extinct one, and it too lived through only this narrow time zone. If surveyors found the same species of *Hildoceras* in different parts of the English countryside, they know that both fossils were from the same strata of rock.

Ammonite species were world travelers, which adds to their value as Jurassic timekeepers. As soon as a new ammonite species came into being, it spread rapidly over huge tracts of ocean. So its fossil remains were dropped into the bottom sediment from Russia to Germany to France to England. Other life forms changed rapidly, too—Smith found oysters useful for dividing Jurassic time—but no clan of creatures were as important as ammonites.

In 1815, Smith published the first complete geological map showing the strata of England. His map was so good that it remains a basic resource for modern studies.

More importantly, the self-taught fossil hunter had grasped the single greatest truth of paleontology: Life changed rapidly in regular, predictable ways as strata were deposited. Smith's principle of *biochron-*

ology, in which fossils are used to divide geological time, is still the most important rule in studying rocks today.

Fossils of a warm Earth

Fossils of Jurassic animals had another story to tell: the saga of shifting world climate. In the late 1700's, geologists found Jurassic coral reefs along English shores. Coral does not grow in cold waters, so the fossil reefs were evidence that the Earth had once been much warmer.

Plant fossils told the same tale. Miners in Yorkshire dug up seams of coal that contained large preserved fronds of tropical ferns nearly identical to those found in balmy Malaysia. Elsewhere in England, diggers found fossilized trunks of cycad trees. Cycad trees, which have leaves like palm trees but are more closely related to pine trees, grow only in warm habitats of the present world. And in the 1880's, geologists exploring Spitsbergen, a frigid island in the Arctic Ocean, found fossils of tropical forests. Today, Spitsbergen's plant life is limited to wind-stunted bushes and lichens clinging to rocks.

Those fossil discoveries showed that the Jurassic was one of the warmest episodes of geological history, when most of the Earth was frost-free. During that time, all trees were *conifers* (cone-bearing trees), cycads, or tree ferns. There were no oaks, elms, or birches. Jurassic plant life had another peculiarity: no flowers. To this day, no one has discovered a single leaf, stem, or pollen grain that came from a Jurassic-era flowering plant. All the Jurassic undergrowth was composed of ferns, horsetails, and ground pine—with not a single dandelion or daisy or blade of grass. To modern eyes, Jurassic forests would appear dull and monotonous, with green hues unbroken by the reds and yellows seen today in tropical flowers.

The discovery that past climates were fundamentally different from today's shocked philosophers of the 1800's. Most civilized cultures had assumed that the world had existed more or less unchanged all through its history. The Jurassic fossils dispelled that myth forever.

Sea dragons of the English coast

The Jurassic had even more shocking discoveries to offer in the first decades of the 1800's—sea dragons! An amateur fossil hunter named Mary Anning found the first evidence of them. Anning, who lived in Lyme Regis, was one of the most famous collectors of fossil sea shells. Local legend had it that a bolt of lightning struck Anning's baby carriage when she was an infant, killing her nurse and giving Anning a supernatural skill in detecting rare fossils.

Anning's success in finding ammonites was already well established when she astonished the scholarly community in 1830 with the discovery of a skeleton of a giant sea lizard. The creature was an oceangoing reptile—a cold-blooded, scaly animal that breathes with lungs. It must have looked something like today's porpoises. William Daniel Conybeare, one of many amateur paleontologists who were also clergymen

Discovering Jurassic sea lizards

The discovery of a giant sea lizard in 1830 by England's amateur fossil hunter Mary Anning, *right,* provided the first indication that Jurassic seas were filled with monsters. Anning's lizard was later named *Ichthyosaurus* ("fish lizard").

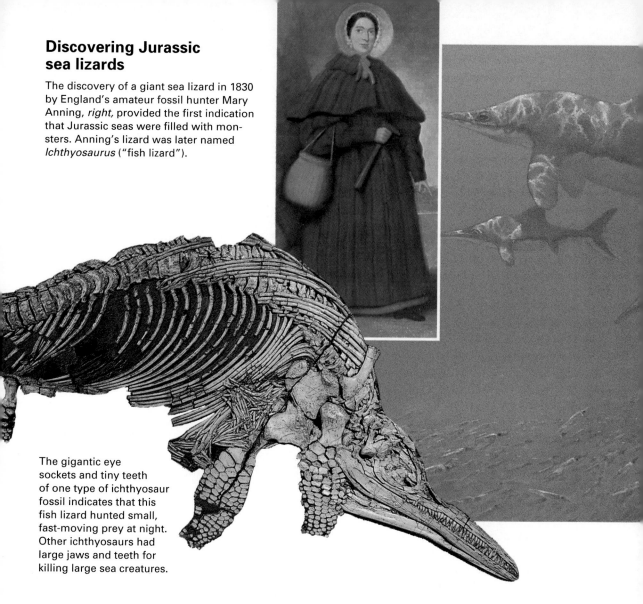

The gigantic eye sockets and tiny teeth of one type of ichthyosaur fossil indicates that this fish lizard hunted small, fast-moving prey at night. Other ichthyosaurs had large jaws and teeth for killing large sea creatures.

in the Church of England, published an article calling the beast *Ichthyosaurus* ("fish lizard").

Later finds showed the Jurassic to have been the golden age of ichthyosaurs, which came in many varieties. Some late Jurassic species had bodies similar in design to that of today's fastest fish: the tuna, mako shark, and porbeagle shark. Those speedy fish lizards could probably reach 40 knots in an underwater sprint. Up to 2 meters (6.5 feet) long, the fish lizards had gigantic eyes, with bony eye sockets as big as dinner plates, and tiny teeth. The small teeth and big eyes suggest that they hunted small, fast-moving prey at night. Other Jurassic ichthyosaurs found between 1821 and 1850 had faces like swordfish, with a long, sharp upper beak for slashing prey. Still others had gigantic jaws and massive cutting teeth for killing and dismembering other large sea creatures.

A few years after finding her fish lizard, Anning dug up another

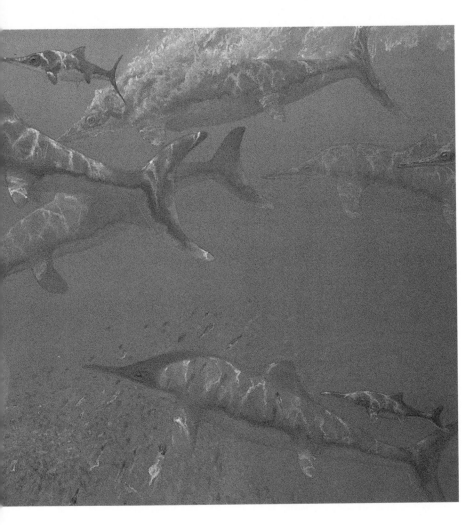

Living ichthyosaurs (shown in an artist's rendering) may have looked similar to the porpoises of today's oceans. The bodies of some Jurassic ichthyosaurs were similar in design to that of today's fastest fish. Their flexible backbones and powerful tails allowed them to speed through the water.

Jurassic sea dragon, this one of a profoundly different design. The four flippers were long, pointed, and backswept at the tip like the wings of penguins. The tail was small, and the neck was long. Conybeare named the beast *Plesiosaurus* ("nearer to a lizard"), because its skeletal structure was more similar to modern lizards' than was the ichthyosaur's.

A great variety of plesiosaurs inhabited Jurassic seas. All had two sets of penguin-style flippers, one forward, one aft. Because penguins are fast and nimble swimmers, plesiosaurs must have been capable of outstanding submarine acrobatics. The long-necked species had small heads and upwardly facing eyes, for attacking schools of squid from underneath. The short-necked species had heads that were 3 meters (10 feet) long, with huge cutting teeth. These gargantuan *carnivores* (meat-eaters) could overpower anything else in the sea.

Fossil hunters discovered yet another clan of sea reptile along the English Channel coasts in the 1820's and 1830's—crocodiles with short legs, long snouts, and powerful swimming tails. The sea crocodiles, like the fish lizards and plesiosaurs, achieved their highest levels of diversity during the Jurassic Period. Some sea crocodiles were covered from head to tail-tip with thick, bony armor that protected their back and belly and made them nearly invulnerable to any bite from another sea reptile. As the sea crocodiles evolved, some types lost their armor entirely, developing more flexibility and speed. These species were shaped like reef sharks and probably lay in ambush with their bodies curled up in crevices, waiting to lurch out and snag unwary passers-by.

Flying dragons

There were Jurassic dragons in the air, too. Anning scored a third Jurassic triumph when she discovered in the Lyme Regis area a jumbled mass of thin, hollow bones that formed a shape vaguely reminiscent of a sea gull's. In 1829, William Buckland, an Anglican clergyman and fellow at Oxford University, identified the specimen as the first large *Pterodactyl* ("wing finger") ever found.

Buckland, who was to play an important role in building the picture of the Jurassic, was one of the more colorful fossil sleuths. An eccentric genius, he was famous at Oxford for his sense of humor as well as his lectures on geology and anatomy. For formal university gatherings, Buckland dressed up his pet bear, Tilgath Pileser, and introduced it to near-sighted senior faculty as a newly arrived undergraduate.

According to Buckland, Anning had discovered a flying dragon, a reptile with long, pointed wings held up by elongated sets of finger bones. Like bats, the pterodactyl's front and hind limbs were connected to its wings, and both appendages were used to power the wings. Bird anatomy, by comparison, is less efficient in its use of muscle energy, because birds use only their front limbs for flapping.

In Jurassic times, pterodactyls filled the ecological role of sea birds, soaring over the ocean, scanning the waves for small fish and squid. The large, gull-sized species Anning found steered by means of a long tail with a vertical appendage at the end that acted as a rudder. Smaller pterodactyls, whose fossils had been found in Germany, were nearly tailless. Their anatomy would have made them much quicker in a turn but more dependent on wing movement for stability.

Dinosaurs!

The discoveries on the English coast had shown that Jurassic seas and skies were filled with reptiles, but what of the land? Land animal fossils were rare in the oceanic sediments. However, inland near Oxford, quarrymen found giant bones in what was called the Stonesfield Slate, a sandstone formation laid down by Jurassic rivers.

Buckland studied the Stonesfield Slate bones in 1822 and declared them to be from a *carnivorous* (meat-eating) beast armed with lizard-style teeth shaped like steak knives. He named the Stonesfield monster *Megalosaurus* ("giant lizard"). It was the first full dinosaur fossil ever dug up. Buckland thought it would have looked like a huge version of the short-legged monitor lizards living now in Southeast Asia.

When more megalosaur bones were found in Oxfordshire and

across the English Channel in Normandy, France, the creature proved to have a strange mixture of features. Although it had teeth with long roots set in sockets, like crocodiles, it also had hip and thigh muscles far more powerful than any reptile's, more like a bird's.

By the mid-1800's, our present view of the Age of Dinosaurs had begun to take shape. A few decades earlier, geologists working in the Jura Mountains of Europe, where rocks and fossils of the period are widespread, had coined the word *Jurassique* to describe the middle period of the Mesozoic. By 1850, the *Jurassic Period* was a well-established term among geologists. But some important gaps in knowledge remained. For example, a complete land ecosystem needs plant-eaters for the carnivores to prey upon. But European fossil hunters never found a rich deposit of Jurassic dinosaurian *herbivores* (plant-eaters). That discovery was left for the Western United States.

The Jurassic and the Wild West

Fossil hunting began in earnest in the American West in 1877. That year, a schoolteacher and a U.S. Navy officer came across a Jurassic dinosaur graveyard at Oil Creek in central Colorado. At the same time, two station agents of the Union Pacific Railroad stumbled upon brontosaur skeletons at Como Bluff, a long ridge in southern Wyoming.

The Great American Dinosaur Rush began when the nation's best-known dinosaur scholars—Othniel Charles Marsh of Yale University in New Haven, Conn., and Edward Drinker Cope of Philadelphia—received telegrams and express mail packages from the Colorado and Wyoming sites. Cope and Marsh could be called dinosaur robber barons, like the ruthless and wealthy American "robber baron" businessmen of their day. Both Cope and Marsh were independently wealthy. Both used all of their inherited fortunes in digging for dinosaurs. Both managed to get big government grants to support digs in the West. Both discovered near complete remains of new Jurassic giants. And they hated each other.

Cope and Marsh apparently tried every trick, legal and illegal, to beat each other in finding new dinosaurs. What is likely to have been the only case of dinosaur rustling occurred at Como Bluff in 1879, when Cope hired two drifters, the Hubbell brothers, to steal skeletons from Marsh's quarries. The brothers apparently sneaked up the east side of Como Bluff while Marsh's men were guarding the west end of the ridge a few kilometers away. The rustlers found what appeared to be a nearly complete megalosaurian skeleton. They dug it up, put it in boxes on their pack mules, and silently led them to a railroad station, where the bones were shipped to Cope in Philadelphia. The rustled dinosaur turned out to be the first good specimen of the Jurassic meat-eater *Allosaurus* ("other lizard"), an advanced cousin of *Megalosaurus*. It was the best carnivore skeleton found until that time.

But in the end, Marsh triumphed in the Wyoming-Colorado dinosaur wars. Out of Marsh's Jurassic quarries spilled an entire menagerie of herbivores and carnivores. They included *Apatosaurus* (also called *Brontosaurus*), *Barosaurus, Camarasaurus, Diplodocus,* and *Stegosaurus.* Marsh's field excursions unearthed Jurassic small fry as well, such as *Laosaurus* ("stone lizard"), a family of delicate, birdlike herbivores. Some laosaurs weighed only 9 kilograms (20 pounds), making them the smallest plant-eating dinosaur of the period.

The most dramatic Jurassic mini-fossils found at Como were the jaws and teeth of mouse-sized predators that hunted insects in the dark underbrush. These were Jurassic representatives of Mammalia, the class of warm-blooded, hairy creatures that today includes such species as chipmunks, dogs, elephants, and human beings. The size of the Jurassic mammal fossils puzzled paleontologists. Before the mid-1800's, experts had agreed that mammals were the highest class of *vertebrates* (animals with backbones). They thought this because mammals have big brains and complex hearts and lungs, because mammal parents spend a great deal of time caring for their young—and because human beings are mammals. Also, in our world, most large land animals are mammals. Reptiles, on the other hand, are mainly small creatures.

Jurassic mammal fossils turned those rules upside down. In Germany in the 1850's, the earliest strata of the Jurassic yielded fossil mammal teeth as small as pinheads. In England, Buckland identified tiny mammals among the Stonesfield fossils, preserved side-by-side with gigantic dinosaurs like *Megalosaurus.* And when Marsh's men combed the slopes of Como Bluff, they found equally small mammal jaws among the dinosaur bones in the latest time zones of the Jurassic. For the entire Jurassic Period, all the warm-blooded mammals had been the size of present-day mice and squirrels, with not one mammal species reaching 0.5 kilogram (1 pound). Mammals did not even begin to evolve into large creatures until almost 75 million years later.

When Marsh finished his Como Bluff studies in the 1890's, the first century of Jurassic research ended, and a more formal style of science took over. Universities and museums established positions in paleontology, and the work of amateurs became less important. Fossil discoveries continued in the early and mid-1900's, but most merely supplied more details to the picture of Jurassic life worked out in the 1800's.

Studying the Jurassic today

In the late 1900's, however, amateurs began returning to the study of the Jurassic. Many donated their time and energy to working for new museums dedicated to fine-scale, stratum-by-stratum analysis of how creatures changed during the Jurassic. One is the College of Eastern Utah Prehistoric Museum in Price, Utah, near the Cleveland-Lloyd Dinosaur Quarry, from which the remains of 44 allosaurs have been removed. Another is the Tate Mineralogical and Earth Science Center museum in Casper, Wyo., located near outcrops that yield brontosaurs and Jurassic crocodiles. And in 1994, the Dinamation International Society planned to open the Devil's Canyon Science and Learning Center at Fruita, Colo., home to spectacular fossils of Jurassic mammals and small dinosaurs.

Digging for Jurassic dinosaurs

Fossil hunters in the Western United States have made many important discoveries about the dinosaurs that lived in the Jurassic Period.

Fossil hunters in the late 1800's in Wyoming, *left,* prepare the backbone of a *Brontosaurus* (also called *Apatosaurus*), a large, plant-eating dinosaur first discovered in America in the 1870's. Before transporting the bones back East for study, workers encased them in plaster, which was chipped off when the bones reached their destination.

Diggers in Montana in 1993, *right,* use plaster to protect the bones of a newly discovered fossil sauropod, a member of the group of dinosaurs that includes *Brontosaurus* and other large, long-necked dinosaurs. Among the many types of dinosaurs discovered in America was *Seismosaurus, below,* one of the largest known dinosaurs, first discovered in New Mexico in 1986.

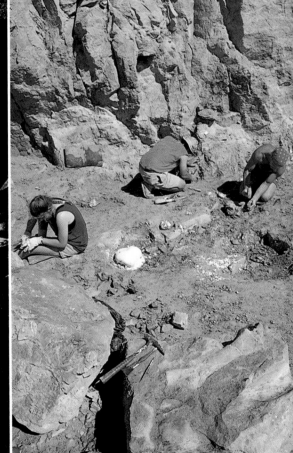

Already today's amateur fossil hunters, working carefully and under the direction of experts, have made important finds. In 1992, James Siegwarth, a volunteer for Dinamation, found a gigantic member of the *Megalosaurus* family at Como Bluff. The fossil is a late Jurassic carnivore as big as a *Tyrannosaurus rex.* The new megalosaur species was discovered near the bones of three other big predators—two allosaur species and a ceratosaur, a megalosaur with a horn on its nose. Jim Filla, a volunteer for the Tate Museum and the Dinamation Society, in 1990 uncovered a new *Brontosaurus* species, older than any discovered by Marsh. In 1992, Robert Gaston, volunteering for the Price museum, discovered two creatures that lived just after the end of the Jurassic. One was the predator *Utahraptor* ("Utah's raptor"), a 6-meter (20-foot) killer with sharp-edged claws on its forelimbs and feet. The other was the herbivore *Gastonia*, a one-ton, bony dino-tank.

Why are fossil hunters finding so many new species? Because evolution, the process by which complex organisms develop from simpler forms of life, proceeded quickly in the Jurassic. New clusters of species cropped up every million years or so. Because the Jurassic was more than 60 million years long, there was time for 60 waves of new species.

The Jurassic started and ended with evolutionary bangs. When the Jurassic began, the worldwide ecosystem was rocked by the extinction of ammonites, primitive sea reptiles, early dinosaurs, and ancestors of mammals. During the early Jurassic, there was an evolutionary rebound. Dozens of new groups of species debuted: new forms of ammonites, plesiosaurs, ichthyosaurs, sea crocodiles, megalosaurs, brontosaurs, stegosaurs, pterodactyls, and the first true mammal. This rich assortment of creatures evolved vigorously until the end of the Jurassic. Then another mass die-off eliminated most of the dinosaurs on land and reptiles in the oceans. In the next geologic period, the Cretaceous, there was a second rebound, with a new wave of sea monsters, dinosaurs, and flying dragons. Then a final, late Cretaceous extinction wiped out all ammonites, sea lizards, dinosaurs, and pterodactyls.

So the Jurassic Period appears to have been one natural unit of evolution, punctuated by mass extinctions. The search for the cause of these extinctions is one of the most pressing questions in geology.

There are many more mysteries about the Age of Dinosaurs, and we have just scratched the surface of Jurassic history. Geologists and museum curators say they could put an army of volunteers to work finding fossils and mapping strata. With 1990's versions of William Smith and Mary Anning, we could unearth the clues the early fossil hunters unwittingly left for us to discover.

Opposite page: A *Brontosaurus* towers over other prehistoric animals in a 1994 depiction of life in the Jurassic Period. A pterodactyl called *Wyomingopteryx* flies above the water, as the rat-tailed mammal *Zofiabaatar* and the ring-tailed *Foxraptor* climb on low branches. Underwater swim a *Uluops* turtle and a small laosaur about to fall prey to a lungfish called *Ceratodus robustus.* On the shore, a hungry *Goniopholis* crocodile is also on the attack.

For further reading:

Bakker, Robert T. *The Dinosaur Heresies.* Morrow, 1986.
Lambert, David. *The Ultimate Dinosaur Book.* Dorling Kindersley, 1993.
Rudwick, Martin J. S. *Scenes From Deep Time.* University of Chicago Pr. 1992.

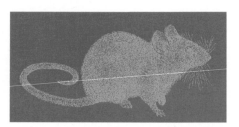

Scientists have been cloning frogs, mice, and cows for years, but cloned people and dinosaurs are far from reality.

Cloning Research on the March

BY ROBERT GILMORE McKINNELL

Glossary

Asexual reproduction: Reproduction in which an offspring gets its genes from one parent.

Blastomere: A cell of a young embryo.

Chromosome: DNA, packed in protein, in a cell's nucleus. Chromosomes carry the genes.

Clone: A group of organisms descended from one organism through asexual reproduction.

DNA (deoxyribonucleic acid): The molecule of which genes are made.

Embryo: An organism in the early stage of development.

Enucleation: The process of removing a cell's nucleus.

Gene: A section of DNA containing the instructions for making a protein. Genes are the units of heredity.

Gene expression: The production of a protein specified by a gene.

In vitro fertilization (IVF): A technique in which an egg is fertilized by a sperm in a laboratory.

Micropipette: An extremely thin glass tube.

Sexual reproduction: Reproduction in which an offspring gets its genes from two parents.

Zona pellucida: A membrane that surrounds mammalian eggs and helps hold the cells of a developing embryo together.

The author:
Robert Gilmore McKinnell is professor of genetics and cell biology at the University of Minnesota in St. Paul.

In October 1993, a pair of researchers at George Washington University Medical Center in Washington, D.C., made a startling announcement: They had cloned very young human *embryos* (organisms in the earliest stage of development). Hoping to avoid controversy, the scientists had performed their cloning experiment using abnormal embryos that had no chance of survival. Although the resulting clones lived for only a few days, news of the researchers' work caught the attention of the world. Some people hailed the experiment as significant because of the ethical questions it raised, and the work won top honors at a 1993 conference sponsored by the American Fertility Society. Other people registered alarm at the possibility of mass-producing people.

The announcement was just the latest incident to stir up visions of the possibilities of cloning. It followed close on the heels of the 1990 novel *Jurassic Park* by Michael Crichton and the 1993 motion picture of the same name, both of which dealt with the fictional cloning of dinosaurs. Given the fanciful nature of that story, many readers and audience members no doubt considered cloning to be in the realm of science fiction.

But as scientists first showed in 1952, cloning is not science fiction, though the technique has strict limitations. So far, researchers have been unable to clone cells from fully developed *vertebrate* (back-boned) animals of any species, be they dinosaurs, laboratory rats, or human beings. So at the present time, the dream—or nightmare— of creating duplicates of oneself is out of the reach of science. But cloning cells from embryos is another matter. This type of cloning has a long history, and today it is not especially difficult for skilled scientists to perform. Agricultural scientists use embryo cloning to boost the number of offspring from farm animals. Research biologists use cloning to study how animals develop during the early stages of life. And, although many ethical questions must first be resolved, some scientists think we may be approaching a time when human embryos are cloned for certain medical purposes.

Cloning in the plant world

In scientific terms, a clone is a group of organisms descended from an ancestor without sexual reproduction. People also use the word *clone* to mean an organism that has the same genes as another organism. Genes are the components of cells that contain the blueprint for the organisms' characteristics and functions. The genes are located on *chromosomes*, long molecules of DNA (deoxyribonucleic acid) that are packaged with proteins. Most of the cells of plants and animals contain two sets of chromosomes, which are found in the cell's central compartment, the nucleus.

The word *clone* is derived from a Greek word for *twig* or *slip*. That meaning comes from the world of plants, which can reproduce in two ways: sexually, as most animals do, and asexually, which creates a natural clone.

Complex plants such as the African violet or ornamental ivy can re-produce sexually. In nature, this process may be quite complicated. In essence, a sperm cell, which contains a single set of chromosomes, fuses with an egg cell, which also contains only a single set of chromosomes. The merger results in a one-celled embryo containing the two sets of chromosomes necessary for the development of a new plant. That new plant will be slightly different from each of its parents because it contains a different combination of genes than the parents.

Plants can also reproduce asexually. In this process, one part of a plant simply breaks off and grows into another plant. Alternatively, clones may form when underground stems give rise to multiple genetically identical plants. Each new plant is a clone, containing the same genes as its parent. Gardeners can easily create a clone by cutting off a *slip* (branch) of African violet or ivy plant and putting it in water. Eventually, the slip will sprout roots and grow into a new plant, genetically identical to the parent.

Why clone animals?

People have been cloning plants for at least 4,000 years, but animal cloning is a much more recent advance. The reason is that most animals do not form clones in nature. Nevertheless, scientists have worked hard to overcome the obstacles to animal cloning for several reasons.

First, cloning experiments offer insight into *gene regulation*—how genes are turned on and off. Only a portion of an organism's genes are activated at any one time, and the makeup of that portion changes during development and varies from cell to cell. Some genes are turned on early to control embryo growth, but they are turned off later in development. Other genes are expressed late in development to help a cell take on a specialized role. By trying to clone animals at different stages of development, biologists can learn about the course of gene expression and identify the molecules responsible for turning genes on and off. This knowledge may help scientists understand and treat diseases that involve abnormal gene expression, such as cancer.

Researches are also pursuing cloning to boost the productivity of farm animals. Scientists someday hope to use cloning to increase the number of offspring from animals with desired traits, such as lean meat or above-average milk production. The technique, in use since the 1980's, could lead to higher-quality animal products.

Another interest in cloning, specifically human cloning, concerns medical treatment for couples who have difficulty conceiving a child. The problem may stem from several conditions, including a blockage in the woman's reproductive system that prevents the woman from becoming pregnant. Such couples often try *in vitro fertilization (IVF)*, in which physicians surgically remove eggs from the woman's ovaries and combine them with the man's sperm in a dish in a laboratory.

Animal cloning: Facts and myths

Cloning is the production of an organism without *sexual reproduction,* the process in which *genes* (hereditary material) are transmitted from two parents. Scientists can clone animals in the early stages of development, but experiments in which adult animals are cloned belong to the realm of science fiction, at least for now.

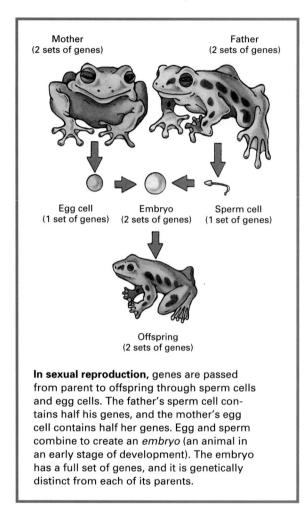

Mother
(2 sets of genes)

Father
(2 sets of genes)

Egg cell
(1 set of genes)

Embryo
(2 sets of genes)

Sperm cell
(1 set of genes)

Offspring
(2 sets of genes)

In sexual reproduction, genes are passed from parent to offspring through sperm cells and egg cells. The father's sperm cell contains half his genes, and the mother's egg cell contains half her genes. Egg and sperm combine to create an *embryo* (an animal in an early stage of development). The embryo has a full set of genes, and it is genetically distinct from each of its parents.

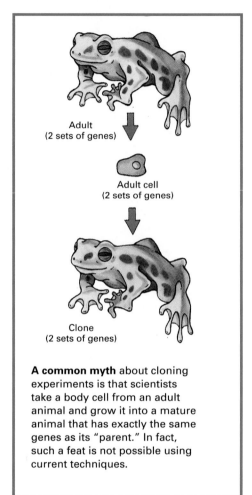

Adult
(2 sets of genes)

Adult cell
(2 sets of genes)

Clone
(2 sets of genes)

A common myth about cloning experiments is that scientists take a body cell from an adult animal and grow it into a mature animal that has exactly the same genes as its "parent." In fact, such a feat is not possible using current techniques.

The doctors then implant the embryos that develop from the fertilized eggs in the woman's uterus. The survival rate of implanted embryos was about 25 percent in 1994, so physicians normally implant several embryos at the same time to increase the chances of a pregnancy. Cloning could increase the number of embryos used for implantation and so raise the likelihood of a successful pregnancy.

Experiments with amphibians

The first vertebrate animals to be cloned were amphibians, the group of cold-blooded animals that includes frogs, salamanders, and toads. Amphibians have long been favorite creatures for scientists

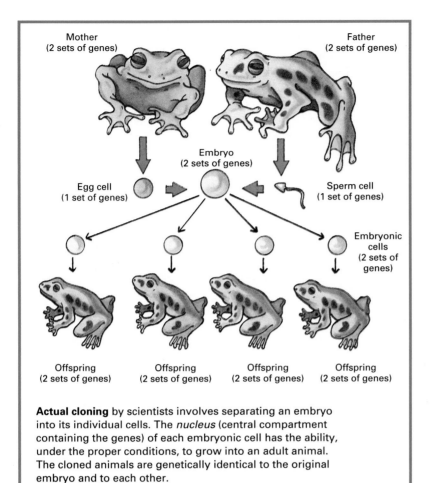

Mother
(2 sets of genes)

Father
(2 sets of genes)

Embryo
(2 sets of genes)

Egg cell
(1 set of genes)

Sperm cell
(1 set of genes)

Embryonic
cells
(2 sets of
genes)

Offspring
(2 sets of genes)

Offspring
(2 sets of genes)

Offspring
(2 sets of genes)

Offspring
(2 sets of genes)

Actual cloning by scientists involves separating an embryo into its individual cells. The *nucleus* (central compartment containing the genes) of each embryonic cell has the ability, under the proper conditions, to grow into an adult animal. The cloned animals are genetically identical to the original embryo and to each other.

studying animal development, in part because amphibian eggs are relatively large. For example, the North American leopard frog has eggs that are up to 2 millimeters (0.7 inch) in diameter. By contrast, the eggs of mammals, such as rabbits, cows, and human beings, are much smaller and only just visible with the naked eye. And amphibian embryos can develop in a water-filled dish in a laboratory just as well as they do in their natural environment, a pond or other body of water. The combination of these two features enables biologists to manipulate and observe amphibian development under the controlled conditions of a biology lab.

The ease of working with amphibian embryos allowed scientists in the early 1900's to try bold experiments to learn how the animals developed. Some scientists cut off part of one amphibian embryo and attached it to another embryo to determine if the part would develop differently at the new site. Others grafted extra limbs onto embryos to learn how nerves grew from the spinal cord into appendages. In 1924, scientists even performed a heart transplant between amphibian embryos.

The success of these experiments led scientists to probe deeper into amphibian development. Instead of working with limbs and organs, which contain cells that have already become specialized, other researchers began to study cells at an earlier stage. They wanted to know how cells with a wide variety of functions arise from a single cell. For example, the biologists wondered if the organism's specialized cells that formed nerves and muscles contained the genetic "blueprint" for the entire organism. Or did they possess only those genes pertaining to "nerveness" and "muscleness"?

In 1938, the German embryologist and Nobel Prize winner Hans Spemann suggested that the best way to find out if a single cell contains the entire genetic blueprint for an organism would be to transplant the cell's nucleus into an egg cell that has been *enucleated* (had its own nucleus removed). Eggs, the female cells involved in sexual reproduction, possess a storehouse of nutrients needed for early development. By replacing the egg's nucleus with the nucleus of another cell, scientists would be giving the egg an entirely new set of genetic instructions. The biologists could then monitor what happened to the egg. If the egg developed normally—by dividing into two cells, then four, then eight, and so on to form an adult—the researchers would know that all the necessary genes in the transplanted nucleus could still be made active. If the egg did not develop, then

Uses of cloning research
Research biologists—such as the author and his co-worker, *below*—may study cloning to learn how genes are turned on and off during development. Those studies could help scientists understand cancer and other diseases that involve abnormal gene expression.

Cloned calves produced at Granada Biosciences, Inc., of Houston were the result of agricultural scientists' work to increase the number of offspring from farm animals with valuable traits, such as lean meat and high-quality milk.

those genes must have been turned off or altered in some other way.

In essence, Spemann was talking about cloning, though he could not envision the experiment's actually being conducted because of the difficulty of performing surgery on cells. But researchers persevered, and in 1952, biologists Robert Briggs and Thomas J. King at the Institute for Cancer Research (now called the Fox Chase Cancer Center) in Philadelphia announced that they had produced tadpoles by nuclear transplantation. In their experiment, they cloned a cell from a frog embryo of a few thousand cells. They chose such a cell because they hypothesized that it would not be very specialized, and so it would still possess most of the same active genes that were in the original fertilized egg.

Briggs and King's cloning experiment involved several steps. They removed the nucleus of an unfertilized frog egg with a very thin needle. Next, they used a *micropipette* (a very thin glass tube) to extract the nucleus from a cell taken from the frog embryo. They accomplished this feat by placing the micropipette next to the cell and drawing the cell into the tube with suction equipment. Because the cell was slightly wider than the micropipette, the cell's outer membrane burst, and the cell's contents, including the nucleus, were freed. The researchers then inserted the micropipette into the enucleated egg cell and ejected the nucleus.

In a few days, Briggs and King's nuclear transplant egg grew into a tadpole. In later experiments, the cloned tadpoles developed into mature frogs. Thus, a single cell from a frog embryo of a few thousand cells still possesses genes that can be activated in the proper sequence to form an adult frog. Furthermore, each of Briggs and King's frogs was genetically identical to the young embryo from which the scientists had taken the cell.

For the first time in history, scientists had cloned a frog. Independent laboratories in China, England, France, Japan, and the Soviet Union quickly reproduced Briggs and King's work, confirming that the experiment had been a success.

But are they really clones?

At this point, a skeptical person might ask how scientists can ensure that the products of cloning experiments are truly clones. Researchers take several precautions. Before they insert new genetic material into an egg, they take great care to remove all of the egg's original genes. To make certain the egg's original genes have been replaced, researchers generally choose embryos and egg cells from animals that have different physical traits. One selected trait in frog cloning is the pigment pattern of the skin. The egg cell comes from a frog with one pigment pattern, whereas the nucleus comes from a frog with a different pattern. If the resulting frog has the second pattern, then the transplanted genes must be responsible for the frog's development.

Scientists can also test the organism to determine whether it is a clone of another animal. They do this by grafting a piece of skin or other tissue from one organism to its clone. All higher animals have an immune system that rejects foreign cells, including tissue that is not genetically identical. But tissue from a clone is recognized as the animal's own. If the animal's body does not reject the transplant, then the transplant donor is indeed a clone.

Attempts to clone older animals

After Briggs and King's groundbreaking work, scientists began performing cloning experiments with other cells, seeking to identify the most developed cell that could still be cloned. So far, only cells from embryos have yielded clones that develop to adulthood. Whenever researchers tried to clone a frog using a nucleus from an older animal, the cloned cell failed to grow into a frog. Furthermore, despite decades of work, scientists still have not found a way to reactivate genes from adult cells in the proper sequence to cause normal development.

Because of that barrier, cloning an adult organism seems out of the question, though scientists have discovered two significant exceptions to that rule. In 1986, biologist Marie A. DiBerardino at the Medical College of Pennsylvania in Philadelphia reported producing tadpoles using cells from adult frogs. In her experiment, DiBerardino used nuclei taken from red blood cells, because those cells are easy to identify and relatively easy to work with. Human red blood cells have no nuclei, but frog red blood cells do.

DiBerardino modified the Briggs and King procedure by exposing the red blood cell nuclei to immature egg *cytoplasm* (the substance of a cell outside the nucleus) before transplanting the nuclei. The resulting embryos developed into tadpoles with all the organs necessary for feeding and swimming, and they even had the buds of hind limbs. However, for reasons as yet unknown, the tadpoles died before reaching metamorphosis, the change from a tadpole into an adult frog. DiBerardino's tadpoles were the most advanced organisms yet cloned using genetic material from adult animals.

Unusual results with cancer cells

In 1991, researchers at the University of Minnesota in St. Paul reported that tissue from cloned cancer cells retained much potential for normal development. Cancer cells are cells that divide uncontrollably. Because repeated cell division is typical of unspecialized cells, scientists think that some genes that are turned off in normal cells are active in cancer cells. The Minnesota scientists undertook their cloning experiment to learn whether the genes in cancer cells could be regulated to result in normal cells.

Researchers had previously transplanted nuclei from frog kidney cancer cells into enucleated eggs. To the scientists' amazement, they found that instead of forming a mass of cancer cells, the eggs grew

How to clone a cow

Since the 1980's, scientists have known how to clone such mammals as cattle, mice, pigs, rabbits, and sheep. The key step involves transferring the nucleus of an embryonic cell into an egg cell that has had its nucleus removed.

First, scientists mate a bull and a cow. After letting the resulting embryo grow and divide for a few days in the cow's reproductive tract, the scientists remove the embryo and place it in a nutrient solution in the lab. Then they apply chemicals that separate the embryo into its individual cells. Each of these cells contains the same genes.

Bull

Cow

Fertilized egg

Embryo in nutrient solution

Next, the scientists remove egg cells from the ovary of another cow. Using a thin glass tube called a micropipette, the scientists *enucleate* (remove the nucleus from) each egg cell. Then they fuse each egg cell with an embryonic cell by means of an electrical pulse. The egg cell now contains the nucleus from the embryonic cell. It thus possesses a full set of genes, just as if it had been fertilized by a sperm in sexual reproduction, and it begins developing like a normal embryo.

Separated embryonic cells

Micropipette

Egg cell donor

Egg cell

Nuclear extraction

Fusion with electrical pulse

The procedure may be repeated with the remaining cells of the original embryo to produce a group of genetically identical cows.

Egg with embryonic nucleus

The scientists let the new embryo grow in a nutrient solution for a few days. Then they implant the embryo into the uterus of another cow, where it develops naturally until the calf is ready to be born.

Foster mother cow

Genetically identical cows

An early attempt at human cloning

In October 1993, researchers announced they had cloned human embryos. To try to avoid controversy over the ethics of cloning human beings, the scientists cloned cells that were abnormal and incapable of survival.

Fertilized egg

Scientists used flawed embryos created during *in vitro fertilization.* As part of that procedure, doctors surgically remove an egg cell from a woman. Using sperm from a man, they then fertilize the egg in a lab dish and let the resulting embryo grow and divide for a few days in a nutrient solution. To clone the abnormal embryos, the scientists first applied chemicals that separated the embryos into individual cells.

Abnormal embryo in nutrient solution

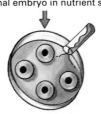

Separated embryonic cells

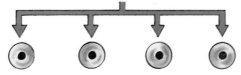

Embryonic cells

The scientists did not transplant the nuclei of the embryonic cells into enucleated eggs—as they do when cloning cows—because human egg cells are too difficult to obtain. Instead, the researchers coated each embryonic cell with a gel-like substance made from seaweed. This substance takes the place of the *zona pellucida,* a jellylike layer that normally surrounds human embryos and keeps them from falling apart.

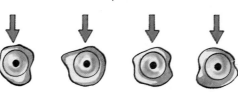

Embryonic cells with artificial zona pellucida

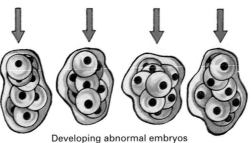

Developing abnormal embryos

The scientists let the new embryos grow in a nutrient solution until they died naturally a few days later. When they died, the embryos consisted of 8, 16, or 32 cells.

into tadpoles. The animals could swim but not eat, and they lived for 10 to 14 days. When fragments of the tadpoles were grafted to normal tadpoles, the cloned fragments developed for an additional 40 days, or about halfway to metamorphosis. The scientists speculated that unidentified factors in the egg cell caused the genes to stop giving rise to cancerous cells and to produce normal cells instead. Discovering those factors could lead to new treatments against cancer.

Problems with the *Jurassic Park* scenario

The limited success of cloning adult cells casts a shadow over the possibility of a real Jurassic Park. In the story, dinosaurs that lived about 70 million years ago are, like Marie DiBerardino's feeding tadpoles, cloned from the genetic material in red blood cells. The fictional scientists obtain the dinosaur DNA from ancient bloodsucking insects preserved in amber.

Researchers point out serious problems with the *Jurassic Park* scenario aside from the matter of cloning cells from fully developed animals. First, although paleontologists have located prehistoric DNA—up to 120 million years old—researchers have never cloned an animal using isolated DNA. They have succeeded only with whole nuclei, which contain more than just chromosomes. A cell's nucleus also contains molecules that bind to the chromosomes to activate or inactivate the genes in the proper sequence during development. Researchers have no way of knowing all the molecules that were present in the nuclei of dinosaur cells. Therefore, to clone a dinosaur, scientists would need an intact dinosaur nucleus, not just DNA.

In addition, successful cloning requires an egg cell that is very closely related to the donor nucleus. The genes must work in harmony with the nutrients in the egg for development to proceed. But scientists do not know how well modern-day eggs would serve as recipients for prehistoric dinosaur DNA. The differences between the dinosaur eggs of millions of years ago and the eggs of modern birds and reptiles, for example, may be so great that the ancient genes would not function properly. Another problem is that the eggs of reptiles and birds tend to be so large that they cannot be easily enucleated.

The tricky process of mammal cloning

Such problems did not stop researchers from trying cloning procedures on mammals, however. Working with mammalian cells proved possible, though tricky. For one thing, mammalian eggs are smaller than amphibian eggs. Mammalian eggs are also enclosed in a tough membrane called the zona pellucida, which holds the cells of the young embryo together.

A common method for enucleating mammalian eggs is *surgical aspiration*, in which a micropipette with a sharpened tip is inserted into an egg cell, and the nucleus is sucked into the micropipette and removed. Researchers then use a micropipette to place a cell containing a nucleus inside the zona pellucida, and they apply a slight electrical pulse to the egg. The electricity fuses the egg with the cell containing the nucleus.

Another complexity in cloning mammals is that the fertilized eggs must be implanted in an adult female's uterus to develop. Thus, a cloned embryo requires a foster mother. Scientists insert the embryo into a foster mother nonsurgically, by inserting the cloned egg through the birth canal with a micropipette.

By 1993, scientists had cloned five types of mammals—cows, mice, pigs, rabbits, and sheep. All were cloned using nuclei from embryonic cells. Researchers have had no success using nuclei from any type of cell taken from adult mammals.

Controversy over human embryo cloning

In theory, human embryos could be cloned the same way as other mammals. Scientists have been working with human embryos for decades, and many of the techniques developed for IVF could be used for human embryo cloning. But there is a hitch: Human eggs are difficult to obtain in large numbers. Each donor nucleus must be placed in a separate egg cell. But women can produce only a few eggs per month, even using fertility drugs, and scientists must perform surgery on the women to obtain the eggs, a cumbersome procedure. The lack of a ready supply of recipient human eggs was a major obstacle to human cloning.

Then a group of scientists headed by Jerry Hall, current director of the In Vitro Fertilization and Andrology Laboratory at George Washington University, made a key advance. Hall and his colleagues developed an artificial zona pellucida for human embryos from seaweed. Like the real zona pellucida, the new substance keeps the cells of a young embryo from falling apart.

In 1993, Hall teamed with colleague Robert Stillman to test whether the artificial zona pellucida could do away with the need for recipient egg cells in human cloning. They began with 17 human embryos that consisted of two, four, or eight cells. The embryos, which came from the IVF clinic at the university, were chosen because they had been fertilized with more than one sperm and so would have died in a few days.

Hall and Stillman separated the young embryos into their individual cells, which are called *blastomeres*. Then they coated each blastomere with the artificial zona pellucida and placed it in a nutrient solution that matched the fluid in a woman's fallopian tube, where the first few days of development occur while the fertilized egg travels to the uterus.

The scientists obtained a total of 48 new embryos. Blastomeres taken from eight-cell embryos developed in the nutrient solution as far as the eight-cell stage, then they died. Blastomeres from four-cell embryos made it only to 16 cells. Blastomeres from two-cell embryos

The 1993 motion picture *Jurassic Park* conjured visions of cloned dinosaurs, but experts say scientists do not have the materials they would need to clone a dinosaur. Dinosaur cloning would require not only dinosaur DNA but an entire nucleus from a dinosaur cell. In addition, scientists would have the difficult task of finding a compatible egg from a living animal to transfer the dinosaur nucleus into.

reached the 32-cell stage, and then those cells died, too. Hall and Stillman were not sure why the cloned blastomeres died, but many scientists blamed the fact that the cells were abnormal to begin with. Eggs fertilized by more than one sperm rarely develop normally.

Hall and Stillman's experiment was widely heralded as successful human cloning, but in reality it only set the stage. For one thing, the embryos were not implanted in women, so the researchers do not know what other problems might have prevented the embryos' development into fetuses. However, most scientists considered that step relatively simple, because the procedure for transferring an embryo from a laboratory dish into a woman's uterus has already been established for use in IVF. The true barriers to human cloning, scientists say, are not technical in nature but ethical. Cloning touches upon personal notions of the sanctity of human life and the uniqueness of individuals.

A survey taken shortly after Hall and Stillman's announcement found that 75 percent of Americans opposed human cloning, and almost half favored making it illegal. Hall and Stillman themselves said they would not proceed any further until scientific organizations such as the American Fertility Society and the American Association of Bioethics established guidelines for human cloning. Scientists say such guidelines are vital if cloning researchers are to continue to hold the public trust.

Potential uses of human embryo cloning

Nevertheless, experts say that human cloning might lead to improvements in medicine. One possible use for cloning is the one that Hall and Stillman were pursuing, to boost the number of embryos that can be implanted in a woman in an IVF operation. A second, related use is for screening IVF embryos for genetic defects. Doctors currently perform such tests by removing one cell from an embryo and testing the genes in that cell. The genetic tests might be more reliable if cloned two- or four-cell embryos were used for analysis, because there would be more genetic material to work with. Some scientists argue that cloning embryos for the purpose of genetic diagnosis would be improper. But other researchers do not see much difference between using single embryonic cells and using two- or four-cell clones.

Other potential uses of clones are much more far-fetched. For example, parents in the future could have one or more "spare" embryos created at the conception of a child using IVF. The couple would then have the option of giving birth to the first child's "twin" at a later date, perhaps to provide compatible organs if the first child needed a transplant. Or the couple could sell the cloned embryos to other families, who would get an indication of how their embryo would turn out based on the characteristics of the first child. Although the vast majority of ethicists do not see these improbable uses of clones ever becoming acceptable, they offer them as extreme cases for discussion.

Ethical concerns

Many of our concerns about human cloning stem from discomfort with the idea of precisely replicating a human being, personality and all. In fact, that will never be possible. Genes are just part of the ingredients that go into making an individual. A person's upbringing and experiences also play an important role. Identical twins come from a single embryo and so are essentially clones of each other. Yet they mature into distinct people, molded by unique events. Similarly, cloned human embryos might grow into adults who look alike, but they would probably possess many different likes, interests, and talents.

Still, some experts say that cloning is better viewed as a means of learning about cell biology than as a technique to produce more frogs or more people. Understanding how an embryo gives rise to a variety of cell types may provide new insights into a number of medical conditions that have plagued humanity, not the least of which is cancer. Researchers originally devised cloning to help them in this type of investigation, and society may come to decide that the focus of cloning research should remain there.

For further reading:

"Clone Hype." *Newsweek*, Nov. 8, 1993, pp. 60-67.
"Cloning: Where Do We Draw the Line?" *Time*, Nov. 8, 1993, pp. 65-70.
McKinnell, Robert Gilmore. *Cloning of Frogs, Mice, and Other Animals*. University of Minnesota Press, 1985.

■ ■ ■

Questions for thought and discussion

Suppose a scientific organization such as the American Association of Bioethics asked you to chair a committee to establish guidelines for human cloning. The guidelines will have a far-reaching effect, because physicians will be barred from offering their patients services that go beyond the guidelines. Your aim is to allow doctors and patients the greatest possible freedom without permitting the unethical use of human cloning.

Questions: Under what circumstances, if any, would you allow couples undergoing in vitro fertilization to have embryos cloned? Would you approve of the technique if it were used to increase the chances that an infertile couple could have a baby? What if the couple did not have fertility problems but wanted to ensure that they had identical twins? What are your reasons, both scientific and ethical, for making your decisions?

The Biggest Eruptions on Earth

BY JOHN H. LATTER

Volcanic eruptions of almost unimaginable size shook the Earth in prehistoric times. Geologists say we may live to see another big one.

hen Mount Pinatubo in the Philippines began erupting in June 1991, the catastrophe made headlines around the world. Almost 300 people died during the initial blasts, and eventually hundreds of thousands lost their livelihoods. It was the fourth-largest volcanic eruption of the 1900's. Geologically speaking, however, the Pinatubo eruption was comparatively small in scale. Thousands of times during Earth's history, volcanic eruptions have erupted at least 100 times more lava, ash, and dust.

Fortunately, eruptions on this scale occur at widely spaced intervals. According to most estimates, only one has happened since recorded history began. That disaster struck in April 1815, when Indonesia's Mount Tambora exploded. The volcano blasted into the sky a column of rock and ash so huge that it completely blocked the sun for 600 kilometers (370 miles) around the volcano. Even larger eruptions occurred during prehistoric times at Yellowstone Lake in Wyoming, Long Valley in California, and Valles volcano in New Mexico's Jemez Mountains. At these sites—and in virtually every other country where there are volcanoes—eruptions from time to time have buried the landscape deep in ash and debris. Some of those eruptions disrupted weather patterns around the globe, and some may even have killed off entire species of plants and animals.

At present, no one can tell where the next massive eruption will occur, or whether any person living today will be around to see it. But geologic history indicates that, sooner or later, another gigantic blast or huge flood of lava will break out somewhere in the world.

Evidence of giant eruptions

Experts say that if they understood the processes leading up to an eruption better, they could identify in advance the danger signs, and people could take steps to avoid the worst of the catastrophe. Many researchers worldwide devote their careers to this study. Some concentrate on finding evidence of prehistoric eruptions, a branch of geology known as *tephrochronology*. Other scientists learn about the smaller eruptions that occur at various sites every year. Their studies concentrate on the geologic activity that produces all eruptions, no matter what size.

In the late 1800's, geologists first began looking for evidence of huge eruptions. Since then, they have identified about 80 volcanoes that at one time have erupted at least 100 cubic kilometers (24 cubic miles) of rock and gas, which is about 20 times the volume erupted by Mount St. Helens in Washington state in 1980.

Many more sites of massive eruptions go undetected, because the largest and most violent eruptions produce the least visible volcanoes. Only relatively weak eruptions allow rock, ash, and other debris to pile up around a crater, building the steep, cone-shaped formation that typically marks a volcano. An extremely violent eruption, on the other hand, blasts its lava far away. Such an eruption will most likely create a depression in the ground where the surface collapsed to partially fill

Preceding pages: If a massive volcanic eruption were to occur today, it would cause enormous devastation within hundreds of kilometers of the volcano. Ash and rock blown high into the atmosphere would block out sunlight. Flows of hot ash and gas would explode outward over the landscape, burning up plants and buildings in their path. If the flows hit the sea, they would create waves big enough to submerge low-lying islands and shorelines.

The author:
John H. Latter is a volcanologist and retired research associate at the Institute of Geological and Nuclear Sciences in Wellington, New Zealand.

the void where molten rock had been. Volcanic depressions, called *calderas,* can be so large—some 100 kilometers (60 miles) across—that the complete circular outline can be detected only by looking at a satellite image of the Earth.

Once geologists discover the site of an ancient eruption, they begin studying the volcanic rock on the ground. Mapping the distance of the deposits from the volcano enables geologists to determine the force of the eruption. By identifying the layers of ash, lava, and other material in the rock, geologists can determine the order in which the debris erupted. Measuring the thickness of the layers indicates how much material was thrown out.

Finally, dating the deposits provides an estimate of when an eruption occurred and how much time elapsed between eruptions if there was more than one. The best method of dating volcanic rock is a technique called *argon-argon dating,* in which scientists measure the ratio of two radioactive forms of argon in the rock. One form of argon changes into another over time at a known rate, so measuring relative amounts of each is a way of calculating the rock's age.

The forces underground

These examinations, as well as studies of present-day eruptions, have helped geologists develop theories about the forces that cause massive eruptions. The eruptions probably begin in the same way that smaller ones do—with currents of heat rising from especially hot points far below Earth's surface. These hot points are thought to exist along the boundary between Earth's inner core and the *mantle* (the middle layer, sandwiched between the core and the outer crust).

As a current of heat rises slowly through the mantle over periods lasting millions of years, some of the mantle rock melts. The molten rock, called *magma,* contains dissolved gases, which make it lighter than the solid rock surrounding it. Being lighter, the magma works its way upward. It continues until it reaches the base of Earth's crust, which varies from about 8 to 80 kilometers (5 to 50 miles) below the surface. Crustal rock is less dense than the magma, so the crust often acts like a ceiling, blocking the magma's path and causing it to pool at the top of the mantle.

The magma may remain trapped under the crust for a very long time. As fresh magma wells up from below, the pool gradually becomes larger. The reservoir eventually becomes so huge and so hot that the lower crust begins to melt. Because molten crustal rock is buoyant, it begins moving upward, through the crust. The magma eventually rises toward the surface, where it is stopped by upper crustal rocks. Barred from further upward movement, the magma collects in a pool called a magma chamber.

Massive eruptions owe their size to the enormity of their magma chambers, a fact scientists learned by "measuring" the chambers below various volcanoes. To do that, geophysicists monitored *seismic waves* (vibrations from earthquakes). The vibrations are affected differently

Glossary

Caldera: A very large depression in the ground created when the surface of a volcano collapses after a major eruption.

Lava: Molten rock erupted from a volcano.

Magma: Molten underground rock and gas.

Pyroclastic flow: A rapid, nearly horizontal, flow of ash, rock, and gas that can sweep out of a volcano after an explosive eruption.

Tephra: Airborne volcanic debris.

Welded tuff: A dense rock formed by the rapid accumulation of hot ash.

by passing through molten rock compared with solid rock. By monitoring the seismic waves that pass through the region below a volcano, scientists can map out the contours of the volcano's magma chamber. In the 1960's and 1970's, for example, seismic studies of the huge volcano in Yellowstone National Park revealed that its magma chamber was about 100 kilometers (60 miles) across. A chamber that size could hold about 80,000 cubic kilometers (20,000 cubic miles) of magma.

Clues to the type of eruption

Just as seismic studies tell scientists how much magma a volcano may hold, examining the composition of volcanic rocks gives clues to exactly how the magma reached the surface. Certain types of rock indicate the volcano erupted in an explosive blast, and other kinds show that the lava poured out more smoothly, in a fiery flood.

Pumice rock is the telltale sign of an explosive blast. This lightweight, frothy looking rock is solidified lava. The rock contains tiny holes where gas escaped violently from the lava as it was erupted.

Pumice forms from types of magma called rhyolite and dacite. Both contain high levels of silica, which makes magma "sticky," in that it holds dissolved gases. Before an explosive eruption, this sticky magma carries trapped gases with it as it moves up through the Earth. Eventually, huge quantities of hot magma pool inside the magma chamber. The reduced pressure in the top few kilometers of the Earth's crust frees gases from the magma. As the gases begin to escape at a furious rate, the pressure of the gas trapped inside the chamber becomes greater and greater. Finally, the pressure causes an explosion, ripping a hole in the surface of the Earth.

If geologists discover that all or most of the rock near a volcano is a type called *basalt*, on the other hand, they assume that the eruptions were much less explosive. Basalt, which forms chiefly in the mantle, contains much less silica than rhyolite and dacite and therefore is not very sticky. Another difference is that basaltic magma is hotter than the other types. A magma chamber filled with basaltic magma does not develop the high gas pressure of a chamber containing rhyolite and dacite, and thus it is much less likely to explode. Instead, the growing pool of magma continues melting the rock above it until it finally breaks through to the surface, often at several deep cracks many kilometers long.

An explosion that shakes the Earth

What would it be like to live through a massive eruption? Historical records of the Tambora eruption, as well as evidence gathered from present-day smaller volcanic blasts, have helped geologists understand how the catastrophe would unfold. For an explosive eruption, the first signs of disaster would be an intense swarm of earthquakes. Then there would be a tremendous rush of gas out of the vent. The gas, dense with rock particles and propelled by the force of the explosion,

Comparing eruptions

One way to understand just how big volcanic eruptions can be is to compare the amount of *magma* (molten rock and gas) that collected below the surface before various volcanoes erupted. The world's biggest eruptions tapped underground stores of more than 50 cubic kilometers (12 cubic miles). The eruption of Mount Pinatubo in the Philippines in 1991 was less than 10 percent of that size. One of the biggest eruptions known to scientists happened at Yellowstone, in what is now the United States.

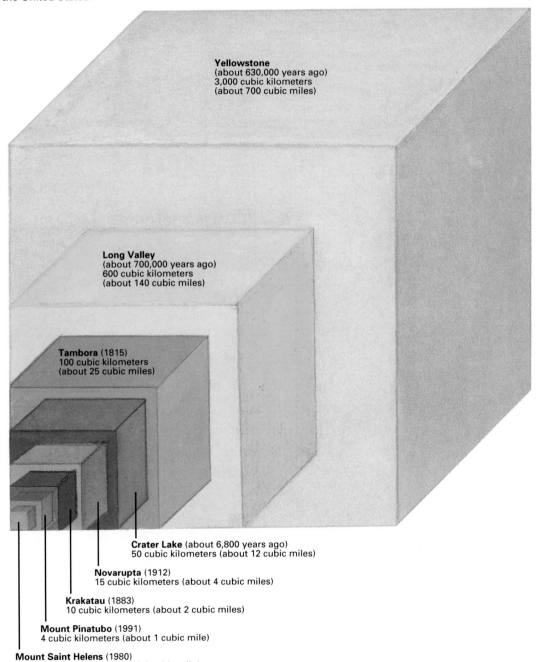

Yellowstone
(about 630,000 years ago)
3,000 cubic kilometers
(about 700 cubic miles)

Long Valley
(about 700,000 years ago)
600 cubic kilometers
(about 140 cubic miles)

Tambora (1815)
100 cubic kilometers
(about 25 cubic miles)

Crater Lake (about 6,800 years ago)
50 cubic kilometers (about 12 cubic miles)

Novarupta (1912)
15 cubic kilometers (about 4 cubic miles)

Krakatau (1883)
10 cubic kilometers (about 2 cubic miles)

Mount Pinatubo (1991)
4 cubic kilometers (about 1 cubic mile)

Mount Saint Helens (1980)
2.7 cubic kilometers (about 0.6 cubic mile)

The forces behind the eruptions

Massive eruptions take the form of explosive blasts or gigantic floods of liquid lava. These events occur when magma pushes up through an opening in Earth's surface. In massive eruptions, the volume of magma is so huge that it triggers gigantic explosions of gas, rock, and ash, *top row,* or tremendous floods of lava, *bottom row.*

Both explosive and flood eruptions may be fed by currents of heat rising from the boundary between Earth's core and the *mantle* (the layer between the core and the outer crust). The rising currents of heat melt some of the mantle rock in their path, forming magma. For tens or hundreds of thousands of years, the magma accumulates at the top of the mantle, forming a huge reservoir.

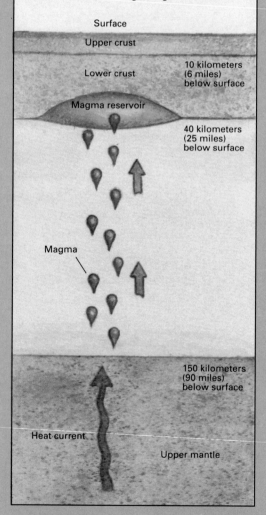

Surface

Upper crust

Lower crust

10 kilometers (6 miles) below surface

Magma reservoir

40 kilometers (25 miles) below surface

Magma

150 kilometers (90 miles) below surface

Heat current

Upper mantle

Stages of an explosive eruption

Before a massive explosive eruption, the magma at the top of the mantle gradually melts rock in the lower crust. The crustal magma, which has high levels of dissolved gases, is less dense than mantle magma and so can force its way upward. For tens or hundreds of thousands of years, the magma collects in a magma chamber from 3 to 10 kilometers (2 to 6 miles) below the surface.

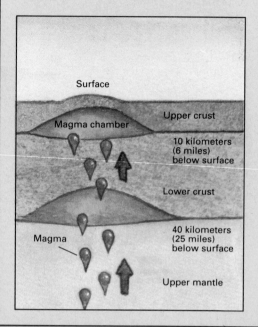

Surface

Upper crust

Magma chamber

10 kilometers (6 miles) below surface

Lower crust

40 kilometers (25 miles) below surface

Magma

Upper mantle

Stages of a lava flood eruption

In flood eruptions, the volume of magma in the magma reservoir is so huge and so hot that it melts and merges with the rock in the lower crust.

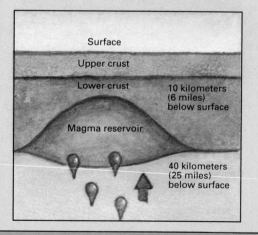

Surface

Upper crust

Lower crust

10 kilometers (6 miles) below surface

Magma reservoir

40 kilometers (25 miles) below surface

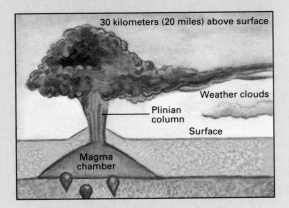

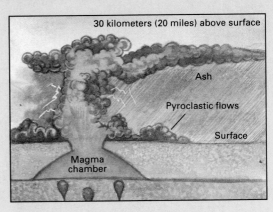

Eventually, the gas pressure in the magma chamber builds to such tremendous levels that the volcano explodes. Propelled by escaping gases, a gigantic column of ash and rock, called a *Plinian column*, blasts into the atmosphere, reaching an altitude of at least 30 to 40 kilometers (20 to 25 miles).

As gas pressures within the Plinian column drop, the column collapses, and about half the ash and rock falls back to earth. Huge clouds of hot gas, rocks, and ash, called *pyroclastic flows*, sweep out from the volcano in all directions at speeds of about 300 kilometers (200 miles) per hour.

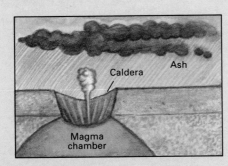

The eruption drains only about 10 percent of the magma in the magma chamber. But the loss is enough to cause the ground above the volcano to collapse, forming a huge depression called a *caldera*.

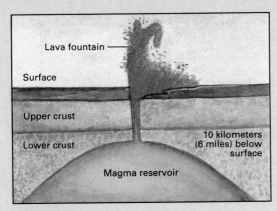

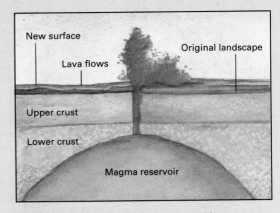

Eventually, the magma breaks through the crust, creating cracks several kilometers long. Lava flows over the surface, and molten rock shoots skyward in spectacular lava fountains.

Repeated eruptions, sometimes occurring over several million years, bury the landscape in layers of lava up to several kilometers thick.

Where massive eruptions occurred

At least 80 massive explosive eruptions (red dots) have occurred at various sites throughout the world during the past 2 million years. In those eruptions, huge amounts of ash, dust, and rocks were blown violently into the atmosphere. Scientists have also found evidence of gargantuan flood eruptions (purple areas), in which enormous sheets of lava poured out of the Earth. The lava from the flood eruptions, all of which happened more than 2 million years ago, covered vast areas, with repeated eruptions over millions of years building huge plateaus on land or on the ocean floor.

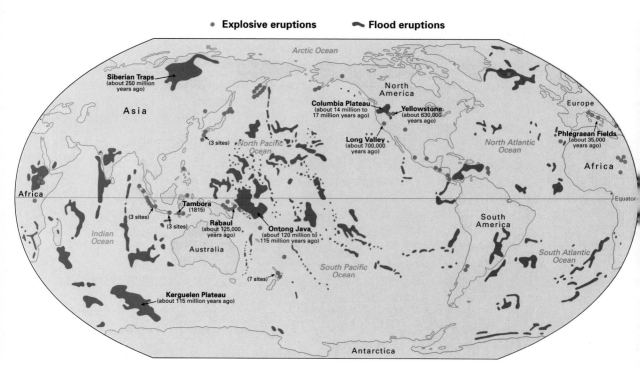

• Explosive eruptions   ➤ Flood eruptions

travels so fast that it creates a sonic boom. The highly destructive blast levels almost everything in its path, flattening trees and wiping bare most of the landscape for perhaps 1,500 to 2,000 square kilometers (600 to 800 square miles) around the vent.

Fragments of lava, ash, and other debris explode from the vent at the same instant. Rocks fly out to distances of more than 5 kilometers (3 miles). Fast-moving clouds of steam, gas, and rock particles burst horizontally from the vent. Most of the debris, however, is propelled straight up into the sky in a gigantic column. This spectacular formation of hot, buoyant debris is called a *Plinian column* after the Roman scholar Pliny the Elder, who died when Mount Vesuvius erupted in A.D. 79.

By measuring the distance of debris from the vents of ancient volcanoes, geologists learned that Plinian columns may rise up to 50 kilometers (30 miles) into the air—higher than jet airplanes fly, higher even than the ozone layer in the upper stratosphere. At the top of the Plinian column, the debris is spread by the wind into an immense canopy, which acts like a huge blanket, obliterating the sun and creating total darkness for hundreds of kilometers around the volcano.

A day or two after the start of the eruption, the gas pressure in the magma chamber drops, and the Plinian column finally begins to collapse. About half the ash and rock in the column falls to the ground and then sweeps out in all directions in what geologists call *pyroclastic flows*. Each pyroclastic flow pours over the landscape on a cushion of turbulent hot gases. It races at speeds of up to 300 kilometers (190 miles) per hour, and its tremendous momentum can easily carry it over hills and may propel it for distances of 50 to 150 kilometers (30 to 90 miles) or more.

After the passage of a large pyroclastic flow, the countryside appears totally changed, with all structures and all living things destroyed. The flow leaves behind hot ash that levels off the landscape by filling valleys and depressions to great depths while thinly covering hills. If this ash is hot enough, and if it accumulates rapidly enough, it forms a dense rock called *welded tuff*, which looks like concrete when it has cooled.

If a pyroclastic flow slams into a lake or river, a huge mudflow will surge downstream and over low-lying ground, destroying everything in its path. If the pyroclastic flow sweeps into a very large lake or an ocean, it may create giant waves called *tsunami* that swamp low-lying coastal areas and islands.

Scientists call airborne volcanic debris *tephra*, a term that describes fine ash as well as boulders tens of meters across. The boulders and other large particles fall quickly back to the ground close to the volcano. Finer tephra falls to Earth after being dispersed by the wind, and the ash may travel an amazing distance from the vent. About 50 kilometers (30 miles) away, the ashfall from a massive eruption of 50 cubic kilometers (12 cubic miles) will cover the ground to a thickness of 10 meters (33 feet). At 175 kilometers (110 miles), the ash may be 1-meter (3-feet) thick. Even as far as 2,250 kilometers (1,400 miles) away—the distance between New York City and Houston—the ashfall may be 1-centimeter (0.4-inch) thick.

The aftermath

A single volcano may erupt in this fashion several times, though one eruption in a single period of activity is usually much bigger than the others. Eventually, unless the supply of magma is renewed from deeper levels, most of the gas-rich magma is ejected. The remainder then cools and solidifies underground over a period that may be as long as several thousand years. Shrinkage cracks form as the rock cools, opening the way for the underlying basaltic magma to break through. This cycle of events has happened at least three times at Yellowstone, with lesser volumes of basalt following eruptions of thousands of cubic kilometers of rhyolite. Where the supply of basaltic magma is especially large, basaltic flood eruptions may take place.

Lava floods and fire fountains

Although flood eruptions do not produce Plinian columns or pyroclastic flows, a massive flood eruption would be a spectacular sight. The basaltic magma pours through surface cracks in huge glowing red sheets. "Fire fountains" of lava shoot up high into the air. The heat can cause adjacent forestland to erupt into flame. If the lava flows into rivers and lakes, it creates mudflows, tsunami, and gigantic eruptions of steam. Airfall tephra and poisonous gases are a hazard to plant and animal life even at great distances.

The largest known flood eruptions in North America began 17 million years ago and continued, on and off, for the next 3 million years. These eruptions produced a total of about 200,000 cubic kilometers (50,000 cubic miles) of lava. That rock is the Columbia Plateau, which covers large portions of Idaho, Oregon, and Washington.

By dating some of the layers of lava produced during these eruptions, scientists estimated that up to 100 cubic kilometers (24 cubic miles) erupted in a single week, which means that lava was flowing from the volcano on average at about 165,000 cubic meters (6 million cubic feet) per second. At such a rate of flow, one week would be enough time to cover an area the size of the state of Washington knee-deep in lava.

Gigantic eruptions of basalt on the sea floor dwarf even those that created the Columbia Plateau. Sea-floor eruptions tend to be of monstrous size, probably because the crust on the ocean floor is thinner, and thus more easily melted through, than the crust that makes up the continents. For example, seismic studies of two underwater plateaus formed by flood eruptions about 115 million years ago—Ontong Java, north of the Solomon Islands in the southwestern Pacific, and Kerguelen in the southern Indian Ocean—revealed that those features were each formed by eruptions of about 250 times more lava than created the Columbia Plateau.

Eruptions that warm the Earth

Submarine eruptions such as these may discharge so much volcanic gas that they significantly alter the chemistry of the oceans and the atmosphere. The eruptions at Ontong Java and Kerguelen, for example, released vast amounts of carbon dioxide, sulfur, phosphorus, and nitrogen.

According to a theory proposed by scientists Ken Caldeira and Michael Rampino of New York University in New York City, those eruptions may have indirectly led to the creation of much of Earth's petroleum deposits. Petroleum deposits are formed from layers of dead plant and animal matter subjected to extreme pressure as

Evidence of big blasts

The giant caldera that formed after Yellowstone erupted 600,000 years ago, *right,* is so large that a satellite view is necessary to see its complete outline. Later lava flows have obscured the edges of the caldera, which is 75 kilometers (47 miles) wide in places. Thick deposits of rock formed from ash in New Mexico's Bandelier National Monument, *below,* are another sign of a massive explosive eruption. The rock, called welded tuff, formed after the Valles volcano in the nearby Jemez Mountains erupted massively about 1 million years ago.

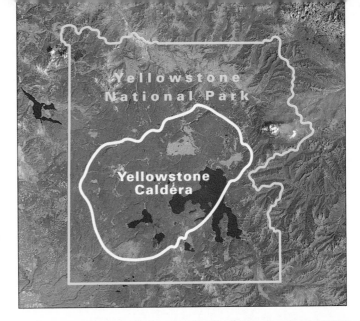

they are buried in sedimentary rock over millions of years.

Caldeira and Rampino set forth the following scenario. First, the eruptions released gases including carbon dioxide, one of the so-called *greenhouse gases*. In the atmosphere, greenhouse gases trap energy from the sun somewhat like the windows in a greenhouse. According to Caldeira and Rampino, the extra carbon dioxide in the atmosphere helped cause an increase in average global temperatures and spurred plant growth. As polar ice melted and as lava spilled out on the sea floor, sea levels rose. Tiny marine organisms called plankton flourished in the warming waters, which now contained large amounts of nitrogen and other chemical nutrients released by the volcanoes. When those marine organisms died and settled to the sea floor, they provided the raw material that eventually became the petroleum deposits.

Eruptions that cause a cooling effect

Several massive eruptions of the explosive type, on the other hand, have been followed by unusually cool weather. The process begins as sulfur dioxide and other volcanic gases sent high into the atmosphere combine with hydrogen and oxygen to form droplets of sulfuric acid. These drops, which may remain aloft for years, scatter incoming radiation from the sun. At the same time, airborne dust particles absorb heat radiating from the Earth. Both lead to lower average temperatures at the surface.

Many scientists believe that even the relatively small eruption of Mount Pinatubo temporarily cooled the world's weather. The more severe Tambora eruption caused a much greater temperature decrease. Historical records show that the year after the blast was known as "the year without a summer." In the Northern Hemisphere, summertime snows and frost ruined crops.

A few geologists have even proposed that series of gigantic explosive eruptions may have triggered the *ice ages* (periods during which enormous sheets of ice covered huge areas of Earth). Geological records do show a link between the timing of some of the largest known eruptions and the beginning of the most recent ice age about 2 million years ago.

Another small group of experts argue that the relationship is reversed: the ice ages triggered volcanic activity. Those researchers say that the build-up of ice creates great stress on Earth's crust, which leads to the eruptions. It may even be possible that both theories are correct. The ice ages may trigger eruptions, which further cool the climate, causing the ice ages to be more intense and prolonged than they would have been otherwise.

The debate will probably not be resolved until scientists discover a way to determine much more precisely when the ice ages began and when the known massive eruptions occurred. Until then, determining whether there is a relationship between the two—and, if so, what it is—is virtually impossible.

A link to mass extinctions and dinosaurs

Massive eruptions may be involved in yet another geologic mystery—why large numbers of plant and animal species suddenly died out during at least five periods in the past 245 million years. One of the most recent of these extinction periods occurred about 65 million years ago, when the last of the dinosaurs died off.

Many theories have been proposed to explain one or more of the extinctions. The most popular current theory is that the extinctions happened after a comet or asteroid struck the Earth, throwing up huge clouds of dust that blocked the sun and cooled Earth's climate or destroyed the ozone layer. In the cold and darkness that followed, many plants and animals perished. A second and less-popular theory is that massive volcanic eruptions causing dramatic temperature changes were to blame.

In the late 1980's, some experts attempted to combine the two arguments by linking comet showers to flood eruptions. These scientists proposed that several mass extinctions were caused by comet showers that jolted Earth severely enough to trigger intense outpourings of lava. The combination of eruptions and impacts would have disrupted the environment so severely that many species and even entire families of organisms would have become extinct.

In 1990, geologists reported the discovery of what appeared to be a huge crater on the coast of Mexico's Yucatán Peninsula, a finding that supports the theory that an asteroid impact led to the mass extinction about 65 million years ago. But scientists continued to evaluate evidence that volcanoes may have played a direct role. One clue was reported in a 1991 study of one of the largest known eruptions, an outpouring of about 1.6 million cubic kilometers (400,000 cubic miles) of basalt lava in Siberia. Researchers Asish R. Basu of the University of Rochester in New York and Paul R. Renne of the Institute of Human Origins in Berkeley, Calif., found that this eruption occurred between 248.3 million and 247.5 million years ago, about the time of Earth's most devastating mass extinction, when up to 95 percent of all marine animal species died out.

Predicting the next big one

A huge eruption occurring in the future is likely to cause serious problems. An explosive blast at Yellowstone, for example, would produce enough ash to cover places as far away as New York City, Boston, and Montreal to a depth of more than 3 centimeters (1 inch). The falling ash would create intense electrical disturbances, blacking out television, radio, and telephone signals. Electric power systems would shut down as ash collapsed transmission lines and clogged generators. And because tephra causes jet engines to stall, travel by air would be impossible.

These problems would only trouble people living outside an approximately 40-kilometer (25-mile) ring around the volcano. Those inside that ring would almost certainly perish in the initial blast or the

New Zealand's uninhab-
ited Curtis Island is one
of several possible sites
of Earth's next massive
eruption. The volcanic island's surface rose 7 me-
ters (23 feet) during a 34-
year period, a sign that
the pool of molten rock
and gas underground is
pressing upward.

later pyroclastic flows. But even people living on the other side of
the world might suffer from the eventual temperature drop and poor
harvests.

Fortunately, scientists see no immediate threat from Yellowstone or
any other volcano. But experts do believe there is a need to identify
likely sites of future massive eruptions, in order to recognize early
signs of activity and give emergency workers time to plan.

Since the 1960's, geophysicists have developed new instruments and
techniques for monitoring the activity of volcanoes before and during
eruptions. These advances have greatly improved scientists' ability to
forecast eruptions both large and small. For example, using gas ana-
lyzers, geochemists can measure changes in the composition and
amount of gases escaping from a vent, changes that may signal an im-
pending eruption. Tiltmeters and strain gauges can detect the expansion of the surface of a volcano. Such expansion means that gas pressure is increasing, a sign that an eruption may soon occur. Extremely
sensitive *seismometers,* instruments that record seismic waves, allow experts to track the movement of magma under a volcano and estimate
when it may begin to break through to the surface. These techniques
enabled geologists to forecast in advance all eruptions at Mount St.
Helens after the initial blast in May 1980. Geologists had similar success in forecasting the major eruption of Mount Pinatubo and the ongoing eruptions at Kilauea in Hawaii.

Where will the next massive eruption occur? One possible candidate is the little-known Curtis volcano in the Kermadec Islands near New Zealand, whose surface rose 7 meters (23 feet) between 1929 and 1964. Another is the volcano that formed the Japanese island of Iwo Jima, where a similar uplift of the surface has amounted to about 8 meters (26 feet) since 1945. Other possibilities include volcanoes at Long Valley in California, the Phlegraean Fields caldera in Italy, Rabaul in Papua New Guinea, and Yellowstone.

There are doubtless many other sites, as yet undetected, where geological unrest will one day lead to a massive eruption. The real question is *when*, because big eruptions happen at intervals so long that a species like ours may evolve, flourish, and die off without ever experiencing one. Some 600,000 to 800,000 years elapsed between each of the three most recent major eruptions at Yellowstone, for example. The last big eruption there took place about 600,000 years ago. Although the numbers indicate that Yellowstone might erupt on a massive scale at any time, no one should be surprised if it remains quiet for tens of thousands of years.

But the menace of dormant volcanoes continues to haunt us. After all, Earth is ringed with thousands of volcanoes, and geologists have identified only some of these sleeping giants. It is entirely possible that somewhere on Earth, sometime in our lifetime, a volcano will erupt with such fury that Mount Pinatubo will pale into insignificance.

For further reading:

Blong, Russell J. *Volcanic Hazards. A Sourcebook on the Effects of Eruptions.* Academic Press, 1984.

Bullard, Fred M. *Volcanoes of the Earth.* University of Texas Press, 1984.

Simkin, Tom, and Fiske, Richard S. *Krakatau 1883. The Volcanic Eruption and Its Effects.* Smithsonian Institution Press, 1983.

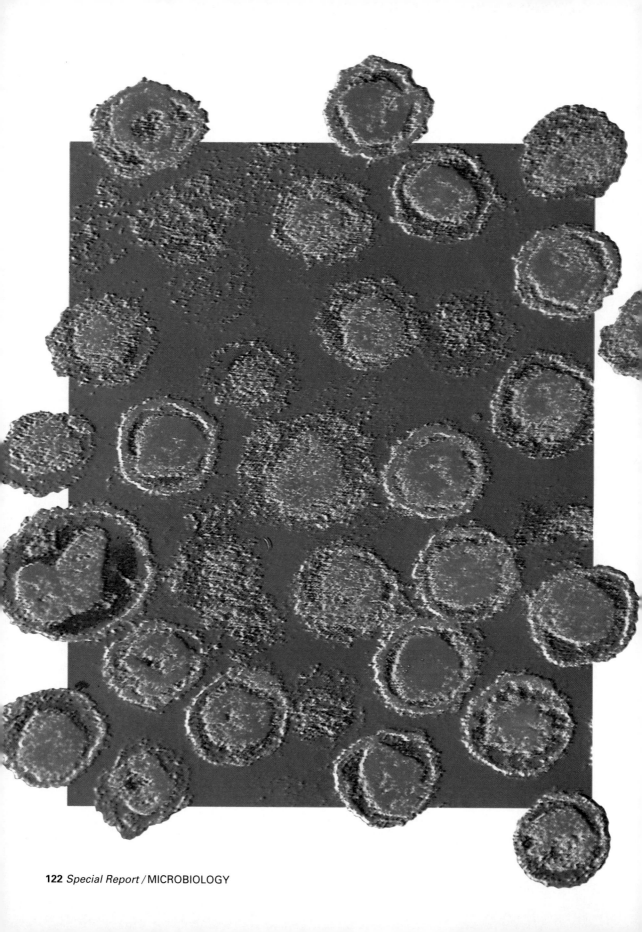

The AIDS epidemic has put the retrovirus—the microbe that causes this deadly disease—at the forefront of medical research. But scientists are probing these viruses for other secrets as well.

Exploring the Mysteries of the Retrovirus

BY JOHN M. COFFIN

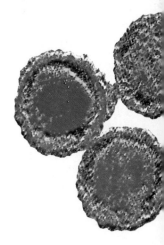

A single virus particle, carried in a tiny droplet of blood on a used syringe, has found its way into a vein on the left arm of a young drug user. The virus, less than a billionth of a billionth as large as its human host, courses through the man's bloodstream until it attaches to a white blood cell and enters it. This cell's usual job is to help protect the body from infection. Now it turns to another task, as the virus uses the cell's machinery to make thousands of copies of itself. Within a few days the cell dies, but not before the newly made viral copies have moved on. They infect many more of the man's white blood cells, which together churn out millions of copies of the virus. These viruses infect still more cells.

Within a few weeks, the young man's disease-fighting immune system brings the infection under control, and he recovers from the fever and aches it had caused. For most viruses, such as those that cause influenza or the common cold, that would be the end of the story.

But this virus is not defeated. It continues to infect and kill white blood cells, destroying the body's defenses so slowly that the young man continues to feel well. Eventually, however, the man's immune

The author:
John M. Coffin is American Cancer Society Research Professor of molecular biology and microbiology at Tufts University in Boston.

system can no longer stop the spread of the virus or combat infections caused by bacteria, fungi, parasites, or other viruses. He has more and more trouble recovering from the constant assault of infections. Finally, some years after the first infection, he dies, yet another victim of acquired immunodeficiency syndrome, or AIDS.

Although AIDS and the human immunodeficiency virus (HIV) that is its cause are among the most dangerous threats to public health today, they are but the latest chapter in the story of an unusual group of infectious agents called retroviruses. Retroviruses, like other viruses, are tiny, simple-looking microbes compared with microorganisms such as bacteria. But retroviruses are endowed with special abilities that give them a unique place in biology. As a group, retroviruses cause not only AIDS in human beings but also cancer and other diseases in a variety of mammals, birds, and even snakes and fish. Retroviruses are also capable of altering the genetic material in living cells with no obvious ill effects. In the 1990's, scientists began using that unique ability as a tool to treat or cure disease.

The nature of viruses

Scientists regard retroviruses and all other viruses as the least complex infectious agents. Viruses are so simple, in fact, that most *virologists* (scientists who study viruses) do not consider them living things. Unlike plants and animals, viruses are not made of cells. Viruses also are unable to react to their surroundings, to use food to produce energy, or to reproduce on their own—three attributes that most biologists agree are essential to life.

Viruses can reproduce when they come into contact with the tools and materials found in living cells, however. Although there are many kinds of viruses, all have as their essential task the job of reproducing inside a host cell. In the process, the virus may change or kill the cell, events that can lead to disease. People tend to think of viruses in terms of the illnesses they cause, but cell killing and disease are only side effects of a virus's real job—using living cells to reproduce.

As a simple analogy for this process, imagine the cell as a computer with a hard disk that contains software instructions used to operate the machine. A virus is like a floppy disk containing different software. When inserted into the computer, the instructions on the floppy disk can take control.

The control center of a real cell is its nucleus, the part of the cell that contains the organism's genetic material in the form of DNA (deoxyribonucleic acid). Each DNA molecule is a long strand that may carry hundreds or thousands of genes, the units responsible for the transmission of inherited characteristics.

The function of most genes is to carry instructions for producing proteins, compounds that make up many cell structures and regulate and carry out the body's chemical processes. To make a protein, the cell first creates a "twin" of the corresponding gene's DNA. The twin molecule, termed RNA (ribonucleic acid), then travels out of the nucleus to a structure in the cell called a ribosome. The ribosome moves along the RNA strand, "reading" the molecule as if it were a code and directing chemical building blocks to link up to form the needed protein.

Viruses lack the ribosomes and chemical building blocks they would need to build their own proteins. Instead, viruses typically consist of just two main parts. An inner core is made of genetic material inside a *capsid*, a casing made of proteins. For most viruses, the core is enclosed in an "envelope," which consists of a mixture of proteins and fatlike substances. Just as a floppy disk is encased in a hard plastic coating that protects the information it carries from damage, a virus's envelope protects the microbe's genetic information during the passage from cell to cell. The envelope also contains proteins that help the virus attach to a host cell and that assist in penetrating it.

As the virus enters the cell, its envelope is absorbed into the cell membrane. Then the virus's genetic material uses the cell's resources and machinery to make proteins and duplicates of the virus's own genetic material. These molecules combine to form new viral cores. The copies then pass through the cell membrane in a process called *budding*, wrapping some of the membrane around themselves as they do so. The membrane, along with viral proteins, forms the viral envelopes.

Why the retrovirus is unique

All viruses can be grouped into two main categories—those that store their genetic information as DNA and those that store it as RNA. (In contrast, the cells of plants, animals, bacteria, and other living things store their genetic information only as DNA.) The main difference between the two groups comes into play when the virus creates RNA for protein building. In most DNA viruses, the viral DNA is copied into RNA using *enzymes* (proteins that carry out chemical reactions) in the cell, in the same way as the cell copies its own DNA into RNA. In most RNA viruses, enzymes of the virus make more RNA copies of the viral RNA.

Retroviruses are a special type of RNA virus. For these microbes, replication begins when an enzyme in the retrovirus copies the viral RNA into DNA, a process that is the reverse of what happens in living

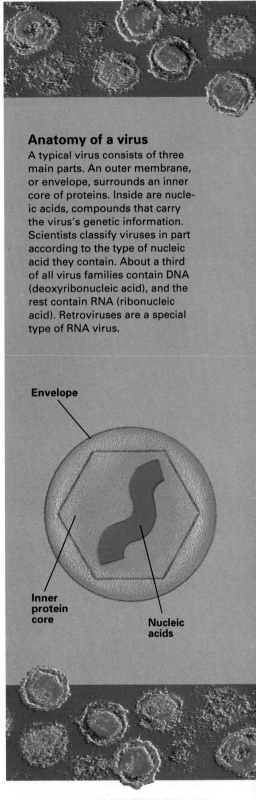

Anatomy of a virus
A typical virus consists of three main parts. An outer membrane, or envelope, surrounds an inner core of proteins. Inside are nucleic acids, compounds that carry the virus's genetic information. Scientists classify viruses in part according to the type of nucleic acid they contain. About a third of all virus families contain DNA (deoxyribonucleic acid), and the rest contain RNA (ribonucleic acid). Retroviruses are a special type of RNA virus.

Envelope

Inner protein core

Nucleic acids

things. Indeed, the prefix *retro* in *retrovirus* comes from the Latin word meaning *reverse.*

Once a retrovirus has copied its genetic material into DNA, the microbe does something else that is unique. The retrovirus DNA travels inside the nucleus of the host cell. There, another viral enzyme cuts open the cell's DNA and splices in the retrovirus DNA, a process known as *integration.* Through integration, the viral DNA becomes, in effect, part of the genes of the host cell. Like the cell's own genes, the viral DNA is made into RNA copies, which in turn go to the ribosomes to direct the manufacture of proteins needed to make more copies of the virus.

Cancer research: Opening a window on the retrovirus

Scientists learned about these special properties of retroviruses as they studied the role of the microbes in causing disease, especially cancer. In fact, the early history of *retrovirology* (the study of retroviruses) is an important part of the history of cancer research. The first retrovirus was discovered in 1910, when a New York City medical researcher named Francis Peyton Rous was studying *sarcomas* (cancers that arise in connective tissue, such as muscle, cartilage, or bone) in chickens. Rous suspected that a chicken sarcoma was caused by an infectious agent that could be passed from one bird to another. To discover what kind of agent was involved, he ground up a sarcoma tumor and passed it through a filter fine enough to remove bacteria and fungi but not fine enough to filter out viruses. When Rous then injected the filtered tumor into a healthy chicken, the chicken developed the sarcoma, showing that the cancer must have been transmitted by a virus.

Because most scientists could not believe that cancer could be caused by an infectious agent, they did not immediately recognize the importance of Rous's finding. But by the 1960's, the virus Rous discovered, called *Rous sarcoma virus,* had become a cornerstone of virology and cancer research. Its study brought Rous and other researchers a total of four Nobel Prizes.

Researchers learned that a retrovirus could also cause cancer in a mammal in the 1930's, when they discovered a retrovirus that causes breast cancer in mice. In the following years, investigators discovered many new retroviruses.

But the real breakthrough in retrovirus research came in 1970, when two virologists—Howard M. Temin of the University of Wisconsin Medical School in Madison and David Baltimore of the Massachusetts Institute of Technology in Cambridge—independently discovered the viral enzyme, called *reverse transcriptase,* that enables retroviruses to copy their RNA into DNA. Temin's and Baltimore's work proved that retroviruses are capable of that process, something most scientists had previously considered impossible. The discovery unleashed a whirlwind of research into the secrets of retrovirus biology and, therefore, into the mechanisms by which retroviruses transform healthy animal cells into cancerous ones.

How retroviruses can cause cancer

One puzzle researchers faced had to do with the rate at which different retroviruses give rise to cancer, which involves the uncontrolled growth of cells. Many animal cancers caused by retroviruses develop in six months to a year. That is the equivalent, given the animals' brief life spans, of many years in human beings. But certain retroviruses, such as the Rous sarcoma virus, produce cancers that develop extremely quickly, killing the animal within two weeks.

To solve this puzzle, scientists had to crack the code of the retrovirus *genome*, the set of genes that contain instructions for building the proteins that help make up viruses. One gene, researchers discovered, codes for the proteins that make up the core of the virus. A second gene is responsible for reverse transcriptase and other proteins that aid in retrovirus reproduction. A third gene codes for the proteins that help make up the viral envelope.

In the early 1970's, scientists compared the genomes of the fast-acting and slow-acting cancer viruses and found that the slow-acting retroviruses contained only the genes for the viral proteins. All the fast viruses, by contrast, had an additional gene, one that caused the host cell to divide out of control, eventually producing a tumor.

Researchers named the first such gene they found *src* (pronounced *sahrk*) because it occurs in the Rous sarcoma virus. Soon, they isolated different genes in retroviruses that cause various types of cancer in animals. Scientists call these cancer-causing genes *oncogenes,* from the Greek word *onkos,* meaning *tumor.*

In the mid-1970's, a group of molecular biologists at the University of California in San Francisco made another unusual finding: The DNA of healthy chickens contains a form of the *src* gene. Instead of causing cancer, this form of the gene helps regulate cell division. To explain the seeming coincidence, the researchers concluded that the retrovirus *src* gene must have originally come from a chicken. At some point in the past, the researchers realized, a retrovirus integrated itself into the DNA of a chicken cell next to the *src* gene. Then, when the viral DNA was copied onto RNA, the chicken *src* gene was copied, too. That unusual event produced an abnormally long RNA strand that became the genetic material for a newly formed retrovirus. It reproduced, creating thousands of retroviruses that harmlessly carried the extra gene. Eventually, however, the retrovirus *src* gene was *mutated* (changed) into a slightly different form. This form did not disturb the function of the virus, but when integrated into chicken DNA, it could cause a cell to divide uncontrollably.

Researchers soon determined that all the cancer genes in quick-acting retroviruses are altered forms of genes that normally help the host animal control cell growth. And although slow-acting retroviruses do not contain cancer genes, they too cause cancer by affecting host genes. That fact was discovered in 1980, when a group of researchers examined the DNA of chickens that were sick with a kind of *leukemia* (cancer of the blood-forming tissues) caused by a retrovirus. The researchers found that in the cancerous cells, the viral DNA had lodged

Retroviruses attack a cell

Retroviruses—and all other types of virus—infect the cells of living organisms and use the cell's machinery to make duplicates of themselves. With retroviruses, this process also permanently changes the genetic material in the infected cells.

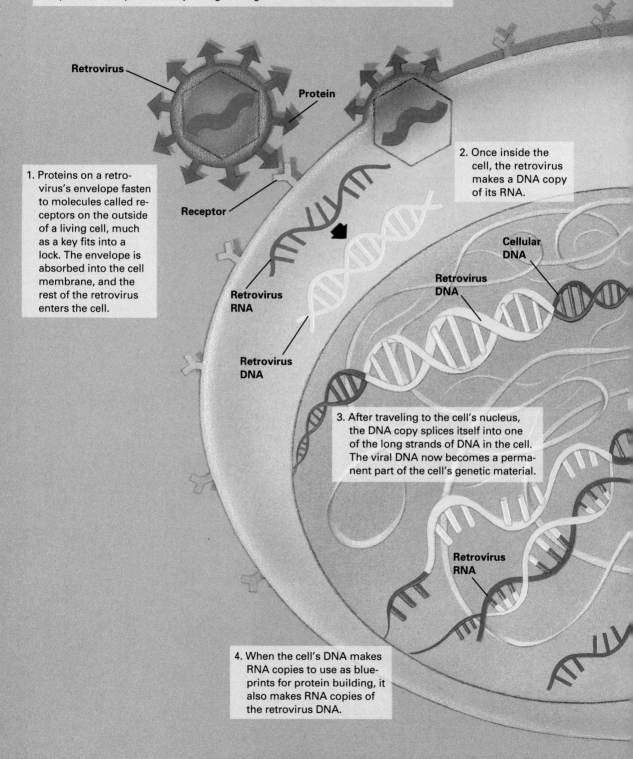

Retrovirus

Protein

Receptor

1. Proteins on a retrovirus's envelope fasten to molecules called receptors on the outside of a living cell, much as a key fits into a lock. The envelope is absorbed into the cell membrane, and the rest of the retrovirus enters the cell.

Retrovirus RNA

Retrovirus DNA

2. Once inside the cell, the retrovirus makes a DNA copy of its RNA.

Cellular DNA

Retrovirus DNA

3. After traveling to the cell's nucleus, the DNA copy splices itself into one of the long strands of DNA in the cell. The viral DNA now becomes a permanent part of the cell's genetic material.

Retrovirus RNA

4. When the cell's DNA makes RNA copies to use as blueprints for protein building, it also makes RNA copies of the retrovirus DNA.

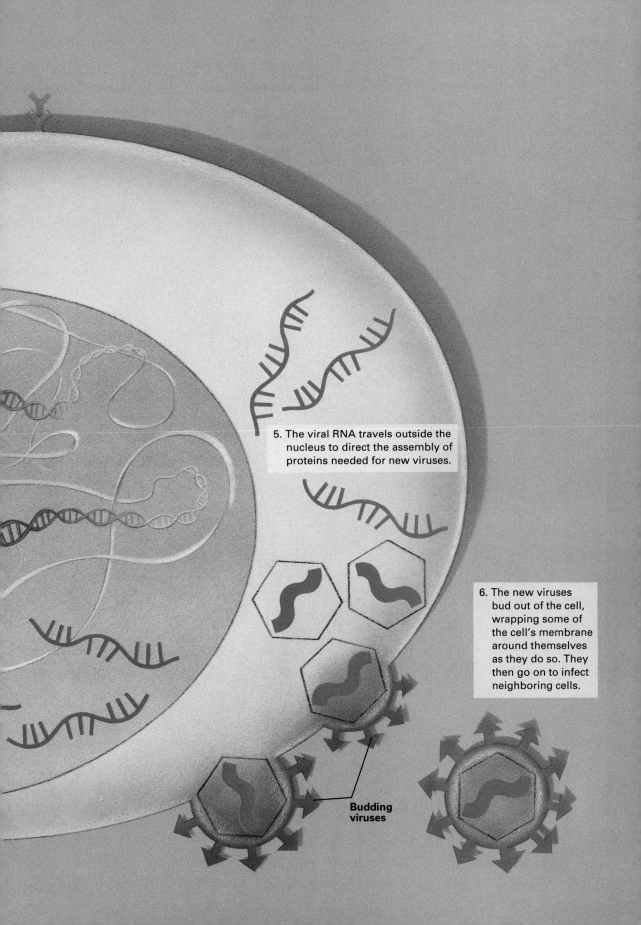

5. The viral RNA travels outside the nucleus to direct the assembly of proteins needed for new viruses.

6. The new viruses bud out of the cell, wrapping some of the cell's membrane around themselves as they do so. They then go on to infect neighboring cells.

Budding viruses

How retroviruses can cause cancer

Two main types of retroviruses can cause cancer in certain animal species. Both types involve a cancer gene, an altered form of a gene that is normally responsible for helping to regulate cell division.

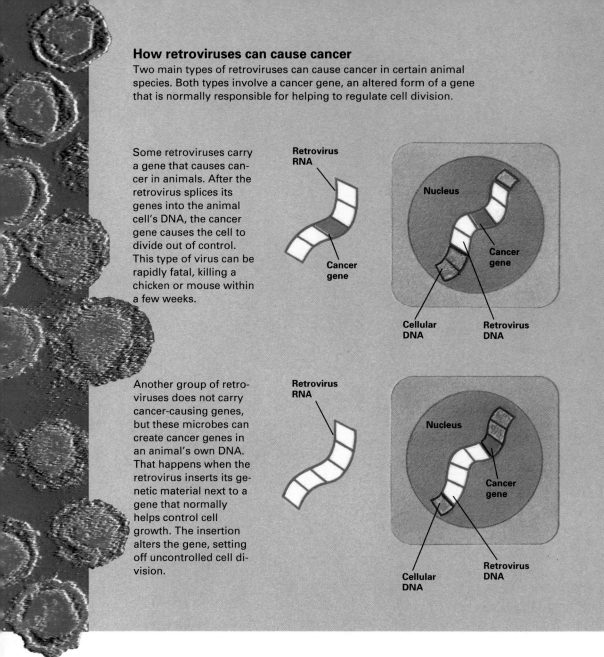

Some retroviruses carry a gene that causes cancer in animals. After the retrovirus splices its genes into the animal cell's DNA, the cancer gene causes the cell to divide out of control. This type of virus can be rapidly fatal, killing a chicken or mouse within a few weeks.

Another group of retroviruses does not carry cancer-causing genes, but these microbes can create cancer genes in an animal's own DNA. That happens when the retrovirus inserts its genetic material next to a gene that normally helps control cell growth. The insertion alters the gene, setting off uncontrolled cell division.

next to a gene responsible for regulating cell growth. Insertion there made the chicken gene cause cancer. Because only one retrovirus in a million was likely to insert its DNA in just that place, the leukemia progressed more slowly than cancers caused by a retrovirus that can turn every infected cell into a cancer cell.

Discovering the first human retrovirus

As scientists sharpened their understanding of the mechanisms by which retroviruses produce cancer in animals, the researchers identified hundreds of cancer-causing retroviruses. But could retroviruses be a cause of cancer in human beings? Many scientists thought so, and they began to direct their efforts to the isolation of retroviruses in people. However, despite numerous false leads (jokingly called "human rumor viruses"), investigators could find no human disease that was linked to a retrovirus. By the early 1980's, most scientists had given up the search.

Among those who kept looking were researchers at the National Cancer Institute in Bethesda, Md., and at Kyoto University in Japan. In 1981, Bethesda virologist Robert Gallo and his colleagues announced that they had isolated a retrovirus in cell cultures obtained from people with a rare form of leukemia. Gallo's team determined that the virus infects a type of white blood cell called a T cell, which plays a central role in the body's immune response to infection. For this reason, Gallo called the virus *human T-cell leukemia virus* (HTLV). Soon afterward, researchers at Kyoto University reported that they, too, had isolated a retrovirus from patients with the leukemia, which is more prevalent in parts of Japan. Soon, the Japanese researchers showed that their virus was HTLV as well.

HTLV differs from most other cancer-causing retroviruses in a number of ways. For one thing, the virus tends not to be passed from person to person in the form of individual viruses. Rather, it normally infects people through the transmission of infected cells—for example, through blood transfusions, during sexual intercourse, or in the milk of nursing mothers. Also, the virus typically infects a person for 20 to 40 years before leukemia develops. Even then, less than 1 percent of infected individuals show signs of the disease. Finally, HTLV is unusual among cancer-causing retroviruses because it does not contain a cancer gene and its DNA does not integrate next to a potential cancer gene. More than a decade after it was discovered, researchers are still trying to determine exactly how HTLV infection leads to cancer.

The story of HIV and AIDS

Despite the apparent minor role of retroviruses in human cancer, the study of retroviruses would soon prove very important to human health. In 1981, doctors in the United States began reporting the first cases of the disease now known as AIDS, in which the immune system loses the ability to defend the body against infection. AIDS researchers soon discovered that patients with AIDS had reduced levels of the very type of T cells targeted by HTLV.

At first, scientists only guessed that AIDS might be caused by a retrovirus. Then, in 1983, virologists led by Luc Montagnier at the Pasteur Institute in Paris discovered that adding blood samples from AIDS patients to cultures made from T cells killed the cells, indicating that the blood carried an infectious agent. Montagnier's team, and later the Gallo laboratory, soon showed that this agent was a new retrovirus, now called HIV. Since then, many studies have firmly established HIV as the cause of AIDS.

As is the case with HTLV and leukemia, scientists still do not fully understand how HIV causes AIDS. They do know that HIV, like HTLV, infects a particular kind of T cell called a CD4 cell. Researchers have advanced a number of theories to explain how HIV infection causes CD4 cells to die. Some scientists believe that one of the proteins in the virus poisons the cell. Others suggest that the virus, by reproducing rapidly within the cell, prevents the cell from making enough of the proteins the cell needs to stay alive. Still another theory is that HIV infection sets off a signal that causes the cell to shut itself down, effectively killing itself.

In addition, although the killing of T cells seems to lie at the heart of AIDS, researchers debate whether this is the whole story. One puzzle is that HIV infects only a small percentage of the body's T cells at any one time, and the immune system normally replaces T cells as fast as they die. Over time, however, the virus destroys the body's ability to replace lost T cells. Some evidence indicates that the virus does this by gradually destroying the lymph nodes, the organs where much of the immune response to infection takes place.

HIV and HTLV are the only retroviruses known to cause disease in people. However, both viruses can give rise to more than one condition. HTLV, for example, can cause a nervous system disorder involving paralysis of the arms and legs. HIV can give rise to *dementia* (a mental disorder involving confusion and loss of memory). According to research reported in April 1994, HIV also may cause one rare form of leukemia. The researchers found that HIV seems to cause the leukemia by lodging next to a potential cancer gene in the host cell and activating it, much as slow-acting retroviruses can cause cancer in animals.

In animals, retroviruses can also cause many illnesses in addition to cancer, including *anemia* (the loss of red blood cells), arthritis, and AIDS-like illnesses that affect mice, cats, and monkeys. For the most part, scientists know even less about the mechanisms behind these diseases than about AIDS.

Using retroviruses to treat and cure disease

Even as some scientists work to unveil the means by which retroviruses harm health, other researchers are putting their efforts into using retroviruses to benefit patients with certain diseases. Geneticists have identified many disorders that arise when an individual is missing a particular gene or has a defective copy of a gene. Doctors can treat some of these disorders, but actually curing such a disease would require supplying the patient's cells with a permanent copy of the normal gene, a technique called *gene therapy*. Because retroviruses have the unique ability to insert foreign genes into a cell's DNA, the viruses can be used to carry needed genes into the body.

In late 1990 and early 1991, geneticists at the National Institutes of Health (NIH) in Bethesda, Md., performed the first such experiments in human beings. The patients were two Ohio girls afflicted with a rare form of *severe combined immunodeficiency disease* (SCID). This deadly inherited disorder results from a defective form of the gene that codes for *adenosine deaminase* (ADA), an enzyme produced by T cells that breaks down chemicals harmful to these cells. Without ADA, the human immune system fails to develop, making SCID patients vulnerable to even the slightest infection.

For the NIH experiments, scientists used a retrovirus that normally infects mice. First, the researchers removed the genes that enable the virus to reproduce. By disabling the retrovirus in this way, the scientists hoped to reduce the risk that the virus would later cause disease in the treated children. The scientists then inserted normal ADA genes into the disabled retrovirus and, in a third step, inserted the virus into genetically altered mouse cells. The altered cells contained all the retrovirus genes and were thus able to make virus particles containing the ADA gene.

Next, the doctors removed some of the girls' T cells and infected them with the specially prepared retrovirus particles. After allowing the infected T cells to multiply in the laboratory, the researchers injected

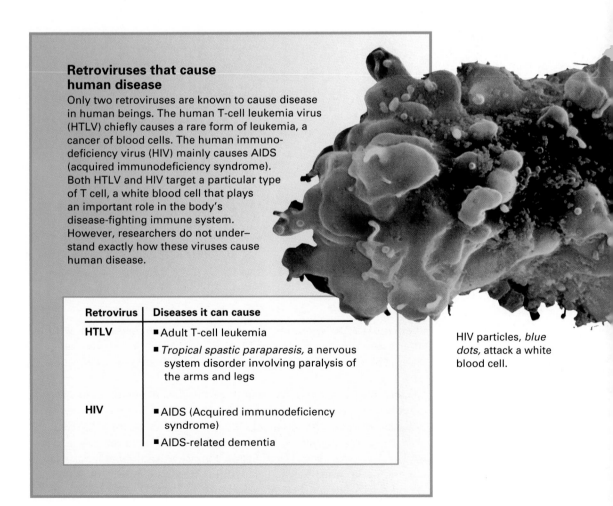

Retroviruses that cause human disease

Only two retroviruses are known to cause disease in human beings. The human T-cell leukemia virus (HTLV) chiefly causes a rare form of leukemia, a cancer of blood cells. The human immunodeficiency virus (HIV) mainly causes AIDS (acquired immunodeficiency syndrome). Both HTLV and HIV target a particular type of T cell, a white blood cell that plays an important role in the body's disease-fighting immune system. However, researchers do not under–stand exactly how these viruses cause human disease.

Retrovirus	Diseases it can cause
HTLV	▪ Adult T-cell leukemia
	▪ *Tropical spastic paraparesis,* a nervous system disorder involving paralysis of the arms and legs
HIV	▪ AIDS (Acquired immunodeficiency syndrome)
	▪ AIDS-related dementia

HIV particles, *blue dots,* attack a white blood cell.

Harnessing retroviruses for gene therapy

Scientists are working to harness retroviruses to treat or even cure diseases that arise when a person is missing a particular gene or has a defective copy of a gene. To treat a disorder of the blood, for example, doctors might use retroviruses to carry healthy copies of a defective gene into a patient's white blood cells.

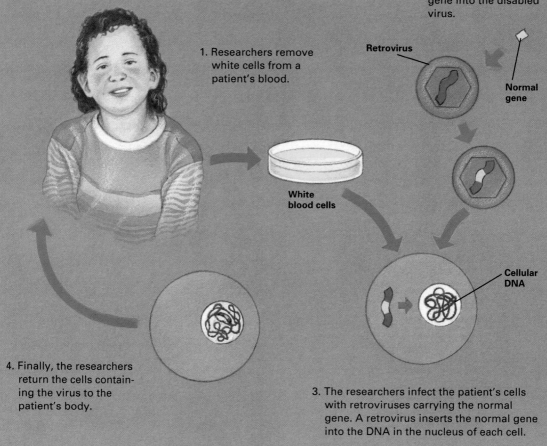

1. Researchers remove white cells from a patient's blood.

2. The scientists disable a retrovirus so that it is unable to cause disease. Then they splice a normal copy of the patient's defective gene into the disabled virus.

Retrovirus

Normal gene

White blood cells

Cellular DNA

4. Finally, the researchers return the cells containing the virus to the patient's body.

3. The researchers infect the patient's cells with retroviruses carrying the normal gene. A retrovirus inserts the normal gene into the DNA in the nucleus of each cell.

them into the girls and waited to see if the experiment worked. Within 10 months, blood tests showed that the girls' bodies were producing ADA. The retrovirus had successfully inserted the ADA gene into the girls' cells.

Unfortunately, T cells live only a few months, so gene therapy that targets these cells must be repeated several times a year. For this reason, scientists in 1993 began an experimental therapy for SCID that uses *stem cells*—permanent cells, located in the bone marrow, that give rise to the many types of blood cells. The scientists were able to isolate the stem cells, which normally are difficult to distinguish from other blood cells, using a technique developed in 1991. One group of doc-

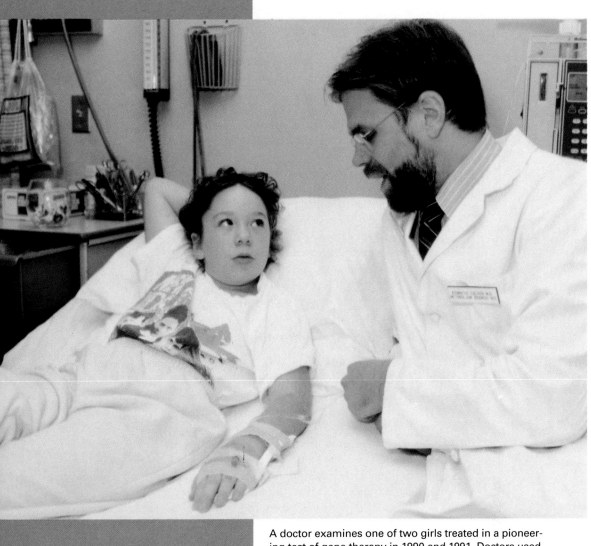

A doctor examines one of two girls treated in a pioneering test of gene therapy in 1990 and 1991. Doctors used genetically altered retroviruses to successfully carry healthy genes into the girls' white blood cells.

tors treated one of the Ohio girls, using a retrovirus to alter some of her stem cells and then injecting the cells into the bloodstream. The investigators hoped that the altered cells would travel to the bone marrow and give rise to many generations of T cells. Another group of researchers tried the procedure on several newborns with SCID, retrieving stem cells from the blood in the babies' umbilical cords. As of mid-1994, doctors were still waiting to see whether the altered stem cells would indeed produce a permanent supply of T cells equipped with the ADA gene.

Scientists are working on harnessing retroviruses to treat a small number of inherited diseases besides SCID—a number that may be likely to grow as researchers identify the genes responsible for more disorders. Investigators are also studying the use of retroviruses in gene therapy for diseases that are normally not inherited, such as AIDS and cancer. One trial on cancer patients was launched in December 1992, when a group of NIH researchers began infecting brain tumor cells with a retrovirus carrying a gene that makes the tumor vulnerable to drug treatment. As the study continued into 1994, the researchers reported that the tumors in some of the trial patients had shrunk following the treatment.

Although only retroviruses are capable of permanently making genes part of a cell's genetic material, using retroviruses for gene therapy is considered riskier than using other types of viruses to insert genes into cells. Some experts fear that even a disabled retrovirus may prove capable of causing cancer or some other disease in patients, perhaps many years after treatment. If a disabled retrovirus inserted its DNA next to a human growth gene, for example, it is possible that the human gene might then cause cancer. Researchers say it may take years of study to determine whether such an event is indeed likely.

Unsolved mysteries: Retroviruses, genes, and evolution

While some scientists seek to learn more about how to harness the special abilities of retroviruses, other experts are intrigued by entirely different mysteries. One involves the role retroviruses might have played in influencing the makeup of human genes. Scientists have discovered that some retroviruses can infect sperm or egg cells, which carry the genetic information passed from parent to offspring. In such cases, the descendants of an infected organism may also carry the virus genes in their DNA. Such inherited viral genes are normally inactive, but their presence can affect the workings of nearby genes.

Scientists have identified thousands of inherited viral genes in human beings, and at least some are known to have had an effect on certain human genes. For instance, all animals, including people, carry a gene that directs the production of an enzyme called *amylase*, which helps convert starches to sugar during digestion. In most animals, this enzyme is made only in the pancreas. In people, however, amylase also occurs in the saliva, and its presence there is the reason that starchy foods taste sweet when chewed for a long time. In 1992, scientists examining the amylase gene in human beings found that the gene had been altered by neighboring viral DNA. The virus changed the gene so that it directed the salivary glands as well as the pancreas to produce the enzyme.

Some scientists believe retroviruses might even have played a role in the evolution of human beings and other species. At some early point in the development of the species, the scientists reason, a retrovirus might have picked up a gene from one portion of the DNA of a host cell, just as some retroviruses became capable of causing cancer by picking up genes from a host cell. Later, the copies made by that retrovirus might have infected a sperm or egg cell and inserted the gene into another place in the DNA, changing the way in which the gene worked. Under this scenario, all the descendants of the original individual would carry a copy of the gene in the new place. A retrovirus might even carry a gene from the DNA of one species to the DNA of another. As yet, however, scientists have no evidence that retroviruses have influenced the evolution of any species by moving genes around in this way.

Another unsolved mystery concerns the origin of retroviruses themselves. Scientists know that retroviruses are very old. Indeed, some researchers believe that retroviruses evolved from the original life forms on Earth. Most evolutionary biologists believe that the first living things arose from simple RNA molecules that developed the ability to copy themselves. Later, these simple forms of life evolved into more complex organisms that stored their genetic information as DNA. But RNA molecules could never have been converted into DNA without some form of reverse transcriptase. Some scientists suggest that the reverse transcriptase in today's retroviruses evolved from that ancient enzyme.

Although such questions continue to fascinate scientists, retroviruses are at the forefront of medical research in the 1990's primarily because of the AIDS epidemic. Since the disease was discovered, learning how to prevent and cure retrovirus infections has become one of the most important activities of medical science. Already, however, the study of retroviruses has provided scientists with a wealth of other information, most notably the discovery of cancer genes. Such genes are a key to understanding virtually all cancers, even those not caused by viruses.

Indeed, despite their simplicity, retroviruses have been a source of knowledge and insight unmatched by any other type of virus. Putting that knowledge to work will provide challenges to researchers for many years to come.

For further reading:

Gallo, Robert. *Virus Hunting: AIDS, Cancer, and the Human Retrovirus.* Basic Books, 1991.
Levine, Arnold J. *Viruses.* Scientific American Library, 1992.

One of the world's most honored—and wittiest—physicists looks back on a career spent among the quarks and leptons.

Conversation with a Particle Smasher

An Interview with Leon Lederman
Conducted by Jinger Hoop

Science Year: You're one of the most highly acclaimed scientists alive today—the physics community's equivalent of a five-star general. During your career, you've been director of the Fermi National Accelerator Laboratory, president of the American Association for the Advancement of Science, and the recipient of dozens of awards, including the Nobel Prize for physics. When you look back today, at age 71, what do you consider the most satisfying moments of your career?

Leon Lederman: Probably the times when I suddenly realized one of my experiments was going to be successful. Not that it was going to be a socko-smash, but just that I was going to get useful data. In the earlier days of my career, I might go two or three years before getting any data out of an experiment, years spent working intensely with other people and making decisions of all kinds. Finally, there would be the crisis of taking the data. Does it come in right? If something's wrong, could we fix it? When I suddenly knew that the experiment was working, I always felt enormous relief and satisfaction.

SY: And if the data showed you'd discovered something important?

Lederman: Now that's incredibly exciting. If it happens to come when you're all alone at 3:00 a.m, it's even more thrilling. And later of course,

you have the enormous pleasure of telling people about it. If scientists were sworn to secrecy, so that they couldn't tell anybody about their discoveries, they'd do something else for a living.

But if everyone had to have moments like that in his or her career, nobody would become a physicist. Because those things on average don't happen. Most physicists will go through their whole life and never make a major discovery. Still, you get satisfaction from small things, the day-to-day pleasures of seeing that some new equipment is working, some progress toward your goal is being made. Or perhaps you're sitting around with some graduate students and one of them gets a good idea. You can take a great deal of pleasure in that.

SY: In your field, physicists generally describe themselves as belonging to one of two camps—those who develop theories, and those who perform experiments to gather data that tests the theories. When did you decide to join the experimenters?

Lederman: In college. Little by little it became clear to me that my insights were in things rather than theories. Not that I'm very good with my hands. The main thing is to sort of "feel" apparatus and "feel" experimental situations. I was also more interested in reading about experimental discoveries than theoretical ones. And I probably didn't have the mathematical and analytical abilities it would take to be a competent theorist.

SY: The machines you used for your experiments were particle accelerators—huge, complex devices that speed particles and then smash them together, creating showers of subatomic particles.

Lederman: Accelerators dominate the field of particle physics. The founder of Fermilab, Robert R. Wilson, used to compare them to medieval cathedrals. He said that we put the same creativity and engineering effort into building particle accelerators that people in the Middle Ages put into building the great cathedrals. You could even say that accelerators and medieval cathedrals were motivated by similar feelings of faith and hope. Certainly when we build a new accelerator, we have faith and hope that the machine will benefit humanity.

SY: As an experimenter, how do you develop a "feel" for such massive and complex equipment?

Lederman: When you're in the middle of an experiment, it's by letting the machine run your life. Unless something breaks, the accelerator is going for 24 hours a day, seven days a week. So you sleep on a cot in the laboratory or maybe even leaning against a wall. You do this for five, six, seven days at a stretch, thinking about the experiment as you comb your hair, shave, and do everything else. You get obsessed.

SY: What are some of the discoveries you made that way?

Lederman: The first was my thesis experiment, when I was in graduate school at Columbia University in 1950. That was the experiment I was the most nervous about. What worried me was that I was trying a brand new way of collecting data, and I was using a brand new machine, Columbia University's Nevis synchrocyclotron, the world's most powerful accelerator at the time. When I started getting some interesting data from the experiment, I knew I was really going to be a physicist.

Another high point was in 1961, when I and six colleagues at Columbia did the experiment that led to winning the Nobel Prize for physics. That one was a lot of fun. We created a steel wall 40 feet thick, using scrap steel from decommissioned Navy ships, and then aimed high-energy particles at it. The experiment got noticed for a couple of reasons. The only thing that could pass through the steel wall was an elusive little particle called the neutrino. Our arrangement created the first artificial beam of neutrinos. By doing so, we were able to discover that there was more than one type of neutrino. Because of that finding, scientists learned that all elementary particles come in pairs.

SY: In those days, the physics department at Columbia was virtually crawling with Nobel Prize winners and other scientists who would go on to win the prize.

Lederman: Yes, it was a fabulous time. Columbia was a spectacular place to learn, and physics itself was explosive in its development after World War II. The number of Nobelists on the faculty was so large that some of us wore buttons we had made that said "Not Me" or "Not Yet."

SY: You were awarded the prize in 1988. What was the best thing about winning?

Lederman: The money. No, really, I guess it was just being announced, getting that 6:00 a.m. phone call saying I'd won. Meeting the Queen of Sweden wasn't bad, either.

SY: Was there a down side?

Lederman: Yes. It really interferes with whatever else you want to do. For me, it wasn't too disruptive, because I won late in life. But it takes enormous strength of character to turn down all the invitations and opportunities the Nobel Prize brings with it. Once you have a Nobel Prize, if you get ideas about how to improve the Chicago schools, as I did, then people open doors to enable you to try those ideas. So instead of doing physics, I end up trying to convince bureaucrats in Washington, D.C., that we need more money to help the Chicago public schools, and that what we're doing in Chicago may work in Washington, Detroit, and elsewhere. Since winning the prize, I find myself doing a lot of things I'm not really good at, just splashing around.

SY: Now that you're on the sidelines of physics research, what experiments strike you as the most interesting?

Lederman: That's like asking, "What's the best food?" It comes down to personal preference. But the most exciting physics around has been at Fermilab this year: the attempt to discover the top quark, the last elementary particle. To look for it, they used two humungous particle detectors to examine all the different particles produced by collisions of protons and their antimatter counterparts. Everyone knew that the more massive the top quark was, the less likely it was that any one collision would produce it. At first, we expected the top would be twice the size of the heaviest known quark, called bottom, which I helped discover in 1977. So physicists or-

> If scientists were sworn to secrecy, so that they couldn't tell anybody about their discoveries, they'd do something else for a living.

Leon M. Lederman

As a child, Leon M. Lederman was a "molecules kid," a boy who developed an interest in chemistry from reading books on the physical sciences and watching his older brother experiment with a chemistry set in the family basement. After high school, Lederman drifted toward physics, in part, he claims, because the physics students in college were a funnier crowd and better athletes.

Lederman was born on July 15, 1922, in New York City, the son of Russian immigrants. He graduated from the City College of New York in 1943, with a major in chemistry and a minor in physics. During World War II (1941-1945), he served three years in the U.S. Army Signal Corps, part of the time stationed in France and Germany and part of the time at the Massachusetts Institute of Technology in Cambridge, where he helped invent Doppler radar, a method of tracking moving objects. After the war, Lederman resumed his studies in physics at New York City's Columbia University. He received a Ph.D. in physics in 1951 and then stayed on at Columbia as a researcher and professor.

In 1961, Lederman and his colleagues performed the experiment for which they were awarded the 1988 Nobel Prize for physics. Using a new accelerator at the Brookhaven National Laboratory on Long Island, N.Y., Lederman and his co-workers demonstrated that there is more than one type of neutrino, an elementary particle in the same family as the electron. This "two-neutrino experiment" indicated that elementary particles come in pairs, or "doublets," a finding that is a cornerstone of present-day understanding of particle physics.

In 1979, Lederman became director of the Fermi National Accelerator Laboratory (Fermilab) in Batavia, Ill. There, physicists send subatomic particles hurtling along a ring 6 kilometers (4 miles) in circumference beneath a restored prairie that is home to cranes, swans, geese, and even a herd of buffalo. As Fermilab's director, Lederman oversaw construction of the first particle accelerator that makes use of superconducting magnets. That accelerator, called the Tevatron, was completed in 1983 and is the most powerful "atom smasher" in existence.

Even before the Tevatron was completed, Lederman proposed the next generation accelerator, which he originally dubbed the Desertron and which later came to be called the Superconducting Super Collider

Lederman poses with a magnetic device at the Fermi National Accelerator Laboratory.

King Carl XVI Gustaf of Sweden awards
Lederman the 1988 Nobel Prize in physics.

Academy offer courses in science instruction to Chicago teachers. The academy also provides computer networks linking schools with each other and with universities and museums. Lederman hopes eventually to take the concept to other cities.

Since retiring from his post at Fermilab in 1989, Lederman has served as president of the American Association for the Advancement of Science, Frank E. Sulzberger Professor at the University of Chicago, and Pritzker Professor at the Illinios Institute of Technology, also in Chicago. In addition to winning the Nobel Prize, Lederman has received numerous other honors. Among them are the U.S. National Medal of Science (1968), Israel's Wolf Foundation Prize in Physics (1982), and the U.S. Department of Energy's Fermi Prize (1992).

In the physics community, Lederman is well known for his sense of humor. His classroom lectures have the easy banter of a stand-up comic, and he entertains professional colleagues as well as students with a vast supply of jokes. A good way to describe him, acquaintances say, is part Albert Einstein, part Mel Brooks.   [J. H.]

(SSC). The new accelerator, which was to be built in Waxahachie, Tex., was designed to be 87 kilometers (54 miles) in circumference and 20 times as powerful as the Tevatron. Until the U.S. Congress voted to cut off funding for the SSC in October 1993, Lederman was a chief public spokesman for the SSC, spending much of his time talking to the public and politicians about the benefits of building the huge machine.

Lederman takes a passionate interest in science education. In 1986, he helped create the Illinois Mathematics and Science Academy, a residential public high school for gifted children from all parts of the state. In 1990, he founded the Teachers Academy for Mathematics and Science in Chicago, an institution whose aim is improving science education in Chicago public schools. To do that, experts at the

Lederman and a colleague, *above*, relax in 1977 after completing the experiment that led to the discovery of the bottom quark, one of the basic building blocks of matter. Lederman celebrates a birthday, *left*, with a group of elementary school students.

> **We need something simple and to the point that explains the universe. It might be an equation of a few words, but it would have to be crystalline in its clarity.**

ganized collisions that would have produced the top if it was 2 times heavier than the bottom. When that didn't work, they increased the sensitivity of the collisions to produce the quark if it was 3 times heavier, and then 4. But the top quark didn't show up. They tried 6, 8, 20 times bigger, but still it didn't show up. The only thing you can do to improve the odds of finding such a massive particle is build a bigger accelerator or make more collisions. At Fermilab they made many more collisions. Finally, at about 40 times heavier than the bottom quark, they found it. That's enormously heavy. It's the Fridge of particles.

SY: Would you have liked to work on the search for the top quark?

Lederman: Personally, I'd rather do a somewhat smaller kind of experiment, one that takes a look at the properties of the bottom quark. The special properties of that quark have become a hot subject lately. But to really study them, you need to devise an experiment where you can look at billions and billions of bottom quarks. We'd have to build a special machine to do that, a bottom quark factory.

SY: Let's talk about another machine you tried to get built—the Superconducting Super Collider, the world's biggest and most powerful particle accelerator, which was under construction near Waxahachie, Tex., until late in 1993. How did you feel about the U.S. Congress's decision to cut off funding for the Super Collider?

Lederman: It's going to take some time to get the necessary perspective on the disaster. We worked on the SSC for 10 years, obtaining international commitments and the enthusiastic support of three U.S. Presidents. And then Congress says "No, we're not going to vote for it," and that's that. The problem was that Congress was obsessed with the budget deficit. They needed to show voters they could cut something out of the budget, and there was strong opposition from a small number of legislators who felt that the SSC was just not worth the cost since it produced only pure knowledge. And then management problems at the SSC surfaced, and they were serious enough not to help. But even the opponents agreed that the scientific objectives had merit. It's ironic because the same Congress voted to build two submarines that even the Navy said it didn't want. But building them would keep up employment in Connecticut. And so the submarines were funded, at about the same cost as the SSC.

SY: What was the purpose of the SSC?

Lederman: To solve an important problem concerning the standard model of physics—the concise summary of everything we know about matter in the universe and the forces that act on it. According to the standard model, matter is made up of six quarks and six particles called leptons, and four fundamental forces act upon them. Now as concise summaries go, that's a complicated and ugly one. It's also mathematically inconsistent. All the data coming out of all the accelerator laboratories are in agreement with the standard model. But if you consider what would happen if the particles were accelerated to higher speeds, the standard model predicts nonsense.

So we know that something has been left out of our equations. It turns out that a new kind of force called the Higgs field could account for the complexities and allow us to make clean predictions as to what would happen in those extreme circumstances. The Super Collider was designed to produce the Higgs field as a particle that we could study and try to understand.

SY: Was finding the Higgs field a priority for anyone other than particle physicists?

Lederman: Cosmologists, who study the birth and evolution of the universe, were also very excited about it. That's because if the Higgs field exists, it has to play a crucial role in our universe. The questions the SSC was designed to answer all had to do with the obsession with the world in which we live. When I listen to children in elementary schools, I hear the same type of questions. Why is the sky blue? Why are clouds white? What keeps them up? How many words do I have inside of me? If I talk too much will I use them all up? That kind of curiosity was the motive for building the SSC.

SY: In your book *The God Particle*, you say that your chief ambition is to live long enough to see all of physics reduced to a formula brief enough to be written on a T-shirt.

Lederman: Sure. We need something simple and to the point that explains the universe. It might be an equation of a few words, but it would have to be crystalline in its clarity. Out of that equation would flow everything we know about the universe: the big bang that started everything, the quarks and leptons, the fundamental forces, and the basis for such complex things as the periodic table of the elements, DNA, and everything else we know.

SY: How long will it take physicists to find that simple formula?

Lederman: It's hard to say because it's like the song about the bear that went over the mountain. What did he see on the other side? Yet another mountain. Right now we see the Higgs field as a certain peak ahead of us, but we don't know what's beyond that. The loss of the SSC undoubtedly set us back a decade or so. But whether the decade is a small or large chunk of time compared with the overall length of our journey, I don't know. It might be quite short. And there are some people who think we'll never be able to find a simple formula, that we'll just keep finding new complexities.

SY: Does your belief that nature is fundamentally simple affect the way you look at the universe?

Lederman: Yes, I think so. If you share the optimism, you begin to see things as part of a pattern that's mystifying in its own way. I think Albert Einstein was talking about that when he said the most inexplicable thing about the universe is its explicability.

SY: But would your T-shirt formula really be able to explain everything? Or do you think there are limits to what physicists will ever be able to learn?

Lederman: It may be that what happened in the earliest moments of the universe will forever be unknown, though our formula might give us some options. And the formula will not show us how to cure the common cold or fix a downtown traffic jam. It's sort of satisfying that we know that DNA molecules consist of atoms, and atoms are made of protons and neutrons and electrons. And protons and neutrons are made of quarks. But it won't help you analyze DNA to know that ultimately it's made up of quarks and electrons.

Still, it's handy if you know an obnoxious kid who keeps asking "Why? Why? Why?" You say, "Humans think," and he says, "Why?" You say, "Because people's brains have cognitive functions." Again, the kid says, "Why?" So you talk about nerve cells and memory retrieval. If he keeps asking, eventually you get down to the properties of atoms, and then finally you tell him about quarks. And if he still says "Why?" you punch him in the nose.

SY: You sometimes joke that most people think that your Nobel-Prize-winning "two-neutrino experiment" is the name of an Italian dance team.

Lederman: And they think I won the Nobel *Peace* Prize for it.

SY: Is it frustrating to find that so many people don't understand what you do?

Lederman: It's more than frustrating. Not in a personal sense, because you get your kicks by having the praise of your peers. But what's frustrating is that if the general public doesn't develop a higher level of comprehension of science, then we are not going to be able to solve the problems that the world is facing: economic problems, social problems, environmental problems, natural resource problems, education problems. People are just terribly ignorant about science.

SY: Do you think the mass media is partially to blame?

Lederman: Of course. Think about how scientists are portrayed on the movie screen—wearing a white coat and glasses, stroking a cat, and muttering, "Tomorrow we destroy the world!" And lately there has been a series of movies that portray scientists very negatively, all the way from the silliness of *Honey, I Shrunk the Kids*, where the scientist is portrayed as a nerd, an unrealistic and slightly dangerous nerd, to *Lorenzo's Oil*, which says the medical establishment doesn't know anything. And our culture is dominated by television, but the science on network TV is virtually nonexistent. There is a lot of good science programming on public TV and cable, but most people watch the networks.

Things are so bad that I and some colleagues went to Hollywood to talk to writers and producers recently. We talked about the excitement of science, about how it really doesn't have to be boring, and about how scientists really aren't all nerds. We said to the president of CBS, for example, why not locate one of your sit-coms in a graduate dormitory? Or have a *This Week in Science* program, co-hosted by Bill Cosby and Sally Ride, just to pick two names at random. But trying to change Hollywood is going to require a long-term campaign.

SY: Before funding for the SSC was cut off, you had said publicly that U.S. science was in a state of malaise, or unease. Do you still feel that way?

Lederman: It's gotten much worse, incredibly bad. The mood in the scientific community is as bad as I've ever seen it. There is a belief that the nation's leadership is not interested in science, that what science we are interested in must be focused on immediate needs. Forget the idea that researchers should satisfy their own curiosity, which is virtually the definition of science. U.S. industry doesn't seem to be interested in science and has been dropping out of research. Universities are in financial trouble and downsizing. Government's support of science is still strong but lukewarm. When military budgets start being cut, the military reduce their research. From the point of view of scientists, it's all economic bad news. And the loss of the Super Collider increases the sense of malaise.

SY: What advice would you give a high school student who wants to become a scientist but is scared by the discouraging job prospects?

Lederman: It's true that at this moment the job prospects for scientists and engineers are not rosy. It's a spooky time. But I was in college during the Great Depression, and compared with that, this is a piece of cake. Unemployment rates were 20 percent then, not 7 percent. None of us students expected to get jobs, so we just decided to study subjects that interested us. "What are you going to be unemployed in?" we'd ask each other. "I'm going to be unemployed in physics," I'd say. "It's a lot more fun than being unemployed in biology."

No one is going to guarantee you a living in anything you do, so you might as well do something you think will give you a rewarding life. And to do that, you have to know a little bit about your-

The mood in the scientific community is as bad as I've ever seen it. There is a belief that the nation's leadership is not interested in science, that what science we are interested in must be focused on immediate needs.

self. What do you feel like doing when you get up in the morning? What are you enthusiastic about? What drives you? Unfortunately, most kids don't spend much time finding out what things make them happy.

SY: Do you think the job shortage for scientists is likely to persist?

Lederman: No, I really don't. My guess is that countries such as Korea, Brazil, and India, which are improving their technological capabilities, will soon become competing centers for scientists. And if you look at all the problems we have—global warming, ozone depletion, the need for energy sources that don't pollute—there is tremendous opportunity for science and technology over the next 20, 30, or 40 years. So in the long term, prospects for scientists and engineers look very good.

SY: What about job prospects for would-be physicists in particular?

Lederman: As a physicist, I have to say humbly that if you major in physics, you'll be able to do anything. During World War II, physicists became the leaders of the engineering groups in all the war laboratories because physicists are so adaptable. They know the basics. They even become chemists. And a lot of the new biology, which deals with genes and DNA and thus molecules, has been done by physicists. A physicist goes into any profession with an admission card that says, "I understand computers, atoms, instruments, electronics. . . . I eat neutrinos for breakfast."

SY: Although you've retired from active research, do you still teach?

Lederman: I was up until 1:00 a.m. last night grading final exams from my freshman physics class.

SY: It's surprising to hear of a Nobelist teaching an introductory course.

Lederman: I love doing it, because the kids in those classes are the biggest challenge. I like particularly to teach liberal arts students, because they have to be brought kicking and screaming into a physics course. "Oh, my God," they say. "Math! I can't stand it!" That's ridiculous. Those law students and liberal arts students are going to be the politicians and the TV announcers of tomorrow. They need some sense of science and how it works. That's why I believe all college students should be required to take four years of science, though I usually put on my bullet-proof vest before I say so in public.

SY: Assuming the students would stand for it, what would be the advantage of having future artists take four years of science classes?

Lederman: You'd have an educated citizenry, something we desperately need. You open up the newspaper, and you see stories about health care, gene mapping, Russia's nuclear weapons, global warming. These are life-and-death issues, but most people's eyes glaze over when confronted with them. This is why we need more science education: for the public to become science wise, in the sense that city dwellers need to be streetwise.

SY: Can't citizens be adequately trained in science in high school?

Lederman: I've found that high school graduates usually come to college badly trained. Sometimes I wish the high schools didn't even try to teach kids science if they aren't prepared to do a good job of

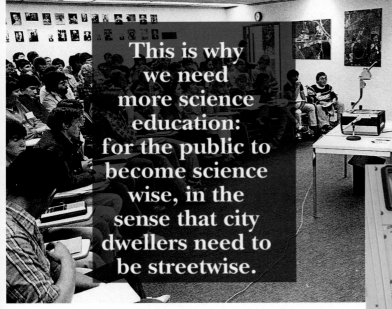

This is why we need more science education: for the public to become science wise, in the sense that city dwellers need to be streetwise.

it. Of course, what we really have to do is make the schools much better.

SY: Is that why you became involved in working to improve the Chicago public school system?

Lederman: Yes. In 1990, we founded the Teachers Academy for Mathematics and Science to help teachers do a better job of teaching science. Already we see positive results. I love going into an elementary classroom and seeing that the teacher is comfortable and having a good time with the lesson, and the kids are laughing and enjoying themselves. That's what school should be like. If you could get that atmosphere in every classroom, or 90 percent of them, what a change that would be! Working on that project is one of the more important things I've done.

SY: What project has been the most important? What do you see as your greatest contribution in your career as a scientist?

Lederman: The experimental stuff is okay, and I have five or six really nice experiments in the books. But I'd like to think that my greatest contribution was not being too bad an influence on my students and young Ph.D.'s. Over the years, I've taught 52 Ph.D. students and what seems like billions and billions of undergraduates. And to my knowledge, not one of them is in jail.

For further reading:

Lederman, Leon M., and Schramm, David N. *From Quarks to the Cosmos.* Scientific American Library, 1989.

Lederman, Leon, with Teresi, Dick. *The God Particle.* Houghton Mifflin Co., 1993.

Wolkomir, Richard. "Putting a New Spin on Pitching Science to Kids," *Smithsonian*, April 1993, 104-8.

Is It Worth the Risk?

BY JOHN G. TRUXAL

Modern life is filled with risks, from common activities as well as potentially catastrophic ones. Engineers and scientists can help us to understand these risks and to make decisions about them.

I t's Saturday morning, and you have a busy day ahead of you. You get up early and ride your bike to the soccer field, where you play goalie for your school team. After the game (your team wins), you ride home and jump into the shower. Still wet, you use the hairdryer, which is plugged into a bathroom outlet. You race downstairs for lunch: a peanut butter sandwich. You relax at home for a while, then head to the doctor's office for a tetanus shot. Back home again, you sneak a taste of the cookie dough on the kitchen counter and make arrangements for a ride to a party that evening.

Later that night, safely home and preparing for bed, you might reflect on the actions you've performed during the day. Each one has been very ordinary. And yet each has carried some risk—some chance of resulting in injury, illness, or death. You risked a serious accident bicycling, driving, running downstairs, even playing soccer. Using your

Glossary

Carcinogen: A substance that can cause cancer.

Probability: The likelihood that a given event will occur at a given time.

Risk assessment: The process by which scientists and engineers measure risk.

hairdryer in the wet bathroom put you at risk of electrocution. Your lunch exposed you to aflatoxin, a natural *carcinogen* (cancer-causing substance) found in peanut butter. Your house may contain another carcinogen: radon, a natural radioactive gas that can enter homes through cracks in basement walls or floors. Your tetanus shot, like any vaccine, carried a small risk of harmful side effects. And the raw eggs in the cookie dough could have given you a dangerous case of food poisoning.

If you're like most people, you willingly accept these and other risks in your daily life. You may take steps to reduce certain risks—for example, by wearing an automobile seat belt or bicycle helmet, or by sealing your basement against radon. But you recognize that you can't completely avoid risk, and that to try to do so would drastically change the way you live.

There are certain risks, however, that people are less willing to accept. These hazards seem more frightening than others—more dangerous, or harder to avoid. Many people, for example, are concerned about the possible effects of living near a hazardous waste disposal site. They fear that chemicals burned or stored at such facilities could pollute the air or poison the water supply. Others wonder how safe their food is: Does it contain dangerous levels of pesticides or food additives? And the risk of accidents at nuclear power plants has created strong opposition to nuclear energy. Such risks are often the focus of political debate and community activism.

The scientific study of risk

Societies, like individuals, have to make choices about the risks they face. They must decide, for example, whether to give up the benefits of a new technology in order to eliminate its risks. Sometimes, they must choose between competing technologies carrying different kinds of risks. Or they must decide whether the number of people who might be affected by a hazardous activity justifies the cost of taking action to reduce the risk.

To help make these decisions, engineers and scientists have developed tools that allow them to measure and compare risks. Scientists approach questions of risk in measurable terms. How many people, they ask, will die prematurely as a result of a risky activity, technology, or substance? How many will become seriously ill? How many people will benefit? How much money will society save?

The scientific study of risk is known as *risk assessment*. The study is based on the branch of mathematics concerned with *probability*—the likelihood that an event that occurs randomly will happen at a given time. Probability theory was developed in Europe in the 1600's, as a way to help gamblers make bets in dice-rolling games.

The first major problem in risk analysis arose in Europe in the late 1700's. At that time, smallpox—an infectious disease—was one of the leading causes of death, killing hundreds of thousands of people a year. Physicians knew they could make people immune to smallpox by

The author:
John G. Truxal is professor of engineering at the State University of New York at Stony Brook.

Using statistics to calculate risk

Some risks, such as the risk of death caused by car travel, are easy to measure because statistics on the risk have been kept for many years. Here is how experts calculate the risk of dying in a car accident in the United States. (The figures have been rounded slightly.)

- In 1992, some 21,300 automobile drivers and passengers were killed as a result of traffic accidents.

- Also in 1992, all automobiles in the United States covered 1,600,000,000,000 miles (2,570,000,000,000 kilometers), and each car had an average of about 1.7 occupants.

- Americans thus traveled 1,600,000,000,000 × 1.7 miles in 1992, or about 2,700,000,000,000 passenger miles.

- The number killed divided by the number of passenger miles is 21,300 ÷ 2,700,000,000,000 = 0.0000000079, or about 79 deaths for every 10,000,000,000 passenger miles. This can be rounded to 0.8 death for every 100,000,000 passenger miles.

- Americans travel by car, on average, about 11,000 miles (17,700 kilometers) per person a year. Multiplying miles per year by deaths per passenger miles gives us $11,000 \times {}^{0.8}/_{100,000,000} = {}^{88}/_{1,000,000}$, or about $^1/_{11,400}$. Of any 11,400 motorists, 1 is likely to die in an auto accident each year.

inoculating (deliberately infecting) them with a mild form of the disease. But inoculation carried a risk of giving the person a more serious form of the illness, which could result in death. Leading mathematicians and scientists used probability theory to help them weigh the risks of inoculation until physicians developed a less dangerous vaccine in the 1800's.

The modern field of risk assessment began to emerge in the early 1900's, chiefly in the United States. In the 1920's, concern about the growing use of pesticides in agriculture led scientists to begin using laboratory animals to test the safety of chemical compounds. But the new science of risk assessment received its most important boost beginning in the 1960's, amid growing fears about the hazards of nuclear radiation and the emergence of the environmental, consumer protection, and worker safety movements.

Today, governments play an important role in protecting individuals from excessive risk. For example, the U.S. Food and Drug Administration (FDA) administers standards for the labeling of food products and the content of processed foods. The Environmental Protection Agency (EPA) regulates the public's exposure to health risks from pollution and other environmental hazards. And the Occupational Safety and Health Administration (OSHA) oversees regulations covering workers' exposure to potentially hazardous substances and conditions on the job.

Estimating unknown risks

Some risks, such as that of large amounts of radioactivity escaping from a damaged nuclear reactor, may have never happened before or have happened only rarely. In such cases, experts cannot compile statistics that could be used to directly calculate the likelihood of a future occurrence. Instead, experts calculate the risk by considering separately all the risk factors for possible events that might lead to the hazard.

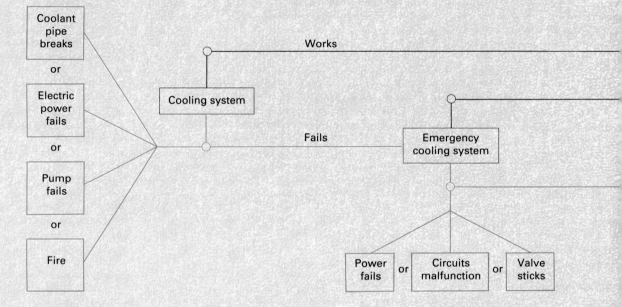

To calculate the probability of a nuclear reactor accident releasing radioactivity into the atmosphere, experts might first consider all events, such as a pipe breaking, that could cause the vital cooling system to fail. The experts use statistics to calculate the probability of each of these events.

If the cooling system fails, the reactor switches off and an emergency cooling system should keep the core from overheating. But a sticking valve or other problem could cause the emergency system to fail, leading to a core meltdown. The experts calculate the probability of each of these possible problems.

Measuring risk directly

Agency officials and other experts who deal with risk say there are two main types of risks: those that are directly measurable and those that must be calculated indirectly. Experts use different tools to assess the different kinds of risks.

Risks are directly measurable if the consequences of a risky activity occur in large enough numbers for statisticians to accumulate data on their frequency. For example, hospitals keep records of the number of patients who die of lung cancer and other illnesses that can be caused by smoking. Scientists can use these data, along with other statistics about smokers and nonsmokers, to calculate the health risks of smoking. These calculations tell researchers that, for example, a pack-a-day smoker is up to 30 times more likely to develop lung cancer than someone who has never smoked. The data also show that smoking is a probable cause of 17 percent of all deaths in the United States.

No radiation released

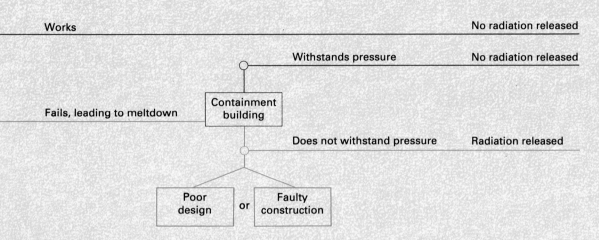

Works   No radiation released

Withstands pressure   No radiation released

Containment
building

Fails, leading to meltdown

Does not withstand pressure   Radiation released

Poor
design   or   Faulty
construction

In the United States, nuclear reactors are enclosed in a contain-ment building designed to keep radioactivity from escaping in case of a meltdown. The containment building should be able to withstand the high pressure a meltdown would create. The experts figure the probability that such factors as poor design or faulty construction will make the containment building un-able to withstand this pressure, causing it to leak or explode.

Experts add and multiply the probabilities they have calculated for each stage according to math-ematical formulas. By doing so, they determine the likelihood of radioactivity being released as the result of an accident.

To learn how scientists calculate directly measurable risks, let's look at the risk of death caused by automobile travel. Statistics show that in the United States, some 21,300 automobile drivers and passengers die annually as a result of traffic accidents. Other data—collected by, for example, electronic highway counters—indicate that, taken together, all the automobiles in the United States travel a total of about 1,600 billion miles (2,570 billion kilometers) each year. These units are called *vehicle miles.*

To estimate the probability of dying in an auto accident during a giv-en year, we also need to know how much automobile traveling Amer-icans do. Statisticians compile this information as *passenger miles.* One passenger mile is the transportation of one person for one mile. Trans-portation surveys show that, on average, each car carries about 1.7 pas-sengers (including the driver). So 1.7 passengers traveling 1,600 billion vehicle miles per year gives us about 2,700 billion passenger miles.

The next step is to calculate the number of deaths per passenger miles. To do this, we divide 21,300, the annual number of deaths, by 2,700 billion. This calculation yields 0.0000000079, or 79 deaths for every 10 billion passenger miles.

Now, suppose you expect to travel 35,000 miles (56,000 kilometers) in 1995. Your chance of suffering a fatal accident during that year is $35,000 \times 0.0000000079$, or about 0.00028. Expressed as a fraction, this can be reduced to about $\frac{1}{3,570}$, or 1 chance in 3,570. Like any probability, this can also be expressed as a percentage, 0.028 percent.

Of course, the likelihood of any specific person becoming an accident victim may be greater or smaller than the average we just calculated. If you are a driver, your precise risk depends on how safely you drive, whether you wear a seat belt, whether you drink before driving, the weight of your car, and other variables. Experts can gather data on such variables to determine, for instance, the effectiveness of seat belts in preventing fatalities and thus reducing the risk from car travel.

Calculating the risks of rare events

The risk of dying in an auto accident can be calculated directly because auto fatalities occur in large numbers, so small variations from year to year do not affect future expectations. But many other hazardous activities result in fatalities or other health consequences infrequently, making direct statistical analysis impossible.

In the United States, for example, some 150 to 200 of the nation's approximately 500,000 bridges annually suffer the collapse or partial collapse of one or more spans. Fewer than 12 people die each year as a result of such failures. However, the consequences of a single bridge collapse could be disastrous, especially if the bridge is large and heavily traveled. For this reason, it is important that engineers have some way

Estimating risk by analogy

Many risks are difficult to estimate because few people are affected and because levels of exposure are small. This makes historical data hard to gather. Estimating the risk to human health from exposure to a chemical compound, such as pesticide residues in food, poses such a problem. To collect data on which to base their risk assessments, researchers often use laboratory animals, usually rats and mice.

0.01 gram per day   0.005 gram per day   0 grams per day

Laboratory rats are fed varying doses of the pesticide to determine whether it can cause health problems, such as cancer, and to determine the smallest dose at which the health problem will appear. Some of the animals might be fed 0.01 gram (0.0004 ounce) per day, while others might receive half that amount. A third group might not be given the pesticide at all.

to determine the likelihood that any particular bridge might collapse.

Engineers know that in most cases, a bridge collapse results from a series of smaller events that are themselves not uncommon. For example, flooding can allow water to accumulate on a bridge deck. Or debris may build up in the drains, blocking them. The water can then corrode the steel and other structural elements of the bridge. In cold weather, water freezing inside the bridge deck can cause it to crack, while salt or other deicing compounds can increase corrosion. Meanwhile, heavy loads on the bridge can cause additional cracks, especially where the structure has been corroded. And boats colliding with the bridge can weaken its support structures.

One way to assess the probability of an event such as a particular bridge collapsing is to calculate the likelihood of each step in any possible combination of events that might lead to the disaster. Engineers can use historical data to estimate the probability of such events as flooding followed by freezing temperatures. Then, using mathematical formulas, they can multiply these numbers to get the probability that all of these steps will occur. Likewise, engineers can calculate the probability for all other series of events that might result in bridge failure. They can then add the probabilities of each of the different chains of events to come up with a total probability for the accident during a given period of time.

Using analogy to measure risks

Some risks must be measured indirectly not only because they occur infrequently, but also because data on these risks are hard to collect. The risk of cancer due to exposure to certain substances often falls into this category. It is impossible to determine the specific origin of most cases of cancer because 20 or more years may elapse between the

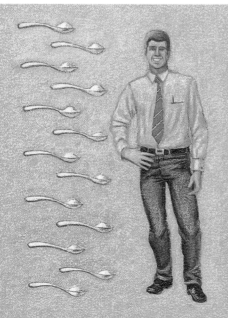

Scientists use these tests to help assess the risk to human beings of equivalent amounts of the pesticide. If the rats developed cancer when fed a dose of 0.01 gram per day, for example, the equivalent, in human consumption, might be 1 gram (0.04 ounce) per day. However, this dose may be far greater than people would be exposed to in real life. Scientists believe that most chemical pesticides are present in human food at levels no higher than 0.000001 gram (0.00000004 ounce) per day.

Researchers use complex mathematical models to estimate how much of the pesticide might cause cancer in human beings exposed to small doses over long periods of time. Experts typically regard a dose that would cause cancer in a tiny percentage of people, such as 1 in a million, as being safe.

time a person is exposed to a carcinogenic substance and the time the cancer is diagnosed. In addition, the large number of cancer deaths from all sources makes it difficult to isolate common factors—such as exposure to a particular substance—that might have caused cancer in many different patients.

If scientists want to determine whether a chemical compound may pose a health risk such as cancer, they can test it in the laboratory. First, they might test the compound to see whether it can cause *mutations* (genetic changes) in bacteria. Cancer is thought to begin with changes involving genes.

The scientists then test the effects of the compound on laboratory animals. In these studies, they give high doses of the chemical to a small number of animals, usually rats or mice. (The scientists use high doses because lower doses would cause illness in few animals, requiring hundreds of animals for each test.) Rats and mice make good subjects for such tests because they have short life spans, so changes in their health show up quickly. The scientists divide the animals into groups, give each group a certain amount of the compound, and so determine the smallest daily dose that will cause some of the animals to develop tumors or other disorders. The researchers calculate the daily dosage that would pose an equivalent risk to human beings exposed to the compound over a lifetime. They can then calculate the risk people would face from smaller exposures.

Scientists use sophisticated computer models to estimate how much exposure to the compound different groups of individuals might actually have. For example, when solid wastes are burned in an incinerator, workers at the facility are likely to be exposed to higher doses of any hazardous compounds produced than are people who live nearby but work elsewhere. The scientists use the models to help estimate the maximum amount of a compound different groups of people might come into contact with over a lifetime. Then, they compare data from the computer models with data from the animal studies to determine whether the compound should be regarded as hazardous.

The uses and limitations of risk assessment

Risk assessment has proved a useful tool in helping societies make decisions about risk. For example, the U.S. Federal Aviation Administration (FAA), the agency that oversees aircraft safety, used risk assessment when it decided in 1992 not to require the use of safety seats for infants in commercial airplanes. Data on crash fatalities had shown that the regulation would save, on average, the life of 1 child every 10 years. But the rule would have forced parents to purchase a ticket for an extra seat, encouraging many parents to travel by car instead. The FAA found that the resulting increase in auto travel would cause 5 additional infant deaths each year, or 50 over 10 years.

But decisions are not always so simple. One problem is that risk assessments can be uncertain, leaving citizens and policymakers unsure how dangerous an activity really is. When experts calculate risks based on statistics, the data leave little room for opinion. But when scientists evaluate risks indirectly, their findings may not be so clear-cut. Because experts must rely on assumptions, estimates, and judgments to make these assessments, many such evaluations are highly controversial.

Consider, for example, the risk of a major accident at a nuclear power plant. Estimates of the likelihood of such an accident vary widely, from 1 chance in 10,000 to 1 chance in 1 million annually per plant. This is partly because probability estimates on such complex activities as nuclear power generation depend on large numbers of smaller estimates, which may themselves be uncertain. For example, much of the technology involved in nuclear power has never been applied to any other industry, so experts have little direct experience to help them estimate the likelihood of a problem. Another problem is that engineers cannot foresee every possible combination of events that might occur in a complex system. Many critics also charge that risk assessments often ignore the possible contributions of human error to an accident.

There is also uncertainty about risk assessments based on animal studies. For example, scientists assume—unless they know otherwise—that a compound with harmful effects on animals has similar effects on human beings. But research has shown that many compounds act differently on different species. One such compound is the artificial sweetener saccharin, which studies in the 1970's linked to bladder cancer in rats. Today, some biologists believe saccharin promoted the disease because it stimulates rats' bodies—but not those of human beings—to produce another substance, which in turn causes cancer. If this is so, saccharin may not pose a cancer risk to humans.

Animal studies may in other ways make certain compounds seem riskier than they really are. Many critics point out that laboratory tests rely on exposures far higher than would ever be found in real life. They argue that a compound may be dangerous at high levels but safe in low doses. Some researchers even believe that the act of ingesting massive doses of certain compounds, rather than anything in the compounds themselves, may trigger body cells to change in ways that can result in cancer.

Other experts say animal studies may lead researchers to underestimate risks. They argue that some chemicals can accumulate in the body, causing long-term harm undetectable by studies using animals with extremely short life spans. Critics also say the studies may fail to take into account the fact that one substance may be more hazardous in the presence of another. Cigarette smoking, for example, has been shown to increase the toxic effects of many compounds. Finally, animal studies are most often performed solely for cancer risks, so any other health effects of a substance may go unnoticed.

Making decisions about risks: The case of pesticides

Most experts believe that animal studies, though imprecise, are still the best tool for estimating chemical risks. They say that scientists can avoid underestimating most risks by leaving a margin of safety in their

Rank the risks
How would you rank the risk of death caused by the following activities or substances?

- Air pollution
- Cigarette smoking
- Commercial aircraft travel
- Car travel
- Radon gas
- Nuclear waste

List the six items in order from most risky to least risky. Then turn the page to see what experts think about these and other risks.

How people perceive risk

Public policy decisions about risk are often complicated by the fact that the public perceives risk differently from scientists and other experts in risk assessment. For example, many nonexperts tend to minimize the danger of a risk they take on voluntarily compared with a risk they feel is forced upon them. People also tend to be more fearful of risks that may cause many casualties at once than of risks whose effects are spread out over time. When a group of college students and a group of experts were asked to rank activities and objects from most risky (1) to least risky (10), the results were vastly different.

College students	Experts
1. Nuclear power	1. Motor vehicles
2. Handguns	2. Smoking
3. Smoking	3. Alcohol
4. Pesticides	4. Handguns
5. Motor vehicles	5. X rays
6. Alcohol	6. Pesticides
7. Police work	7. Electric power (nonnuclear)
8. Commercial aviation	8. Commercial aviation
9. X rays	9. Police work
10. Electric power (nonnuclear)	10. Nuclear power

Source: Adapted from "Rating the Risks," by Paul Slovic, Baruch Fischhoff, and Sarah Lichtenstein. *Environment* 21:3, April 1979, pp. 14-20, 36-39.

estimates—for example, by basing them on maximum possible doses.

Nevertheless, scientists recognize that they still have a very imperfect understanding of some risks. This failing sometimes puts consumers, producers, environmentalists, scientists, and regulators at odds. This is true, for example, in the case of chemical pesticides. These compounds allow farmers to produce abundant, inexpensive agricultural goods. But studies have found that some of these chemicals pose both health and environmental risks. On the basis of such studies, the EPA has banned the use of many such compounds in the United States.

One health risk posed by some pesticides is cancer. Some experts who argue against strict government control of pesticides point out that the cancer risk from most artificially produced pesticides may be minuscule compared with the risk from natural pesticides made by plants as protection against insects, plant-eating animals, and bacteria. Biochemist Bruce N. Ames of the University of California at Berkeley, a leading expert in carcinogenic risks, has estimated that these natural compounds make up more than 99 percent of all pesticides in the American diet.

Many environmentalists and others who call for stricter pesticide regulation argue that cancer is not the only known risk of using artificial pesticides. Some types of pesticides have been found to cause other toxic effects, such as nervous system disorders and, possibly, birth defects. In addition, they say, some pesticides accumulate in the envi-

Which is riskier?

or

Air pollution from motor vehicles, industry, and electric power plants can aggravate lung conditions and increase the risk of lung disease for children, the elderly, and people with weakened immune systems. Scientists believe air pollution may contribute to at least 5,000 to 50,000 deaths in the United States each year.

Cigarette smoking is the leading cause of lung cancer and a major cause of heart disease in the United States. According to the U.S. Centers for Disease Control, some 450,000 smokers in the United States die of smoking-related illnesses each year, as do some 50,000 nonsmokers exposed to cigarette smoke.

or

Automobile travel. Traveling about 100 miles (160 kilometers) by car increases a person's risk of death by 1 chance in a million.

Airplane travel. Flying about 2,000 miles (3,220 kilometers) in a commercial aircraft increases the risk of death by 1 in a million.

or

Radon is a natural radioactive gas that can enter homes through cracks in basement floors and walls. The American Lung Association believes radon may cause 7,000 to 30,000 lung cancer deaths a year in the United States.

Nuclear wastes are highly radioactive, and their risks are controversial. But many engineers say that if properly stored, such wastes would cause a maximum of 1,000 cancer deaths over 100,000 years.

ronment and may devastate fish, birds, and livestock. Furthermore, some scientists argue, chemical pesticides may pose unique risks to children, whose growing bodies and smaller body weights may make them more vulnerable to certain substances than adults are.

Researchers have developed safer, less-polluting ways to control some pests—for example, through techniques that disrupt the reproductive cycles of insects. But such methods require a different approach for each insect, so they are far more expensive than chemical pesticides. As a result, a society that decides to eliminate chemical pesticides must pay the price at the grocery checkout counter. And this could cause many people to reduce their consumption of fruits and vegetables, resulting in poorer nutrition and, possibly, an overall decline in health.

When perceptions of risk collide

The pesticide issue, like many others, is complicated by the fact that people's perceptions of risk often differ sharply from those of the experts. Psychologists, sociologists, and others who study how people think about risks have found, for example, that individuals more willingly accept risks they take on voluntarily than risks over which they feel they have no control. They tend to fear new hazards more than familiar ones and poorly understood risks more than sure ones. People are also more concerned about risks that might affect them or their families personally than about risks affecting strangers. Finally, nonexperts tend to view risks that might cause many casualties at once with more dread than risks whose effects may be spread over time.

These psychological factors sometimes lead people to make what many experts regard as irrational judgments about risks. Nuclear power is a case in point. Until such energy sources as wind or solar power become more efficient, energy experts say, the United States must continue to rely on two main sources of power: nuclear energy and the *combustion* (burning) of fossil fuels, chiefly coal and petroleum. Both technologies carry risks—but comparing them may surprise you.

The world's largest nuclear accident occurred in 1986, when an explosion and fire destroyed the reactor at a nuclear power plant in Chernobyl, near Kiev, Ukraine. Some 30 people died of radiation poisoning after the accident, and experts believe the radiation released may eventually contribute to as many as 20,000 cancer deaths.

A high estimate of the likelihood of a major accident in the United States is 1 chance in 10,000 annually per reactor. This means that with 100 U.S. reactors operating (the approximate number in use in 1994), such an accident might be expected about once every 100 years. Even a major U.S. accident would probably not lead to a significant release of radiation, however, because of the way nuclear power plants in the United States are constructed. Experts believe that the chance of an accident so severe that significant radiation is released is only $\frac{1}{10}$ to $\frac{1}{100}$ of the overall accident risk. These odds mean that a deadly accident might occur once in 1,000 to 10,000 years.

Citizens may also be concerned about nuclear energy because of the risks from radioactive waste, or because of the possible effects of low-level radiation exposure on people living or working near a nuclear reactor. But engineers estimate that if nuclear waste were properly and permanently stored, it would be likely to cause no more than 1,000 cancer deaths during the entire 100,000-year period that such waste is radioactive. Experts also point out that radiation levels around a nuclear plant are hundreds of times lower than a person's average radiation exposure from such natural sources as radon and from medical and dental X rays.

People generally regard fossil fuels as much safer than nuclear power. But unlike nuclear power, fossil fuel combustion is responsible for highly dangerous forms of environmental pollution. Burning the fuels produces chemical compounds—sulfur dioxide and nitrogen oxides— that form the chief pollutants in acid rain, a major source of damage to forests, rivers and lakes, and the wildlife that depend on them. Air pollution from nitrogen oxides and ozone, another compound that is released by fossil fuel combustion, can cause or worsen lung disease, contributing to between 5,000 and 50,000 deaths a year, according to some estimates. Fossil fuels also release carbon dioxide, which accumulates in Earth's atmosphere. Many scientists believe this accumulation may cause *global warming*, in which excess heat is trapped in the atmosphere, increasing Earth's average surface temperature.

Of course, if a nuclear disaster might occur once in 10,000 years, it is as likely to happen tomorrow as on any other specific day during the next 10,000 years. But the question scientists say policymakers and consumers need to ask is whether we, as a society, should make such a small risk the basis for our decisions about the future—especially in light of the amount of risk we live with every day. After all, they say, a risk is like a reverse kind of lottery. Each week, lotteries sell millions of tickets, one of which may bring its owner a windfall. But for the other 9,999,999 or so ticket buyers, nothing changes.

If you're the person who wins the lottery, of course, it doesn't matter what the odds were—just as the odds don't matter if you're the one person in a million to suffer the effects of a risky activity. That's why experts say it's important to be aware of hazards, so that we can act, when possible, to reduce them. But it's important to remember, too, that society cannot eliminate all risks. It can only compare the risks and benefits of all alternatives—and then try to make the best choice possible.

For further reading:
Lewis, H. W. *Technological Risk*. W. W. Norton & Company, 1990.
Readings in Risk. Ed. by Theodore S. Glickman and Michael Gough. Resources for the Future, 1990.

Gearing Up for the Information Superhighway

BY HERB BRODY

A vast communications network, now being developed, may someday link every telephone, television, and computer in the world.

At the beginning of 1993, few people in the United States had ever heard of the "information superhighway." But that soon changed. Throughout the year, the media trumpeted the coming of the superhighway, and companies hoping to cash in on it announced one multimillion-dollar business deal after another. By year-end, the Administration of U.S. President Bill Clinton had pledged to help turn the vision into reality.

What exactly is the information superhighway? According to leaders in computer science and communications, it will be a far-reaching system of computer networks connecting every home, business, and institution in the nation—and ultimately the world—to every other one. Users will hook up to the network with an "information appliance," an electronic device that some experts envision as a cross between a telephone, a computer, and a television set. Information, translated into computer data, will travel as pulses of electricity through copper wires or as light signals through glass fibers. Powerful computers called servers will store great quantities of data and transmit it on demand.

The mammoth network should give people access to an incredible variety of services and diversions. Researching a term paper? If expectations are correct, you'll be able to browse through the Library of

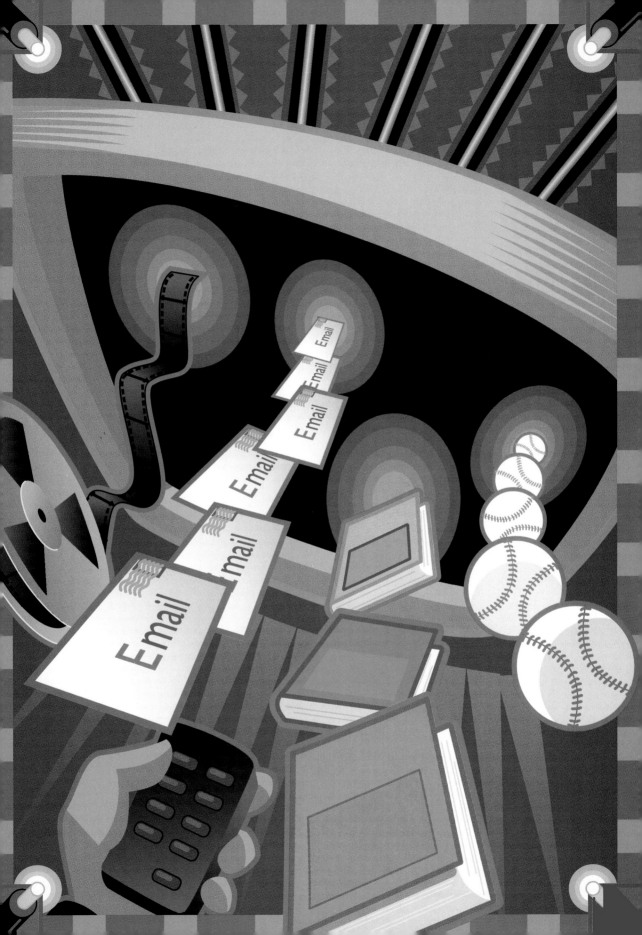

Glossary

Asymmetric digital subscriber line (ADSL): A system for reducing electrical interference between neighboring copper telephone wires so the lines can be used for video transmissions.

Digital compression: Transmitting a digital TV image in highly abbreviated form by sending information only on the parts of the image that change from one moment to the next.

Digital format: The language of computers—the translation of information into a string of 1's and 0's, known as bits.

Internet: A worldwide system of interconnected computer networks.

Optical fibers: Extremely transparent strands of glass used to transmit digital information as pulses of light.

Video on demand: A service that will enable television viewers to see TV programs and movies at times of their choosing.

Video server: A special computer that holds movies and TV shows in digital form and conveys them to viewers when they order them.

The author:

Herb Brody is a senior editor at *Technology Review* magazine.

Congress without leaving home. Looking for entertainment? You'll call up any movie you want, whenever you want, without having to make a trip to the video-rental store. Enjoy video games? You'll pit your skills against partners across town or on the opposite side of the globe. How about shopping? The superhighway will enable you to take a video stroll through hundreds of stores or flip through electronic catalogs, ordering merchandise with the push of a button.

The information superhighway could even bring a revolution in the way we get an education and earn a living. It might become unnecessary for students to congregate every day in a school building, for example. Teachers could offer lessons "on line," with students able to listen, ask questions, and interact with schoolmates just as they do in a traditional classroom. And companies might find that their employees could conduct meetings and do many other parts of their jobs just as well from home as at the office.

For now, these ideas are largely speculation. Although the information superhighway is now being built from today's telephone, cable TV, and computer networks, no one knows exactly what the full-fledged version of the superhighway will be like or when it will be completed. Some experts predict, however, that the first widely available multimedia services will be available by the end of the 1990's, with many more to follow in later years. Telecommunications companies have already begun testing various new information services. As those trials proceed, observers will be able to make more accurate predictions about how the system will shape up—and how it may affect our lives.

Building the electronic superhighway is possible today in large part because of two technical advances. One is the ability to efficiently convey sound and video—the substance of TV transmissions—in the language of computers. The other is the ability to transmit that information as pulses of light.

Digital technology

For decades, TV signals have been sent to the home as an *analog* signal—that is, as a continuous electronic wave. In the 1960's, computer scientists learned how to translate audio and video information into computer data. They do this by converting the sound and pictures into *digital* format—a series of 1's and 0's, which are referred to as *bits*. In the standard code used by most computers, the letter A, for example, is represented in eight bits as 01000001. Every point in a color video image and every instant of sound can also be expressed as such a string of numbers.

Digital format is ideal for electronic communications, because the strings of 1's and 0's can be transmitted by a series of "on" or "off" signals. An "on" signal, such as a pulse of electricity or light, can indicate a 1. An "off" signal—the lack of a pulse—can stand for 0. Information in this form is also easy to store electronically. Television programs and movies that have been digitized—converted to digital format—can be held in the memory of a computer as easily as text documents.

But computer engineers had to overcome a stumbling block before the digital transmission of television pictures could become practical. Encoding TV images requires an enormous number of 1's and 0's. One *frame* (still image) of a color-TV picture takes up about 3 million bits. Television signals are broadcast at the rate of 30 frames per second, so sending one TV signal digitally means transmitting 90 million bits per second. With that rate of transmission, it would take several channels to convey a single digital TV signal.

Then in the late 1980's, engineers made great progress in developing a technology called *digital compression,* which allows pictures to be transmitted in a highly abbreviated form. With most video pictures, the image in one frame is pretty much identical to that in the previous frame. For example, the background of the picture often remains the same for many consecutive frames, and the actors may move only slightly from one frame to the next. So instead of transmitting the entire image again, a compression system sends only the parts of the picture that have changed. Digital compression makes it possible to represent a continuous color-TV signal with as few as 10 million bits per second.

This technique makes the digital format a vast improvement over analog. Today's analog cable TV systems can provide about 50 television channels over coaxial cables, thick copper wires wrapped with insulation and encased in metal tubes. Digital compression will boost that number to as many as 500 channels, without requiring any additional cable.

The transition to digital technology has some way to go, however. Most recorded entertainment, such as movies and old TV shows, is stored in analog form and would have to be converted to digital before it could be transmitted on the information superhighway. And engineers are still perfecting the specially adapted computers, called video servers, that will hold huge collections of movies and other programs in digital form and transmit them to users.

Transmitting data with light

The other key technology being used to create the electronic superhighway is *fiber optics,* the most advanced method available for transmitting digital information. Fiber optics employs hair-thin strands of glass to carry data as pulses of light. These optical fibers, first developed in the 1970's by American scientists, are made of high-purity glass that is extremely transparent. The great transparency of optical fibers enables light waves to travel for long distances through them without fading away. The glass in today's optical fibers is so transparent, in fact, that if seawater were equally clear, you could see to the bottom of the deepest ocean.

A fiber-optics system can transmit incredible amounts of information. A pair of plain copper wires is able to carry just one telephone conversation, traveling as electrical impulses. A pair of optical fibers, conveying light pulses at the rate of hundreds of millions of bits per

New technologies pave the way

Advanced techniques for sending and receiving data are making the information super-highway possible.

Optical fibers, hair-thin glass strands, can carry vast amounts of information, transmitted as pulses of light. By 1994, engineers had designed fibers that could convey 300,000 simultaneous telephone conversations. A pair of copper wires, in comparison, can carry just one. Optical fibers are also ideal for transmitting TV signals.

Digital technology, which has long been the language of computers, will be the basis of all communications on the information superhighway. With digital technology, any kind of information—a television image, for example—is translated into a series of *bits*, 1's and 0's. The bits can be sent over optical fibers as pulses of light. They can also be transmitted as electrical signals over conventional wires or as broadcast signals over the airwaves.

Digital compression enables transmissions using as few as 10 percent of the bits normally required. The technique, developed in the late 1980's, takes advantage of the fact that although a TV picture changes 30 times a second, much of the image remains the same from one frame to the next. Only the parts of the image that change are transmitted as bits.

Digital Converter

10101010111010
01010101101010
11101101010011
01011001110101

Portion of image that has changed

Digital Converter

01001101101001

Television terminals that give TV's computing power were under development in 1994. A terminal will receive digital video information over telephone lines and convert it into images displayed on the viewer's TV. A wireless remote control will enable the viewer to select programs and to take part in interactive services, such as home shopping and video games.

second, can handle more than 15,000 simultaneous conversations. The transmission of so much data is possible because the waves of light keep their shape in the glass fibers, even over long distances. This regularity and predictability makes it possible to interweave light signals representing many conversations into a single stream of pulses.

Technical improvements, such as ever-purer glass fibers and new methods of feeding light pulses into the fibers, have produced constant increases in the carrying capacity of fiber-optics systems. A fiber-optic cable laid under the Atlantic Ocean in the 1990's by the American Telephone and Telegraph Company (AT&T), one of the world's largest communications companies, transmits 5 billion bits per second over each of two pairs of fibers. That is enough capacity for 320,000 simultaneous conversations. Experts predict transmission rates of more than 1 trillion bits per second in the future.

In the United States, telephone companies have been replacing their old electrical transmission lines with optical fibers at a rapid pace. For decades, the telephone network was nearly all copper wire, not much different from what Alexander Graham Bell used when he invented the telephone in the 1870's. Then in the 1980's, U.S. phone companies began laying fiber-optic cables in earnest. By 1994, the nation was crisscrossed by an optical-fiber network for long-distance communications, and fiber optics had become the technology of choice for those long-haul transmissions. Nevertheless, because replacing the wires with optical cables would cost billions of dollars, copper wires continue to carry the signal the last mile or so to most home and office telephones. The situation is like having six-lane highways linking the nation's cities and towns, while local traffic still uses gravel roads.

Making copper wire work harder

Throughout the 1980's, those "gravel roads" kept telephone companies from offering video services over the phone lines. Even with digital compression, copper wire simply was not adequate for transmitting video. Interference—known as "crosstalk"—between neighboring copper wires caused a video signal to become progressively muddled. In the early 1990's, however, telephone-industry researchers developed a new technology called *asymmetric digital subscriber line* (ADSL) that provided a way around the copper-wire obstacle. ADSL uses specially designed transmitters and receivers to reduce the interference between wires. With ADSL, copper phone lines can deliver compressed digital video transmissions with quality indistinguishable from that produced by a typical videocassette recorder. And the same wires can continue to be used for ordinary conversations.

What ADSL does not permit, however, is two-way video communications, a necessity for interactive services in which the user transmits as well as receives video. For that reason, experts predict that the full flowering of the information superhighway will have to wait until fiber optics is extended to every telephone customer, sometime after the year 2000.

Incredible variety on the superhighway

As it is envisioned today, the information super-highway will bring into the home a tremendous array of electronic services provided by TV networks, libraries, and other suppliers. The super-highway will also offer many ways for consumers to communicate directly with one another.

Video games
Interactive games with multiple players will link opponents at distant sites.

Suppliers will provide a variety of electronic services, entertainment, and databases. They will relay transmissions digitally to local cable TV and phone companies, either through the airwaves or via fiber-optic cable. The local companies will then route the digital information to homes along optical fibers. Many transmissions, such as movies and TV programs, will be stored in computers and sent to consumers whenever they order them. With interactive video services such as electronic shopping and video games, data will travel out of the home over the same fibers.

Business meetings
Teleconferencing will enable people to hold meetings with distant co-workers.

Local cable TV company, telephone company, or both

Special programs
A wide array of concerts and other events will be offered on a pay-per-view basis.

Electronic malls
Shoppers will browse by "walking" through video representations of stores.

Customized news
"Smart" TV's will sort through news items and select news that interests each viewer.

Motion pictures
Thousands of movies will be available whenever viewers want to see them.

Television shows
Viewers who miss a TV program will be able to order a rerun at a time they select.

Research help
Consumers will be able to look through the holdings of data banks and libraries.

Personal affairs
Consumers will do their banking, travel planning, and other chores electronically.

Catalog shopping
Electronic catalogs will make it possible to order products at the click of a button.

Reading material
People will read books and magazines on video screens or make printouts of them.

Video phone calls
Video phones will become common, and calls may someday come through the TV.

A TV, telephone, and computer all in one

Electronics engineers think that by the time the fiber-optics network is completed, they will have made another important advance: creation of an all-purpose communications appliance that blends the functions of the television, telephone, and computer. The new device may look like a television—or like a picture on the wall—but it will transmit information as well as receive it. One way experts envision data being transmitted over the information appliance is through an "air mouse," similar to an ordinary remote control unit, that could be pointed at choices listed on the screen. With interactive shopping, for example, the press of a button on the mouse will bring more information on any item of interest, perhaps a video of someone modeling a sweater or demonstrating an appliance. To place an order, a viewer will simply click on a "yes" box on the screen. The consumer's name and address and other relevant information, encoded in the computer's memory, will be relayed directly to the store along with the order.

A "rough draft" for the superhighway

Although the major elements of the information superhighway are ready, or soon will be, how will they come together? The telephone system, which reaches virtually every home and business in the United States and most other parts of the world, is the most obvious "rough draft" for the highway. Telephones are everywhere and easy to use, and millions of electronic switches instantly link any home or business in the world with any other one. In fact, industry analysts say that only the telephone system has the worldwide network needed for a true information superhighway. By contrast, most cable TV systems are limited to providing entertainment and information to homes from a central supplier—they cannot link individual homes to one another.

To imagine how the phone system could form the backbone of the information superhighway, consider the Internet. This global web of thousands of interconnected computer networks—a network of networks—operates over telephone lines. The Internet evolved from ARPAnet, a computer network that was established by the Department of Defense in the 1960's. ARPAnet enabled scientists working on military projects at separate government laboratories to transmit data to one another under conditions of security. In the mid-1980's, the National Science Foundation built high-speed communications links between five supercomputers in different parts of the nation and, at the request of the Defense Department, linked them to ARPAnet. The result was the Internet.

Until the late 1980's, the new network remained the province of a high-tech elite at government and university laboratories, but then other groups with common interests established their own networks and linked them to the Internet. The system grew without any real direction or organization. By 1994, an estimated 15 million people in 50 countries were users of "the Net," and if current growth rates continue, the number of users will reach 100 million by 1999.

Anyone with a computer connected to a *modem* (a device linking a computer to a telephone line) can join the Internet, though a fairly high degree of skill is necessary to navigate the system efficiently. Users are able to send electronic-mail messages to other subscribers and tap into computer databases anywhere in the world. They can also take part in any of thousands of on-line discussion groups, called newsgroups, on topics ranging from politics to physics to television shows. The Internet is starting to look like a full-fledged information superhighway as users are increasingly able not only to exchange written information but also to talk face-to-face and to send and receive full-motion videos. But the extension of these advanced applications to the general population will require the installation of higher-capacity lines—particularly fiber-optic cables—to homes.

The role of cable TV companies

For most people, the first taste of the information superhighway will come through their cable TV provider. In the mid-1990's, many cable companies were building hybrid networks consisting of both optical fibers and coaxial cables. In such a system, programming from the networks and dozens of cable channels is relayed via optical fibers to distribution points in neighborhoods. From there, the existing coaxial cables carry the TV signal to individual homes. This approach makes it possible to provide a variety of video-based services to viewers without the huge expense of laying optical fiber to individual homes.

Companies such as Tele-Communications Incorporated (TCI), the nation's largest cable company, were also gearing up to equip their customers' homes with devices that "decompress" signals sent through the cable in compressed form. By 1996 or soon thereafter, this technology will enable cable networks to carry the 500 video channels that have been promised by digital compression.

Most of those channels will be used for a scaled-down version of interactive television, in particular a service known as "video on demand." Telecommunications experts envision video on demand as a way to allow viewers to call up any TV program or movie, at any time. When fully operational, video on demand could make TV programming schedules a thing of the past. Every household would choose from among a galaxy of offerings listed in on-screen catalogs. When a viewer orders a movie or TV program, it would be sent digitally to the viewer's information appliance and stored in its memory circuits. Viewers could watch the show whenever they wanted and stop or replay parts of the action, just as they do now using videocassette recorders.

Cable companies are planning to use some of the new channels for expanded home shopping services. Department stores and other major retailers may establish separate channels to showcase their wares. Other new shopping services may offer computer software that is delivered directly to the purchaser's computer, along with an electronic instruction manual. Musical recordings could be also delivered to a home computer, which would transfer the music to a recordable com-

Cruise control

In mid-1994, several companies were testing ways to make it simple for people to navigate the information superhighway.

Stargazer, a cable TV system being tested by the Bell Atlantic Corporation of Arlington, Va., allows viewers to choose movies with the press of a button, *right*. Other services include grocery shopping, *below*.

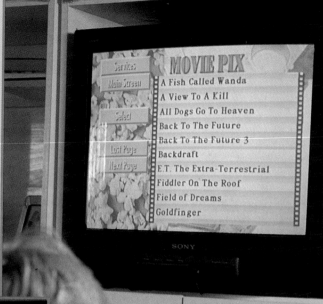

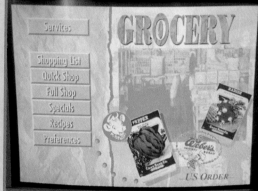

In a system being tested in Florida by Time Warner Cable, the TV displays a computer-generated aerial view of buildings that represent options and services. Information services, for example, are depicted by the book-shaped building. Viewers can zoom in on a building, enter, browse, and make a selection.

pact disc. Car buyers, too, may be able to shop without leaving home. The customer would choose a basic model automobile and then select from a list of colors, options, and interiors, creating an image of the resulting car on the video screen.

In some parts of the United States, small interactive cable systems were already being planned or tested in 1994. For example, Time Warner Cable, one of the biggest cable companies in the United States, was developing what it calls a "full-service video network" that was to be provided to several thousand customers in Orlando, Fla. Company executives said the first trials would focus on shopping and entertainment, including video on demand. Users will retrieve programming from at least a dozen video servers.

Making the driving easier

While some companies were working to create new services for the information superhighway, other businesses were designing software that will make the superhighway simpler to use. A leader in that line of research is the Bell Atlantic Corporation, one of the seven regional phone companies created in 1984 by the court-ordered breakup of AT&T. A Bell Atlantic team in Arlington, Va., is developing an interactive system called Stargazer, for shopping and other services, that it hopes will be widely adopted when the superhighway is in full operation. The goal of the Bell Atlantic researchers is to allow consumers to find their way through an electronic marketplace as easily as they now use the telephone.

Shopping and using other electronic services may eventually be even simpler than that. Researchers at a number of companies and laboratories were aiming at developing software "agents" to do consumers' bidding. An agent, which would essentially be an electronic servant, might be represented as a computer-generated image of a human being that appears on the video screen and responds to spoken commands. If the user asks what airline flights are available from Boston to London on a coming Saturday, for example, the agent would locate the information in computer databases that list airline schedules. Then the agent would report back with the answer—perhaps by knocking politely on the computer screen and reciting the available flights. The agent could also place a ticket order for whichever flight the consumer chose. But further technological advances, including computer software that can recognize human speech, will be required before we will see electronic agents that seem like living helpers rather than just clever computer programs.

Challenges to be solved

Making the network easier to navigate is just one of several challenges ahead. One of social scientists' biggest worries about the information superhighway, for example, is the danger that it could be used to invade people's privacy. The price of tapping into a rich artery of in-

Roadblocks ahead

Building the information superhighway is a complex undertaking that presents challenging problems. How those problems are solved will shape the superhighway and determine who has access to it and how they will use it.

Problems	Possible solutions
▪ Difficulty in navigating computer networks and obtaining needed information and services.	▪ Easy-to-use operating systems, perhaps including electronic "agents" that travel the superhighway to find what a user is looking for and special systems to help the disabled and the elderly.
▪ Difficulty keeping electronic communications private.	▪ Technology enabling users to send coded transmissions and laws giving people the right to use that technology.
▪ Inequalities resulting from the expense of services, which could cause society to divide into informational "haves," who can afford electronic services, and "have-nots," who cannot.	▪ Competition among service providers to drive down costs; government subsidies for the poor.
▪ The need to convert printed information in books, periodicals, and other documents into digital form before they can be made available on the superhighway.	▪ Use of text-scanning technology, though this will be a time-consuming and costly process.
▪ Legal disputes regarding copyright infringement on materials electronically accessible anywhere in the world.	▪ Court decisions establishing the ownership rights of creators whose work is available on the superhighway and mechanisms for protecting those rights.
▪ Lack of access to the superhighway for people who want to provide services or information.	▪ Public-access channels, or laws limiting the rights of TV, cable, and telephone companies to restrict the content of information transmitted over their lines or channels.
▪ Incompatible operating systems among electronic networks, preventing people on different networks from communicating with one another.	▪ Standards, available to everyone, for connecting computer networks.

formation and commercial offerings is that every transaction leaves an electronic trail. Every purchase, every airline reservation, every request for information will be recorded. If these records are freely available, businesses, political organizations, and other groups would be able to assemble highly detailed rundowns of people's habits, tastes, and activities by monitoring their comings and goings on the superhighway.

Another privacy issue surrounds the difficulty of keeping the content of electronic communications confidential. For example, businesses using the superhighway to communicate with employees might fear that computer hackers could listen in and discover company secrets. Techniques to encode computer transmissions could ensure privacy, however. The sender of a transmission would use a mathematical code that scrambles the digital bits in the message, making them gibberish without possession of a decoding "key," which would be known only to the intended recipient. Such a system worries law enforcement agencies because it would make it difficult to carry out wiretaps on suspected criminals and terrorists. The Clinton Administration in 1994 was pushing for a standard coding system that would keep a decoding key in the hands of the government, but that idea ran into strong opposition from privacy advocates.

Other concerns about the electronic revolution have to do with its possible effects on the cohesiveness of American society. Advocates of the superhighway talk of the "shared experiences" that the new technology will bring. Most of the services that are being envisioned do not support that notion, however. Video on demand, for example, will lessen the chance that someone has seen the same shows as his or her neighbor. And electronic shopping offers none of the opportunities for mingling with other people that come with strolling through a shopping mall. Some experts fear that many users of the superhighway, with the world at their fingertips, will feel that they have no need to leave home. If that happens, the new technology is likely to make people feel more, not less, isolated.

Beyond that, what about those who cannot afford to cruise the superhighway? Amid all the hoopla surrounding the new technology, the probable costs for consumers have been glossed over. The many electronic services that will be available, and the hardware needed to obtain them, may be unaffordable for many people. We would thus risk becoming a nation divided between information "haves," who can get the data they need to do well in work and school, and "have-nots," who are shut out.

To combat that problem, social scientists are already proposing ways to give everyone a chance to get onto the information superhighway, regardless of income. One solution would be to give government vouchers, similar to food stamps, to low-income individuals so that they can pay for information services. Another possibility would be to give those people direct subsidies for basic services. The money for the subsidies could come from a surcharge levied on high-priced services that are used mainly by the affluent.

Experts may find ways to make the information superhighway accessible to everyone, but it is still not clear exactly how people will use it. When the United States built the interstate highway system, it did so in large part to make sure the country could mobilize quickly in case of military attack. Planners did not set out to empty the populations of the nation's cities into the suburbs, but that was one result of that massive project. Similarly, people will no doubt find their own uses for the electronic interstate system, and that makes the long-term impact of the information superhighway impossible to foresee.

For further reading:

Brody, Herb. "Information Highway: The Home Front." *Technology Review*, August/September 1993, pp. 31-40.
Stix, Gary. "Domesticating Cyberspace." *Scientific American*, August 1993, pp. 100-110.

Science Studies

The Promise of Renewable Energy

BY ARTHUR FISHER

The need for cleaner, inexhaustible energy sources
will grow as world electricity use increases.
Advocates say renewable energy can meet that need.

Introduction

We use energy in a thousand ways: to heat our homes, to cook, to provide light, to manufacture products, and to run the electronic systems upon which modern society depends. As the world's population has grown, our energy use has increased as well. Experts predict that our energy needs will increase dramatically in the next century.

Increased energy use will almost certainly highlight the problems of producing energy in the usual way—by burning *fossil fuels* (coal, oil, and natural gas). These fuels produce air pollution that can kill forests, harm rivers and lakes, damage lungs, and potentially disrupt Earth's climate. And fossil fuel deposits are limited. Nuclear energy offers an alternative to fossil fuels, but that technology has drawbacks of its own.

Despite these problems, the world continues to rely on fossil fuels. Modern societies use vast quantities of oil-derived fuels such as gasoline for transportation. The amount of energy used to produce electricity surpasses that used for other purposes in some nations, however, and it is a particularly good example of our fossil fuel dependence. In 1991, nearly two-thirds of the world's electricity came from the burning of fossil fuels.

But alternatives can supply power as long as the sun shines, winds blow, water flows, and trees grow. These so-called *renewable energy* sources are capable of providing inexhaustible supplies of power for electricity production and other needs, in most cases emitting far less pollution than fossil fuels. The most common renewable energy sources are *hydropower* (energy from falling water); *biomass power* (energy from wood and other plant matter); *geothermal power* (energy from heat within the Earth); *solar power* (energy from the sun); and *wind power* (energy from the wind).

Many obstacles prevent the widespread use of renewable energy. They range from the cost of new energy technologies to opposition from groups with financial interests in the use of fossil fuels. But as traditional ways of producing electricity become less acceptable, experts say, we will increasingly turn toward renewable energy.

The author:
Arthur Fisher is the science and technology editor of *Popular Science* magazine.

The Case for Renewables

To provide the electricity needed to keep our complex society from grinding to a halt, the world relies mainly upon fossil fuels. Among those fuels, coal accounts for 38 to 40 percent of the world's total electricity output, natural gas produces about 13 percent, and oil accounts for about 11 percent.

The three energy sources are called fossil fuels because they derive from the remains of plants and animals that died millions of years ago. Most coal formed between 345 million and 280 million years ago from the compressed remains of vegetation. As those remains became buried under sediment, they hardened into their present form. Oil and gas deposits were created in a similar process that began when tiny plantlike organisms in the seas that covered Earth millions of years ago died and settled to the sea floor. As sediment compressed these organisms, they turned into a waxy substance called kerogen. The extreme pressures far underground eventually caused the kerogen to separate into liquid (oil) and gas (natural gas).

The energy of fossil fuels originated in the sun. The ancient plants and organisms that formed fossil fuels harnessed energy from sunlight during *photosynthesis,* the process by which plants convert carbon dioxide and water into food. Burning fossil fuels, whether to produce electricity or to fuel the engines of cars, trucks, and airplanes, releases the energy stored in the plants millions of years ago.

To produce electricity from coal or oil, power plant operators burn the fuel in a combustion chamber to heat a water supply piped through the chamber. The heated water produces steam, which spins the blades of a turbine. In natural gas power plants, a mixture of gas and air ignites to produce a rush of hot gas. The gas spins the blades of the turbine. In both types of plants, the turbine is connected to a generator. A generator is a device that turns mechanical energy into electricity by moving a coil of wire through a magnetic field.

The advantages of fossil fuels

The main advantages of fossil fuels are their accessibility, ease of storage, and low price. Coal, oil, and natural gas deposits can be found in many parts of the world.

Since the 1970's, engineers have developed increasingly efficient ways to explore for oil and natural gas and have designed more efficient power plants that waste less fuel. Such improvements have helped keep prices of fossil fuels lower than those of nearly all other common energy sources.

The drawbacks of fossil fuels

Despite their popularity, fossil fuels are far from perfect energy sources. One problem is that reserves are limited. The world is consuming fossil fuels 100,000 times faster than geological processes can replace them. Estimates of the amount of fuel remaining in the Earth vary considerably, but some experts believe that at current levels of use there may not be enough oil to last beyond 2100. Natural gas reserves may be depleted about the same time. Without new discoveries, coal reserves may not last beyond 2300. Increased demand could deplete supplies faster.

Another problem is that supplies of the fuels are not evenly distributed across the Earth. The Organization of Petroleum Exporting Countries, a group of 12 nations that depend heavily on their oil exports for income, contain about 59 percent of the world's combined reserves of oil and natural gas but consume only about 4 percent of the world's energy. Other nations, such as Japan, have few fossil fuel supplies and must import almost all they require.

As a result of this lopsided distribution, 44 percent of all the oil consumed in the world, 14 percent of the natural gas, and 11 percent of the coal must be shipped from one country to another. Nations have gone to war over this unequal distribution and may continue to do so as fossil fuel reserves diminish.

But the biggest problem with fossil fuels is that their combustion produces by-products that pollute the air. One by-product is carbon dioxide. All fossil fuels contain carbon, and during combustion, that carbon combines with oxygen to form carbon dioxide gas. Carbon dioxide occurs naturally in Earth's atmosphere, where it, water vapor, and several other gases help keep Earth warm enough to sustain life by trapping more than 80 percent of the planet's heat that would otherwise escape into space. That process corresponds to the way glass walls trap heat in a greenhouse, and so the atmospheric gases are called *greenhouse gases.*

Many scientists fear that the increasing use of fossil fuels releases so much carbon dioxide into the atmosphere that Earth's average surface temperature will begin to rise, a scenario called *global warming.* Global warming could produce widespread droughts, shift prime farmland farther

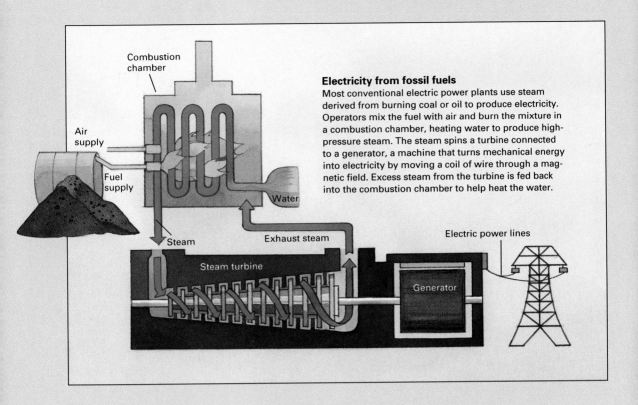

Electricity from fossil fuels

Most conventional electric power plants use steam derived from burning coal or oil to produce electricity. Operators mix the fuel with air and burn the mixture in a combustion chamber, heating water to produce high-pressure steam. The steam spins a turbine connected to a generator, a machine that turns mechanical energy into electricity by moving a coil of wire through a magnetic field. Excess steam from the turbine is fed back into the combustion chamber to help heat the water.

north, and melt some polar ice, leading to a rise in sea levels that would flood many coastal cities and islands.

The amount of carbon dioxide released into the atmosphere by burning fossil fuels varies with the fuel. The combustion of coal produces nearly twice as much carbon dioxide as does natural gas combustion and about 1¼ times as much as oil. Burning enough coal to provide electricity for an average household in the United States creates about 790 kilograms (1,740 pounds) of carbon dioxide emissions per month.

Fossil fuel combustion causes other pollution problems as well. Sulfur dioxide and nitrogen oxides are released when the fuel is burned, and these gases can combine with moisture in the air to form sulfuric and nitric acids that fall to Earth in snow or rain. Sulfuric acid produces so-called *acid rain* or *acid deposition* that hinders plant growth, contributes to the death of trees, and damages life in lakes and rivers.

The nuclear power option

One alternative to fossil fuels is nuclear energy. By 1993, nuclear power plants generated about 17 percent of the world's electricity. These facilities produce electricity by harnessing the energy

of *nuclear fission*—the splitting of *nuclei* (cores) of atoms. In most nuclear reactors, *neutrons* (one of the two types of particles in atomic nuclei) bombard fuel pellets containing uranium. The neutrons split uranium atoms, producing energy in the form of heat and releasing even more neutrons that hit and split other atoms, creating a "chain reaction." The heat is used to turn water into steam. As in a fossil fuel power plant, the steam powers a turbine connected to a generator.

A main benefit of nuclear power is that it releases almost no carbon dioxide or other air pollutants. Producing electricity through nuclear power rather than fossil fuel combustion prevents about 1.7 billion metric tons (1.9 billion short tons) of carbon dioxide from being added to Earth's atmosphere each year.

Nevertheless, nuclear power does have drawbacks. Nuclear fuel is radioactive—that is, it emits hazardous radiation that can damage living cells. Used fuel pellets from nuclear plants will be radioactive for thousands of years. Safely disposing of such waste is a difficult problem that engineers still have not adequately solved.

In addition, although malfunctions at nuclear power plants are rare, they are potentially far more dangerous than accidents at fossil fuel power plants. If a nuclear plant's cooling system mal-

A coal-burning power plant obscures the horizon in South Africa, *above*. Worldwide, coal is the most popular fossil fuel used to generate electricity. Coal is easy to burn and relatively cheap, and in many areas of the world, such as in Logan, W. Va., *right,* supplies are abundant and easy to reach.

functioned and backup safety measures also failed, molten fuel might burn through the reactor's containment wall, an occurrence called a *meltdown.* If molten fuel reached underground water supplies, it could create a massive steam explosion, sending radioactive gas and debris over a wide area.

Finally, building nuclear power plants is enormously expensive. The high cost as well as concerns about safety have prevented any new orders of nuclear plants in the United States since 1978.

A different form of nuclear power—fusion energy—holds promise as an alternative to fission energy. Nuclear fusion is the process that fuels the sun and other stars. Fusion reactors create extremely high temperatures—up to 300,000,000 °C (540,000,000 °F)—to *fuse* (combine) the nuclei of atoms. Physicists fuse *hydrogen isotopes* (forms of hydrogen that have different numbers of neutrons) called deuterium and tritium in fusion reactors. Fusing these elements produces helium, energy, and a neutron.

Fusion reactors are safer than fission reactors, because fusion produces far less radioactive waste than does fission, and fusion cannot produce an uncontrolled chain reaction. Wide-scale use of fusion reactors is many years away, however. Experimental fusion reactors produced short bursts of energy in the early and mid-1990's, but they consumed more power than they produced.

Despite the problems with our traditional sources of fuels, demand for electric power is ex-

A pine tree damaged by air pollutants resulting from burning fossil fuels withers in southern Germany. When burned, fossil fuels emit sulfur dioxide, nitrogen oxide, and other pollutants that can harm plants and animals, including human beings.

The pros and cons of traditional power sources

Coal	Oil	Natural gas	Nuclear power

Advantages

Coal	Oil	Natural gas	Nuclear power
■ Supplies are readily accessible in many areas of the world and easy to use. ■ Coal-fired power plants are less expensive than most large-scale power plants to build. ■ Coal can be treated to burn more cleanly. ■ Except for carbon dioxide, emissions can be controlled.	■ Oil is cheap to drill and transport and easy to burn. ■ Oil-fired power plants are relatively cheap to build. ■ Except for carbon dioxide, emissions can be controlled.	■ Natural gas burns more cleanly than coal or oil. ■ Gas can be mixed with coal to reduce coal-fired electric plants' emissions and raise their efficiency. ■ Gas-fired power plants can be more efficient than coal or oil plants.	■ Nuclear plants produce very little air pollution. ■ Nuclear energy reduces dependence on fossil fuels.

Disadvantages

Coal	Oil	Natural gas	Nuclear power
■ Coal-fired plants produce sulfur dioxide and nitrogen oxides, which can cause acid rain. ■ Burning coal releases carbon dioxide, which can contribute to to global warming. ■ Burning coal produces *particulates* (airborne particles, which can cause health problems when inhaled). ■ Burning coal releases toxic metals, such as mercury and arsenic, which can damage lakes. ■ Mining degrades land and nearby lakes and rivers.	■ Oil-fired plants produce sulfur dioxide and nitrogen oxides. ■ Burning oil releases carbon dioxide, toxic metals, and particulates, but not as much as coal. ■ Transporting oil in ships can cause harmful oil spills and leaks. ■ Supplies are limited.	■ Burning natural gas releases carbon dioxide. ■ Supplies are limited.	■ Nuclear plants produce radioactive wastes. ■ Plants are very expensive to build and take out of service. ■ Accidents pose risks to workers and people living in the path of airborne radioactive emissions.

A nuclear power plant delivers power to the city of New Orleans. Unlike fossil fuel plants, nuclear power plants emit almost no air pollution during operation. Nuclear plants are very expensive to build and take out of service, however. Accidents also pose the risk of dangerous radiation exposure for workers and those who live in the path of airborne emissions.

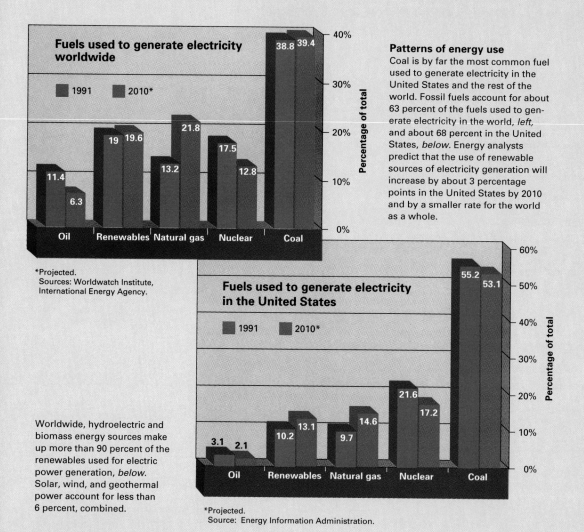

Fuels used to generate electricity worldwide

■ 1991　■ 2010*

Oil	Renewables	Natural gas	Nuclear	Coal
11.4 / 6.3	19 / 19.6	13.2 / 21.8	17.5 / 12.8	38.8 / 39.4

Percentage of total

*Projected.
Sources: Worldwatch Institute,
International Energy Agency.

Patterns of energy use

Coal is by far the most common fuel used to generate electricity in the United States and the rest of the world. Fossil fuels account for about 63 percent of the fuels used to generate electricity in the world, *left*, and about 68 percent in the United States, *below*. Energy analysts predict that the use of renewable sources of electricity generation will increase by about 3 percentage points in the United States by 2010 and by a smaller rate for the world as a whole.

Fuels used to generate electricity in the United States

■ 1991　■ 2010*

Oil	Renewables	Natural gas	Nuclear	Coal
3.1 / 2.1	10.2 / 13.1	9.7 / 14.6	21.6 / 17.2	55.2 / 53.1

Percentage of total

*Projected.
Source: Energy Information Administration.

Worldwide, hydroelectric and biomass energy sources make up more than 90 percent of the renewables used for electric power generation, *below*. Solar, wind, and geothermal power account for less than 6 percent, combined.

Renewable fuels used for electricity production worldwide*

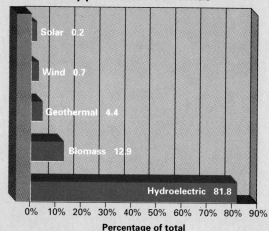

	Percentage
Solar	0.2
Wind	0.7
Geothermal	4.4
Biomass	12.9
Hydroelectric	81.8

0%　10%　20%　30%　40%　50%　60%　70%　80%　90%

Percentage of total

*1990.
Source: World Information Systems.

pected to grow. According to the Worldwatch Institute, an environmental research organization in Washington, D.C., world electricity production grew by about 125 percent between 1971 and 1991, a rate three times faster than human population growth during that time. As the world population increases in the coming century and poorer countries become richer, demand for electric power is likely to explode.

Renewable energy sources—hydropower, biomass, geothermal, solar, and wind—may fill the gap. These energy sources not only avoid most of the pollution that fossil fuel combustion creates, but also the risks presented by nuclear power. Although renewable energy sources have drawbacks of their own, engineers and policymakers have begun to view them as increasingly important ways to produce electricity.

Hydroelectric Power

Hydropower is perhaps the simplest of all forms of renewable energy to understand. Power is derived from the *kinetic* (moving) energy of falling water. As long as the sun's heat lifts water into the air through evaporation, rain and snow will cause riverbeds to fill with water. And as long as gravity pulls the water in rivers downstream, the water's kinetic energy can be harnessed to do work.

A water wheel is a very simple example of hydropower technology. For centuries, people constructed water wheels along rivers. The flowing water turned the wheel, providing the force needed to operate machinery. Textile mills in particular relied heavily on water wheels for power during the Industrial Revolution of the 1700's and early 1800's in Europe and the United States.

Today, hydropower is the most widely used source of renewable energy for electricity generation, employing hydroelectric plants in dams. To construct a plant, engineers dam a river, creating a reservoir of water that may be hundreds of meters deep. Water from the reservoir falls down pipelines or tunnels through the dam. Near the bottom, the rushing water drives a turbine. The turbine is connected to a generator, which produces electricity. The energy of 3.8 liters (1 gallon) of water per second falling 30 meters (100 feet) can generate about 1 kilowatt of electricity. (One kilowatt is the rate at which energy must be used to light ten 100-watt light bulbs or to power a typical hairdryer.)

Hydroelectric plants are built in different sizes, depending on how much water is available to operate the turbines and the distance the water falls. Some hydroelectric dams can supply power to a few thousand people. Others, such as the massive 6,000-megawatt Grand Coulee Dam on the Columbia River in Washington state, supply millions of people.

Advantages of hydroelectric power

Hydroelectric power offers several important advantages over fossil fuels. Although it can be expensive to construct a hydroelectric plant, actually producing electricity at an existing facility costs little. The "fuel" for the plant—water—is free. Electricity production from hydropower plants can thus be less than half as expensive as production at traditional fossil fuel plants, according to the United States Department of Energy (DOE) in Washington, D.C.

Hydroelectric plants also provide significant environmental benefits. Unlike fossil fuel power plants, hydroelectric plants emit no air pollution.

Today, hydroelectric plants account for about 18.4 percent of the world's electricity. Producing the same amount of electricity by burning fossil fuels would release about 2 billion metric tons (2.2 billion short tons) of carbon dioxide into Earth's atmosphere each year, according to World Information Systems, a consulting firm in Boston that specializes in environmental and energy research.

Hydroelectric dams also provide important benefits beyond electricity production. For example, a dam may help prevent flooding downstream, and it can supply water for recreation and human consumption.

Disadvantages of hydroelectric power

Hydroelectric power does have drawbacks, however. Huge hydroelectric dams flood hundreds or even thousands of square kilometers upstream, forcing the people living in the area to leave their homes. In China, for example, officials estimate that the nation's Three Gorges hydroelectric dam, which is scheduled to be completed around 2010, will submerge dozens of towns and cities and force the relocation of 1.3 million people.

A dam may also devastate wildlife. The flooding can destroy spawning areas for some fish species, and the dam itself may block other fish species trying to swim upstream to spawn. Land creatures may be harmed as well. A massive hydroelectric project under consideration in Canada, for example, would divert water from five rivers that flow into the James Bay area at the southern end of Hudson Bay. The dam is expected to flood 4,400 square kilometers (1,700 square miles) of wilderness area, currently home to black bears, polar bears, moose, and many kinds of ducks and migrating birds.

A hydroelectric dam can upset ecosystems in less obvious ways, for instance by blocking the flow of silt and nutrient-rich sediment down a river. This can lower the fertility of farmland downstream and reduce the productivity of ocean fisheries near the mouth of the river. Such a blockage has built up, for example, at the Aswan High Dam, constructed in the 1960's along the Nile River in Egypt.

The structural failure of a hydroelectric dam would be particularly catastrophic. Hydroelectric dams are designed to withstand the tremendous weight of water behind them, as well as shocks from earthquakes. But severe earthquakes may threaten some dams. Because of their high visibility, hydroelectric dams could also be appealing targets for terrorists. Terrorist acts could destroy a dam and produce devastating floods many miles downstream.

Worldwide use of hydroelectric power

Despite those drawbacks, some nations with an abundance of suitable rivers rely nearly exclusively on hydroelectric power for their electricity. According to World Information Services, Norway derives nearly all of its electricity from hydropower; Nepal gets 95 percent; Brazil, 94 percent; New Zealand, 78 percent; and Canada, 58 percent. Canada alone accounts for about 13 percent of the world's hydroelectric production.

The world's largest hydroelectric plant is the 12,600-*megawatt* (million watts) Itaipu Binacional plant on the Paraná River between Brazil and Paraguay. Completed in 1991, the plant cost $18 billion and supplies electricity to Paraguay and much of Brazil, including Rio de Janeiro and

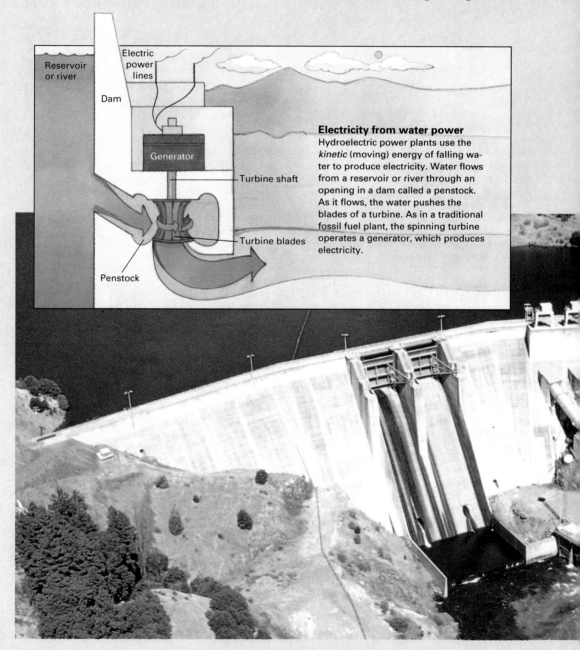

Electricity from water power
Hydroelectric power plants use the *kinetic* (moving) energy of falling water to produce electricity. Water flows from a reservoir or river through an opening in a dam called a penstock. As it flows, the water pushes the blades of a turbine. As in a traditional fossil fuel plant, the spinning turbine operates a generator, which produces electricity.

São Paulo, Brazil's two largest cities.

In the United States, hydroelectric plants provided 8.9 percent of the total electricity produced in 1992, according to the Energy Information Administration, a research branch of the DOE. That year, hydroelectric power accounted for about 76 percent of the electricity produced from renewable sources in the United States.

Hydroelectric plants deliver power in nearly all areas of the United States, but they are more common in mountainous areas with abundant rivers. That is because most dams are designed to be built between two high points. Idaho,

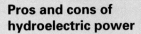

Pros and cons of hydroelectric power

Advantages

- Supplies of water for hydroelectric use are abundant.
- Dams produce virtually no pollution.
- Hydropower is the cheapest form of large-scale electricity production.

Disadvantages

- Building hydroelectric projects requires flooding large tracts of land, forcing people to relocate and endangering wildlife.
- Levels of rainfall and snowfall affect energy output.
- The pressure of water in large hydroelectric dams may cause earthquakes in susceptible areas.

Washington, Oregon, California, New York, Maine, and New Hampshire are the states with the most hydroelectric plants. In Canada, the province of Quebec derives much of its electricity from hydroelectric plants.

The best prospects for hydroelectric power plants are in the developing world and the nations of the former Soviet Union. Nations of the former Soviet Union have built power plants on only about 6 percent of the rivers that are technically and economically usable. Developing nations (those with limited industry and very low earnings per person), such as Vietnam, Madagascar, and Sudan, use as little as 3 percent. In North America, by comparison, about 55 percent of usable rivers have been tapped.

There are limits to the expansion of hydroelectric power in the developing world, however. Among the most significant problems are the high cost of building large hydroelectric plants and opposition from people living in the area who are concerned about the changes the dam will bring. Although construction costs for hydroelectric plants are, on average, only about 30 percent more than for advanced coal plants, many of the nations that could most benefit from hydroelectric plants are already heavily in debt, and any added expense would be a large burden.

Nevertheless, energy analysts agree the world could generate four times more energy using hydroelectric power than is currently produced. No one can say whether that will occur, but some obstacles could be overcome by building smaller plants that require less money and that affect the environment less drastically. Experts say that to encourage developing nations to build any type of plant, however, industrial nations will need to provide financial assistance. Only then will hydroelectric power become a leading contributor to the growth of the world's electric supply.

A hydroelectric dam on the Pit River in northeast California supplies power to about 30,000 homes.

Biomass Energy

Burning wood is probably humanity's oldest way of producing energy. Hundreds of millions of people around the world rely on wood as their primary source of energy. Combustion releases the biomass fuel's stored chemical energy in the form of heat. The same process occurs when fossil fuels are burned, the difference being the age of the once-living fuel.

Heat from burning wood can be used not only to warm a hearth or roast a marshmallow but also to power an electricity plant. Scientists call wood or any other plant matter burned for this purpose *biomass* fuel. In a biomass power plant, operators burn fuel in a boiler to produce steam. The steam drives a turbine, which turns a generator to produce electricity.

Engineers also fuel some older coal plants with a mixture of biomass and coal, a practice called *cofiring*. Cofiring helps reduce the power plants' emissions of sulfur dioxide, a major contributor to acid rain, because most biomass fuels contain much less sulfur than coal does.

Wood is the most common fuel for biomass electricity generation. About 88 percent of biomass fuels come from wood chips and residues from lumber mills, pulp and paper manufacturing plants, and other industrial wood users, according to the DOE.

Another common biomass fuel is municipal solid waste. At least 40 percent of such waste is paper and paper products, which are themselves derived from wood. More than 130 electric plants burn municipal solid waste as fuel in the United States and Canada.

Some by-products of agriculture, normally considered bothersome wastes, can also supply fuel for biomass power. Bagasse (*buh GAS*), the portion of sugar-cane plants that remains after the sugar-bearing juice has been extracted, is the most common. Bagasse combustion supplies large amounts of electricity in Hawaii and Louisiana, and it holds great potential in many developing countries that grow sugar cane. In Brazil, 150 sugar-cane distilleries signed an agreement in September 1993 with the state government of São Paulo to sell bagasse to three major state-run electric utilities. The deal will eventually increase the amount of electricity produced from burning bagasse in the state of São Paulo by 15 times.

Today, biomass energy provides about 1 percent of the total electric generating capacity in the United States, according to the DOE. About 1,050 wood-fired power plants operate in the United States, mostly in heavily forested regions, such as Vermont, Maine, New Hampshire, and states in the Pacific Northwest. Private firms such as paper plants that generate their own electricity use the majority of biomass power. Biomass is a much less common fuel for electric utilities, but the world's largest biomass electric plant is in Burlington, Vt. This 50-megawatt plant uses wood chips as fuel and provides electricity for about 50,000 people.

Benefits of biomass fuels

Biomass electricity generation provides several environmental benefits. Biomass combustion releases fewer nitrogen oxides—a group of compounds that contribute to acid rain—than do fossil fuels. Burning biomass fuels also produces less ash and fewer *particulates* (airborne particles

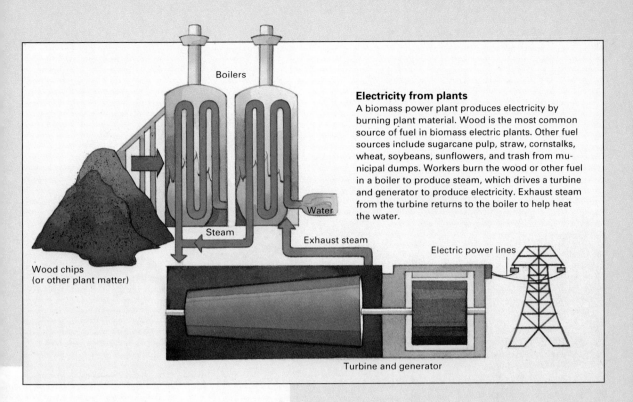

Electricity from plants
A biomass power plant produces electricity by burning plant material. Wood is the most common source of fuel in biomass electric plants. Other fuel sources include sugarcane pulp, straw, cornstalks, wheat, soybeans, sunflowers, and trash from municipal dumps. Workers burn the wood or other fuel in a boiler to produce steam, which drives a turbine and generator to produce electricity. Exhaust steam from the turbine returns to the boiler to help heat the water.

Boilers

Water

Steam

Exhaust steam

Electric power lines

Wood chips
(or other plant matter)

Turbine and generator

A biomass power plant supplies electricity to a factory in Woodland, Calif.

that can be harmful if inhaled) than does the combustion of coal.

Burning plant material does release carbon dioxide, a major greenhouse gas. But when replacement plants grow, they take in carbon dioxide for photosynthesis. Plants may release more carbon dioxide when they burn than they take in while growing, however.

Drawbacks of biomass fuels

Biomass has other disadvantages as a power source. Combustion causes some of the natural chemicals in plant matter, such as potassium and silicon, to condense on burner walls and boiler tubes. There, they cause troublesome deposits that interfere with the efficient transfer of heat from the burning fuel to the water.

Plantations of crops grown as biomass fuel can interfere with surrounding habitats. Pesticides and fertilizers can pollute streams and lakes, affecting a wide range of wildlife. If biomass crops are new to an area, they may also attract unfamiliar pests that could pose a threat to other plants.

In addition, most biomass facilities are not as efficient as fossil fuel plants. As a measure of energy efficiency, scientists determine the percentage of a fuel's heat that a power plant can harness for useful work, in this case electricity. Biomass fuels are currently about 25 percent efficient, compared with about 30 to 35 percent for coal and between 45 and 50 percent for natural gas. The lower efficiency of biomass is primarily due to its relatively high moisture content. Extra energy is required to evaporate the water during combustion.

High-efficiency systems

Advanced biomass systems now under development by the DOE offer efficiencies approaching 50 percent, twice as high as current technologies. One of the most promising of the new techniques is *gasification*, in which a biomass fuel is mixed with a limited amount of air or oxygen and heated to high temperatures. Chemical reactions transform the fuel into a mixture of carbon monoxide, hydrogen, and small amounts of methane, which is then burned in a gas turbine. This process yields higher efficiencies, because combustion of the gas produces force to turn the turbine directly, rather going through the intermediate step of producing steam first.

Growing energy crops

Many energy experts believe that growing biomass fuels as crops offers the best prospects for boosting worldwide biomass energy production. For example, 100 biomass energy farms of 260 hectares (640 acres) each could supply enough fuel to continuously run a 150-megawatt power plant, yielding enough power to serve about 150,000 people.

In the 1990's, several electric utilities in the United States began experimenting with projects to grow trees as energy crops to be used as biomass fuel. Suitable trees include fast-growing, clean-burning species such as poplar, willow,

maple, sycamore, and sweet gum, all of which can grow to a size suitable for harvesting in as little as five to seven years.

Using modern techniques, farmers could create highly productive biomass plantations on their unused or underused agricultural land. New methods for pest control, fertilization, and soil improvement have enabled agricultural researchers to grow hardwood trees taller, more quickly, and more closely together. According to Edwin White, dean of forestry research at the Syracuse University in New York, researchers can grow twice as many tons of hardwood trees per hectare in 1994 than could be grown in the early 1980's and 10 times more trees than grow naturally in forests.

On a biomass farm, a practice called coppicing would permit repeated tree harvesting without the expense of replanting. Coppicing entails cutting hardwood trees very low to the ground and allowing shoots to grow up from stumps. As the shoots mature, they too can be harvested to produce energy.

Other options for biomass crops are fast-growing grasses such as switchgrass. The plants regenerate quickly after cutting, and a single planting can supply many years of crops. In addition, farmers could use conventional farm equipment to harvest the grasses.

Experts say that short-term prospects for biomass energy in the United States look good. The DOE aims to double biomass electricity production by the year 2000 through the agency's National Biomass Power Program. The DOE created the program in 1992 with the goal of producing 12,000 megawatts.

Biomass energy may become even more prominent. In older coal plants, cofiring with wood is likely to assume a larger role through 2010, according to the National Renewable Energy Laboratory in Golden, Colo. The utility-funded Electric Power Research Institute in Palo Alto, Calif., predicts that biomass electric power capacity in the United States could reach 50,000 megawatts by 2010. And the DOE foresees a potential worldwide production of more than 600,000 megawatts from biomass by 2004, with heavy growth in Asia, Africa, and Latin America.

Pros and cons of electricity from biomass

Advantages

- Supplies of biomass fuels are abundant.
- Levels of sulfur dioxide and nitrogen oxide pollution are lower than fossil fuels produce.
- Biomass fuel sources such as poplar and willow trees can be grown on deforested land to help restore it.
- Biomass facilities can supply jobs in rural areas.
- Particulates caused by burning biomass can be drastically reduced by filtering emissions.

Disadvantages

- Supplies are not available everywhere.
- Growing fuel requires large amounts of land.

Geothermal Energy

Volcanic eruptions, which emit molten rock, and geysers, which shoot heated water and steam from underground, are two of the most visible examples of the power of geothermal energy. This power comes from the natural heat underground. The word *geothermal* means *Earth's heat.*

For thousands of years, people have used water from hot springs for heating. In the 200's and 100's B.C., Romans used it to heat water for bathhouses. Today, many people in Iceland, New Zealand, the Western United States, and elsewhere continue that practice, using water from hot springs to heat houses and other buildings.

People first used geothermal energy to produce electricity in the early 1900's. In that process, heat from the Earth turns water into steam. Then, as in most other electric power plants, the steam drives a turbine, which turns a generator to produce electricity.

Geothermal energy may be considered renewable because Earth contains vast stores of heat that are maintained by natural processes. Rock deep inside the Earth first became molten in the intense pressures and high temperatures during the formation of the planet some 4.5 billion years ago. Radioactive decay has provided the heat energy to keep much of Earth's inner layers in a molten state. In radioactive decay, atoms of elements such as uranium, radium, and thorium change into other elements and release energy through nuclear fission in the process.

Tapping into the Earth's heat stores

Hot springs and geysers are not found at many places on Earth's surface, so engineers must usually drill deep into the Earth to capture geothermal energy. Temperatures rise about 30 Celsius degrees (54 Fahrenheit degrees) for every kilometer below the surface. But deep drilling is technically difficult and expensive, so the drill holes usually do not extend lower than the top 4 kilometers (2.5 miles) of Earth's crust.

The most promising places to drill are areas where molten rock rises close to the Earth's surface. That typically occurs near the intersection of *tectonic plates* (gigantic plates that make up Earth's crust). Such regions include the western portions of much of North and South America, many areas in the western Pacific Ocean, and the eastern Mediterranean Sea.

Engineers tap geothermal heat in four ways. The most common involves drilling to find hot water at relatively shallow depths. Such sources, called hydrothermal reservoirs, may be only a few

hundred meters below the surface or as deep as 4,300 meters (14,000 feet). Even at the shallower depths, the pressure of rock above the water prevents it from boiling. If conditions are right, the liquid's temperature may be as high as 300 °C (600 °F), much hotter than its boiling point at Earth's surface. Most underground superheated water temperatures are between 150 and 300 °C (300 and 600 °F), however.

Such sources of superheated water are often so extensive that they can provide energy for thousands of years. If people remove water faster than it is replaced, a geothermal reservoir may gradually become depleted, however.

For the most common type of geothermal power plant, called a *hydrothermal plant*, operators pump the pressurized, superheated water from underground to a collection tank on the surface. The pressure is lower in the tank than underground, permitting the water to boil instantly into steam. Engineers then use the steam to produce electricity.

Other methods to recover geothermal energy were still under development in 1994. In one method, engineers drill into sandstone between 3,000 and 6,000 meters (10,000 and 20,000 feet) below the surface and extract hot *brine* (very salty water). The heat produced by this technique is called *geopressured energy.* Engineers can also drill into *magma* (molten rock) in areas where it is close to the surface. Heat obtained this way is called *magma energy.* Finally, a method called *deep heat mining* allows engineers to heat water by pumping it down into fractures created in hot, dry rocks and pumping it back out for use.

Benefits of geothermal power plants

The major environmental benefit of geothermal electric plants is the low level of carbon dioxide emissions that the facilities produce. According to the Geothermal Division of the DOE, a geothermal plant emits about 90 percent less carbon dioxide than a coal plant of the same size. And advanced geothermal plants currently under development produce almost no carbon dioxide emissions.

Geothermal plants also require less land to yield the same amount of power than any other kind of electric plant. That is because geothermal plants do not need to occupy very much land to gather energy, as wind farms and solar plants do. Nor do geothermal plants require mines to support them, as coal plants do. A typical geothermal plant requires nine times less land than a coal plant to produce the same amount of electricity, if the amount of land necessary for coal mining is taken into account, according to the World-watch Institute.

Finally, the potential of geothermal electricity production is vast. Estimates vary, but energy analysts agree that just a small percentage of U.S. geothermal resources could supply the entire nation's electricity needs for decades.

Environmental concerns

Geothermal plants do present some environmental concerns, however. Plants often can emit hydrogen sulfide, a compound that smells like rotten eggs and that is *toxic* (poisonous) at high concentrations. Hydrogen sulfide can also break down in the atmosphere to form sulfur dioxide, a major contributor to acid rain. Although engineers can avoid this problem by treating emissions with special chemical filters, the chemicals

Flash tank

Generator

Steam

Turbine

Hot water

Exhaust steam

Pressure nozzle

Condenser

Water reinjected

Pump

Rock

Superheated water

Tapping geothermal energy
Superheated water provides the energy to produce power in most geothermal electric plants. Engineers pump water from deep underground into a tank on the surface. Pressure applied during pumping and through a pressure nozzle keeps the water from boiling until it enters the tank. There, reduced pressure allows some of the water to *flash* (boil by reducing pressure) and produce steam, which is used to drive a turbine and generator. After steam leaves the turbine, operators inject it into a condenser, where it turns into water. A pump injects this water, along with water from the flash tank that did not boil, farther underground.

Pros and cons of geothermal electricity production

Advantages

- The supply of geothermal energy is vast.
- Geothermal plants produce very low carbon dioxide emissions.
- Geothermal plants usually require less maintenance than fossil fuel plants.

Disadvantages

- Geothermal resources are difficult to find and tap.
- Controls to limit emissions of hydrogen sulfide, which can lead to acid rain, are sometimes necessary.
- Geothermal plants are expensive to build.
- Water extracted by some geothermal plants may contain toxic chemicals—such as boron, arsenic, lead, and mercury—which must be disposed of.

that filter sulfur can themselves be hazardous and must be taken to approved disposal sites. Experts say this is not a major obstacle to geothermal energy production, however.

Water extracted from deep underground also may contain hazardous metals, such as arsenic, mercury, and lead. Operators can reinject this water into the ground, but they must be careful that the metals do not accidentally contaminate underground water supplies or lakes and rivers.

Geothermal plants around the world

In 1994, world electrical generating capacity from geothermal energy was about 6,000 megawatts, according to the Geothermal Resources Council, an organization in Davis, Calif., that studies and promotes geothermal energy. This was enough power to supply the needs of 6 million people at the rate used in the developed world.

About half of the world's geothermal electric generating capacity is in the United States. The world's largest geothermal electric plant is in the Mayacamas Mountains about 100 kilometers (60 miles) north of San Francisco. In 1990, this facility, called the Geysers, had a capacity of 2,000 megawatts, about 75 percent of the U.S. geothermal electric capacity and about 22 percent of the world capacity.

The next largest amount of electricity generated from geothermal sources was in the Philippines. About 15 percent of the islands' electricity in 1990 was derived from geothermal energy, and that rate may increase to 30 percent by 2000, according to the United Nations. Mexico, Italy, Indonesia, and New Zealand also produce large amounts of electricity from geothermal sources.

Although the total electrical generating capacity from geothermal sources in 1991 was far less than 1 percent of the world's electrical generating capacity, prospects for geothermal energy are good in areas where underground heat reservoirs are abundant. Most of the new production is likely to be in developing nations.

Prospects in the United States may depend largely on the price of fossil fuels. The price of natural gas, a major competitive fuel source for electricity production, is a particularly important factor. Energy analysts agree, however, that as newer technologies lower the cost of producing geothermal power, it could become a much more significant source of electricity.

A hydrothermal geothermal electric plant in California's Imperial Valley harnesses heat from underground sources of superheated water to produce electricity.

Solar Energy

The sun is our greatest source of energy. In 20 days, more energy reaches the Earth from the sun than is contained in the planet's entire coal, oil, and natural gas reserves. The United States receives more energy from the sun in 40 minutes than is provided by burning a year's worth of fossil fuels.

Primitive people used energy from the sun in the simplest way possible: by warming themselves in rays of sunlight. Later, ancient builders oriented dwellings to best capture the sun's heat. Today, solar power plants harness the power of the sun to produce electricity.

A major benefit of solar power is that it produces no carbon dioxide, sulfur dioxide, nitrogen oxides, or radioactive wastes. Solar power plants also make no noise. And, like other renewables, solar energy is free and plentiful.

Solar plants do have some drawbacks, however. They require a great deal of land, and some solar electric plants are as much as 5½ times more expensive to build than fossil fuel plants. Once the plants are built, solar energy is between 2 and 7 times more expensive to produce than the average cost of power, depending on the type of solar plant, according to data provided by the Electric Power Research Institute. However, even at this cost, solar energy can be cheaper than extending existing power lines in remote areas.

Engineers have two very different methods for producing electricity from sunlight. One technique uses devices called solar concentrators that focus sunlight. The sunlight heats water to produce steam, which turns a traditional turbine and generator to create electricity. The other method of producing electricity takes advantage of photovoltaic cells, devices that when exposed to sunlight produce a useful electric current.

Solar concentrators

To build a solar concentrator plant, engineers first choose a suitable site. The plant must be located where there are many days of the year with bright sunshine and few clouds—such places as southern California or Arizona. Even in those areas, however, normal sunlight is too weak and diffuse to produce enough heat to be efficiently converted to electricity. To collect the most possible sunlight, concentrator devices are typically motorized so that they can follow the sun. When the weather is cloudy, natural gas or propane is often needed as a backup fuel to produce electricity. Some plants in remote areas may also store excess energy in batteries for use during cloudy weather.

There are three basic kinds of solar concentrators—parabolic trough systems, parabolic dish systems, and central receivers. (A parabola is a type of curve.) Parabolic trough systems use rows of semicircular or U-shaped reflective enclosures to focus sunlight onto a metal or glass tube filled with oil or another heat-absorbing fluid. The focused sunlight heats the fluid to between 200 and 400 °C (390 and 750 °F). Pumps transport the heated fluid to a central area, where the fluid heats water to produce steam.

Trough solar concentrators capable of producing about 354 megawatts were installed in southern California from 1984 through 1991—the largest amount of this kind of solar electricity generation in the world. That is enough electric power for a community of 355,000 people. The facility accounts for 95 percent of the world's electricity from solar concentrators.

Trough systems are considered the most well-established concentrator technology and the most versatile. But parabolic dish systems and central receiver systems can produce higher temperatures. They thus hold more promise for generating large amounts of electricity.

Parabolic dish collectors are bowl-shaped devices lined with mirrors or reflective film that measure between 7 and 15 meters (23 and 49 feet) in diameter. The mirrors focus sunlight onto a fluid-filled receiver in the front of the dish. Oil or liquid sodium serves as the heat-absorbing fluid, which circulates through the receiver. The collector can heat fluid up to 800 °C (1500 °F).

Central receiver systems use an array of *heliostats* (large, flat reflective surfaces) to focus sunlight onto a fluid-filled receiver at the top of a central tower. The typical central receiver system heats water that passes through the receiver in glass or metal tubes. Other types of central receiver systems use air or molten salt to collect and transport heat. In systems that use water, it boils, producing steam at about 510 °C (950 °F).

The world's largest central receiver is in southern California near Daggett. The California Energy Commission, along with the DOE and several California electric utilities, sponsored the construction of the 10-megawatt demonstration plant in the early 1980's and operated it until 1988. Called Solar One, the plant consisted of 1,800 heliostats that heated water piped through the central receiver at the top of the tower. In 1989, operators began reengineering Solar One to test molten salt as the fluid that collects and transports heat. The new plant—Solar Two—is scheduled to begin producing electricity by early 1996.

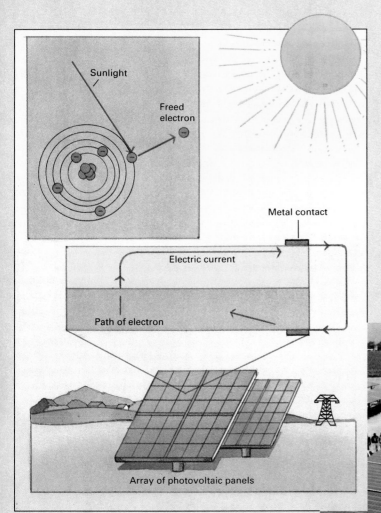

Sunlight

Freed electron

Metal contact

Electric current

Path of electron

Array of photovoltaic panels

From sunlight to electricity

A photovoltaic solar cell can directly harness sunlight to create electricity. Cells are usually constructed in panels that are arranged in groups called arrays, *below.* Cells, *left,* are most often made up of two thin slices of the semiconductor material silicon that are treated with different chemicals to create an electric field between them. The energy in sunlight knocks electrons free from atoms in the bottom semiconductor. The electric field forces the freed electrons into the top semiconductor. That flow of electrons can be harnessed as a useful electric current. A metal contact conducts the freed electrons from the top semiconductor into transmission lines to provide useful power. Electrons return to the bottom semiconductor to fill spaces created by other freed electrons.

The efficiency of the various types of solar concentrator power plants ranges from 12 to 25 percent. Those figures correspond to the rate at which the devices convert the sunlight that strikes the collectors into generated electricity. Parabolic dishes have the highest efficiency at 20 to 25 percent, followed by central receivers at around 15 to 18 percent and parabolic troughs from 12 to 15 percent, according to the DOE's Office of Solar Energy Conversion.

Photovoltaic electricity production

Unlike solar concentrators, photovoltaic (PV) cells produce electricity directly from sunlight. This ability results from the *photovoltaic effect,* whereby the energy in sunlight causes *electrons* (negatively charged subatomic particles) to flow through layers of a conductive material to produce a useful electric current.

The French physicist Edmond Becquerel dis-

covered the photovoltaic effect in 1839, but it remained just a curiosity until U.S. scientists at Bell Laboratories developed a PV cell capable of producing a useful amount of electricity in 1954. The U.S. National Aeronautics and Space Administration began using PV cells in 1958 to power electrical components on satellites.

Conventional PV cells are made with two thin slices of extremely purified silicon, the semiconductor material used to make computer chips.

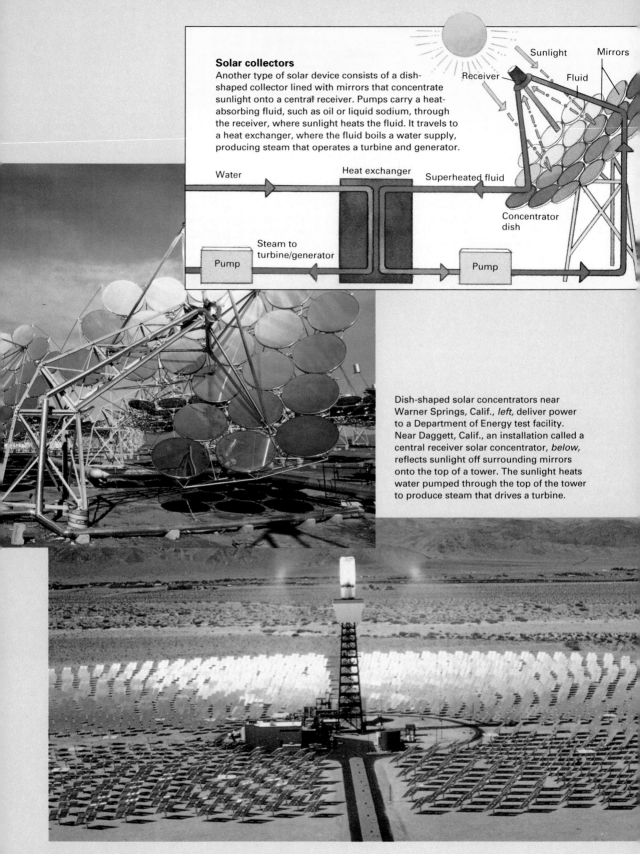

Solar collectors

Another type of solar device consists of a dish-shaped collector lined with mirrors that concentrate sunlight onto a central receiver. Pumps carry a heat-absorbing fluid, such as oil or liquid sodium, through the receiver, where sunlight heats the fluid. It travels to a heat exchanger, where the fluid boils a water supply, producing steam that operates a turbine and generator.

Sunlight

Mirrors

Receiver

Fluid

Water

Heat exchanger

Superheated fluid

Concentrator dish

Steam to turbine/generator

Pump

Pump

Dish-shaped solar concentrators near Warner Springs, Calif., *left,* deliver power to a Department of Energy test facility. Near Daggett, Calif., an installation called a central receiver solar concentrator, *below,* reflects sunlight off surrounding mirrors onto the top of a tower. The sunlight heats water pumped through the top of the tower to produce steam that drives a turbine.

Impurities are added to the layers as they form so that an electric field exists where the two layers meet. When a ray of sunlight strikes the PV cell, the sunlight dislodges electrons from the silicon atoms. The electric field separates freed electrons from one layer and forces them into the other layer, where they are collected by a metal contact at one end of the PV cell. The movement of these electrons through a closed circuit constitutes an electrical current that can perform work.

The major appeal of using photovoltaic cells to generate electricity is the technique's simplicity. There is no intermediate step in which heat is transformed into mechanical energy, as there is when a solar-heated gas must spin a turbine. This approach is not only simpler, but also theoretically capable of much higher efficiency, because every time one form of energy is converted to another, some efficiency is lost. Despite important improvements, most PV technology is still less efficient than solar concentrators, however.

The main drawback of PV cells is the high cost of manufacturing them. The three most common types of PV cells are crystalline silicon cells, polycrystalline silicon cells, and amorphous silicon cells. Each type requires a different manufacturing method.

Crystalline silicon is the most widely used PV cell, accounting for about 48 percent of those sold in the United States in 1993, according to the DOE. Crystalline silicon PV cells are so named because every atom in the cell is part of a single crystal structure. According to the DOE's Office of Solar Energy Conversion, these cells are expensive to make, but they convert about 14 percent of the sunlight that strikes them into electricity—a high rate of efficiency for today's PV cells.

Technicians make crystalline silicon PV cells by dipping a silicon crystal into a molten silicon solution. The molten silicon collects and cools around the crystal, eventually forming a larger, cylindrical piece of silicon that can be sliced into wafers to make PV cells.

Polycrystalline silicon PV cells are easier and cheaper to make, but they are about 2 percent less efficient than crystalline silicon. To make polycrystalline cells, technicians pour molten silicon into a mold. As the solution cools, it forms a block of silicon that can be cut up into blocks and sliced into wafers. Polycrystalline cells are so

Pros and cons of solar electricity

Advantages

- Supplies of solar energy are free.
- Using solar devices produces almost no pollution.
- Solar panels are nearly maintenance-free.
- Solar panels can be mass produced.
- Solar panels can supply limited power to remote areas without the need to build large, expensive power plants.

Disadvantages

- Solar electricity is very expensive.
- Some solar plants do not work well in cloudy climates.
- Solar panels require a large area of land.

named because many crystals form in the silicon as it cools.

Amorphous silicon cells are the cheapest to make, but they have the lowest efficiency— typically about 5 percent. Technicians produce these cells by depositing hydrogen and silicon from a *plasma* (hot gas) onto a base made of stainless steel, ceramic, or glass. As the plasma cools, a layer of solid silicon forms on the base. No crystals form in the silicon during this process, so the wafers have no internal crystalline structure. Amorphous silicon cells can be as much as 200 times thinner than single crystal slices—a fact that reduces costs for materials.

Prospects for amorphous silicon cells improved in January 1994, when the United Solar Systems Corporation of Troy, Mich., announced that it had set an efficiency record for amorphous silicon cells: 10.2 percent. Engineers reportedly achieved this efficiency by stacking three layers of silicon, each with the ability to convert a different part of the spectrum of sunlight to electricity. (The spectrum is all the rainbowlike colors of visible light.) In this way, more of the sun's energy performs work than in conventional PV cells, which are sensitive to just one part of the spectrum.

Today, PV cells are used for electricity generation mostly in remote areas, where extending electric power lines would be too difficult or too costly. The cells are used to operate such devices as remote weather stations, irrigation pumps, and ocean navigation aids.

Prospects for solar energy

Electric utilities throughout the United States began to see benefits in solar energy in the early 1990's, as prices for PV panels fell and as new federal laws increased penalties on heavy air polluters. In September 1992, 67 U.S. electric utilities formed a consortium that agreed to buy enough PV cells to produce 50 megawatts.

In 1994, the DOE continued to push the development of PV and solar concentrator technologies through its Solar 2000 program. This program aims to add 1,000 additional megawatts of PV capacity in the United States and 500 more megawatts around the world by the year 2000. If the program is successful, solar power may become more of an everyday reality.

Wind Power

People have been using the power of the wind for thousands of years. One of the first uses of wind power was for propelling boats. The earliest known depiction of a wind-driven craft is a 5,000-year-old drawing, found in Egypt, of a sailboat on the Nile River.

Eventually, enterprising workers realized that they could harness wind power on land, too. They built windmills by mounting sails on vertical masts that turned a large round stone. As early as 200 B.C., such windmills were used to grind grain in the area that is now Iran.

Beginning in the mid-1800's, farmers and other landowners throughout the Midwestern and Western United States built millions of small windmills to pump water. Later, windmills also provided electricity. Many thousands of these windmills are still in use.

Today's windmills for producing electricity are often called *wind turbines*. In a wind turbine, the wind turns a *rotor* (one or two rotating blades) that converts the force of the wind into the rotation of a horizontal or vertical shaft. The process is the reverse of the way a fan motor turns a shaft to spin a fan blade, which pushes air. In the windmill, the shaft's rotation spins a generator to produce an electric current. Wind power plants then distribute the electricity through transmission lines for use in homes and businesses.

The benefits of wind power

Like other renewables, wind energy is free and inexhaustible. In addition, wind power provides environmental benefits. Because no fuel is burned, a process that leads to air pollution, regions that rely on wind power to replace some of their fossil fuel electric plants can reduce their pollution levels.

In California, for example, more than 15,000 wind turbines meet about 5 percent of the state's residential electricity needs. If fossil fuel plants had provided that energy in 1992, an additional 1.2 billion kilograms (2.7 billion pounds) of carbon dioxide and 7.3 billion kilograms (16 billion pounds) of sulfur dioxide and nitrogen oxides would have been added to the air.

Wind power's disadvantages

But giant wind turbines can undesirably affect the local environment, most obviously by their high visibility. Wind turbines must be located where they can capture the maximum velocity and amount of wind. Such areas are often on mountain passes or across plains. With *hubs* (the center of a turbine's rotor) often at least 30 meters (100 feet) above the ground and each blade 15 meters (50 feet) long, wind turbines are visible from far away, and some people consider installations of hundreds of them an intrusive presence.

Noise can be another problem. The sound created by the whirling blades can be heard up to about 400 meters (1,300 feet) from the turbines. However, energy engineers say the noise is not likely to be significantly louder than the noise of the wind itself and is much quieter, for example, than the sound of traffic on highways near wind power plants.

Large, older wind turbines with metal blades can also reflect television signals and interfere with reception. This problem usually does not occur more than 400 meters away from a turbine, however, and newer rotors, which are typically

Wind power is one of humanity's oldest sources of energy. Windmills in Rhodes, Greece, *below*, were built in the late 1500's.

Wind turbines near Altamont Pass in California deliver electricity to nearly 1 million people.

Electricity from the wind

Windmills for electric power generation use the power of wind to turn turbine blades. The turbine blades spin a shaft that operates a generator, producing electricity. Sets of gears in the gearbox allow operators to change the speed of the turbine blades under varying wind conditions to provide a relatively constant power output to the generator.

Gearbox

Turbine rotor blades

Generator

Transmission wire

Tower

To electric power lines

made of fiberglass or wood, do not cause any television interference.

Another problem for the local area is that some wind turbines can kill birds. A 1992 report by the California Energy Commission estimated that wind turbines in California's Altamont Pass had killed 500 birds, including 78 golden eagles, in two years. Engineers are working to solve this problem, which has not been detected at other wind farms.

The problem of inconsistent winds

Engineers must also contend with the inconsistency of wind as an energy source. Winds vary enormously, not just from place to place but even at the same place, and so the wind may not be blowing when energy is needed. Solar energy and hydroelectric power also depend on the consistency of their "fuel"—sunlight and water from rain and snow. If an inconsistent source of power reduces the amount of energy available during critical periods, utilities must turn on backup generators, usually fueled by natural gas.

Unless better methods for storing wind energy for use during calm periods are developed, engineers say, wind turbines will not be suitable as a utility's primary source of power. In addition, engineers have found it difficult to design wind turbine generators and other mechanical systems to derive the most energy possible from changing wind conditions.

Overcoming technical problems

High equipment costs and mechanical unreliability slowed the growth of wind power in the 1980's. Engineers of early wind turbines underestimated the force that wind would produce. The rotors of early large wind turbines often broke in high winds or strong gusts, destroying generators, gearboxes, and other critical parts.

Engineers overcame many of these obstacles during the 1980's and early 1990's, however, as they developed less expensive materials and manufacturing methods and developed a better understanding of wind force. Engineers also redesigned rotors to extract more energy from the wind, arranged turbines more carefully in order to capture more wind, and strengthened rotors, gears, and other critical components to withstand the stress of wind turbulence.

Improved design and materials changes sharply lowered the cost of producing electricity from wind power. In the 1970's, the cost was nearly 50 cents per kilowatt-hour. By mid-1994, the figure had dropped to between 7 and 9 cents per kilowatt-hour, competitive with nearly all other sources except the cheapest fossil fuels.

As with all energy sources, wind power is not perfected. Engineers in 1994 were working on lighter rotor blades that would cost less to build. Other scientists were studying ways to allow rotor blades to rock back and forth like a seesaw to adjust to changes in the angle of wind striking the blades. As technology advances, the cost of electricity from wind power is projected to drop to 5 cents in 1995 and to 4 cents by 2000.

Prospects for wind power

In the early 1990's, wind power generated about 0.8 percent of the electricity needed by residences in the United States, according to the American Wind Energy Association, a promotional organization in Washington, D.C. Energy analysts believe that wind power plants could generate as much as 20 percent of electricity needs in the United States. Most of the wind power plants would be located in the windswept Great Plains, with North Dakota holding the greatest potential, according to studies released by the American Wind Energy Association.

As a step toward increasing this resource, the U.S. Department of Energy and the Electric Power Research Institute announced in August 1993 a $40-million project designed to test advanced wind turbines. Utilities will operate wind turbines from different manufacturers at windy sites in Texas and Vermont in an effort to demonstrate the technology's viability.

Wind power will also continue as an important alternative to fossil fuels in Europe, particularly in Denmark, Sweden, the United Kingdom, and the Netherlands. By the year 2000, energy analysts predict, about 62 percent of the world's wind power installations will be in Europe.

Wind power is spreading beyond Europe and the United States as well. Argentina and the Ukraine plan to have 500 megawatts of wind power in operation by the year 2000, and Mexico, Costa Rica, China, New Zealand, and Australia are also developing wind power projects.

Experts believe that wind power is an important part of any effort to expand the use of renewable energy. As wind power becomes more accepted, many believe that its share of energy production will grow more by the year 2000 than any other form of renewable energy.

Legislation may help accomplish this growth. The U.S. Energy Policy Act of 1992, which sets the nation's energy goals through 2010, grants electric utilities a 1.5-cent-per-kilowatt-hour tax credit for electricity produced from wind turbines installed from 1994 through 1999. Partly as a result of that act, the U.S. Wind Energy Association expects the electric generating capacity from wind power to triple in the United States by the year 2000. Such an increase would be a major step toward establishing the technology's widespread acceptance.

Pros and cons of electricity from wind power

Advantages

- Supplies of wind energy are free.
- Using wind power devices produces almost no pollution.
- The cost of electricity production can be as low as fossil fuels.
- Windmills can supply power to remote areas where large power plants would be too expensive.

Disadvantages

- Areas with little wind are not suitable for wind power generation.
- Harvesting wind energy requires more land than fossil fuel plants.
- Windmills can be noisy.
- Windmills can kill birds.

Energy Economics

Most of the obstacles to renewable energy concern the higher cost of renewables compared with fossil fuels. Although the price of most types of renewable energy fell during the 1980's and early 1990's, most of the technologies are still more expensive than conventional sources.

According to data from the Electric Power Research Institute, a coal-fired plant costs about $1,500 for each kilowatt of generating capacity, a price that includes design and construction. That compares with about $1,800 for a geothermal plant and $2,250 for a biomass power plant. For a PV cell plant, the extra expense is much more daunting—about $8,500 per kilowatt.

These differences mean that adding large amounts of renewable energy generating capacity today would require millions, or even billions, of extra dollars. Adding 1,000 megawatts of biomass generation could cost as much as $750 million more than adding the same amount of coal-fired capacity. Photovoltaic cells would cost an extra $7 billion.

The added expense of renewable energy is especially significant when fossil fuels are cheap, because there is little incentive to search for new energy sources. The price of oil usually drags the prices of other fuels up or down with it, and at about $20 a barrel in early 1994, oil had remained remarkably cheap for about eight years, with the exception of a brief period in 1991. The price of natural gas—the most serious competitor to many renewable fuel sources—remained at levels in 1993 only slightly above those in 1980 for industrial and commercial customers, according to the American Gas Association.

Lowering the costs of renewables

Through research, scientists and engineers can lower the costs of developing sites for renewable energy plants and of designing and manufacturing equipment. A striking example is wind power. Research into better equipment design allowed the cost of electricity from wind turbines to drop from about 50 cents per kilowatt-hour in the mid-1970's to about 7 cents in 1994—nearly equal to the cost of fossil fuels.

Yet equipment manufacturers and utilities often do not have the money or experience to conduct extended research on renewable energy technologies, industry analysts say. According to the DOE's Office of Utility Technologies, at least 50 percent of renewable energy research projects depend on government funding.

Not surprisingly, fluctuating government spending can hamper renewable energy development. In the United States, such spending has indeed varied widely. Spurred by oil embargoes and price hikes in the 1970's, the Administration of President Jimmy Carter increased spending on renewable energy research from virtually zero in 1973 to $718 million in 1980. Spending fell to $110 million by 1990, as the Administrations of Presidents Ronald Reagan and George Bush chose to focus on increasing domestic fossil fuel production. The figure rose again by 1994, when the U.S. Congress approved a budget of $287 million for renewable energy research.

Laws granting financial incentives to private companies and utilities have also helped promote renewable energy production. For example, the U.S. Energy Policy Act of 1992 permanently extended tax credits for businesses involved in solar and geothermal energy production and included a 1.5-cent-per-kilowatt-hour tax credit for wind and biomass electric plants built between 1994 and 1999.

Energy sources for developing nations

The need to find alternative energy sources is an even more pressing problem in the developing world, where some 4.3 billion people—about 77 percent of Earth's population—live. Increased energy efficiency is expected to decrease electricity use per person in the United States and other developed nations by 2025, but energy use is predicted to more than double in developing nations as they expand their economies and populations, according to John P. Holdren, physicist and energy analyst at the University of California at Berkeley. This growth in energy use calls not only for more renewable energy use but more efficient production from conventional systems.

How much renewables will contribute to the energy needs of developing nations is uncertain, however, because developing nations can rarely afford the extra costs of building renewable facilities. A large fossil fuel plant can cost $1 billion or more, but a renewable energy facility can be substantially more expensive. The high cost of operating fossil fuel plants compared to most renewable plants brings the lifetime cost of fossil fuel and renewable electricity plants closer, however.

The cheapest alternative for developing countries is to use energy more efficiently, avoiding the need to build too many expensive new plants of any type. Most developing nations waste fossil fuels through inefficiencies. In the developed nations, energy use rose just one-fifth as much as

Average cost of building electricity plants

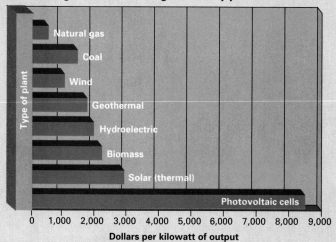

Type of plant

- Natural gas
- Coal
- Wind
- Geothermal
- Hydroelectric
- Biomass
- Solar (thermal)
- Photovoltaic cells

0 1,000 2,000 3,000 4,000 5,000 6,000 7,000 8,000 9,000

Dollars per kilowatt of output

Sources: Figures derived from data from the Electric Power
Research Institute and the U.S. Department of Energy.

The costs of renewable energy
The biggest obstacle to the wide-scale use of renewable sources is the high cost of constructing generating plants, *left*. Wind plants can be less expensive to build than coal-fired generating stations, but other types of renewable plants can cost significantly more. Once a plant begins operating, however, some forms of renewable energy, such as hydroelectric, wind, geothermal, and biomass, can rival traditional fuels in the cost of producing electricity, *below*. Environmentalists point out that neither of these comparisons takes into account the costs of health problems and environmental damage caused by burning fossil fuels.

Average cost to produce electricity

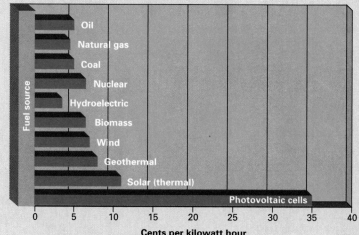

Fuel source

- Oil
- Natural gas
- Coal
- Nuclear
- Hydroelectric
- Biomass
- Wind
- Geothermal
- Solar (thermal)
- Photovoltaic cells

0 5 10 15 20 25 30 35 40

Cents per kilowatt hour

Sources: Figures derived from data from the Electric Power
Research Institute and the Energy Information Administration.

A significant shift is likely to occur in the pattern of the world's energy use by 2010, *below*. If present trends continue, developing regions of the world, such as Asia, Africa, and Latin America, will by 2010 expand their energy use to nearly half of the world total, because these regions hold the vast majority of Earth's population. The developing nations' choice of fuels will dramatically affect the environment. But their limited financial resources may prevent their switching to wide-scale renewable sources of energy.

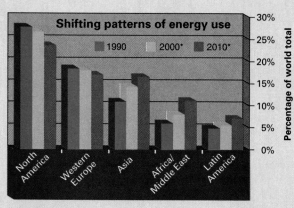

Shifting patterns of energy use

■ 1990   □ 2000*   ■ 2010*

Percentage of world total

30%
25%
20%
15%
10%
5%
0%

North America   Western Europe   Asia   Africa/ Middle East   Latin America

*Projected.
Source: Organization for Economic
Cooperation and Development.

economic growth between 1973 and 1989. But in developing countries, energy use grew 20 percent faster than economic growth in the same period, according to the Worldwatch Institute. The developing world requires 40 percent more electricity than industrial nations to produce the same quantity of materials, such as steel, glass, and fertilizer.

According to energy analysts at the Lawrence Berkeley Laboratory in Berkeley, Calif., developing nations could avoid spending $1.75 trillion in new power plants, oil refineries, and other energy-related construction by the year 2025 if the nations spent $350 billion in efficiency improvements. The savings would come from the use of more efficient manufacturing equipment, commercial heating and cooling equipment, and consumer products.

Nearly all energy analysts agree that the degree to which developing nations adopt renewable energy depends on how much money the industrial nations offer to support technological assistance and research. According to a 1989 estimate by the World Bank, an international lending agency affiliated with the United Nations, developing countries will require about $1 trillion to meet their desired demand for traditional electricity generation through the year 2000. The World Bank estimated that cost is about five times more than developing countries can supply. Building renewable energy plants would likely put the cost even farther out of reach.

Calculating the true costs of energy use

These issues seem to cloud the future of renewables as a solution to our energy troubles. Yet the true costs of producing electricity with fossil fuels continue to rise. Economists do not always calculate the costs of health problems and environmental damage caused by fossil fuels when considering the expense of various energy sources.

But many experts believe that these costs could amount to billions of dollars, making traditional electricity production more expensive than using renewables. Such costs include those associated with respiratory problems and other illnesses caused by breathing suspended particulates in polluted air; agricultural damage from acid rain and toxic metals; oil spills in oceans, lakes, and rivers; and possible damage to croplands and coastlines from global warming. As more people consider these costs of using fossil fuels, a cleaner environment and better health may seem worth the expense of renewable energy—for the developed as well as the developing world.

Experts say there is still a long way to go before renewables become commonplace, however. Setting aside hydroelectric power, the renewable energy sources account for a mere 0.3 percent of the world's electricity production. Most energy analysts agree that the potential for renewables is much greater, however, with some predicting that by 2050, renewables could fuel as much as 60 percent of the world's electricity production. But researchers, electric utilities, and policymakers must overcome many obstacles to reach such a lofty goal.

Study Guide and Reading List

Study questions:

1. What are the advantages and disadvantages of producing electricity with fossil fuels?
2. What are the main advantages of the various renewable energy sources? What are the drawbacks?
3. How does geography determine whether certain renewable energy sources can be effectively used?
4. Which renewable energy sources appear to be the most feasible for widespread use by utilities in the near future? Why?
5. How does electricity production with each type of renewable energy resemble electricity production in a fossil fuel plant? How does it differ?
6. Discuss how a country's population and level of affluence influence the types and amount of energy it uses.

For further reading:

Brower, Michael. *Cool Energy: Renewable Solutions to Environmental Problems.* MIT Press, 1992.

Brown, Lester; Kane, Hal; and Ayres, Ed. *Vital Signs: The Trends That Are Shaping Our Future.* Norton, 1993.

Carliss, Jennifer. *Renewable Energy.* Walker, 1993.

Dower, Roger, and Kozloff, Keith. *A New Power Base: Renewable Energy Policies for the Nineties and Beyond.* World Resources Institute, 1993.

Golob, Richard, and Brus, Eric. *The Almanac of Renewable Energy.* Holt, 1993.

Lenssen, Nicholas. *Empowering Development: The New Energy Equation.* Worldwatch Paper No. 111. The Worldwatch Institute, 1992.

Rosenberg, Paul. *The Alternative Energy Handbook.* Fairmont, 1993.

Scientific American: Energy for Planet Earth. Special issue, September 1990.

Science Year contributors report on the year's major developments in their respective fields. The articles in this section are arranged alphabetically.

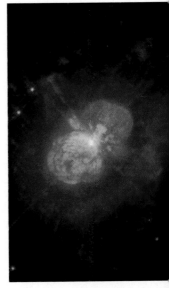

Agriculture

The United States Food and Drug Administration (FDA) approved the first genetically engineered product for use in commercial livestock on Nov. 5, 1993. The product is an artificially produced version of a natural growth hormone, called bovine somatotropin (BST), that increases milk production in dairy cows.

Milk-producing hormone. Agricultural scientists have known since the 1930's that BST in cows enhances milk production. But it was not until the 1980's, after the techniques of genetic engineering were developed, that BST could be manufactured in large enough quantities and at a low enough cost to launch research into its commercial use. To make BST, scientists insert into bacteria the cow gene that controls production of the hormone. The fast-growing bacteria produce large quantities of BST.

Injecting a cow with the genetically engineered BST causes the animal's milk production to increase by 10 to 20 percent or more. According to industry studies, the milk from BST-treated cows looks the same, tastes the same, and has the same nutritional value as milk from untreated cows. Because treated cows produce more milk without requiring an equivalent amount of extra food, dairy farmers who use BST can produce milk more efficiently than before.

Some experts and consumer groups voiced strong opposition to the FDA move, however. One concern was that the milk of treated cows would contain BST and that ingesting the hormone could harm human health, particularly the health of children. Another concern was that by increasing milk production, BST would lead to health problems in cows, and that those problems would ultimately affect the health of people.

Advocates of FDA approval pointed out that BST had undergone extensive study in the decades since it was first detected. They said that recent research had demonstrated that the milk from treated cows is safe for adults and infants. According to the National Agricultural Biotechnology Council, trace amounts of BST occur naturally in all types of cow's milk, and there is no detectable difference between the BST found in milk from treated cows and

Preventing erosion
Before-and-after tests of soil treated with an inexpensive powder called polyacrylamide show the powder's ability to prevent irrigation water from carrying topsoil and fertilizers off fields and into irrigation furrows. In research conducted by the U.S. Agricultural Research Service in 1994, untreated water picks up soil as it washes into a test cone at the end of a sloping furrow, *right*. But adding just 10 parts per million of polyacrylamide to the water almost eliminates the sediment in the runoff, *far right*. Studies of the powder's long-term effects on soil were planned.

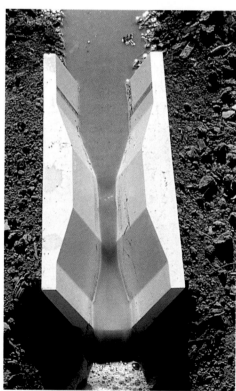

Sheep carry satellite-positioning equipment that monitors their location while they graze in England's Lake District. In August 1993, British scientists outfitted the sheep to help locate "hot spots" of radioactive contamination that makes some sheep unsalable due to contaminated meat. The radiation problem was caused by the 1986 explosion at the Chernobyl nuclear power plant near Kiev, Ukraine. The explosion produced radioactive dust and gases that were dispersed by the wind, and some of the material fell onto the sheep-grazing region in rain.

the natural BST in the milk of untreated cows. In addition, the council reported, pasteurization destroys 85 to 90 percent of the BST in milk. Whatever amount remains is harmlessly broken down in the human digestive tract.

According to the head of the council, the controversy among the U.S. public stems in part from the lack of understanding of the need for increased milk production. In the United States, the supply of milk is plentiful and relatively inexpensive. In regions of the world that lack those supplies, however, people might be more convinced of BST's benefits. After evaluating the evidence, several U.S. health groups endorsed the use of BST.

Flavr Savr approved. In another controversial move, the FDA on May 18, 1994, approved the first genetically altered food, a tomato called Flavr Savr. The tomato was altered to stay firm longer while ripening on the plant. According to the developer, Calgene Inc. of Davis, Calif., the tomato has better flavor and stays fresh longer than most other commercially grown tomatoes.

Pea gene helps potatoes. After years of work, researchers finally transferred a gene from pea plants to potato plants, giving the potatoes improved resistance to a common and widespread fungal disease. Plant pathologists at Washington State University in Pullman announced their success in June 1993.

The disease, called verticillium wilt, is found in most temperate regions of the world. In addition to destroying potato crops, the fungus harms many other crop plants by clogging the *xylem vessels,* channels that carry water from the roots to the leaves. The plant then turns yellow and dies prematurely. Because potato plants are infected when potato tubers are developing underground, the wilt stops the growth of the tubers.

Scientists have long known that plants of one species can resist most of the microbes that cause disease in other species. To make potatoes resistant to verticillium wilt, plant pathologist Lee Hadwiger and his team first examined 200 genes of pea plants to discover which ones were most centrally involved in helping the plants resist verticillium wilt. This process alone took years to accomplish, but the scientists identified several such genes. They selected one to transfer into two varieties of potato, the Shepody and the Russet Burbank. It took another two years to transfer the characteristics to a potato plant that could reproduce plants resistant to the disease.

In test fields, the potatoes with the pea gene lived two weeks longer after fungal infection than did the plants without the gene. Even though the test plants died, the two extra weeks allowed the potato tubers to develop more fully. In some cases, the yield of altered plants was double that of unaltered ones.

Cloning disease resistance. For the first time, researchers isolated a gene in a crop plant using techniques developed in the Human Genome Project, an effort to map all the human genes. Scientists at Purdue University in West Lafayette, Ind., and Cornell University in Ithaca, N.Y., announced in November 1993 that they had used a technique called map-based cloning to isolate a particular gene in a tomato plant variety. Then, they successfully transferred

the gene, which gives the plant resistance to a disease called bacteria speck, into another tomato plant variety.

The scientists used sophisticated techniques to *clone* (produce identical copies of) a series of small, overlapping segments of the disease-resistant tomato's DNA (deoxyribonucleic acid, the molecule of which genes are made). Then, the researchers transferred the individual segments into tomato plants susceptible to the disease. Some plants then showed resistance to the disease, which demonstrated that the plants had received the resistance gene.

According to the Purdue researcher, agronomist Gregory Martin, map-based cloning is an important technique because it enables researchers to copy specific genes in crop plants for the first time. Being able to copy genes expands the gene pool available to plant breeders. Martin speculated that the breakthrough will bring improved varieties of crops to producers in about five years. [Steve Cain and Victor L. Lechtenberg]

See also BIOLOGY; GENETICS. In WORLD BOOK, see AGRICULTURE.

Anthropology

The first human beings to migrate from Africa into Asia may have done so nearly 1 million years earlier than scientists had thought, according to a report in February 1994. The report was based on a reevaluation of the age of fossils belonging to *Homo erectus,* widely regarded as the most recent ancestor of modern and early modern human beings. The report cast into doubt a long-accepted theory that *H. erectus* arose in Africa about 1.8 million years ago and began migrating to Asia and southern Europe between 1.4 million and 1 million years ago. (Most experts think that *H. erectus* gave rise to *Homo sapiens,* the species to which modern human beings belong, beginning about 500,000 years ago.)

Fossils redated. The *H. erectus* fossils that were the subject of the reevaluation were found at two sites in Java, Indonesia, beginning in the 1930's. Previously, scientists had considered the remains from one site, Mojokerto, to be about 1 million years old and those from the other site, Sangiran, to be 700,000 to 900,000 years old. They based these estimates on a rough analysis of extinct ani-

mal fossils found in the same layer of sediment as the *H. erectus* remains.

The new analysis dated the Mojokerto fossils at 1.8 million years and the Sangiran specimens at 1.6 million years. Researchers led by Carl Swisher III and Garniss Curtis, specialists in geological dating at the Institute of Human Origins in Berkeley, Calif., arrived at the dates by calculating the age of volcanic rock fragments from the *H. erectus* fossil beds at Mojokerto and Sangiran.

The researchers used a dating technique that takes advantage of the fact that after molten lava hardens into rock, any naturally occurring argon in the rock changes at a slow but measurable rate into a radioactive form. By measuring the ratio of stable to radioactive argon in the volcanic fragments, the researchers determined when the rocks had hardened. The researchers presumed that this date closely matched the date when the fragments and the *H. erectus* fossils become incorporated in the same beds.

The new dates make the Javan fossils about the same age as the oldest African

A researcher holds a model of a partial *Homo erectus* skull, one of three sets of *H. erectus* fossils whose reanalysis was reported in February 1994. The fossils had been found at two sites in Java, Indonesia. The new analysis dates the oldest of the fossils to about 1.8 million years, about the age of the oldest *H. erectus* fossils found in Africa. The re-dating suggests that *H. erectus* migrated from Africa to Asia far earlier than scientists had thought.

H. erectus fossils, which are about 1.8 million years old. If the dates are correct, *H. erectus* must have spread eastward from Africa almost immediately after the species evolved. This fact, the researchers noted, could explain why the specialized stone tools associated with *H. erectus* sites in Africa have never been found in Asia. These artifacts, which include double-edged cutting tools known as hand axes, appear to have been invented in Africa between 1.7 million and 1.4 million years ago. They would therefore not have been among the objects that African emigrants carried with them 1.8 million years ago.

The new research also increases the probability that two populations of *H. erectus*, one in Africa and one in Asia, evolved into separate species of *H. sapiens*. Most anthropologists have believed that only African *H. erectus* was ancestral to *H. sapiens*.

However, scientists cautioned against rushing to revise the story of human evolution. They pointed out that the fossils and volcanic fragments were found in sediments from ancient river-

beds that could have formed long after the rocks themselves hardened. As a result, it is possible that the dated volcanic fragments are older than the *H. erectus* fossils. Swisher and Curtis said they planned to analyze many additional fragments from the sites to determine whether they yield similar dates.

Lucy's family. Scientists have discovered two new groups of fossils belonging to *Australopithecus afarensis,* the earliest known hominid species, according to reports in 1993 and 1994. (Hominids include human beings and their close prehuman ancestors.) The new fossils show that *A. afarensis* remained remarkably unchanged from about 3.9 million years ago, the date of its first known appearance, to its latest known existence 3 million years ago.

The finds also help resolve the question of whether fossils attributed to *A. afarensis* indeed represent a single species, as some scientists have argued, or two separate species, as others have claimed. This question arose soon after the discovery of the first *A. afarensis* fossils, including the partially complete female skeleton dubbed Lucy, which were unearthed at Hadar, Ethiopia, in 1974.

In November 1993, anthropologist Tim White of the University of California at Berkeley reported the first of the new discoveries, which were found at the site of Maka, Ethiopia. The Maka fossils date to 3.4 million years ago and include a nearly complete lower jaw and portions of two arm bones. The second set of fossils, reported in March 1994, were found at Hadar and include the first nearly complete *A. afarensis* skull. Expedition leaders William Kimbel and Donald Johanson of the Institute of Human Origins and Yoel Rak of Tel Aviv University in Israel said the new Hadar fossils are between 3.4 million and 3 million years of age.

A. afarensis was first defined in 1978, based on fossils from Hadar and from Laetoli, a site in northern Tanzania. The Laetoli bones were closely associated with humanlike fossil footprints. Together, the Hadar and Laetoli finds indicated that *A. afarensis* walked and ran on two feet, like human beings, but remained apelike in certain features, including its relatively long arms and large *canine teeth* (pointed teeth next to the incisors). However, the Hadar and Laetoli fossils varied greatly in size. Some scholars argued that the size differences among the fossils were too great for them to represent a single species.

White and Johanson, who were two of the scientists who originally defined *A. afarensis,* and their colleagues argued that the size difference among the fossils meant that *A. afarensis* was highly *sexually dimorphic*—that is, the males were on average much larger than the females. The new finds support this conclusion. As a group, they show as great a difference between the smallest and largest fossils as did the earlier specimens, but they include a wider range of sizes between the two extremes. Together, the *A. afarensis* specimens indicate that members of this species were on average no more sexually dimorphic than were other early hominids.

The new Hadar skull also closely resembles a reconstructed *A. afarensis* skull made by White and Johanson in the 1970's from fragments belonging to

A skull of a male *Australopithecus afarensis* is the first nearly complete skull of this early human ancestor to be discovered, researchers reported in March 1994. The skull, which is at least 3 million years old, was found at Hadar, Ethiopia, where the partially complete *A. afarensis* skeleton nicknamed Lucy had been unearthed in the 1970's. The skull was one of several finds in 1993 and 1994 that help prove that *A. afarensis* indeed represents a single species.

several individuals. The new skull thus counters arguments that White and Johanson unintentionally mixed skull bones from two species when they made the earlier reconstruction.

Human evolution in China. A 200,000-year-old *H. sapiens* skull from northeastern China bears some features that resemble those of living people in China, firing a debate over the evolutionary path of modern human beings. In March 1994, researchers led by Chen Tiemei of Beijing University in Beijing described the skull, which was found in the 1980's at the site of Jinniushan.

According to the researchers, the skull exhibits several features common to living people in China, including a broad nose bridge and prominent cheekbones. These features differentiate the skull from specimens of the same age found in Africa and Europe, suggesting that physically modern human beings in China evolved separately from *H. sapiens* elsewhere.

If Chen and his colleagues are correct, the Jinniushan skull at least partly disproves the "Out-of-Africa" theory of modern human evolution. According to this theory, physically modern human beings evolved from their *H. sapiens* ancestors in Africa about 100,000 years ago. From there, they spread to Europe and Asia between 60,000 and 40,000 years ago, replacing other groups of human beings, including Neanderthals in Europe and the descendants of *H. erectus* in Asia.

However, some scholars argued that the Jinniushan specimen does not prove that physically modern human beings evolved separately in China. These experts pointed out that the skull displays large brow ridges, a receding forehead, and other characteristics of earlier human beings. They also noted that overall, the skull differs from skulls of living human beings to about the degree that Neanderthal skulls do. The Jinniushan skull may thus represent a nonmodern population that was eventually replaced by immigrant Africans just as the Neanderthals were.   [Richard G. Klein]

See also ARCHAEOLOGY. In WORLD BOOK, see ANTHROPOLOGY; PREHISTORIC PEOPLE.

Archaeology

A 300-year-long drought may have helped bring about the collapse of the world's first great empire, the Akkadian civilization, which arose in ancient Mesopotamia (located in present-day Iraq, Syria, and southern Turkey) more than 4,000 years ago. Archaeologist Harvey Weiss of Yale University in New Haven, Conn., reported this discovery in August 1993.

First empire's decline. The Akkadian empire arose about 2300 B.C. near what is now Baghdad, Iraq. The empire soon stretched across Mesopotamia, as the armies of Sargon, the founder of the Akkadian dynasty, and his successors conquered the cities that lay along the Tigris and Euphrates rivers. Within a century, however, the empire collapsed.

Previously, excavations in the northern part of the empire showed that the residents of these areas abandoned their homes beginning about 2200 B.C. At the same time, Akkadian texts reveal, tens of thousands of refugees flooded into cities in the south. The influx of refugees strained the water and food supplies and led to internal warfare that toppled Sargon's dynasty. Scholars have cited overpopulation, local rebellions, or similar factors as the possible cause of these events, but they have found little evidence for any specific explanation.

In the new research, Weiss' colleague Marie-Agnès Courty, a soil scientist at the National Center for Scientific Research in Paris, carried out a detailed study of soil samples from three Akkadian sites in Syria. Using a technique called micromorphology, Courty analyzed soil samples under a microscope to determine the composition and structure of ancient sediment layers. Courty found that soil layers dating to the period from 2200 to 1900 B.C. showed signs that the region's climate had been very dry. These signs include a low number of holes formed by earthworms, which thrive under moist conditions, and a large amount of windblown dust.

Weiss and Courty speculated that a sudden drought struck Mesopotamia about 2200 B.C. The drought devastated the wheat-, barley-, and sheep-raising economy of the north, where agriculture and livestock-raising depended on rainfall. Agriculture in the south, which

Archaeology Continued

Uncovering a vanished city

Explorations on Mexico's Gulf Coast revealed a previously unexamined center of ancient civilization, an American archaeologist announced in February 1994. The city, named El Pital after a nearby village, flourished sometime between A.D. 100 and 600, the archaeologist said. A survey of the 104-square-kilometer (40-square-mile) site revealed the remains of more than 150 earth-and-stone pyramids, *right,* which farmers long believed to be natural hills.

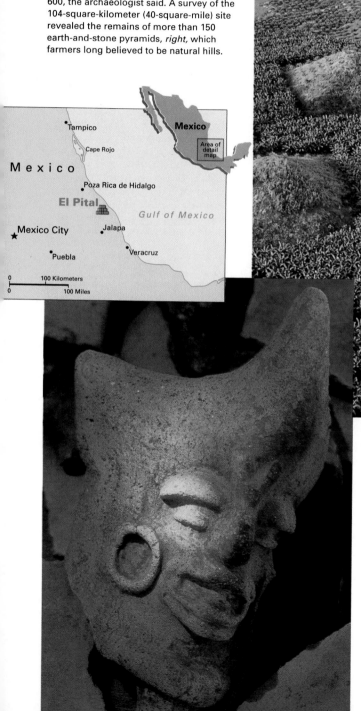

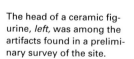

The head of a ceramic figurine, *left,* was among the artifacts found in a preliminary survey of the site.

relied on irrigation, was less affected by the drought, and so cities in that region became magnets for the impoverished northern migrants.

The archaeologists were unsure what caused the 300-year drought. Deposits of volcanic ash in the soil layers indicate that a major volcanic eruption struck the area shortly before 2200 B.C. Ash and dust clouds from volcanic eruptions can remain in the atmosphere for years, blocking sunlight and altering weather patterns. But scientists are divided as to whether such an eruption could have led to a dry spell lasting 300 years. Another possibility, the researchers suggested, is that a large-scale warming of ocean currents disrupted rainfall patterns and led to prolonged drought in the region.

El Pital. The remains of a vast 1,500-year-old city, possibly of a previously unexplored culture, were found in what is now Mexico, archaeologists announced in February 1994. Archaeologist Jeffrey K. Wilkerson of the Institute for Cultural Ecology of the Tropics in Tampa, Fla., began work at the site, located in a river delta along the Gulf of Mexico, northwest of the modern city of Veracruz.

Wilkerson said a preliminary survey of the site, named El Pital after a nearby village, had revealed the ruins of more than 150 earth-and-stone pyramids and other structures, some of them up to 40 meters (130 feet) tall. People now living in the region had long believed that the structures were natural hills, the archaeologist said. The site is at least 104 square kilometers (40 square miles) in size, and the city may have supported a population of more than 20,000.

Archaeologists said El Pital probably flourished between A.D. 100 and 600 and may have served as a major port, controlling trade along the Gulf coast. The stylistic features of ceramic artifacts found at the site suggest that the city may have been influenced by Teotihuacán, a powerful urban center in central Mexico.

El Pital may have played a role in exporting goods produced by the Teotihuacán culture. But its chief exports may have been local crops of beans, squash, cacao, and cotton. Wilkerson's

A fragment of a stone monument found in northern Israel bears the first known mention outside the Bible of the House of David, the Israelite dynasty founded by the Biblical King David about 1000 B.C. An Israeli archaeologist announced the discovery in August 1993. The monument was written in Aramaic—an ancient language related to Hebrew—and dates to the mid-800's B.C., after the Israelites split into the kingdoms of Israel and Judah. Scholars believe the text of the fragment commemorates a victory by Aram (present-day Syria) over Israel and over troops of the House of David, which ruled Judah.

survey suggests that farmers raised these crops in the marshy lowlands near the city, where they created fields by raising islands out of alternating layers of mud and marsh plants.

Archaeologists do not know why this ancient port city declined, though one possibility is that flooding and other natural disasters linked to the weather pattern called El Niño led the population to abandon the site. Wilkerson said the excavations and studies designed to answer the many questions about El Pital would take at least 30 years to complete.

Lost mission found in Texas. The site of a Spanish colonial mission, lost since soon after the mission's destruction in 1758, was discovered near the modern town of Menard, Tex. Archaeologist Grant Hall of Texas Tech University in Lubbock announced the discovery in January 1994.

Spanish settlers established the mission, known as Santa Cruz de San Saba, in 1757 in an effort to convert local Apache Indians to Christianity. About 10 months later, however, warriors from the Wichita and Comanche tribes raided the mission and destroyed it.

Archaeologists had looked for the mission before Hall's attempt. But finding the site was difficult because the mission existed for such a short period of time. The occupants had built few large structures whose remains would now be detectable in archaeological surveys.

Hall's team took a different approach. The team first narrowed their search area by exhaustively reexamining colonial Spanish documents relating to the mission. They then used remote sensing techniques, such as infrared photography, to detect traces of the buried ruins. (In infrared photography for archaeology, special film detects solar radiation reflected by vegetation and soils. The patterns of radiation reveal the shape of subsurface features.) Finally, the team used metal detectors to turn up bits of rusted Spanish colonial artifacts.

After the archaeologists found what appeared to be the site, excavations confirmed that it was indeed the location of the San Saba mission. Among the artifacts unearthed were iron nails and hinges, fragments of pottery made in a Spanish colonial style, a copper medallion with an eroded image of a saint, and numerous musket balls, including

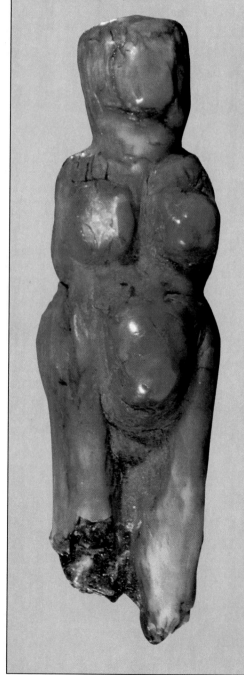

An Ice Age figurine of a pregnant female is one of seven such figures that had been missing since soon after their discovery in Italy in the 1880's, archaeologists revealed in January 1994. A sculptor who purchased the figurines in a Montreal, Canada, antique shop brought them to the attention of archaeologists in 1993. The ivory figures, which are 18,000 to 25,000 years old, are among some 200 so-called Venus figurines that have been uncovered across Europe. The figures may have played a role in prehistoric religious practices.

A fragment of cloth unearthed in southeastern Turkey is the oldest fabric ever found, American and Turkish archaeologists announced in July 1993. The fragment dates to about 7000 B.C., making it at least 500 years older than any other known cloth. The fabric, which is probably linen, was wrapped around a tool handle made from an antler.

some that had been flattened, presumably in the 1758 raid. The excavators also found large chunks of hardened mud. Spanish documents indicate that residents of such missions strengthened the wooden walls of the mission buildings by packing them with mud.

Ancient Indians in the Arctic. A nearly 12,000-year-old site provides new insights into early cultures in Beringia, the region of Alaska that lies east of the Bering Strait, according to a February 1994 report. Most archaeologists believe that prehistoric people first settled the Americas more than 12,000 years ago by crossing the Bering Strait, which was then a land bridge between North America and Asia.

In the February report, archaeologists Michael Kunz of the U.S. Bureau of Land Management and Richard Reanier of the University of Washington in Seattle discussed the results of their excavations at the Mesa site, a ridgetop overlook in the foothills of northern Alaska's Brooks Range. Artifacts from the site included nine hearths, a number of stone tools, and several distinctive spear-

points, as well as numerous flakes produced as waste when spearpoints were made. Using a technique that enabled the scientists to date tiny bits of charcoal, Kunz and Reanier discovered that eight of the hearths were about 10,000 years old and one was up to 11,700 years old. The commanding view from the site, along with the large number of waste flakes found, suggests that prehistoric hunters used the ridge as a temporary campsite where they repaired broken spears and watched the movements of animal herds below.

The Mesa site offers clues to the origin of ancient Indian cultures of southern Canada and the United States, including the so-called Clovis culture of the southwestern United Sates, which existed about 11,200 years ago. Many archaeologists believe the Clovis people were the earliest inhabitants of North America. However, the relation between the Clovis culture and its supposed ancestors has been the subject of debate. Besides Mesa, three ancient Indian sites in Beringia are at least 11,000 years old, but scholars are divided over their pre-

New Light on the Maya

In spring 1993, archaeologists working at the ruined city of Aguateca, deep in the rain forest of northern Guatemala, uncovered a scene of violent destruction. Inside the remains of a burned palace about 1,250 years old, they found a wealth of artifacts—jewelry of shell and stone, elegant vases and plates, and human bones—that lay smashed in heaps. In one room, excavators found a broken war trophy: part of a human skull decorated with a carved text celebrating the victories of an ancient king of Aguateca.

Far to the north, at the Mexican site of Yaxuna, archaeologists in summer 1993 exposed a jewel of gleaming jade in a 1,600-year-old tomb. The jewel adorned a 15-year-old girl, a princess who had been ritually murdered with a blow to the head. Along with the princess were 10 other sacrificial victims, all wearing royal jewels.

In spring 1994, excavators worked cautiously in a two-chambered tomb deep below an ancient temple at Copán, Honduras. The entire tomb had been coated with cinnabar, a powdery red pigment. Cinnabar contains the poisonous chemical mercury, so excavating the tomb was hazardous and slow. But the excavators worked eagerly because the carved text on the threshold of the tomb contained the name of an important king.

In 1993 and 1994, archaeologists at these three sites—and many others—were unearthing the legacy of the Maya, a Native American people who created one of the great civilizations of the ancient world. The new archaeological findings, combined with breakthroughs in the understanding of ancient Mayan inscriptions, had begun to yield new insights into the rise and fall of the warlike Maya kingdoms.

Archaeologists have long known that the ancient Maya lived in what are now southern Mexico and Central America. The first Maya kingdoms arose about 1000 B.C. in the lowlands of the Yucatán Peninsula, centering in northern Guatemala. During the peak of Maya culture from about A.D. 250 to 900, a time known as the Classic Period, Maya kingdoms covered more than 310,000 square kilometers (120,000 square miles), extending from southeastern Mexico to parts of Honduras and El Salvador. The Maya civilization began to decline toward the end of the Classic Period, though Maya rulers continued to control certain areas until the arrival of Europeans on their shores in the 1500's. Today, at least 4 million Maya still live throughout the lands their ancestors began to settle about 3,000 years ago.

The Maya writing system consisted of pictorial symbols known as *glyphs*. During the Classic Period, Maya scribes produced lengthy texts that were often carved in relief on stone monuments. But after the 1500's, the Maya lost the knowledge of how to read their language. As a result, the inscriptions lay unread for centuries.

Epigraphers (specialists in ancient writing systems) began deciphering the Mayan glyphs in the 1820's. The first glyphs that yielded to their efforts were those representing numerals and mathematical symbols. With this knowledge, scholars were able to interpret the complicated calendars and astronomical tables that the Maya produced with their sophisticated mathematical system.

Scholars finally began to decipher the other glyphs in the late 1950's. Until that time, epigraphers were hindered by a belief that Mayan inscriptions were written in a secret code concerned with astronomical observations and religious thought. This hindrance disappeared when scholars realized that the glyphs were transcriptions of the language the Maya still speak. Scholars also realized that Maya writing included two kinds of glyphs: picture symbols that represented whole words, and phonetic signs that stood for consonant-vowel combinations, such as *pa* and *ka*.

By 1994, scholars had deciphered about two-thirds of the estimated 800 Mayan glyphs. Their work has enabled them to read the Classic Period inscriptions recording the deeds of powerful leaders, as well as stories of ancestral gods and heroes. The glyphs also provide researchers with clues to a central mystery about the Maya: what caused the decline of the Classic Period dynasties. In the late A.D. 700's, kingdoms in a broad swath of territory at the base of the Yucatán Peninsula suddenly began to collapse. Within a century, the Maya had all but abandoned their heartland in northern Guatemala and neighboring lowland regions.

Nikolai Grube of the University of Bonn and independent scholar Simon Martin, two experts in deciphering Mayan glyphs, have helped shed light on this dark time. The scholars' analysis in the 1990's of texts carved at major Maya capitals revealed that protracted wars of conquest raged for centuries across the Maya lands, eventually unleashing destructive social chaos.

Grube, Martin, and many other experts met in March 1994 to pool their insights into Maya warfare. The general picture that emerged was that the Maya civilization was dominated by two grand alliances headed by large cities, Tikal in northern Guatemala and Calakmul in Mexico.

In mid-1994, several archaeological expeditions were seeking evidence of how those rival cities vied for power through war and diplomacy. Archaeologist Arthur Demarest of Vanderbilt University in Nashville, for example, was continuing

Unearthing the world of the ancient Maya

A wealth of discoveries in the 1990's have deepened archaeologists' understanding of the Maya civilization, which was at its peak from A.D. 250 to 900. In August 1993, for example, archaeologists announced the discovery of four new Maya sites in the Maya Mountains of Belize, *right,* in a region that scholars had thought too rugged to sustain large settlements.

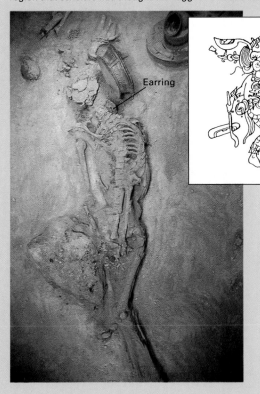

Earring

Earring

The skeleton of a king dating to the A.D. 300's, *far left,* was found in 1993 at Yaxuna, in Mexico's Yucatán Peninsula. The king wears shell earrings that resemble those worn by Chac, a god of rain and war, in Maya art, *left.* The Maya sometimes depicted kings sacrificing victims while wearing the earrings and other ornaments associated with Chac. Such finds suggest that the Maya were more warlike than scholars had once believed.

his explorations into the rapid rise and fall of an ambitious royal family with capitals at Aguateca and Dos Pilas. At Dos Pilas, archaeologists had unearthed inscriptions showing that the city fought on Calakmul's side in the alliance wars. Texts found at the site boast of victories over nearby kingdoms and even over Tikal itself.

In 1993, Demarest reported unearthing grim evidence of the collapse of the Dos Pilas kingdom. According to inscriptions, two conquered cities rebelled against Dos Pilas in about 760. Excavations show that as the conflict neared its climax, desperate defenders of the capital stripped temples and palaces of their stones to throw up crude defensive walls against encircling enemies. Toward the end, farmers had to build stone walls to defend even their crops against lawless marauders. Eventually, the common folk left the area altogether. By that time, the royal family had retreated to Aguateca. The war ended when the rebels captured the king of Dos Pilas.

Work at the Yaxuna site in Mexico has revealed that the Maya living there also fought fierce wars during the Classic Period. In 1993, Charles Suhler, a graduate student in archaeology at Southern Methodist University in Dallas, discovered two tombs in pyramids at Yaxuna, both dating to the A.D. 300's. One tomb contained the remains of a single king laid out in majestic attire. The king was wearing the shell earrings of a Maya god named Chac, who is depicted as an ax-wielding executioner in sacrificial scenes painted on Maya pots. The other tomb contained the remains of the mass sacrifice that included the young princess with the jade jewel. The princess was one of 10 men, women, and children killed to accompany a beheaded king. Clearly, the penalty for defeat in war was sometimes death for Maya royalty.

The quest for wealth and power led Maya governments to foster commerce as well as war. To learn more about that aspect of Maya life, archaeologist Peter Dunham of Cleveland State University in Ohio was in 1994 exploring the Maya Mountains of Belize in search of mines and quarries, where the Maya dug minerals and precious stones for use in tools and ornaments. The Maya traded such items among themselves and other groups. In 1993, Dunham had discovered the ruins of four Maya centers in these rugged mountains, testimony to the importance of the resources there.

War and peace, prosperity and devastation marked the lives of the ancient Maya as they do those of all civilizations. But the new findings about the Maya have also begun to reveal insights about the character of these powerful and determined people, from farmers, artists, and scribes to warriors and kings. [David A. Freidel]

The discovery in western China of a 3,000-year-old mummy with European features suggests that contact between China and the West began far earlier than scholars had thought, an American researcher announced in spring 1994. The mummy, preserved by the dry temperatures of China's Xinjiang region, was one of more than 100 specimens unearthed by Chinese archaeologists since 1978 but not reported outside China until the 1990's.

Archaeology Continued

cise ages and their relationship to the more southern cultures. Because the Mesa spearpoints exhibit features that resemble those of spearpoints from Clovis and other ancient Indian cultures, the Mesa finds strengthen the argument that the mid-American cultures developed from cultures in Beringia.

Early domestication of pigs. Pigs may have been raised for food about 10,000 years ago, some 1,000 years earlier than sheep and goats, once thought to be the first domesticated food animals. Archaeologists working at the site of Hallan Cemi, in southeastern Turkey, reported this finding in May 1994.

Analysis of the many pig bones found at the site revealed that the pigs had smaller molars than wild boars, a sign of domestication. Also, a large proportion of the bones were of young males, suggesting that most males were slaughtered for food while females were kept for breeding.

The finding opens new perspectives on the Neolithic, the period in which hunting and gathering gave way to settled ways of life based on agriculture. The people of Hallan Cemi appear to have domesticated pigs before they began cultivating grains. Among other Neolithic populations in the Middle East and western Asia, the transition to agriculture was based on grain cultivation.

Caucasian mummies in China. The discovery in western China of more than 100 mummified corpses with European features, some of them 4,000 years old, suggests that contact between China and the West began far earlier than had been thought, an American researcher reported in April 1994. Chinese archaeologists had begun unearthing the mummies in 1978 but did not report the finds outside China. Victor Mair, a professor of Chinese language and literature at the University of Pennsylvania in Philadelphia, noticed some of the mummies in a Chinese museum in 1987. He began studying them in collaboration with Chinese scientists in 1993.

According to Mair, the mummies, which Chinese archaeologists date to between 2000 and 300 B.C., were found in four main sites in the Xinjiang region of northwestern China. The dry climate of this largely desert region naturally preserved the bodies after they were buried.

With blond or light brown hair, long

Excavations in Egypt's eastern desert uncovered a mining town dating to the A.D. 400's and 500's, when Egypt was part of the Byzantine Empire based in present-day Turkey. Archaeologists who announced the find in June 1993 said the size of the site, called Bir Umm Fawakhir, indicates that Byzantine Egypt was more prosperous than scholars had believed.

noses and skulls, and deep-set eyes, the mummies show features characteristic of Europeans. The mummies were clothed in garments of leather and wool, and some wore tall, peaked hats of felt. Studies of the garments suggest that the wool was spun from the coarse outer hair of sheep or goats, then dyed blue, green, and brown and woven into plaid designs. Scholars believe that such techniques are of European origin.

Some of the burials also yielded evidence of the use of horses. Archaeologists found the remains of metal and wooden bits, leather whips and reins, a leather saddle, and a wooden wagon wheel. Most scholars believe that people began using horses for riding and drawing vehicles in Europe about 4000 B.C.

To Mair and other archaeologists and linguists, the discovery of the mummies and the horse-related artifacts offers support for a theory that the spread of mobile, horse-riding peoples from Europe helped account for the spread of the Indo-European family of languages. These languages are spoken in Europe, western Asia, and India.

The archaeology of language. A January 1994 article offered an archaeological perspective on the spread of the world's languages and language families. Linguists have identified numerous families of related languages, including the Indo-European language family, that arose in part as populations moved apart and their common language changed in different ways.

Traditionally, linguists have relied on comparisons of vocabulary, grammar, and similar features to explore the relations between languages. These experts did not concern themselves with the mechanisms by which languages spread. For their part, archaeologists played little role in the discussion of language formation, because most early cultures left behind no traces of the language they spoke.

In the January article, archaeologist Colin Renfrew of Cambridge University in England argued that by studying cultural changes, archaeologists can shed light on how languages developed and spread. Renfrew suggested three main ways in which cultures could have ex-

When the fragment is viewed in visible light, *above,* no writing can be deciphered.

An electronic camera sensitive to infrared light reveals the phrase "He wrote the words of . . . ." Much of the next word is obscured by a flap of parchment.

A second technique separates the flap and the text beneath it according to the degree to which they reflect infrared light. A computer enhances the difference to expose the hidden word and complete the sentence: "He wrote the words of Noah."

Archaeology Continued

panded over wide areas, taking their languages with them. First, climate changes following the end of the Pleistocene Ice Age about 10,000 years ago made some areas less habitable than they had been and opened other areas to settlement. Renfrew speculated that populations migrating due to such climate change caused the spread of the language families of the Arctic, including the Eskimo-Aleut languages spoken from northwestern Russia to Greenland.

A second source of change was the spread of farming, also beginning about 10,000 years ago. In such cases, populations might have expanded as new agricultural technologies enabled them to thrive in other environments. Also, as nearby hunting and gathering groups adopted new farming technologies, they might have gradually adopted the language of the farming culture as well. Renfrew's studies suggest that the Indo-European languages of Europe became widespread as farming peoples moved northwest from what is now Turkey.

As early farming cultures evolved into complex societies, a third form of cultural change—military conquest—became important in spreading languages, Renfrew suggested. In such cases, local populations may have chosen or been forced to adopt the language of the ruling group. For example, the conquests of Genghis Khan, a Mongol ruler who lived about A.D. 1200, played an important role in spreading the Altaic language family over central Asia.

Renfrew argued that languages that do not belong to one of the world's large language families must derive directly from the language spoken by the first members of *Homo sapiens sapiens,* the subspecies to which living people belong. These languages include some African languages, some American Indian languages, and the Basque language spoken in parts of France and Spain.

Renfrew and some anthropologists believe that *H. sapiens sapiens* arose in Africa about 100,000 years ago, and that from there people spread to Europe, Asia, Australia, and eventually the Americas. Other anthropologists, however, believe that *H. sapiens sapiens* evolved independently in Africa, Asia, and Europe. [Thomas R. Hester]

See also ANTHROPOLOGY. In WORLD BOOK, see ARCHAEOLOGY.

Astronomy

The discovery of what may be a planetary system surrounding a bright nearby star called Fomalhaut was announced in March 1994 by an international team of astronomers. The astronomers—S. Alan Stern of Southwest Research Institute in San Antonio, David Weintraub of Vanderbilt University in Nashville, and Michel Festou of the Mid-Pyrenees Observatory in Toulouse, France—used a new radio telescope in Spain to detect the glow from a disk of dust and rocky debris orbiting the star.

New planetary disk? Fomalhaut lies some 21 *light-years* from Earth. (A light-year is the distance light travels in one year—about 9.5 trillion kilometers [5.9 trillion miles].) Although it was impossible to make out dim, planet-sized objects at that distance, the investigators concluded from the characteristics of the disk that large bodies may be present in the system.

Astronomers have long thought that planetary formation is a natural by-product of star formation, and there is ample indirect evidence for that theory. Many stars, for example, have been found to emit greater-than-expected amounts of *infrared* (heat) radiation and radio waves, which are attributed to the presence of a disk of warm, dusty debris in the vicinity of the star. Before the 1994 announcement, astronomers had directly observed only one other stellar disk—a very large cloud of dust particles discovered in 1984 around a star called Beta Pictoris.

Using the sensitive new radio telescope, Festou, Stern, and Weintraub were able to determine that the dusty region around Fomalhaut is a disk much like the one around Beta Pictoris. The astronomers estimated the width of the disk to be about 120 billion kilometers (75 billion miles)—approximately 10 times larger than the diameter of Pluto's orbit about the sun.

The researchers assumed that the disk is a long-lived phenomenon, not something that existed briefly and just happened to be there when they looked. But a dusty disk around a star could not exist very long unless the supply of dust was continually renewed, because the tiny orbiting particles collide with each other, lose speed, and gradually spiral into the star.

The astronomers thus concluded that large bodies must be orbiting Fomalhaut along with the dust, because those bodies are the most likely source of new dust particles necessary to maintain the disk. The bodies might be comet-sized objects consisting of ice and rock, which occasionally collide with one another. The collisions would break the objects apart, contributing new clouds of dust and icy debris to the disk. If cometlike bodies are present in the disk surrounding Fomalhaut, the astronomers speculated, then perhaps actual planets are there as well.

Another planetary system around a distant star was reported in April 1994 by a research team led by astronomer Alexander Wolszczan of Pennsylvania State University in University Park. Wolszczan reported that at least two, and perhaps four, planets are orbiting a distant collapsed star known as a pulsar.

Wolszczan and another American astronomer, Dale A. Frail of the National Radio Astronomy Observatory in Socorro, N. Mex., first reported in 1992 that the pulsar, PSR1257+12, apparently had planets around it. Their finding was based on an analysis of radio waves emitted by the pulsar. In the latest announcement, Wolszczan offered additional observational data that he said removed any doubt about the discovery.

Bright nova in Cassiopeia. A new nova was spotted in the constellation Cassiopeia on Dec. 7, 1993, by Japanese amateur astronomer Kazuyoshi Kanatsu. A nova is a star that suddenly flares up, becoming up to a million times brighter than it had been.

Astronomers examining older photographs of the Cassiopeia region identified the star in its prenova state. They determined that the star's brightness had increased by about 100,000 times. The nova was named Nova Cas 1993.

Astronomers think a nova is caused by the sudden outbreak of nuclear reactions on the surface of a tiny, dense star called a *white dwarf*. A white dwarf is the collapsed remnant of a medium-sized star like the sun that is slowly becoming dimmer and cooler. Nuclear reactions are the mechanism by which stars in the prime of life release energy to produce light and heat. The reactions transform one type of atomic nucleus into another type, primarily hydrogen nuclei into helium nuclei.

Ordinarily, a white dwarf has exhausted its store of nuclear fuel, and no more reactions take place. But if matter is drawn to the star, the matter can fuel more nuclear reactions. For an isolated white dwarf, such an occurrence is all but impossible. But a white dwarf that is part of a two-star system may sometimes acquire matter from its companion star.

As that happens, the white dwarf's immense gravity accelerates the gas and pulls it to the star with great force. The gas's *kinetic energy* (energy of motion) is then converted to heat—enough to ignite nuclear reactions in the gas. The reactions proceed at a rapid rate, quickly consuming all the new matter and releasing an immense amount of energy. That energy release causes the star to flare into a nova. The brilliance soon fades, however, as the nuclear reactions stop and the star cools again.

During a nova outburst, gas is ejected at high speed from the white dwarf. In February 1994, observers at the Astrophysical Institute of the Canary Islands noted that the gas streaming away from Nova Cas 1993 had condensed into solid form, creating tiny dust particles. That process has been observed in many novae. Astronomers believe that novae, even though they are relatively rare, create much of the dust that fills the Milky Way and other galaxies.

Astronomers will continue to monitor Nova Cas 1993 as it fades. They will try to learn how much dust the nova has produced, what elements were formed in the nuclear reactions on the surface of the white dwarf and ejected into space, and what shape the expanding cloud of gas and dust is taking.

Gamma-ray bursts. Since the 1970's, astronomers have been puzzled by mysterious flashes of high-energy radiation called gamma rays detected by astronomical satellites. In January 1994, data from a satellite called the Compton Gamma Ray Observatory (CGRO) indicated that these short bursts of radiation come from distant galaxies, not from stars in our own Galaxy.

Gamma rays are a type of electromagnetic radiation, which also includes visible light, infrared and ultraviolet radiation, radio waves, and X rays. Gamma rays have the shortest wavelengths and the highest energies of any form of electromagnetic radiation.

The energy of gamma rays is so immense that only nuclear reactions can produce significant amounts of the rays. Thus, when astronomers began observing gamma-ray bursts from space in the 1970's, they knew that the bursts must be coming from some kind of explosive process involving nuclear reactions. But the satellite-borne gamma-ray detectors used at the time were not sophisticated enough to determine exactly where the radiation bursts were coming from.

The CGRO, launched in April 1991, was designed to survey the entire sky for gamma-ray bursts and to provide improved, though still not very precise, information on the location of detected sources. By 1994, the CGRO had detected about 1,000 bursts. Those data have given astronomers the raw material needed to test some of their hypotheses about gamma-ray bursts.

It was evident from early CGRO observations that the bursts do not come from the disk of the Milky Way galaxy. Still, that finding left open the possibility that the bursts could originate elsewhere in the vicinity of the Milky Way, perhaps in the spherical "halo" of matter surrounding it.

But a powerful argument that gamma-ray bursts arise in the far reaches of the universe emerged in January 1994 from CGRO observations reported by astronomers Robert Nemiroff of George Mason University in Fairfax, Va., and Jay Norris of the Goddard Space Flight Center in Beltville, Md. Nemiroff and Norris analyzed CGRO data and discovered that the gamma rays in many bursts were of relatively low energy. They noted further that the bursts of longest duration had the longest wavelengths and the lowest energy.

Nemiroff and Norris, citing theoretical work in 1992 by two other astronomers—one an American and the other an Israeli—said these findings indicated that gamma-ray bursts originate far outside the Galaxy. The other astronomers had shown that gamma rays should become stretched out and drained of energy as they travel across long distances.

The stretching effect is caused by the stretching of space itself—the universe has constantly been expanding since the big bang, the explosion of matter and energy that gave birth to the universe some 15 billion years ago. Due to the stretching phenomenon, a short burst of high-energy gamma rays would gradually become a long burst of low-energy rays. The farther the rays traveled, the astronomers said, the more pronounced the changes would be.

Thus, the observational evidence from the Compton Observatory strongly supports the theory that gamma-ray bursts were produced by events that occurred extremely far away. The events must also have occurred long ago, because it would have taken billions of years for them to reach us, traveling far across space at the speed of light. But it still must be determined what energetic, explosive processes created the gamma-ray bursts in the first place. Astronomers will now try to answer that question.

Galactic mergers. The Hubble Space Telescope provided new evidence in 1993 that galaxies can fall together, creating new, larger galaxies. Astronomer Bradley Whitmore of the Space Telescope Science Institute in Baltimore announced in June that the galaxy NGC 7252 appears to be the result of such a merger.

NGC 7252 is a large elliptical galaxy. Elliptical galaxies, which are round or oval with relatively smooth boundaries, are one of the two major types of galaxies in the universe. The other type consists of spiral galaxies, which have a pinwheel shape. Our own Milky Way is a spiral galaxy, as are many of the most prominent galaxies in the sky.

Ellipticals are common in large clusters of galaxies and tend to be concentrated near the crowded centers of the clusters. That fact led astronomers to suggest several years ago that elliptical galaxies may be the result of the collision and merger of smaller galaxies.

Whitmore examined images of NGC 7252 taken with the Hubble Space Telescope and made a surprising discovery. He found that the inner region of this galaxy consists of a small spiral structure rotating in the opposite direction from the rest of the galaxy. This "mini spiral" embedded in the core of the large elliptical galaxy appears to have been created by the collision and merger of two smaller galaxies. When the galaxies merged, Whitmore speculated, their

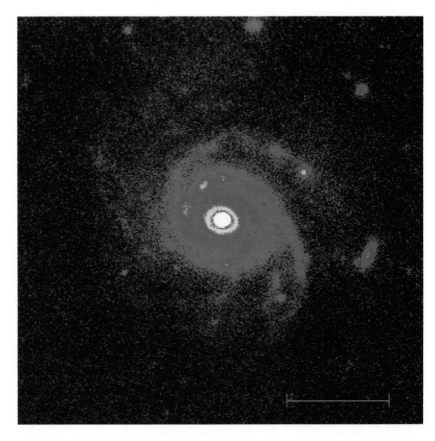

A galaxy discovered in late 1993 by astronomers at the University of Arizona in Tucson contains more stars and hydrogen gas than the Milky Way but is extremely faint because its stars are spread across a much larger volume of space. (The scale bar indicates the width of the Milky Way.) Sensitive electronic devices now enable astronomers to detect and study these giant, low-density galaxies, which may provide important clues to how galaxies form and evolve over time.

MACHO's: Clues to the Dark-Matter Mystery

Astronomers in 1993 and 1994 found important new clues in their quest to solve one of the greatest mysteries about the universe: the nature of dark matter. Stars and luminous clouds of gas and dust make up the visible part of the universe, but astronomers have evidence that these objects are only a fraction of the matter in the universe. Something else must account for at least 90 percent, and perhaps as much as 99 percent, of the universe's mass. Because that matter cannot be seen, it is known as dark matter.

The first indication that the universe contains dark matter came in the 1930's, when astronomers studied *clusters* (large groups) of fast-moving galaxies. Calculations showed that the gravitational attraction among the galaxies is not powerful enough to keep the galaxies from drifting apart. For the galaxies to remain bound together, the researchers determined, they must contain far more mass than is in their visible stars.

Since then, studies of the motions of stars and gas clouds in galaxies, including our own Milky Way, continued to point to the presence of dark matter in the universe. The most recent such finding was reported in June 1993 by three University of California astronomers—Douglas Lin, Burton Jones, and Arnold Klemola—who had been studying the Large Magellanic Cloud, one of two small galaxies that orbit the Milky Way. The researchers measured the speed at which the Large Magellanic Cloud is orbiting the Milky Way. That speed relates directly to the gravitational pull of the Milky Way—and thus to its mass. They found that the Milky Way's total mass must be at least five times that of its visible stars.

Lin, Burton, and Klemola made another discovery that involves the dark matter mystery. They analyzed the orbital path of the Large Magellanic Cloud and found it to be *elliptical* (oval). They said the shape of the orbit indicates that dark matter is present throughout the Milky Way's halo, the vast volume of space surrounding the Galaxy's visible disk of stars and gas clouds. The halo of dark matter seems to extend far beyond the Large Magellanic Cloud.

What might the dark matter consist of? Some experts have theorized that it is made up of subatomic particles left over from the creation of the universe some 15 billion years ago. Astronomers may yet discover such particles. But the new findings indicate that much—though probably not all—of the universe's dark matter is far less exotic than that.

These findings support the theory that a great deal of dark matter is in the form of countless large objects made of ordinary matter. Those objects might be Jupiter-sized planets or *brown dwarfs*, gaseous bodies that never got hot enough to become actual stars. Astronomers use the term MACHO's (*m*assive *c*ompact *h*alo *o*bjects) to refer to these bodies.

By their very nature, MACHO's should be invisible to even the largest telescopes. But astronomers in the 1980's realized that the dim objects might be observed indirectly with the aid of gravitational lensing. Gravitational lensing is a phenomenon in which the gravitational field of very massive objects bends light rays, much as a glass lens does.

A gravitational lens is a massive object in the sky that lies directly between Earth and a distant star or galaxy. The gravitational lens bends light rays coming from the distant object, distorting its appearance to observers on Earth. Some gravitational lenses cause the light to appear as a ring, for example, or as multiple images of the distant star or galaxy.

Most of the known gravitational lenses are galaxies. But in 1986, astronomer Bohdan Paczynski of Princeton University in New Jersey pointed out that stars or planets could also be gravitational lenses. Paczynski said that such a "microlens," if precisely aligned with a more distant background star, would create multiple images of the star. The images would be so close that they would blend together, producing a single image of greatly intensified brightness.

Here was the perfect tool with which to search for large, dark objects—or MACHO's, as they were soon dubbed. Astronomers could look for MACHO's in and around the Milky Way by watching for stars whose brightness increased and then returned to normal. The change in brightness would presumably be caused by a MACHO passing between Earth and the star.

Paczynski proposed searching for this effect by observing stars in the two Magellanic Cloud galaxies. Light from the galaxies' billions of stars passes through the halo of the Milky Way on its way to Earth. If the halo is indeed filled with dark objects, a considerable number of them should pass between Earth and various stars in the Magellanic Clouds each year. Paczynski calculated that for every million stars observed over the course of a year, there should be dozens to hundreds of alignments that cause gravitational lensing.

By 1993, a team of astronomers from the Lawrence Livermore National Laboratory in California, the University of California at Berkeley, and the Mount Stromlo Observatory in Canberra,

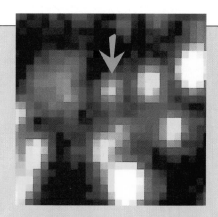

The sign of a MACHO?

A sequence of computerized images of a star (arrows) in a nearby galaxy called the Large Magellanic Cloud indicate the presence of a large object—perhaps a dark gaseous body known as a brown dwarf—between Earth and the star. Astronomers think the star's light was bent and magnified by the object's gravity, causing the star to temporarily appear much brighter than normal, *center*. Objects such as this one, called MACHO's, may constitute much of the universe's *dark matter*, unseen matter that makes up as much as 99 percent of the universe's mass.

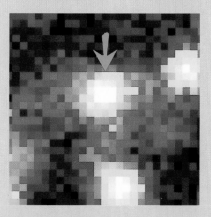

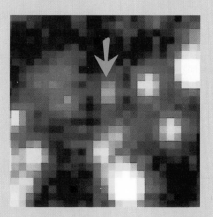

Australia, was involved in an intensive search for MACHO's. Working at the Mount Stromlo facility and using a telescope connected to electronic detectors, the researchers made multiple images of four regions of sky centered on the Large Magellanic Cloud. The instruments produced images of about 1.8 million stars in the four fields of view.

French astronomers at the European Southern Observatory in Chile conducted a similar search. That group photographed stars in the Large Magellanic Cloud with two telescopes, one of which had a wide field of view encompassing about 8 million stars.

The two research groups used computer analyses of the images to reveal whether any of the stars had changed in brightness. That immense task was complicated by the fact that the light from some stars varies naturally. But such stars could be recognized by other characteristics, including frequently recurring changes in brightness. The investigators eliminated those stars from the search and concentrated on finding stars that brightened and then faded just once.

In September 1993, both groups reported success. The French astronomers announced that they had observed two stars that had apparently brightened due to gravitational microlensing. The California-Australia team reported finding another. Over the course of one to two months, the stars had brightened and then dimmed again. The astronomers said that the foreground objects causing this effect may have been brown dwarfs or very dim normal stars.

In 1994, the search for MACHO's continued as astronomers sought to determine how common dark objects are in the Milky Way. The frequency with which MACHO's are sighted should make it possible to estimate how numerous they are in our Galaxy—and presumably in other galaxies as well.

One observing team, made up of American and Polish astronomers, including Bohdan Paczynski, was looking for MACHO's in a different direction: toward the star-packed center of the Milky Way. Those researchers, working at the Las Campanas Observatory in Chile, also met with success. By April 1994, they had detected seven gravitational microlenses in the central region of the Galaxy. Analysis indicated that the objects were brown dwarfs or faint normal stars.

All three teams planned to keep searching for MACHO's. They hoped that with hard work and some luck, they would be able to determine once and for all if MACHO's could account for a significant proportion of the dark matter in the universe. [Theodore P. Snow] mutual gravity tore them apart, producing whirling streams of gas that developed into the spiral-shaped structure.

Whitman also noted that NGC 7252 is surrounded by spherical clusters of bluish stars. Blue-colored stars are extremely hot and live only a few million years before using up all their nuclear fuel. The stars in the clusters must therefore be quite young.

Whitmore said this finding also supports the conclusion that NGC 7252 was created by the joining of two galaxies. When the smaller galaxies came together, Whitman said, streams of gas from the galaxies collided and became concentrated enough to form new stars through gravitational contraction. Most galaxies, including the Milky Way, are also surrounded by star clusters, but the stars in them are typically very old.

Galaxies adrift. The expansion of the universe is apparently not uniform, according to evidence reported in April 1994. Astronomers have known since the late 1920's that the universe is expanding and that all the galaxies in it are rushing away from each other. They think this outward motion is the result of the big bang.

Until the 1994 report, the expansion of the universe was assumed to be uniform in all directions, with variations occurring only within small regions of space. Then astronomers Tod Lauer of the National Optical Astronomy Observatories in Tucson, Ariz., and Marc Postman of the Space Telescope Science Institute in Baltimore reported that the universe seems to contain many large regions in which galaxies follow paths that are somewhat independent of the overall expansion. Our own Milky Way may be part of such a region.

The two astronomers surveyed the motions of galaxies in our part of the universe. They found that the Milky Way and its neighboring galaxies are all moving in the same direction. Astronomers had previously detected that movement, but their observations indicated that the only galaxies affected were in a relatively small region extending a few tens of millions of light-years from Earth.

The survey carried out by Lauer and Postman included galaxies that are

Dense clumps of glowing, electrically charged gas stream from the region of an apparent explosion in the Great Nebula in Orion. Astronomers in Australia reported in 1993 that the blast—which they said must have occurred within the last 1,000 years—may have been either a sudden outburst of energy in an infant star or the explosion of an aging massive star.

A mystery in Andromeda

An image produced by the Hubble Space Telescope in July 1993, *right,* shows two bright spots at the center of the Andromeda galaxy, indicating that the galaxy has two nuclei—dense central clusters of stars. Astronomers said the brighter nucleus may be the remnant of a galaxy that collided and merged with Andromeda. Alternatively, they said, the two bright spots may be parts of a single nucleus that is divided by a dark band of dust.

Andromeda galaxy

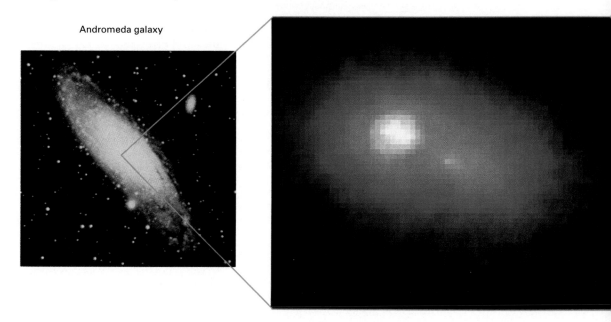

much farther away—up to 500 million light-years from Earth. The fact that all of the galaxies in so large a volume of space are moving in unison suggests that the universe, in addition to expanding outward, may be fragmented into large regions that move in other directions. If that, indeed, is the case, how could these multiple independent motions have arisen? Experts say that question will be a puzzle for *cosmologists* (scientists who study the birth and evolution of the universe) to solve.

An endless expansion? Another question raised by the expansion of the universe has long challenged astronomers: Will the expansion go on forever or will the universe at some point begin to contract toward a "big crunch"? Research reported in January 1994 by astronomer Ruth Daly of Princeton University in New Jersey indicates that the expansion will never end.

When discussing the ultimate fate of the universe, astronomers usually describe the alternatives as being an open, closed, or flat universe. An open universe is one in which the expansion nev-

er ends. In a closed universe, the expansion eventually stops, and then the universe contracts. If the universe is flat, the expansion slows but never quite comes to a halt.

Daly conducted a study of *radio galaxies,* galaxies that emit most of their energy as radio waves. In most cases, the radio waves are emitted from two huge clouds of hot gas, called radio lobes, on opposite sides of the galaxy. The radio lobes are created by rapidly moving jets of *ionized* (electrically charged) gas streaming out of the core of the galaxy.

Daly had studied the radio emissions and shapes of several radio galaxies and had determined how far apart each galaxy's radio lobes are. By comparing the true distance between a galaxy's radio lobes with their *angular separation*—the apparent distance between them as seen from Earth—she was able to calculate how far away the galaxy is. This technique is similar to determining how far away a mountain is on Earth by comparing the peak's actual height to its apparent size on the distant landscape.

Once Daly had calculated the distance to a number of radio galaxies, she measured the galaxies' velocities. She found that nearby galaxies are moving nearly as fast as very distant galaxies. Because the distant galaxies are seen as they were a long time ago, when the universe was younger, Daly's finding indicates that expansion of the universe has not slowed very much. If her findings are correct, then the universe's rate of slowing is so small that the expansion will never stop—the universe is open.

This conclusion, however, is far from certain. Astronomers will now try to confirm or refute Daly's finding.

Mars probe lost. Engineers at the National Aeronautics and Space Administration (NASA) Jet Propulsion Laboratory in Pasadena, Calif., lost contact with the Mars Observer space probe in late August 1993. The loss of the spacecraft just days before it was to go into orbit around Mars and begin sending back data was a tremendous blow to the exploration of the red planet. (See SPACE TECHNOLOGY.)

Comet impact on Jupiter. In mid-July 1994, astronomers had their telescopes trained on Jupiter to observe the effects of a predicted collision of a disintegrated comet with the planet. Fragments of Comet Shoemaker-Levy 9 were expected to smash into Jupiter during a seven-day period, from July 16 to 22. The comet had an earlier encounter with Jupiter in July 1992, when it passed close to the planet. Jupiter's gravity broke the comet into at least 19 fragments and put the pieces on a collision course with the solar system's largest planet.

Observations indicated that the chunks of Comet Shoemaker-Levy 9 were up to roughly 4 kilometers (2.5 miles) in diameter. The pieces traveled toward the planet in line, like a string of pearls, and were expected to strike Jupiter at a speed of about 60 kilometers (37 miles) per second. At that speed, the cometary fragments carried as much energy as 100 million megatons of TNT, 10,000 times as much as in all the nuclear weapons on Earth during the height of the Cold War.

Astronomers had predicted in 1993 that the impacts from the comet would occur on the side of Jupiter turned away from Earth, and so they would be hidden from direct observation. Scientists had to be content with viewing the after-

effects on Jupiter's thick atmosphere as the impact sites rotated into view some minutes after each collision. However, they anticipated obtaining direct, though distant, images of the impacts from the Galileo and Voyager space probes.

During the year, astronomers around the world were preparing to study the effects of the impacts on the chemistry and cloud structure of Jupiter's atmosphere and on the vast region of electrically charged particles that surround Jupiter, trapped by the planet's magnetic field. The opportunity to prepare for such an impact well in advance was unique in the history of astronomy.

A moon of an asteroid. The United States spacecraft Galileo, which is heading toward a 1995 rendezvous with Jupiter, in August 1993 photographed the first known moon orbiting an asteroid. The discovery was announced in March 1994 by researchers at the Jet Propulsion Laboratory.

The asteroid, Ida, is a potato-shaped body roughly 60 kilometers long. Its moon, designated Ida-2, is an irregular chunk of rock roughly 1 kilometer (0.62 mile) across that is orbiting the asteroid at an estimated distance of 100 kilometers (62 miles).

Galileo sent back images of Ida and the moon as the space probe passed through the asteroid belt, a ring of rocky debris between Mars and Jupiter. Because Galileo's main antenna is stuck in a closed position, the spacecraft has had to relay data to Earth with a backup antenna, which operates very slowly. For that reason, the images containing Ida-2 were not received until early 1994.

For some time, astronomers had accepted the notion that asteroids might have tiny moons surrounding them, but because of the small size of such objects, none had been observed. Ida-2 is much too small to be seen from Earth.

The main belt of asteroids consists of vast numbers of rocky bodies that most likely failed to come together to form a planet. Members of the asteroid belt sometimes collide with other debris that happens to cross the asteroid belt, and astronomers speculate that such collisions may sometimes produce a fragment that goes into orbit around a larger body. Ida-2 may have been created in that way.

Comet crash on Jupiter

A string of comet fragments, *below*, streak through space en route to a predicted collision with Jupiter in July 1994. The comet, Shoemaker-Levy 9, broke apart after passing close to the giant planet in 1992. A computer simulation, *right*, predicted that each collision would send huge ripples through Jupiter's atmosphere.

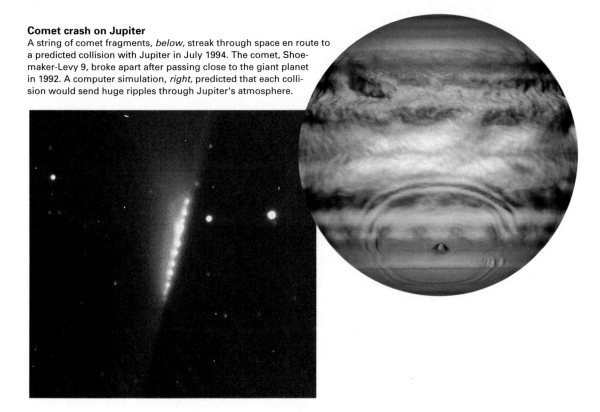

Because Ida-2 is so close to Ida, and because the larger asteroid has such an irregular shape, it is possible that the little moon's orbit is not stable over a very long time. Further analysis may reveal whether Ida-2 is the result of a recent collision and how long it is likely to maintain its orbit around Ida.

Outer solar system revealed. For nearly 50 years, when astronomers were unable to find evidence of planet-sized objects beyond Pluto, they wondered why the outer solar system is apparently so empty. But by 1994, astronomers were becoming increasingly certain that the space just beyond Pluto is not so empty after all—that it may be heavily populated by a new class of objects.

These objects are small icy bodies that orbit the sun just beyond Pluto. Astronomers had long speculated that a ring of such objects, which they called the Kuiper belt, was present in the outer solar system and was the source of many comets. But for years, efforts to confirm the existence of the Kuiper belt could detect no trace of it.

Then, in August 1992, American as-tronomers David Jewitt of the University of Hawaii in Honolulu and Jane Luu of the University of California at Berkeley detected what was apparently a member of the Kuiper belt orbiting the sun at a distance of 6.3 billion kilometers (3.9 billion miles). They called the object 1992 QB1. By late 1993, Jewitt and Luu and other astronomers had discovered several more tiny bodies at roughly the same distance. The objects, thought to be mainly rock and ice, are all an estimated 100 to 200 kilometers (62 to 124 miles) in diameter.

Why did it take so long, after decades of searching for these objects, to find them? Jewitt and Luu said that in previous searches, astronomers simply did not have sensitive enough instruments and did not use the largest telescopes available to them. New electronic devices that enhance the light-gathering ability of large telescopes made the discoveries possible. [Jonathan I. Lunine and Theodore P. Snow]

In the Special Reports section, see THE SEARCH FOR BLACK HOLES. In WORLD BOOK, see ASTRONOMY.

Atmospheric Science

Violent weather caused great damage in much of the United States during 1993 and 1994. Widespread flooding in the upper Midwest drove thousands of people from their homes and caused billions of dollars in damage during the summer of 1993. Later in the year, wind-driven wildfires raked southern California.

Meanwhile, atmospheric researchers monitored the continuing atmospheric effects of the 1991 Mount Pinatubo volcanic eruption and detected another record loss of atmospheric ozone above Antarctica. In addition, through late 1993 and into 1994, scientists considered new evidence that Earth's climate is less stable than previously believed.

Flooding in the Midwestern U.S. Relentless rains during the summer of 1993 caused severe flooding in the upper Midwest. The flooding caused 50 deaths and at least $12 billion in damage to property and crops, according to the Federal Emergency Management Association (FEMA).

Part of the reason for the flooding was that the upper Mississippi River Valley had been unusually wet since July 1992. The amount of precipitation for the winter of 1992-1993 had averaged about 150 percent of normal. By early spring 1993, rains had completely filled streams and rivers and saturated soils throughout the upper Midwest. Heavy rains continued with little letup through the summer and into autumn.

The floods, which began in June and lasted into September, also resulted from an unusually steady weather pattern over North America. Beginning in mid-spring 1993, the jet stream remained strong and persisted, week after week, along the same southwest-to-northeast track across the upper Mississippi River Valley. The jet stream is a current of high-speed winds between 10 and 15 kilometers (6 and 9 miles) above the ground. It normally flows in a more west-to-east route.

The unusual jet-stream path created a pattern of wind and pressure in the lower atmosphere that caused large amounts of water vapor from the Gulf of Mexico to flow north. The water vapor fell to Earth as rain in daily thunderstorms. According to the National Climatic Data Center in Asheville, N.C., an average of 40.97 centimeters (16.13 inches) of rain fell in the upper Mississippi River Valley from April through June, the rainiest such period since scientists began keeping weather records in 1895. Normal rainfall for the period is approximately 28.04 centimeters (11.04 inches).

At the peak of the flooding, the Mississippi River was 11 kilometers (7 miles) wide in places, and the Missouri River swelled to a 32-kilometer (20-mile) width just northwest of St. Louis. By mid-July, the National Weather Service reported that 100 Midwestern rivers had overflowed their banks. About 1,100 levies or flood walls—about 70 percent of those bounding rivers in the upper Midwest—failed in spite of heroic efforts to save them. As a result of the flooding, the federal government declared nine states disaster areas: Iowa, Illinois, Minnesota, Missouri, Wisconsin, South Dakota, Nebraska, Kansas, and North Dakota. (See also PUBLIC HEALTH. In the Special Reports section, see THE COST OF TAMING A RIVER).

California wildfires. Santa Ana winds gusting to 113 kilometers (70 miles) per hour helped fuel wildfires—some of which were set by arsonists—in southern California in autumn 1993. Santa Ana winds are hot, extremely dry winds that blow toward Los Angeles from the high deserts east of the Sierra Nevada. The winds rapidly draw moisture out of the area's dry vegetation, greatly increasing its ability to catch fire. Once a brushfire starts, the high-speed Santa Ana winds fan the flames and spread burning embers that ignite new fires.

On October 27, more than 12 wildfires burned brush and homes in southern and eastern Los Angeles. Then on November 2, fires raced through portions of western Los Angeles, again driven by Santa Ana winds. The strongest of these fires occurred near Malibu, sweeping down canyons to the ocean. By year's end, more than 200,000 acres had been burned and over 1,000 homes were destroyed. At least one person died and more than 120 were injured, according to FEMA.

El Niño lingers. The persistence of El Niño in late 1993 made the latest appearance of this vast cycle of atmospheric and ocean conditions one of the three longest in the 1900's. According to climatologist Gerald Bell of the Na-

Record floods in the Midwest

Unusual weather patterns in summer 1993 brought severe flooding to the Midwestern United States. Many areas suffered the worst flooding since scientists began keeping weather records in the late 1800's.

Atmospheric conditions contributed to the flooding. Two high pressure systems, one over the Pacific Ocean and another over the East Coast, helped bend the *jet stream* (a high-altitude, high-speed current of air) out of position for many months. This allowed a stream of warm, moist air to rush north from the Gulf of Mexico into the Midwest, producing heavy rainfall.

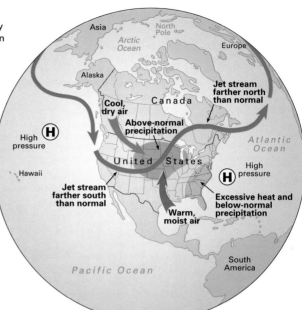

Satellite photographs show the extent of the flooding at the convergence of the Illinois, Missouri, and Mississippi rivers near St. Louis. In early July 1988, *below left*, the rivers appear as dark, slender bands. In the same location in July 1993, heavy rainfall had caused the rivers to flow far out of their banks, *below right*.

July 4, 1988

July 18, 1993

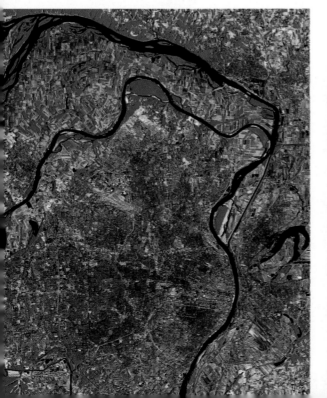

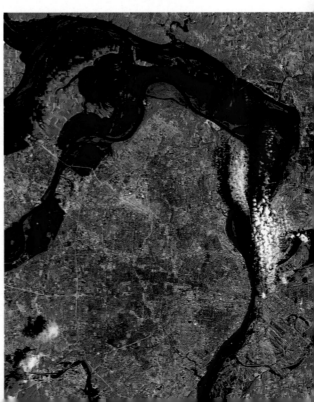

tional Oceanic and Atmospheric Administration's Climate Analysis Center in Camp Springs, Md., the latest El Niño rivaled those of 1911-1913 and 1939-1942.

El Niño occurs every three to seven years, when trade winds that normally blow west from South America along the equator weaken. A huge pool of warm surface water that normally rests in the western Pacific Ocean then moves east along the equator. This warm water helps produce more clouds and thunderstorms than usual over the central Pacific Ocean. This enhanced cloudiness alters the jet stream, affecting weather in many areas of the world, often drastically.

The most recent El Niño began in late 1991. By summer 1992, its effects had weakened, and scientists predicted it would end later that year. But in December, it unexpectedly strengthened, and El Niño persisted until late fall 1993.

Pinatubo's atmospheric effects. Compounds released during the eruption of Mount Pinatubo in the Philip-

pines in June 1991 were still influencing Earth's weather in late 1993. That finding was reported in December 1993 by atmospheric scientists John Christy of the University of Alabama in Huntsville and Roy Spencer of the National Aeronautics and Space Administration (NASA) Marshall Space Flight Center in Huntsville.

The volcanic eruption released 14 to 18 metric tons (15 to 20 short tons) of sulfur dioxide, which produced droplets of sulfuric acid suspended in the *stratosphere* (upper atmosphere). This cloud of droplets covered the globe with a thin veil that very slightly reduced the amount of sunlight that reached the surface. That effect led to a global cooling of surface temperatures. At first, Christy and Spencer said, the droplets warmed the stratosphere as they absorbed sunlight and heat radiated from Earth.

As time passed, the droplets slowly settled out of the high atmosphere, thinning the veil and letting more sunlight through. Christy and Spencer reported that stratospheric air temperatures reached a 28-month low in December

New center for the study of ice cores
Scientists at the new National Ice Core Laboratory in Boulder, Colo., *below,* examine cylinders of ice drilled out of the Greenland icecap. The new lab, which opened in October 1993, will be used to store and study ice cores, which contain samples of ice that formed hundreds of thousands of years ago. By studying the samples, scientists can learn about atmospheric conditions long ago. A scientist at the Colorado lab, *right,* slices through an ice core to prepare it for study.

1993 and then began rising steadily in 1994. That finding indicates that Pinatubo's cooling effect may be over.

Record ozone loss. Levels of ozone in the stratosphere over Antarctica fell to record lows again in autumn 1993. (Ozone is a molecule made up of three oxygen atoms. A layer of ozone gas in the stratosphere absorbs some of the sun's harmful ultraviolet rays.) Ozone levels above Antarctica have dropped each year since scientists began measuring such levels in 1985.

Artificially created chemicals called chlorofluorocarbons (CFC's) are the main culprit in the loss of ozone from Earth's upper atmosphere. CFC's are common gases used as cleaning agents in industry and in many air conditioners and refrigerators. When sunlight strikes CFC molecules, the molecules break down into chlorine atoms, which react with ozone and destroy it. This destruction thins the ozone layer, creating an area of depletion centered over the South Pole. This depleted area is commonly called the "ozone hole."

Scientists have recorded a widening ozone hole every year since 1985. In 1993, measurements using instruments on weather balloons showed that the ozone hole had again grown deeper. The hole was about 15 percent deeper than in 1992, the previous deepest hole, with nearly all of the ozone between 13.5 and 19 kilometers (8.4 and 11.8 miles) above Earth's surface destroyed.

Rapid climate change? For many years, atmospheric scientists thought that changes in Earth's climate came slowly and steadily, with thousands of years passing before global average temperatures changed more than a few degrees. Then in July 1993, the Greenland Ice Core Project, a group representing eight European nations, reported the surprising and controversial news that Earth's temperature may change dramatically in just a few decades.

The Ice Core Project researchers extracted a core of ice from the Greenland ice shelf, drilling down to 3,029 meters (9,938 feet). That extremely deep core provided a record of snowfall and ice formation dating back 250,000 years.

The scientists examined ice layers formed during an *interglacial* (between ice ages) period called the Eemian, which occurred between 115,000 and 135,000 years ago. The scientists wanted to determine whether Earth's climate was as stable then as it has been during the present interglacial period.

To determine average temperatures during the Eemian, the researchers examined the ratio of two *isotopes* (forms) of oxygen trapped in each of the different layers of ice. That ratio varies according to temperature, with a warm year producing more of one isotope than a cool year.

The team determined that average air temperatures in Greenland warmed and cooled by as much as 10 Celsius degrees (18 Fahrenheit degrees) during the Eemian, often in as little as 10 to 20 years. In the most dramatic event, at the height of Eemian, Greenland's average temperature appeared to drop by 25 Celsius degrees (45 Fahrenheit degrees) in only 70 years.

The European scientists reported that abrupt changes in ocean circulation in the North Atlantic Ocean may have triggered the climate variability. The normal warm northward currents may have halted, allowing colder currents to flow farther south. The scientists said they did not know what might have caused the ocean current shifts, however.

If the Europeans' conclusions are true, then Earth's present stable climate may not stay that way. Some atmospheric scientists disputed the findings, however. For example, Richard Fairbanks, a senior scientist at Columbia University's Lamont-Doherty Earth Observatory in Palisades, N.Y., suggested in January 1994 that the actual temperature changes recorded in the ice were not nearly as large as reported by the European team.

Fairbanks claimed that temperature fluctuations are not the only thing that determines the ratio of oxygen isotopes in ice cores. He used complex computer simulations to determine that the mixing of air currents may have caused varying ratios. The actual air temperature fluctuations were probably only half as large as those suggested by the European team, he said. But even those shifts would be quite large, indicating that the temperatures of the last few thousand years have been unusually stable.

[John T. Snow]

In WORLD BOOK, see METEOROLOGY; OZONE.

Advances in the understanding of the genetic code, new techniques used to copy and manipulate genes, and observations that helped confirm the existence of gravity waves were the scientific advances awarded Nobel Prizes in October 1993. For students, major prizes were awarded for the invention of furnaces that recycle plastic, for the evaluation of different science teaching methods, and for many other projects.

The Nobel Prize in chemistry was shared by biochemist Kary B. Mullis, now an independent consultant based in La Jolla, Calif., and British-born biochemist Michael Smith, a professor and a director of the Biotechnology Laboratory at the University of British Columbia in Vancouver, Canada. Mullis was awarded the prize for his work in developing a technique known as *polymerase chain reaction* (PCR). Mullis invented PCR in the 1970's while employed by the Cetus Corporation, a biotechnology company based in Emeryville, Calif. The technique allows laboratory workers to take a trace amount of DNA (deoxyribonucleic acid, the molecule of which genes are made) and quickly make millions of copies of it to use for analysis.

PCR has enabled the study of extremely small amounts of DNA recovered from plant and animal fossils. The Nobel Committee noted that the technique's development helped inspire the premise of *Jurassic Park,* the novel and 1993 motion picture that postulates that dinosaur DNA could be recovered from fossilized insects and used to create living dinosaurs. A less-fanciful application of PCR is creating sufficient quantities of DNA from hair or blood samples to identify criminal suspects.

Smith was honored for his work in developing a method known as *site-directed mutagenesis,* which enables scientists to study how genes work and how to make altered genes. The method involves altering DNA by splicing new *base pairs* (chemicals that code for amino acids, the building blocks of proteins) onto a selected strand of a DNA molecule. These site-directed *mutations* (changes) create predictable alterations in the proteins a gene codes for. For example, plant genes can be altered to create plants with predictable new traits. The Nobel Committee suggested that site-directed mutagenesis may ultimately be used to cure hereditary diseases by altering the defective gene or genes responsible for the disease.

The physics prize was shared by Joseph H. Taylor and Russell A. Hulse, both physicists at Princeton University in Princeton, N.J., for their discovery in 1974 of the first *binary pulsar.* A pulsar is an extremely dense star that gives off a beam of radio waves as it rotates. A binary pulsar is a pair of such stars that are orbiting each other. At the time the two scientists made their discovery, using a giant radio telescope at Arecibo in Puerto Rico, Taylor was a professor at the University of Massachusetts in Amherst, and Hulse was his graduate student.

The physicists' observations of the binary pulsar over a period of four years indirectly confirmed that massive bodies in orbit around one another give off energy in the form of gravitational waves. The existence of such waves had been predicted by the general theory of relativity developed by the German-born physicist Albert Einstein. Taylor and Hulse's observations showed that the two pulsars were moving closer together as the time it took them to orbit each other decreased. That finding indicated that the two stars were losing energy in exactly the amount Einstein predicted would be lost due to gravity waves. The physicists made the discovery in 1978.

The physiology or medicine prize was also shared. The Karolinska Institute in Stockholm, Sweden, awarded the prize to molecular biologists Richard J. Roberts of New England Biolabs in Beverly, Mass., and Phillip A. Sharp of the Massachusetts Institute of Technology (MIT) in Cambridge. The two men in 1977 independently discovered "split genes." They found that genes do not always occur as continuous segments within DNA. Instead, genes may be interrupted by segments called *introns* that have no role in coding for proteins. Introns are common in higher organisms.

"The discovery of split genes has been of fundamental importance for today's basic research in biology," the Nobel Assembly of the Karolinska Institute stated, "as well as for more medically oriented research [on] the development of cancer and other diseases."

After introns were discovered in higher organisms, geneticists developed new theories of how genes evolve. Many sci-

Physicists Russell A. Hulse, left, and Joseph H. Taylor, both of Princeton University in Princeton, N.J., celebrate winning the Nobel Prize in physics in October 1993. The physicists won for their 1974 discovery of a binary pulsar, a twin star system that confirmed the existence of gravity waves.

entists now believe that although introns play no role in producing proteins, they do play a role in creating genetic variation.

Scientists also learned that certain genetic diseases occur as messenger RNA (ribonucleic acid) eliminates, or "splices out," introns during the process of creating proteins. Errors in the splicing process can cause such genetic diseases as muscular dystrophy and beta-thalassemia, a form of anemia.

Science student awards. Winners in the 43rd annual Westinghouse Science Talent Search were announced on March 14, 1994, and winners of the 45th annual International Science and Engineering Fair were named on May 13. Both student competitions are conducted by Science Service, a nonprofit organization based in Washington, D.C. Other student science competitions included international olympiads in chemistry, mathematics, and physics, all held in July 1993, and a computer programming olympiad in October 1993.

Science Talent Search. Forty finalists in the Westinghouse-sponsored competition were chosen from 1,645 entrants from high schools throughout the United States. The finalists were awarded scholarships totaling $205,000.

First place and a $40,000 scholarship went to Forrest N. Anderson of Helena (Mont.) High School for designing and building two furnaces that recycle plastic. Anderson is seeking a patent on the furnaces, which reportedly convert different types of plastic into commercially useful petrochemicals without producing hazardous by-products.

Second place and a $30,000 scholarship were awarded to Jennifer Yu-Fe Lin of Hunter College High School in New York City. Her biology project focused on the role of receptor-binding proteins in cell growth and differentiation.

Third place and a $20,000 scholarship went to John L. Staub of Sisseton (S.D.) High School. He compared the traditional rote-lecture teaching method with a "hands-on" teaching method by designing two versions of a science curriculum for third-grade students. He determined that the hands-on method improved comprehension and interest.

Awards and Prizes Continued

Fourth place and a $15,000 scholarship went to Robert C. Sarvis of Thomas Jefferson High School for Science and Technology in Alexandria, Va.

Fifth place and a $15,000 scholarship were won by Steven D. Sherman of Winona (Minn.) Senior High School.

Sixth place and a $15,000 scholarship were awarded to Flora Tartakovsky of the Bronx High School of Science in New York City.

Seventh place and a $10,000 scholarship went to Janos Zahajszky of Canton (Mass.) High School.

Eighth-place winner of a $10,000 scholarship was Jennifer M. Kalish of Bryn Mawr School in Baltimore.

Ninth place and a $10,000 scholarship were won by Margaret Chalmers Bothner of Falmouth (Mass.) High School.

Tenth place and a $10,000 scholarship were awarded to Jamel Lamonté Oeser-Sweat of Martin Luther King, Jr., High School in New York City.

Science Fair. The 45th annual International Science and Engineering Fair took place in Birmingham, Ala. The 929 participants were selected from students who competed in science fairs in the United States, Puerto Rico, Guam, and a number of foreign countries. Highest honors went to seven students who will attend either the Nobel Prize ceremonies in Stockholm, Sweden; the European Union Contest for Young Scientists in Luxembourg; or the Ninth Feria Internacional de Ciencia y Technologia del Cono Sur in Mendoza, Argentina.

Selected to attend the Nobel Prize ceremonies were Sarita M. James of Homestead High School in Fort Wayne, Ind., and Fred M. Niell III of Lausanne Collegiate School in Memphis. Chosen to attend the ninth international science and technology fair in Mendoza were David A. Bray of T. C. Williams High School in Alexandria, Va., and Daniel A. Colon and Jason R. Sanchez-Gil, both of Colegio San Ignacio De Loyola in Rio Piedras, Puerto Rico. Selected to participate in the European Union Contest were Diego F. Figueroa and Kenna R. Mills, both of Thomas A. Edison High School in Alexandria, Va.

The First Award winners of $500 each in the 13 disciplinary categories were:

Behavioral and social sciences. Reed L. Levine of John F. Kennedy High School in Bellmore, N.Y., and William J. Booher of Westbury High in Houston.

Biochemistry. Heather M. Matthews of Whitney M. Young Magnet High School in Chicago, and Rong Jer Tsay of West Springfield High School in Springfield, Va.

Botany. Neil Ashok Hattangadi of Winter Park (Fla.) High School; Schuyler C. Laws of Clarksdale (Miss.) High School; and Isaac S. Bruck of Cary (N.C.) High School.

Chemistry. Walter N. Simmons of Hedgesville (W. Va.) High School.

Computer science. Ali Reza Anghaie of Buchholz High School in Gainesville, Fla.

Earth and space sciences. Barnas G. Monteith of Randolph (Mass.) High School.

Engineering. Mara L. Carey of Martin County High School in Stuart, Fla.; Nathan D. Holmes of West High School in Davenport, Iowa; Maria-Graciela Hollm of Villa Maria High School in Montreal, Canada; and Rebekah Woods of Ben Lomond High School in Ogden, Utah.

Environmental sciences. Jill S. McCrea of King City (Mo.) R-I High School; David A. Bray; Frederick D. Melendres of Albuquerque, N. Mex.; and Ben Venable of Tallassee, Ala.

Mathematics. Wes A. Watters of South Eugene High School in Eugene, Ore., and Mary K. Clavenna of St. Louis, Mo.

Medicine and health. Griffin M. Weber of Denbigh High School in Newport News, Va.; Zed S. French of William Monroe High School in Stanardsville, Va.; and Kevin B. Jones of Parkway West High School in Ballwin, Mo.

Microbiology. Eden V. Haverfield of Canterbury School in Fort Myers, Fla.; Robert K. Powell of Fort Pierce (Fla.) Westwood High School; and Amita Shukla of Centennial High School in Ellicott City, Md.

Physics. Fred M. Niell III and Ian G. Zacharia of Thomas Jefferson High School for Science and Technology in Alexandria, Va.

Zoology. David I. Crowley of Viewmont High School in Bountiful, Utah; Catherine R. Muller of Samuel Marsden Collegiate School in Wellington in New Zealand; and Frank E. Cohee IV of Covenant Christian Academy in Huntsville, Ala.

The top three winners of the Westinghouse Science Talent Search—left to right, John L. Staub, Forrest N. Anderson, and Jennifer Yu-Fe Lin—display their medals at an awards ceremony in March 1994.

Chemistry Olympiad. The United States finished in the top three in the International Chemistry Olympiad, held in Perugia, Italy, with two gold and two silver medals, the highest finish since the United States began competing in 1984. The other top teams were China and Taiwan. Christopher Herzog of Highland Park (N.J.) High School and Daniel Katz of Torrey Pines High School in San Diego were the gold medal winners. David Hutz of Fox Chapel High School in Pittsburgh, Pa., and Robert West of Oak Park High School in Kansas City, Mo., won the silver medals.

Informatics Olympiad. The Fifth International Olympiad in Informatics, a competition in computer programming, was held in October 1993 in Mendoza, Argentina. First, second, and third place finishes were awarded to Slovakia, Romania, and Russia, respectively. The U.S. team placed seventh and consisted of Hal Burch of the Oklahoma School of Science and Mathematics in Oklahoma City; Eric Pabst of East High School in Salt Lake City, Utah; Mehul

Patel of Langham Creek High School in Houston; and Yonah Schmeidler of MIT.

Math Olympiad. The U.S. team finished seventh in the 34th International Mathematical Olympiad, held in Istanbul, Turkey. The top three teams were, respectively, China, Germany, and Bulgaria. Gold medals were won by Andrew Dittmer of Vienna, Va., and Lenny Ng of Chapel Hill, N.C. Wei-Hwa Huang of North Potomac, Md., and Stephen Wang of St. Charles, Ill., won silver medals. Bronze medals went to Jeremy Bem of Ithaca, N.Y., and Tim Chklovski of Minneapolis, Minn.

Physics Olympiad. The 24th annual International Physics Olympiad was held for the first time in the United States in 1993, drawing 201 high school students from 41 nations to Williamsburg, Va. Dean Jens of Ankeny (Iowa) High School won a gold medal. Daniel Schepler of Beavercreek High School in Ohio won a silver medal, and bronze medals went to Hal Burch and Dmitri Linde of Gunn High School in Palo Alto, Calif.

[Rod Such]

Why living things age is poorly understood, but researchers at Southern Methodist University in Dallas have found evidence that a major culprit is oxygen damage to cells. According to their January 1994 report, the Texas researchers found that fruit flies lived 30 percent longer than their normal life span if they were genetically altered to increase the production of two compounds that remove destructive forms of oxygen from the body.

Oxygen and aging. Some biologists have long believed that the aging process is due to cell damage caused by a type of oxygen molecule called a free radical. A free radical is made up of two or more atoms, one of which has one too many or one too few electrons in its outer shell. Some kinds of free radicals are especially harmful, because they react rapidly with biochemicals, including proteins, fats, and even DNA (deoxyribonucleic acid, the molecule of which genes are made). Some biologists thus theorized that free radicals are responsible for the progressive decline in organisms as they get older.

To test that theory, biologists William C. Orr and Rajindar S. Sohal devised an experiment using fruit flies (*Drosophila melanogaster*). The researchers chose to study fruit flies because the insects have a life span of only about two months and because fruit flies are easy to raise in large numbers. The genetic makeup of the fruit fly is also well understood, and researchers can easily insert foreign genes into them.

Orr and Sohal inserted into their fruit flies extra genes that *encode* (direct the manufacture of) superoxide dismutase and catalase. Both compounds are *enzymes* (proteins that cause or speed up chemical reactions). These enzymes convert chemically active forms of oxygen, including free radicals, into inactive forms. The researchers theorized that fruit flies that were given the ability to manufacture more of these enzymes would age less rapidly.

That hypothesis appeared to be correct. The altered flies lived about 30 percent longer than a group of flies that were not given new genes. Moreover, the altered flies were more active than those in the control group, especially at older ages, and they showed fewer signs of damage to the proteins in their cells.

The researchers concluded that the enzymes had slowed the process of aging.

The gene for right and left. One of the genes responsible for determining how an animal embryo evolves from a simple ball of cells into the more complex structure of a fetus was discovered in 1993 by three research teams working independently. The finding, published in December 1993, was the work of teams headed by researchers at Harvard Medical School in Boston; Harvard University in Cambridge, Mass.; and Oxford University in the United Kingdom.

The Harvard and Oxford teams found a group of four related genes in *vertebrates* (animals with backbones). One of the genes appeared to be of key importance in determining orientation in embryos—that is, what will be the organism's top and bottom and its left and right sides. That gene also controls the early development of the central nervous system in mice, the spinal column in zebra fish, and the wings in chickens. The precise functions of the other three genes have yet to be discovered.

The discovery of the gene helped unravel one of the long-standing problems in developmental biology. Since the late 1960's, developmental biologists have suspected that small groups of cells in the embryo send signals to the rest of the embryo to tell it where to form the spine; where to grow limbs such as hands, fingers, and wings; and where to form other body parts. Those cells were first identified by cutting out patches of cells from a chicken embryo and transplanting them to other parts of the embryo. The nature of the signal used by these cells, however, long defied detection. Researchers now believe that the protein encoded by the newly discovered gene may be the signal, or somehow start the signal, which then passes cell by cell to the rest of the embryo.

The Harvard and Oxford researchers gave their gene the whimsical name *Sonic hedgehog*. The first gene to be named hedgehog was discovered in the fruit fly in 1992. Fly embryos without the gene failed to develop normally and looked like balls covered with spiky hairs, somewhat like tiny hedgehogs. The Harvard and Oxford groups used copies of the fruit fly hedgehog gene to look for similar genes in vertebrates.

The researchers found that vertebrate

A snake species found in the Brazilian rain forest is the first member of the colubrid family of snakes to be observed using its tail to lure prey, according to a July 1993 report. When young, the snake has a bright tip on its tail that resembles a worm, and the snake dangles it to attract small lizards and frogs. As the snake grows, it is able to find larger prey, and the tail tip fades to a drab color.

embryonic cells *expressed* (activated) the Sonic hedgehog gene in precisely the pattern found in fruit flies. Certain embryo cells produced the protein, which then passed to neighboring cells, causing them to secrete another set of proteins that passed on to still other cells.

The Harvard and Oxford teams then altered the genetic material in animal embryos so that the gene was turned on in the wrong place or at the wrong time. The results were greatly altered organisms with extra limbs or other deformities. The researchers thus concluded that Sonic hedgehog is a key gene that guides the embryo during its transformation from a sphere of cells into an elongated body with a top and a bottom and left and right limbs.

Memory's cellular signals. A discovery reported in January 1994 by neurophysiologists may help brain researchers better understand how nerve cells store memory. Erin M. Schuman and Daniel V. Madison of Stanford Medical School in Stanford, Calif., found that when nerve cells in the brain send signals to one another, they affect the signaling

between neighboring cells by releasing nitric oxide, a highly reactive gas.

The brain is made up of nerve cells that send electrical and chemical signals to one another through tiny regions of contact known as synapses. In the early 1970's, researchers discovered one facet of how nerve cells store memories and are responsible for learning. The researchers electrically stimulated nerve cells in a part of the brain called the hippocampus. With repeated electrical jolts, the chemical and electrical signals that passed between the nerve cells became progressively stronger. Moreover, even when the cells were not stimulated for several hours, they still "remembered" that they had been stimulated. Researchers found evidence of that when they discovered the cells' response to renewed electrical jolts was immediately as strong as before.

This was exactly the type of behavior expected for cells involved in memory and learning. Repeated stimulation reinforced the signaling between cells, creating patterns that were progressively easier for the cells to transmit. It is for this reason that repeating a task aids in learning and remembering.

Armed with the earlier findings, the California researchers studied nerve cells in the rat hippocampus. When they stimulated a pair of nerve cells, the signal across the synapse between them became stronger, as expected. The surprise came upon examination of nearby synaptic signals. They too became stronger.

The scientists realized that the stimulated synapse must have released a substance that spread to nearby synapses, reinforcing their signals. The substance proved to be nitric oxide, a gas known since 1991 to act as a chemical messenger between nerve cells. Neuroscientists said that these findings may mean that the brain does not store a specific bit of memory in one location, but instead stores it in a group of closely clustered synapses that act together.

Preventing self-pollination. Scientists in 1994 discovered a key step in how some plants prevent self-pollination. Molecular biologist Te-Hui Kao and co-workers at Pennsylvania State University in University Park reported in February that the flowers of some plants manufacture a compound capable of identifying and rejecting the plant's own pollen, a trait called self-incompatibility. In some ways, self-incompatability resembles the mechanisms the human body uses to distinguish its own cells from transplanted or foreign cells.

In flowering plants, seed production begins when a pollen grain lands on the *stigma,* the flattened area of the *pistil* (the female part of the flower). The pollen grain then germinates, forming a long tube that grows down through the style, the stalklike part of the pistil, to reach the egg-bearing ovary. The pollen tube then releases sperm cells that fuse with egg cells to form embryonic seeds.

In certain plant species, including some petunias, tobaccos, and mustards, the female part of the flower always rejects pollen grains produced on the same plant. This trait promotes cross-pollination, in which a plant's egg cells fuse with sperm cells from another plant. Because cross-pollinated seeds contain genetic material from two different parents, the resulting plants inherit traits from two parents and are more vigorous than single-parent plants.

Researchers have long known that self-incompatibility in some plants is controlled by a gene known as the S locus. In a natural population, the gene takes many different forms, and plants with the same form reject each other's pollen. But exactly how the gene leads to pollen rejection mystified scientists.

To learn more, biologists in the mid-1980's created copies of the S locus gene taken from mustard, petunia, and tobacco plants. The scientists discovered that the gene directs the manufacture of an enzyme that breaks down ribonucleic acid (RNA). RNA is a key player in the transfer of genetic information from the nucleus to the rest of the cell. Scientists named the newly discovered enzyme S-RNase.

In their February 1994 report, the Penn State scientists described experiments in which they transferred the gene for one form of S-RNase into a petunia plant that lacked that form of the gene. After the transfer, the scientists discovered that the petunia plant's pistils contained high levels of the transferred S-RNase. They also found that the plant rejected pollen that carried the gene for that form of S-RNase.

In later work completed in March 1994, the Penn State group altered the S locus gene so that it produced a form of S-RNase that was unable to break down RNA. When the altered gene was transferred into a plant, the plant could no longer prevent self-pollination.

The scientists concluded that the petunia and related plants avoid self-pollination by producing S-RNase in the pistils. The enzyme recognizes pollen tubes containing the same form of the S locus gene and kills those tubes by destroying their RNA.

How plants "see" blue. University of Pennsylvania researchers may have isolated a gene that enables plants to detect blue light. Their results, reported in November 1993, gave clues about the molecular mechanisms that plants and other organisms use to perceive light.

Light affects plant growth in dramatic ways. Exposure to various levels of light from the blue part of the visible spectrum (defined as light with wavelengths between 400 and 500 nanometers) causes plants to flower, grow leaves, halt stem growth, and change in other ways. Other natural responses by the plant

A reconstruction made of bones and skins found in Vietnam shows the first new large mammal discovered since 1937. Biologists confirmed that the animal represents a new genus, *Pseudoryx*, in summer 1993. After months of searching, the scientists found a live *Pseudoryx* calf in Vietnam in June 1994.

Biotechnology

See Genetics

are triggered by light from the red end of the spectrum.

Plant cells absorb light through molecules called photoreceptors. In the 1960's, researchers identified a plant photoreceptor, called the phytochrome, that is specifically responsible for sensing red and far-red light. The location of a photoreceptor for blue light, however, remained elusive. Some scientists dubbed it "cryptochrome," because this photoreceptor stayed cryptically hidden.

The breakthrough, reported by botanists Margaret Ahmad and Anthony R. Cashmore, was the result of research techniques based on genetics, molecular biology, and physiology. First the researchers examined 8,000 specimens of a small weed species called *Arabidopsis thaliana* that had a gene fragment called T-DNA in random locations in the plants' genes. T-DNA has the ability to insert itself into a gene, which causes the gene to mutate, thereby becoming a marker. Researchers use T-DNA to isolate and identify the DNA sequence of an abnormal gene.

Ahmad and Cashmore assumed that

if the T-DNA fragment lodged in or near the gene for the sought-after photoreceptor, the plant photoreceptor gene might not function normally, and the plant might not show the usual response to blue light. So the researchers screened the plants to find those that did not stop their stem growth in the normal fashion when exposed to continuous blue light.

The researchers then examined the genes in these abnormal plants. By comparing the location of the T-DNA fragment in the abnormal plant with the corresponding genetic material in the unaltered wild plants, the scientists tracked down the gene responsible for producing a light-activated protein with a pigment that absorbs blue light. The researchers said that protein is likely to be the elusive blue light photoreceptor.

[Daniel J. Cosgrove]

See also AGRICULTURE; GENETICS; MEDICAL RESEARCH. In the Special Reports section, see EXPLORING THE MYSTERIES OF THE RETROVIRUS; CLONING RESEARCH ON THE MARCH. In WORLD BOOK, see BIOLOGY.

Books About Science

Here are 20 important new science books suitable for the general reader. They have been selected from books published in 1993 and 1994.

Anthropology. *The Origin of Modern Humans* by Roger Lewin summarizes the scientific debate about the origins of human beings, drawing on the fossil, genetic, and anthropological evidence that has contributed to scientists' evolving understanding of how human beings came to be the way they are. (Scientific American Library, 1993. 204 pp. illus. $32.95)

Astronomy. *Newton's Clock: Chaos in the Solar System* by Ivars Peterson tells of the search to understand the motions of Earth's moon and the planets against the starry background. It is also the story of the limitations of mathematics in predicting irregularities observed in the motions of planets, asteroids, and planetary rings. Peterson explores chaos theory to show why such motions are not always predictable. (Freeman, 1993. 317 pp. $22.95)

Biology. *Broadsides from the Other Orders: A Book of Bugs* by Sue Hubbell. Hubbell, a beekeeper and naturalist, provides information on the characteristics and behavior of a wide range of insects, including butterflies, midges and gnats, ladybugs, daddy longlegs, black flies, water spiders, silverfish, katydids, dragonflies, gypsy moths, and camel crickets. (Random House, 1993. 276 pp. illus. $23)

Life Cycles: Reflections of an Evolutionary Biologist by John T. Bonner examines the life cycles of organisms to give readers a more cohesive and comprehensive view of current biological knowledge. Bonner writes of his own interest and research on slime molds and how that research has contributed to his understanding of life cycles. (Princeton University Press, 1993. 209 pp. illus. $19.95)

Signs of Life: The Language and Meanings of DNA by scientist and educator Robert Pollack argues that DNA (deoxyribonucleic acid), the molecule of which genes are made, can be read as a 3-billion-year-old historical text that governs all of life's operations. He explains how biologists and medical researchers are beginning to decipher DNA's messages. (Houghton Mifflin, 1994. 212 pp. $19.95)

Chemistry. *The Norton History of Chemistry* by William H. Brock examines the origins of the science of chemistry and traces its history from alchemy to atomic theory. Included are discussions of methods of teaching chemistry and the applications of chemistry to the arts and to manufacturing. (Norton, 1993. 744 pp. illus. $35)

Cosmology. *Black Holes and Baby Universes and Other Essays* by Stephen W. Hawking contains essays written by the British mathematician and physicist between 1976 and 1992. It also contains an interview with Hawking. The essays reveal Hawking's belief that the universe is governed by an order that can be understood. (Bantam, 1993. 182 pp. $21.95)

The Light at the Edge of the Universe: Leading Cosmologists on the Brink of a Scientific Revolution by Michael D. Lemonick explores new discoveries about the distribution of galaxies in the universe and the finding that much of the matter in the universe is unseen *dark matter* (matter that does not give off light). The author shows how these findings are altering theories about the origin and ultimate fate of the universe. (Villard, 1993. 325 pp. illus. $24)

Through a Universe Darkly: A Cosmic Tale of Ancient Ethers, Dark Matter, and the Fate of the Universe by Marcia Bartusiak places the story of the centuries-long quest to understand the composition of the heavens in a historical context that leads from the ancient Greeks to Nicolaus Copernicus, Sir Isaac Newton, and Albert Einstein. The second half of the book is devoted to the discovery that as much as 90 percent of the matter in the universe could be dark matter. Bartusiak discusses the various theories that have been advanced to explain the composition of dark matter. (HarperCollins, 1993. 383 pp. illus. $27.50)

General science. *The Astonishing Hypothesis: The Scientific Search for the Soul* by British biologist Francis H. C. Crick, who shared the Nobel Prize in physiology or medicine with James D. Watson in 1962 for their model of the molecular structure of DNA. Crick equates the soul with human consciousness, which he considers from the standpoint of how the human brain processes visual information. In order to understand human consciousness, Crick believes we must understand how nerve cells behave and how they interact. (Scribner's, 1994. 317 pp. $25)

Cranks, Quarks, and the Cosmos by Jeremy Bernstein. Bernstein, a physicist and a science writer for *The New Yorker* magazine for more than 30 years, has assembled this book of 16 essays that reveals science as the "experience of recognizable human beings." Bernstein also tells the story of how he became a science writer. The first essay, "How Can We Be Sure that Albert Einstein Was Not a Crank," discusses the problems of distinguishing truly original scientific works from those of cranks. (BasicBooks, 1993. 220 pp. $23)

A Positron Named Priscilla: Scientific Discovery at the Frontier, the third in a series published annually by the National Academy of Sciences, contains 10 chapters that report on the research of scientists at the leading edge of scientific research. The work discussed includes new methods of probing the sun's interior, the science of earthquake prediction, and the results of the Magellan spacecraft mission to the planet Venus. (National Academy Press, 1994. 348 pp. illus. $29.95)

Geology. *To a Rocky Moon: A Geologist's History of Lunar Exploration* by Don E. Wilhelms provides a detailed history of lunar science, emphasizing how much has been learned about the moon from the United States space program and describing how scientists discovered what moon rocks are made of. (University of Arizona Press, 1993. 477 pp. illus. $29.95)

Natural history. *The Last Panda* by George B. Schaller is the first detailed study of pandas in the wild. Schaller studied the lives, courtships, and deaths of pandas for 4½ years in the forests of the Wolong panda preserve in China. With only about 1,000 pandas remaining in their dwindling native habitat, Schaller asks whether this extraordinary creature can survive its own popularity. (University of Chicago Press, 1993. 291 pp. illus. $24.95)

A Natural History of Shells by Geerat J. Vermeij offers a fascinating biological view of shells as products of living organisms, exploring shells as structures, homes, vehicles, and prisons for their occupants. Vermeij shows how shells function, how they are made, and how they evolved, and he reveals the won-

ders of economy and construction that can be seen in them. (Princeton University Press, 1993. 207 pp. illus. $29.95)

Visions of Caliban: On Chimpanzees and People by Dale Peterson and Jane Goodall examines the relationship between chimpanzees and human beings. The book, which notes that the first live chimpanzee was brought to Europe in 1640, describes how chimpanzees today are faring in the wild, and explores the ethical issues associated with their treatment in captivity. (Houghton Mifflin, 1993. 367 pp. illus. $22.95)

Physics. *The End of Physics: The Myth of a Unified Theory* by David Lindley. Much of contemporary particle physics is devoted to developing a final "theory of everything," but Lindley asks whether such efforts are worthwhile, because the resulting theories cannot be subjected to experimental verification. According to Lindley, such approaches have redefined physics as a branch of aesthetics instead of an experimental science. (BasicBooks, 1993. 275 pp. $25)

Public health. *The Forgotten Plague: How the Battle Against Tuberculosis Was Won—and Lost* by Frank Ryan describes the steps leading to the development of effective treatments for tuberculosis and the recent epidemic of antibiotic-resistant strains. (Little, Brown, 1993. 460 pp. illus. $24.95)

Technology. *A Scientist in the City* by James S. Trefil describes the scientific discoveries that have shaped the cities we live in and that will continue to alter the cities of the future. Trefil maintains that the ability to manipulate atoms, the ability to unlock stored energy, and the ability to store and transmit information electronically have had and will continue to have a profound impact on the urban landscape. (Doubleday, 1994. 266 pp. illus. $23.95)

Up the Infinite Corridor: MIT and the Technical Imagination by Fred Hapgood describes the pioneering work being undertaken by engineers at the Massachusetts Institute of Technology in Cambridge. Included are such projects as the development of artificial knees and artificial retinas. Hapgood also provides an interesting account of how engineers think about problems and how they work toward solutions. (Addison-Wesley, 1993. 203 pp. $22.95)

[William Goodrich Jones]

Botany
See Biology

Two teams of chemists in February 1994 announced they had *synthesized* (chemically assembled) the anticancer drug taxol. Taxol is a complex molecule, and chemists hailed the reports as stunning achievements.

Creating taxol. Natural taxol comes from the bark of the rare Pacific yew tree. The compound has been approved in the United States as a drug treatment for ovarian cancer, and the drug has also shown promise against breast cancer and lung cancer. Because the number of yew trees that can be harvested is limited, chemists have been working hard to create taxol in the laboratory.

Chemist Robert A. Holton of Florida State University in Tallahassee headed one of the groups that synthesized taxol. The other group was led by chemist Kyriacou C. Nicolaou of Scripps Research Institute in La Jolla, Calif.

The two research teams used different approaches to assemble the molecule, which consists of four rings of carbon atoms with a number of small *side chains* (chains of atoms) attached to the rings. Holton's group started with camphor, a molecule containing one carbon ring. Through a series of chemical reactions, the scientists added chains of carbon atoms to the camphor molecule, and then connected the ends of the chains to form rings. Finally, the researchers added taxol's chemical side chains at the proper points along the rings.

Nicolaou's group started by making the two larger six-carbon rings of the taxol molecule separately from chains of carbon atoms. Then they subjected nitrogen- and oxygen-containing side groups on the two rings to a long series of chemical reactions to form a third ring. Finally, they built up a fourth ring made of carbon and oxygen from another carbon chain, opened up a fifth ring that had formed during their reactions, and attached a complex group of carbon, oxygen, and nitrogen atoms to one of the remaining four rings.

Experts said the two taxol-production methods were probably too complicated to be used commercially. Nevertheless, the procedures might help chemists create new drugs with structures similar to taxol but with greater anticancer properties and fewer harmful side effects.

New superhard substance. A new material that may be harder than diamond was reported in July 1993 by researchers at Harvard University in Cambridge, Mass. The new material is a *crystal* (tightly organized three-dimensional array) of repeated units of a molecule called beta-C_3N_4. Beta-C_3N_4 is a form of carbon nitride, a compound with three carbon atoms and four nitrogen atoms. Because the atoms in crystals are arranged very compactly, crystals tend to be very hard. Diamond is also a crystal, one made up solely of carbon atoms.

In 1989, physicist Marvin L. Cohen at the University of California at Berkeley had predicted that beta-C_3N_4 would be harder than diamond. Cohen's calculations had shown that the *bond lengths* (distances between atoms) in crystalline beta-C_3N_4 would be even shorter than those in diamond. The shorter the bond lengths, the harder the substance.

After Cohen's report, chemists tried making beta-C_3N_4. The task proved difficult, because it required joining nitrogen molecules to carbon. Nitrogen molecules, which contain two nitrogen atoms, resist reacting with other molecules.

Harvard chemist Charles M. Lieber and his colleagues solved the problem. They used a powerful laser to *vaporize* (turn into a gas) a solid form of carbon called graphite. At the same time, they shot nitrogen molecules through a special nozzle. As the nitrogen molecules left the nozzle, radio waves split them into individual atoms. Some of the nitrogen atoms combined with carbon atoms from the vaporized graphite to form a microscopic film on a wafer of silicon.

Lieber's team was able to show that the film consisted of beta-C_3N_4. However, the chemists could not evaluate the hardness of the substance because the film contained too many impurities. They said the next step was to improve their production technique. If beta-C_3N_4 does turn out to be harder than diamond, it could have many uses, such as superhard coatings for machine tools.

Element 106 named. Element 106, the artificially created element that contains 106 protons, was given the official name of *seaborgium* in March 1994 by the American Chemical Society, an organization of chemists and chemical engineers based in Washington, D.C. The name honored chemist Glenn T. Seaborg, who helped discover a number of elements, including plutonium in 1940.

Microscopic tubes made of *peptides* (fragments of proteins) were created by California chemists, according to a November 1993 report. The tiny tubes formed when an alkaline solution of peptides was made acidic. Because proteins are a basic component of living things, scientists said the peptide tubes could someday be used in living cells, perhaps as channels for delivering drugs.

Unusually stable isotopes found.

The creation of two surprisingly stable *isotopes* (forms) of seaborgium was announced by a team of Russian and U.S. scientists in September 1993. Isotopes of an element contain the same number of protons but different numbers of neutrons. The new finding hinted that there may be undiscovered, superheavy elements that are relatively stable.

The seaborgium isotopes were created by physicist Yuri A. Lazarev and his colleagues at the Joint Institute for Nuclear Research in Russia. The scientists smashed smaller atoms in a *particle accelerator* (a device that speeds particles to very high energies). Some of the particles fused to form the new seaborgium isotopes. A research group at Lawrence Livermore National Laboratory in California provided the instruments used to detect the isotopes.

The only previously known isotope of seaborgium contained 157 neutrons and disintegrated in less than a second through radioactive decay. In contrast, the two new isotopes contained 159 and 160 neutrons and survived for as long as one minute. The greater stability of the heavier isotopes surprised chemists because heavier isotopes tend to be less stable than lighter ones.

A total of 109 elements are currently known to scientists. Only 92 of them are found in nature. Many of the rest have been detected only in laboratories and are unstable, decaying within seconds. But some theoretical physicists have predicted the existence of an "island of stability" around elements with about 114 protons. The unexpected stability of the heavy seaborgium isotopes suggests that an island of stability may indeed exist. If so, chemists say, a range of new and possibly useful elements waits to be discovered.

Microscopic tubes made of *peptides* (fragments of proteins) were unveiled by scientists in November 1993. Other classes of *nanotubes* (microscopic tubes) made up of carbon atoms or the mineral zeolite have sparked much excitement among chemists in the 1990's because of the tubes' unusual structures and their wide range of potential applications.

The peptide nanotubes were created by chemist M. Reza Ghadiri and his colleagues at the Scripps Research Institute. The researchers prepared rings of eight peptide molecules and placed them in an alkaline solution. When the researchers then added acid to the solution, the peptide rings stacked themselves together to form nanotubes. The nanotubes had extremely narrow diameters—about 0.8 nanometers (31 billionths of an inch).

The discovery was interesting for two reasons. First, the Scripps team could adjust the lengths and diameters of the nanotubes simply by changing the ingredients in the solution and the conditions of the reaction. This tight control could pave the way for peptide nanotubes tailor-made for specific applications. Second, because proteins are a common component of cells, peptide nanotubes should be compatible with living tissue. Thus, they could possibly serve as channels for admitting drugs or other compounds past cell membranes.

Fullerenes block HIV. Carbon molecules in the shape of hollow balls can be chemically modified to block a key step in the reproduction of the human immunodeficiency virus (HIV), which causes AIDS (acquired immunodeficiency syndrome). A group of researchers at two branches of the University of California announced that finding in July 1993. The report was the first to indicate that the carbon molecules, called *fullerenes*, may have practical uses in living organisms.

The discovery involved *buckyballs*—soccer-ball-shaped fullerene molecules. Researchers at the University of California's San Francisco campus had noticed that a buckyball is exactly the right size to fit into the hollow pocket of a key HIV protein called HIV protease. HIV protease is an *enzyme* (a protein that carries out a chemical reaction) that helps the virus reproduce inside human cells. The hollow pocket of HIV protease, known as its active site, must be empty for the enzyme to function. If the site is blocked, the virus cannot reproduce. Thus, the researchers reasoned, buckyballs injected into cells might be able to stop HIV from reproducing.

First, though, the researchers had

A *porous metal*—a metal filled with tiny holes—is lightweight yet strong and could find uses in many U.S. industries, according to scientists at Sandia National Laboratory in New Mexico. In late 1993, Sandia scientists planned to begin making porous metals on a large scale. Experts said the materials could be especially useful for aerospace designs, which typically require lightweight components.

to get buckyballs to dissolve in water, which makes up much of the substance of living cells. Chemist Fred Wudl of the school's Santa Barbara campus made a modified buckyball that carried chemical side chains that made it water-soluble. Researchers at Emory University in Atlanta, Ga., then tested the modified buckyball and confirmed that it inhibited HIV reproduction in infected cells.

The researchers cautioned that the modified buckyballs are not AIDS drugs, because no one knows whether they can safely prevent symptoms of AIDS in human patients. However, the scientists said their study may lead to the development of other fullerene molecules that may prove effective against AIDS as well as other diseases.

New superconductivity record? A new material that appears to be *superconducting* (capable of carrying an electric current without resistance) at a temperature of about –23 °C (–10 °F) was reported by a group of French researchers in December 1993. If further tests verify the results, the researchers will have achieved the highest known temperature for a superconducting material, a dramatic jump from the previous high temperature of –140 °C (–220 °F).

The material was created by a team led by materials scientist Michel Laguës of the Centre National Recherches Scientifique in Paris. Like many other superconducting substances, the new material was made of layers of atoms. Researchers had already noticed that the more layers of copper and oxygen atoms in a material, the higher the temperature at which it is superconducting. So the French scientists painstakingly built up a material consisting of eight copper-oxygen layers, sandwiched between nine layers of bismuth, calcium, oxygen, and strontium atoms.

The scientists said the new material showed virtually no electrical resistance when cooled to –23 °C. However, materials with complex structures sometimes give false indications of superconductivity, so the researchers said they needed to perform more tests before they could confirm that their material was superconducting.   [Gordon Graff]

In WORLD BOOK, see CHEMISTRY.

Computers and Electronics

The first computers based on the Power-PC microprocessor were unveiled in March 1994 by Apple Computer, Incorporated, of Cupertino, Calif. The introduction of the new microprocessor set the stage for a showdown in the computer industry, pitting some of the industry's largest companies against each other.

The PowerPC chip. The microprocessor, or "brain" of the personal computer, is the device that performs the calculations and other operations required by software programs. Microprocessors, which are also called computer chips, consist of millions of minute circuits etched onto tiny squares, or chips, of silicon. Microprocessors control the operations of all kinds of devices besides computers—from videocassette recorders and calculators to cars and washing machines.

The two dominant producers of microprocessors are Intel Corporation of Santa Clara, Calif., and Motorola Corporation of Schaumburg, Ill. Intel microprocessors and microprocessors based on Intel designs are used in PC's, a type of computer first introduced in 1981 by International Business Machines Corporation (IBM), which is headquartered in Armonk, N.Y. The Motorola processors are used in Macintosh computers, produced by Apple Computer. PC's and Macintoshes are incompatible—that is, each has different requirements and specifications for software. Computer software makers typically design their programs for one system or the other.

Intel-based microprocessors are the dominant type used in computers, with more than 85 percent of the millions of personal computers worldwide based on Intel chips. Since the early 1990's, IBM, Apple, and Motorola had worked in partnership to develop the PowerPC microprocessor, hoping to put an end to Intel's worldwide dominance of the microprocessor industry.

Computers using the new PowerPC chip can run software written for both PC's and Macintoshes, as well as "native software," which is developed specifically for the new microprocessor. According to the PowerPC's designers and marketers, the new chip is also faster and cheaper than a comparable Intel chip.

The PowerPC was designed to take advantage of a relatively new technology called RISC (*reduced instruction set computing*), which permits computers to process more than one instruction at a time. Because RISC chips can combine computing functions and calculations, the chips are faster than those based on an older technology called CISC (*complex instruction set computing*). Makers of the PowerPC chip claim that the microprocessor offers anywhere from 1.4 to 4.7 times the performance of the most powerful Intel microprocessor, Pentium. Pentium, introduced in 1993, is based upon CISC technology.

The least powerful and least expensive PowerPC microprocessor has 2.8 million transistors arranged on a chip the size of a small fingernail. The Pentium microprocessor has 3 million transistors on a chip the size of a postage stamp.

Generally, the greater the space on which the transistors are placed, the more power they need. The smaller space requirements of the PowerPC

chip offers the advantages of cutting the computer's energy consumption and reducing the amount of heat it produces.

PowerPC microprocessors were priced at around $450, several hundred dollars less than comparable Pentium microprocessors. According to its makers, the PowerPC costs less than the Pentium chip because it works in a simpler fashion and is, therefore, easier to produce. While Pentium and other CISC chips must handle an entire process at once, RISC chips break problems down into smaller tasks.

Because the PowerPC microprocessors cost less, computer manufacturers are able to offer PowerPC-based computers at lower prices than similarly equipped Pentium-based machines. Depending upon the features included in the machines, Power Macintoshes cost from $2,000 to $4,500. Similarly equipped Pentium-based personal computers cost up to $1,000 more than the Power Macintoshes.

The initial market for Power Macintoshes was expected to be people who use large amounts of graphic images, in

PowerPC computing
In March 1994, Apple Computer unveiled the Power Macintosh, *right,* the latest model in its line of Macintosh personal computers. The computer, which can be used to run software designed for Macintosh or IBM-compatible machines, was the first to use the new PowerPC microprocessing chip, *below.* The chip was designed jointly by Apple, IBM, and Motorola.

fields such as magazine and newspaper layout and design as well as desktop publishing.

Industry experts applauded the speed of the Power Macintosh, but cited some drawbacks. The machine's great power is achieved only when running software that has been created for the machine or has been revised to take advantage of the PowerPC chip. Only a few such native programs were available when the Power Macintosh was introduced. Using older Macintosh software, the Power Mac performed as well as the standard Mac, but no faster. And many DOS and Windows programs ran slower on the Power Mac than on IBM-compatible machines.

By the time the PowerPC was introduced, it was becoming clear that Pentium-based personal computers had failed to live up to Intel's sales expectations. There were several reasons for the lack of interest in the Pentium. Chief among them was the continued strong sales and low prices of personal computers based upon Intel's earlier microprocessor design—the 80486, usually called 486, chip. The 486-based personal computers were by far the leading sellers in the computer marketplace in 1993 and 1994. As many as 10 million machines were sold to businesses, schools, and home users. The growth in the home computer marketplace was, in fact, the brightest spot in the computer and consumer electronics industries.

Analysts believed it would take a year or more to know whether or not the Power Macintosh would succeed in restoring Apple to its position of strength in the competitive computer marketplace. The success of the product was believed crucial to Apple Computer, which has suffered financially from poor sales of its existing Macintosh line, as well as the less-than-successful introduction of new products, such as its Newton MessagePad.

Personal digital assistants. Apple's Newton MessagePad, introduced in August 1993, was the first in a new product line known as PDA's (*personal digital assistants*). The Fort Worth, Tex., based Tandy Corporation introduced its own PDA, the Zoomer, in 1993 as well. Typically about the size of a paperback book, most PDA's are capable of performing fairly sophisticated computerlike tasks,

including word processing and linking written commands to stored files of information, sending faxes and electronic mail over phone lines, and receiving wireless pager messages.

One of the most dramatic features of the PDA's is handwriting recognition. Users write on the PDA screen with a stylus and the letters are, at least in theory, recognized by software built into the PDA and then translated into print.

Newton's handwriting recognition feature was the product's most highly touted feature. It also proved to be the machine's greatest vulnerability. Handwriting recognition is a fairly new technology, and it became clear after Newton's introduction that the $700 PDA had difficulty recognizing handwritten input, often wildly mistranslating even simple words, a fact the popular press made light of, damaging Newton's—and Apple's—credibility.

Although initial sales of the PDA were strong, sales figures dropped quickly. By the end of 1993, Newton was considered one of the computer industry's technical failures of the year.

In early 1994, Apple introduced a new, lower-priced Newton with additional functions, longer battery life, and enlarged memory capacity. The existing software was updated to solve some of the problems with the earlier model, particularly the device's handwriting recognition capability, and a much wider range of new software was introduced. These measures, however, failed to increase the public's interest in the PDA.

Other PDA's continued to attract attention. But most industry analysts said that the technology on which PDA's are based needs a few more years of development before the products will finally achieve widespread acceptance.

3DO game machine. Another new addition to the consumer electronics scene was the 3DO game machine. Produced by 3DO Incorporated of Redwood City, Calif., the REAL 3DO Interactive Multiplayer was designed to deliver higher quality and more interesting game and educational programming than was available from other game devices, but at a lower cost than a personal computer.

The difference between the 3DO and other game machines was that the 3DO incorporated CD-ROM (*compact disc-read only memory*) technology. Seamlessly combining graphics, animation, video, and text, CD-ROM discs are capable of carrying far more information than the traditional video game cartridge. It was hoped that the 3DO could take advantage of this capability to run games and educational programming with higher quality graphics and animation, larger "worlds" to explore, more levels, and graphics that approached the quality of television pictures.

Backed by consumer electronics giants, including American Telephone and Telegraph Company (AT&T) of Parsippany, N.J., and Matsushita Electronics of Japan, 3DO was expected to be the consumer electronics story of the year if not the decade. The public, however, failed to embrace the new machine. The retail price was dropped from $700 to around $500 in spring 1994. Even after the reduction, the price was perceived as too high, and there was little public response. Some of the machine's supporters, including AT&T, pulled back their commitment.

Users acknowledged that the 3DO hardware was more than adequate. Besides games, the machine could play music CD's, Kodak photo CD's, and, with an attachment, motion-picture CD's. Critics suggested, however, that the available software, mostly the usual chase-type games, failed to live up to the promise of the 3DO. The public seemingly could find little reason to buy new hardware when the available software was unimaginative and failed to take full advantage of the CD-ROM technology.

Multimedia CD-ROM's. Other types of multimedia became one of the liveliest aspects of the software industry in 1993 and 1994. By mid-1994, the growth in multimedia computing had led to a flood of products, with most of the major software releases incorporating multimedia features.

One popular multimedia title was *Myst,* released in December 1993 by Broderbund Software of San Rafael, Calif. The $60 CD-ROM product, available for both Macintosh and IBM-compatible personal computers, placed the

The REAL 3DO Interactive Multiplayer, developed by 3DO Incorporated and sold by Panasonic, was designed to deliver sharper graphics and faster animation than other video game systems. The 3DO, which hit the market in October 1993, has a CD-ROM (*compact disc-read only memory*) drive. It can play music CD's and educational CD-ROM programs as well as games.

A television set with a 13-inch screen but a thickness of only 9.9 centimeters (3.9 inches) was introduced by Panasonic in January 1994. In conventional TV's, a beam of electrons coming from behind the screen illuminates it. To cover every inch of the screen, the beam source must be positioned several inches behind it. In contrast, the new Flat Vision TV uses nearly 10,000 separate electron beams, each of which can be placed much closer to the screen. The Flat Vision TV was to become available in 1995.

player in a strange and mysterious world, an island filled with extraordinary buildings and technologies. Users exploring the island encountered animation, videos, and sound in an environment that changed and responded to their actions.

In another development, IBM announced in May 1994 that the company had devised a way to increase CD-ROM storage capacity tenfold. The technology, which takes a new approach to how data stored on a CD is read, makes it possible to fit an entire motion picture on a single disc.

Information superhighway. Many of the new home computers sold in 1994 were equipped with a *modem,* the device that enables a computer to transmit and receive information over telephone lines. This capability for telecommunications allows computer users to communicate with each other, with other remote computers, and with huge databases and libraries worldwide.

Such on-line services form the bulk of the traffic on the growing "information

superhighway," which will ultimately link computers and televisions in businesses, institutions, and houses into one gigantic electronic network. The growth of the information superhighway exploded during 1993 and 1994, with estimates of up to 20 million users taking part in on-line activities at any one time.

The spine of the information superhighway is the Internet—a network linking computers in colleges and universities, businesses, government offices, and other institutions. Begun as a military communications system designed to survive a nuclear attack, the Internet was eventually opened to the public. Its population of users grew so fast that experts claim to have lost count at about 15 million. Traffic on the Internet increased at a rate that often strained the system's resources, slowing access times and clogging data networks just as increased traffic can cause jams and delays on real highways. Because of the Internet traffic jams, many computer users paid a private company, called a gatekeeper, for easier access.

Computers and Electronics Continued

Consumer and commercial networks also grew rapidly in 1993 and 1994, leading to even more traffic and increased delays in obtaining information. America Online of Vienna, Va., for example, acquired as many as 50,000 new users per month during 1994. Apologizing for problems created by the flood of users, the company's president announced that the system was delaying the introduction of new services and postponing further efforts to expand the customer base.

Industry experts said that during the next two to three decades, investment by government and business in the "information infrastructure," including telephone and cable television lines, is expected to become a major undertaking, aimed at making movement on the information superhighway smoother and more efficient. (In the Special Reports section, see GEARING UP FOR THE INFORMATION SUPERHIGHWAY.)

Teledesic launched. A fleet of 840 satellites may eventually relay much of the data on the information superhighway. That was the vision of Bill Gates, chief executive officer of Microsoft Corporation of Redmond, Wash., the world's largest software company, and Craig McCaw, head of McCaw Cellular of Kirkland, Wash. The businessmen announced in early 1994 the creation of Teledesic, a company devoted to the satellite project. The two men, considered giants of the computer and telecommunications industries, said they formed their partnership in order to extend the information superhighway around the globe.

By mid-1994, observers said it was unclear when Teledesic would begin launching satellites, or even if the company would receive government permission to do so. It was clear, however, that the information superhighway was becoming a big business, more important to some than the data that moves along it. [Keith Ferrell]

In the Special Reports section, see WELCOME TO THE VIRTUAL WORLD. In the World Book Supplement section, see COMPUTER CHIP. In WORLD BOOK, see COMPUTER; ELECTRONICS; TELECOMMUNICATION.

Conservation

In 1993 and 1994, an important topic for American conservation biologists was the pending reauthorization of the United States Endangered Species Act of 1973. Scientists believed that the outcome would define the nation's commitment to conserving wildlife diversity for years to come.

The 20-year-old act, written to reflect conservation views current in the 1970's, focused on protecting plants and animals on a case-by-case basis—after a species' numbers had dwindled to near extinction. In 1994, many conservation scientists favored a broader approach, one that seeks to protect large areas of an ecosystem while its animal and plant populations are still plentiful. One revision of the Endangered Species Act introduced in 1993 incorporated this idea. As of mid-1994, however, a congressional showdown on the issue was looming.

Another topic of contention was whether the act should be revised to strike a balance between protecting a species and protecting the property rights of those whose lands harbor the endangered plant or animal. Lawmakers in October 1993 defeated a proposal to compensate landowners for financial losses suffered because a protected species lives on their property. Proponents of the bill nonetheless promised to fight for the inclusion of compensation provisions when the U.S. House of Representatives begins debating versions of the reauthorization bill, possibly by the end of 1994.

Ultraviolet risk to amphibians. Increased levels of ultraviolet radiation may be one of the causes of a worldwide decline in some toad, frog, and salamander populations, according to a March 1994 report by researchers at Oregon State University in Corvallis. Biologists began noticing an alarming and mysterious decrease in some amphibian populations in the mid-1980's. Some species completely disappeared even from areas where the natural habitat appears to be undisturbed by human development.

Biologist Andrew R. Blaustein and his colleagues theorized that exposure to high levels of ultraviolet radiation from the sun could be implicated in the amphibian declines. Since the mid-1970's, scientists have believed that chemical compounds formed by various human activities are capable of breaking down the layer of ozone in Earth's upper atmosphere. Ozone is a form of oxygen. In the upper atmosphere, the ozone layer shields Earth from 95 to 99 percent of the sun's harmful ultraviolet rays, making life on the planet possible. A vast area of ozone depletion has been detected each year above Antarctica, but less is known about possible damage to the ozone layer above other areas.

To find out if ozone depletion had played a role in the amphibian deaths, the Oregon State team conducted laboratory experiments with eggs from three species of amphibians that normally lay their eggs in shallow water exposed to sunlight. The researchers shielded some of the eggs with ultraviolet-absorbing filters, and they left other eggs exposed to direct sunlight.

Nearly all the eggs of one species, the Pacific tree frog, hatched whether they were shielded or not. The researchers noted that in the wild, the Pacific tree frog had not suffered population losses.

The researchers found that only 50 to 60 percent of the eggs of the two other species, the Cascades frog and Western toad, hatched when exposed to unfiltered sunlight. Both species are among those with greatly reduced populations and are candidates for designation as threatened species. When the researchers shielded these eggs with ultraviolet-absorbing filters, between 70 and 85 percent of the eggs hatched.

The scientists then examined the eggs to discover why those of the Pacific tree frog seemed better able to withstand exposure to sunlight. They found that the eggs of the Pacific tree frog contained high levels of photolyase, a biochemical known to repair radiation damage to DNA (deoxyribonucleic acid, the molecule that genes are made of). Genes are responsible for a cell's structure and function. Radiation damage to the DNA could thus prevent an egg from developing into a tadpole. The scientists found that photolyase levels in the eggs of the Cascades frog and Western toad were only one-sixth to one-third as high as in the Pacific tree frog.

A Java rhinoceros, which some biologists consider the world's most threatened large mammal, takes its own picture as it steps on a camouflaged pad connected to a hidden camera in the dense jungles of western Java, Indonesia. Wildlife biologists designed the picture-taking apparatus so they could monitor the population of the elusive species. In 1993, the pictures provided evidence that only about 50 Java rhinos survive on the island. Another 15 may exist in Vietnam.

Conservation Continued

Thus, Blaustein's study showed a link between the ability of a species to repair radiation damage to DNA and the capability of the species' eggs to hatch in unfiltered sunlight. Those results support the theory that increased ultraviolet radiation may be contributing to the widespread declines of at least some amphibians. (See also ECOLOGY.)

Protecting Russian Amur tigers. The world's largest subspecies of tiger, the endangered Amur, may have been pulled back from the brink of extinction in January 1994. That was when the World Wildlife Fund, an international conservation group, announced plans to help stop Russian hunters from killing off the animals. Amur tigers can weigh more than 360 kilograms (800 pounds), and some specimens grow to more than twice the size of other Asian subspecies.

Only about 350 tigers remain in their native habitat in Russia. The animals are killed for their bones, which are ground up and sold in China and other Asian countries as alleged treatments for various ailments. Tiger pelts also command high prices. Money from the Wildlife Fund was earmarked to equip two Russian teams in pursuit of poachers.

Whooping cranes in Florida. Five juvenile whooping cranes—offspring of captive adults—were released on the Kissimmee Prairie in central Florida in December 1993 under a new program by the U.S. Fish and Wildlife Service (FWS). FWS wildlife experts then followed up with the release of six cranes on the prairie in February 1994, and eight more in April. The conservation program calls for 20 or more young cranes to be released annually for up to 10 years to establish a nonmigratory population.

FWS biologists used a "soft-release" technique to introduce the birds to the wild. A soft-release technique is one in which the animals were not immediately freed into their new environment. Instead, the biologists put the cranes in predator-proof pens with food and water. Doing so gave the birds time to adjust to their new home. After about a month, the cranes were allowed to fly out and return at will.

The biologists also took measures to prevent bobcats from preying on the newly released cranes. The scientists had discovered that bobcats killed 14 of the 25 birds that had been released in February 1993 at the Kissimmee site. Before freeing the whooping cranes released in December, FWS workers trained the cranes to roost in water, where bobcats would not attack them. In addition, workers mowed the areas near the holding pens to eliminate bobcat hiding places.

The Florida program replaces a foster-parent plan begun in 1975 in which whooping crane eggs were placed in the nests of sandhill cranes breeding in an Idaho wildlife refuge. This effort did not produce enough cranes to justify continuing the program, and it ended in 1989.

The FWS said it hopes to establish two self-sustaining wild populations, one in Florida and the other in Canada. (In addition, Texas is the winter home to a wild flock that has grown from 15 to more than 135 birds.) When the new populations are established, FWS officials say they may propose reclassifying the whooping crane from an endangered species to a threatened one.

Peregrine falcons recover. The Arctic peregrine falcon has been saved from extinction, according to the FWS. In October 1993, the agency proposed that the bird be removed from the U.S. Endangered Species List. After being legally protected for more than 20 years, the Arctic subspecies of peregrine falcon now consists of as many as 10,000 adults, according to government biologists' estimates.

Arctic falcons were among many species harmed by DDT, an insecticide widely applied beginning in the 1940's. Although few falcons died of ingesting DDT, the chemical caused the shells of the eggs the females laid to be abnormally thin. Many egg shells broke during incubation, and few young birds were produced. After the United States banned the use of DDT in 1972, the peregrine population began to rebound.

Wolf control in Alaska. The first year of a controversial three-year program designed to reduce the wolf population in a 10,440-square-kilometer (4,030-square-mile) area of Alaska ended in April 1994. By reducing the number of wolves, Alaskan officials hope to rebuild the area's population of caribou, which the wolves prey upon. Caribou numbers had fallen from 10,700 animals in 1989

Condor moving day

A worker captures one of four surviving California condors in a southern California sanctuary (inset) to transport it to a new location. (The unharmed bird regurgitates as a defensive response during capture.) Four of the eight condors released into the sanctuary since 1992 had been killed by colliding with power lines or drinking spilled antifreeze. In November 1993, workers moved them to a more remote, and presumably safer, California site, *above*.

to about 4,000 in 1993. Because the population had declined so drastically, Alaskan wildlife officials prohibited the hunting of caribou in the area in 1991.

The controversial plan called for about 150 of the estimated 200 wolves in the area to be killed. Officials hoped to then maintain the wolf population at the reduced level for three years. The wolf population would be allowed to increase after the caribou herd recovered.

Wildlife biologists first proposed that the wolves be shot from helicopters. According to Kenneth Taylor of the Alaska Fish and Game Department, aerial shooting is the best and most humane means of controlling the overall wolf population, because it can be used to eliminate entire packs of about eight wolves rather than a few wolves from each pack. Eliminating an entire wolf pack can improve caribou calf survival if the pack's territory includes areas where caribou give birth each year. It takes some time before another wolf pack will move into the vacant territory.

But animal-rights activists opposed aerial shooting, and officials responded by authorizing the use of traps and snares and shooting from the ground. Moose, coyotes, foxes, and even two caribou were among the nontargeted animals caught in the more than 1,000 snares and 24 traps set in the control area. More than half of the snares were designed to release animals other than wolves, and because these worked well, several moose and caribou escaped when they were accidentally ensnared.

State biologists noted that the caribou herd benefited from a reduced level of predation during the first winter of the program. However, they said, the key to caribou recovery lies in improved survival rates for caribou calves. Whether more calves were surviving would not be known until after the calving season ended in summer 1994.

The control program covers less than 1 percent of Alaska's land area. Between 6,000 and 7,000 wolves live in the state.

[Eric G. Bolen]

In the Special Reports section, see THE COST OF TAMING A RIVER; A NEW LOOK AT THE ENDANGERED CHEETAH. In WORLD BOOK, see CONSERVATION.

Deaths of Scientists

Notable scientists and engineers who died between June 1, 1993, and June 1, 1994, are listed below. Those listed were Americans unless otherwise indicated.

Severo Ochoa

Wolfgang Paul

Dixy Lee Ray

Andrews, Rodney D., Jr. (1922-Oct. 19, 1993), chemist known as an expert on the chemistry of *polymers* (large molecules that are made up of identical, smaller molecules).

Bolton, John (1922?-July 6, 1993), British-born astronomer credited with helping establish the field of radio astronomy; discoverer in 1947 of the first *radio galaxies* (galaxies that give off most of their radiation at radio wavelengths); director of the Australian National Radio Observatory from 1961 to 1971.

Carpenter, Frank M. (1902-Jan. 18, 1994), entomologist who was regarded as one of the world's foremost authorities on fossilized insects; Alexander Agassiz professor emeritus of zoology at Harvard University in Cambridge, Mass.

Davis, Bernard D. (1916-Jan. 14, 1994), microbiologist who pioneered in the study of how genes are regulated in bacteria. Davis helped develop several laboratory techniques that were instrumental to later advances that were made in microbiology, genetic engineering, and biotechnology.

Fosberg, F. Raymond (1908-Sept. 25, 1993), botanist known as a leading authority on the flora of tropical islands in the Pacific, Atlantic, and Indian oceans; founder of the Nature Conservancy environmental group.

Gentry, Alwyn H. (1945-Aug. 3, 1993), botanist who was considered one of the world's leading experts on the tropical rain forests of Latin America. Gentry was senior curator of the Missouri Botanical Garden in St. Louis. He was killed in an airplane crash while surveying a rain forest canopy in Ecuador with other scientists.

Gillespie, David H. (1940-Dec. 19, 1993), genetic researcher who helped develop a test that monitors genetic changes in blood, bone marrow, and tumor cells during medical treatment.

Gimbutas, Marija (1921-Feb. 2, 1994), Lithuanian-born archaeologist who was considered an authority on the prehistoric migrations into Europe of Indo-European speaking people. Gimbutas challenged traditional views of prehistoric cultures and became controversial for her theory that early Stone Age societies were centered on women and were peaceful until they were supplanted by patriarchal societies that worshiped warlike gods.

Gordon, Mildred K. (1920?-Aug. 23, 1993), molecular biologist who pioneered in the study of human reproduction. She shed new light on the development of human sperm and on the structure of the inner lining of the human uterus.

Hafstad, Lawrence R. (1904-Oct. 12, 1993), physicist who in 1948 was appointed the first director of reactor development for the Atomic Energy Commission and played a key role in the development of nuclear power plants.

Hirst, George K. (1909-Jan. 22, 1994), virologist who in the early 1940's discovered a way to detect influenza viruses in blood and who pioneered the study of the genetics of animal viruses in the 1940's and 1950's.

Hobby, Gladys L. (1910-July 4, 1993), microbiologist who discovered a technique that made it possible to mass-produce penicillin during World War II (1939-1945).

Hungerford, David A. (1927?-Nov. 3, 1993), cancer researcher who was a co-discoverer in 1959 of the first visible genetic abnormality in cancer cells, having found a damaged *chromosome* (one of the cell's threadlike structures that carry genes) in a type of blood cancer. The discovery helped focus attention on genetic abnormalities as the cause of certain cancers.

John, Fritz (1910- Feb. 10, 1994), German-born mathematician regarded as a leading authority on *partial differential equations,* the mathematical tools that help describe many fundamental laws of physics, such as the laws of electromagnetic radiation.

Kerst, Donald W. (1911-Aug. 19, 1993), physicist who invented the *betatron,* a particle accelerator that was built in the 1940's to probe the structure of atoms and subatomic particles by using electron beams. After the betatron became obsolete as a way to study subatomic matter, it was used for cancer treatment.

Lejeune, Jérôme (1926-April 3, 1994), French geneticist who discovered the cause of Down syndrome, a form of mental retardation. Lejeune found that people with Down syndrome have 47 chromosomes, rather than the normal 46 chromosomes.

Ochoa, Severo (1905-Nov. 1, 1993), Spanish biochemist who shared the Nobel Prize in physiology or medicine in 1959 for his discovery of a bacterial enzyme that can synthesize RNA (ribonucleic acid), a compound that plays an important role in making proteins in the living cell.

Olton, David S. (1942?-Feb. 1, 1994), neuroscientist who was regarded as an expert on the biological basis of memory. Olton was known for his investigations of the role of the *hippocampus,* a structure in the brain, in memory and for his research into drug treatments to stem memory loss.

Parker, Theodore A., III (1953-Aug. 3, 1993), ornithologist known as a leading authority on bird life in Latin America who was renowned for his ability to identify more than 4,000 species by their calls alone. He was killed in an airplane crash with botanist Alwyn Gentry during a survey of plant and animal life in an Ecuadorean rain forest.

Paul, Wolfgang (1913-Dec. 6, 1993), German physicist who shared the Nobel Prize in physics in 1989 for developing a method of isolating electrons and *ions* (electrically charged atoms), enabling scientists to measure them with precision. The Nobel Committee cited work that Paul did in the 1950's to improve a device called an ion trap by suspending ions in electrical fields and illuminating them with laser beams.

Plunkett, Roy J. (1911?-May 12, 1994), chemist who in 1941 received a patent for his invention of polytetrafluoroethylene resin, better known by its trade name, Teflon, thus changing the way millions of people cook and founding a multibillion-dollar industry.

Ray, Dixy Lee (1914-Jan. 2, 1994), marine biologist, former chairwoman of the Atomic Energy Commission, and former governor of the state of Washington. Ray was an outspoken defender of nuclear power and a critic of environmental groups.

Sperry, Roger W. (1913-April 17, 1994), neurobiologist who shared the Nobel Prize in physiology or medicine in 1981 for his finding that many important cognitive functions occur in the right hemisphere of the brain. Sperry was also known for discovering that the role of the *corpus callosum,* a bundle of millions of nerve fibers in the brain, is to pass information between the brain's two hemispheres.

St. Joseph, Kenneth (1912?-March 11, 1994), geologist who was known for pioneering the use of aerial photography in archaeological studies. His research broke new ground in the study of Roman ruins in the United Kingdom, helping locate more than 200 Roman forts.

Steward, Frederick C. (1904-Sept. 13, 1993), British-born botanist and cell biologist whose discovery in 1958 that plants can be completely regenerated in the laboratory from a single cell revolutionized the field of plant cell biology. His finding made it possible to study clones, mutations, and hybrids without the time-consuming process of cultivating cuttings. Steward also did seminal work in how plant roots and tissues obtain nutrients and in how plants synthesize proteins.

Temin, Howard M. (1934-Feb. 9, 1994), cancer researcher who shared the Nobel Prize in physiology or medicine in 1975 for his discovery of *reverse transcriptase,* an enzyme that enables certain viruses to insert their genes into the genetic material of the cells they infect. Temin's discovery proved that some viruses, known as *retroviruses,* carry their genetic information in the form of RNA, which is converted into DNA (deoxyribonucleic acid), when the virus occupies a cell. The discovery of reverse transcriptase proved to be key to identifying other retroviruses, such as the human immunodeficiency virus (HIV), which causes AIDS. The enzyme also became a crucial tool in the biotechnology industry, enabling scientists to clone genes.

Thomas, Lewis (1913-Dec. 3, 1993), physician and popular science writer who won the National Book Award for *The Lives of a Cell: Notes of a Biology Watcher* (1974); former president of the Memorial Sloan-Kettering Cancer Center in New York City.

Vine, Allyn C. (1914-Jan. 4, 1994), oceanographer known for his pioneering role in developing manned submersible research vessels for the study of the deep ocean floor. The first American manned submersible, *Alvin,* was named in honor of him. [Rod Such]

Roger W. Sperry

Howard M. Temin

Lewis Thomas

Drugs

More aggressive treatment of the most severe form of diabetes can slow or prevent the serious complications associated with the disease, according to two studies published in 1993. In the more severe of the two types of diabetes, called Type I, the body cannot produce insulin, the hormone that regulates the use of *glucose* (sugar). The usual treatment for this type of diabetes is one or two daily injections of insulin. But even with treatment, many patients develop serious complications over time, including damage to the eyes, the kidneys, and the nerves in the arms and legs.

Aggressive diabetes treatment. Physicians have long debated whether the complications of diabetes could be prevented with a more intensive use of insulin to bring blood-sugar concentrations closer to normal ranges. Doctors feared that by lowering blood sugar levels they might risk problems caused by blood sugar levels that are too low.

The two studies were designed to explore that issue. In July, a group of Swedish researchers reported that patients who received more aggressive management of their disease appeared to have a lower incidence of diabetic complications. Aggressive management consisted of a program to educate the patients about their disease and about how to monitor their blood sugar levels. The patients in the study also made frequent progress reports to their healthcare providers.

In September, the Diabetes Control and Complications Trial Research Group, a project supported by numerous institutions, published a study of 1,441 young adults that provided very strong evidence that a more aggressive control of blood sugar levels leads to a slower rate of progression of diabetes-related eye and nerve injury. The study evaluated patients who carefully monitored their blood sugar levels and then had three or four injections of insulin each day, as opposed to the usual treatment of one or two injections per day with less frequent monitoring.

Diabetic kidney disease. A drug called captopril may help prevent kidney damage in people with diabetes, researchers from Rush-Presbyterian-St. Luke's Medical Center in Chicago reported in November 1993.

Captopril is a medicine that is commonly used to control high blood pressure. In the study, the drug was given to diabetes patients who did not have high blood pressure. Other diabetes patients in the study received *placebos*, pills that contained no active ingredients. The patients who used captopril showed a slower progression of their kidney disease compared with patients who received a placebo. Based partly on these results, the U.S. Food and Drug Administration (FDA) in February 1994 approved the use of captopril for the prevention of kidney damage in diabetics.

Deaths in hepatitis drug trial. An experimental drug for the treatment of hepatitis B infections was blamed for the deaths of five volunteer patients by September 1993. The drug, called fialuridine, had been thought to be a promising treatment for hepatitis B, a liver disease caused by a virus.

Fialuridine had first been tested on dogs and found to be safe. The FDA then approved testing on hepatitis patients in 1992. At first, the drug seemed equally safe in people, but liver damage and other symptoms began to appear in some of the volunteers. Researchers later stated that the toxic effects of the drug had been masked because they closely resembled the symptoms of the hepatitis that the patients had.

In June 1993, researchers at the National Institutes of Health in Bethesda, Md., halted their clinical trial of 15 patients after two of the patients suffered severe symptoms, including liver and kidney disorders. Patients in trials elsewhere, including one conducted by the makers of fialuridine, Eli Lilly & Co., were also taken off the drug. A number of subjects continued to become ill even after they stopped taking the drug.

In response to the tragedy, David Kessler, commissioner of the FDA, in November recommended changes in the way researchers report drug side effects. Previously, the FDA had required reporting only those side effects thought to be related to the drug. Kessler's report recommended that researchers now be required to report to the FDA all symptoms in patients taking experimental drugs. The new rules could help the FDA more quickly identify unexpected problems with new drugs.

TB drug-resistance clue. A gene in the bacterium that causes tuberculosis

(TB) is a cause of that microbe's resistance to antibiotics. That discovery, which gives researchers their first evidence of how certain TB drugs work, was reported by a team of researchers at Albert Einstein College of Medicine in New York City in January 1994.

The development of drugs to treat TB in the 1950's was a major advance in medicine. By the early 1990's, however, some strains of the bacterium that causes TB had become resistant to the major antibiotics used to treat the infection. The inability of antibiotics to kill those microbes means that physicians have few options for treating patients infected with drug-resistant strains.

The gene discovered by this research team appears to help the bacterium manufacture mycolic acid, a critical component of the organism's cell wall. The researchers believe that antibiotics block the synthesis of mycolic acid. The drug-resistant strains of TB seem to have genetic mutations that allow the microbes to resist this blocking. Researchers said that this discovery is a critical step toward understanding how TB resistance develops and how to design drugs that avoid it.

Heart attack drug debate. Findings published in November 1993 by an international research group known as the GUSTO Angiographic Study fueled an ongoing debate about the best treatment for patients having heart attacks. There are several different drugs, called thrombolytic drugs, that dissolve the blood clots that cause heart attacks. Some of these cost several thousand dollars for a single treatment. Others cost only several hundred dollars.

The GUSTO study compared the benefits of a more expensive drug, TPA, to a cheaper agent, streptokinase. Previous studies had not found TPA to be more effective. The GUSTO study found that 6.3 percent of patients receiving a rapid infusion of TPA died within 30 days of the heart attack, compared with 7.3 percent of the patients receiving streptokinase. The results suggest that the more expensive drug is just a bit better than the cheaper one.   [B. Robert Meyer]

See also MEDICAL RESEARCH. In WORLD BOOK, see DRUG.

Ecology

Ecologists expressed concern—and curiosity—over an unusual ecological experiment carried out in the Pacific Ocean in autumn 1993. The goal was to find out if adding iron to the ocean would stimulate the growth of microscopic ocean plants called phytoplankton. The scientists conducting the research had hoped that stimulating the growth of the plants would reduce the effects of a possible global warming. According to scientists' theories, global warming is a rise in Earth's average surface temperatures due to excess carbon dioxide in the atmosphere.

Adding iron to the ocean. The theory behind the 1993 experiment was that increasing the amount of phytoplankton in the ocean might reverse the buildup of carbon dioxide in the atmosphere. Phytoplankton and other plants use carbon dioxide, water, and sunlight to produce food energy during photosynthesis. According to earlier studies, the growth of phytoplankton—and thus the plants' use of carbon dioxide—was limited only by the lack of iron in the ocean.

To test the theory, marine biologist Richard Barber of Duke University in Durham, N.C., and a team of other scientists dumped powdered iron into the Pacific Ocean south of the Galapagos Islands, where natural iron concentrations are low. About 8 square kilometers (3 square miles) of ocean were affected by the iron dumping.

At first, phytoplankton in the area increased, showing that the plants had indeed needed iron to spur growth. But the effect was short-lived. The dissolved iron began to form small particles, and by the fourth day of the experiment, the particles had sunk to the bottom, taking the iron out of reach of the plants.

Many ecologists were intrigued by the scale of the experiment. But most also expressed some relief that it did not bring the sought-after goal, thereby discouraging other attempts to tamper with ocean ecology.

Milk-producing males. The males of a species of bat in Malaysia appear to be an exception to the rule that only female mammals produce milk to feed their young. Biologist Thomas Kunz of Boston University in Massachusetts re-

Ecology Continued

ported in February 1994 that he and his team had discovered *lactation* (the secretion of milk) in males of Malaysia's Dayak fruit bat. That finding holds interest for ecologists who study the relationship between the males and females in a population.

Kunz's team captured the bats in Pahang, Malaysia. They found that the nipples of the males are smaller than those of the females, but the males nonetheless produce small quantities of milk. The researchers did not observe males nursing their young.

Whether the males actually nurse is a significant question for the field of *behavioral ecology*, the study of social systems in natural populations. Scientists have found that most mammals do not mate for life. Presumably, this social system arose because most male mammals cannot nurse their young and therefore cannot provide much help raising them. In contrast, most birds do mate for life, presumably because both partners can locate food and bring it to the young.

If that theory of animal behavior is correct, then species of mammals in which males can nurse their young should mate for life. Kunz and his colleagues planned to return to Malaysia to see if indeed this is the case in the Dayak fruit bat.

Predator-prey cycle ends. Since 1958, the interactions between wolves and moose on Isle Royale, Mich., have been the world's most studied example of the relationship between predators and their prey. But that opportunity is coming to an end, reported wildlife ecologist Rolf O. Peterson of Michigan Technological University in Houghton. In August 1993, Peterson presented evidence that the ecosystem's wolves will soon die off.

Isle Royale is an island about 72 kilometers (45 miles) long in Lake Superior. For decades, population ecologists have been closely tracking the populations of wolves and moose on the island. When the moose population was abundant, for example, researchers found that the wolves had ample food, and so their population increased in turn. At some point, the moose population would decline, and the wolf population

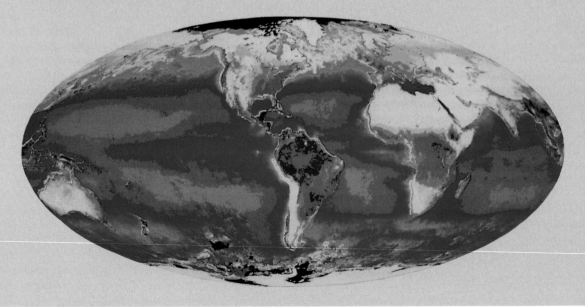

The first map to represent the entire biosphere of Earth was displayed at the Smithsonian Institution in Washington, D.C., in January 1994. Green areas represent the highest concentrations of plant life on the continents, and yellow the lowest. In the oceans, red areas represent the highest concentrations of plankton, and purple the lowest.

would also decrease, due to lack of food.

Peterson reported that the natural predator-prey cycles halted in 1981, when wolves began to die off in large numbers. The population dropped from about 50 animals to about 15 in 1994. The cause of death was probably *parvovirus,* a deadly canine virus. The health of the few remaining wolves is further impaired by *inbreeding,* the mating of close relatives, which may cause cubs to die in infancy or be unusually susceptible to disease. Peterson reported that only four wolf pups were born in the last two years, all to the same female.

In 1994, the moose population, freed from wolf predation, was at an all-time high of almost 2,000. But ecologists expect that the moose will strip the island of so much vegetation that eventually many animals will starve.

Amphibians and acid rain. Acid rain is not the cause of a sharp drop in amphibian populations in the Western United States, according to an autumn 1993 report by biologists Stephen Corn of the U.S. Fish and Wildlife Service and Frank Vertucci of Colorado State University, both in Fort Collins. Amphibians, such as frogs, toads, and salamanders, live both in water and on land. Acid rain is precipitation containing compounds such as sulfuric and nitric acid. Emissions from automobiles, factories, and power plants cause the acids to form in the atmosphere.

The biologists studied the acidity of lakes and ponds in the Rocky Mountains and found that the water becomes more acidic at certain times of the year—for example, after snowmelt in the spring. But those increases did not coincide with the time of year when amphibians are most at risk—the tadpole stage, when they live entirely in the water.

The scientists concluded that pollution was not responsible for amphibian population declines in the American West. The declines may instead be due to destruction of the amphibians' natural habitats.   [Robert H. Tamarin]

See also Atmospheric Science; Biology; Conservation; Environment. In the Special Reports section, see The Cost of Taming a River. In World Book, see Ecology.

Electronics

See Computers and Electronics

Endangered Species

See Conservation

Energy

On May 27, 1994, physicists at Princeton University in New Jersey set a record for the amount of energy produced in a nuclear fusion reactor. The scientists produced 9 million watts in the Tokamak Fusion Test Reactor. The event broke the Princeton team's own records of 6.2 million and 3 million watts, which were achieved on Dec. 9 and 10, 1993. The previous record was 1.7 million watts, set by the Joint European Torus experimental fusion reactor near Oxford, United Kingdom, in November 1991.

Fusion record. Nuclear fusion is the process that fuels the sun and other stars. Fusion occurs when the *nuclei* (cores) of elements *fuse* (combine) under conditions of extremely high temperature and pressure. In the Princeton reactor, tritium and deuterium—two *isotopes* (forms) of hydrogen—fused. For each two nuclei fused, the reaction produces a helium nucleus, energy, and a neutron.

A different reaction, called *fission,* generates energy in today's nuclear power plants. Fission reactions produce energy by splitting atomic nuclei. For decades, researchers have pursued fusion power as a safer and cheaper alternative to fission.

The Princeton scientists started the fusion reaction by passing an extremely strong electric current through tritium and deuterium gas in a tokamak. A tokamak is a hollow, doughnut-shaped vacuum chamber lined with graphite and surrounded by strong electromagnets. Electrical resistance heated the atomic fuel in the tokamak to temperatures several times higher than those in the center of the sun. The high temperature turned the fuel into a *plasma,* a gas made of free electrons and nuclei.

The plasma was so hot that it could have destroyed the walls of the tokamak, so the scientists used magnetism to keep the plasma confined. An electric current flowing through the plasma produced a magnetic field, and the electromagnets in the tokamak repelled the plasma, pushing it away from the walls.

The extreme heat and pressure in the tokamak caused the nuclei to begin to fuse, and the reaction continued for a brief period, until the physicists stopped it. Like all previous fusion experiments, however, the reaction did not produce energy efficiently. The Princeton tokamak required more energy than it yielded. (See also PHYSICS.)

Solar cell efficiency record. A new design allows one of the least expensive types of solar cell to achieve acceptable levels of efficiency, according to a January 1994 announcement. Researchers at United Solar Systems Corporation in Troy, Mich., said that testing showed their design for a photovoltaic cell panel had an efficiency rate of 10.2 percent. The previous record for the same type of cell was 9 percent.

Photovoltaic cells convert sunlight directly into electricity. Most photovoltaic cells are made of purified silicon, the material used to manufacture computer chips. The efficiency of a cell refers to the relative amount of sunlight it converts to electricity.

The Michigan researchers were developing designs for one of the cheapest types of photovoltaic cells, called amorphous cells. Engineers make this type of cell by using a plasma to deposit hydrogen and silicon onto thin sheets of stainless steel, ceramic, or glass. This method allows technicians to make cells up to 100 times thinner than other silicon cells, which results in a considerable savings for materials.

The new United Solar Systems cell is made up of three layers of silicon, each with the ability to convert the sunlight in a different portion of the visible spectrum into energy. The company's previous amorphous cells contained only two layers. The extra layer boosts the cell's efficiency.

Potential users of photovoltaic cells have long viewed 10 percent efficiency as a minimum level for acceptance. Although amorphous cells are among the cheapest photovoltaic cells to manufacture, electric utilities and other potential large-scale users have shied away from them due to their low efficiencies. Other, more expensive types of silicon cells have efficiencies of up to 17 percent. (In the Science Studies section, see THE PROMISE OF RENEWABLE ENERGY.)

Aluminum car. An automobile with an aluminum frame was unveiled in

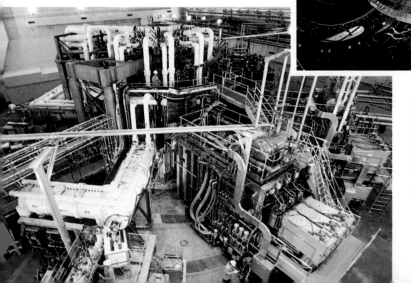

Fusion record set
Physicists at the Princeton Plasma Physics Laboratory in Princeton, N.J., *below,* set the record for producing controlled fusion power on May 27, 1994. Fusion, the joining of atomic nuclei, is the process that fuels the sun and other stars.

A technician inspects the lab's Tokamak Fusion Test Reactor, *above.* The reactor fused two *isotopes* (forms) of hydrogen to produce 9 million watts, the most power ever achieved through a controlled fusion reaction.

March 1994 by the Alcoa Corporation of Pittsburgh, Pa., and the German automaker Audi AG. The A8 luxury sport sedan's aluminum frame is about 40 percent lighter than a steel frame of equivalent strength.

The A8's reduced weight and aluminum construction offer energy savings. Because of the lighter frame, the car requires about 10 percent less fuel to travel the same distance as a steel-framed car of the same size.

Because aluminum is recyclable, the car's frame can be melted down to produce the raw material for a new one. Automobile recycling not only helps reduce the number of hulks in automobile junkyards but also reduces the amount of energy used to mine and process crude ores.

Superconductivity records were reported by two teams of scientists in 1993. Superconductors are materials that offer no resistance to an electric current. The loss of resistance usually occurs only at extremely low temperatures, but since the mid-1980's, scientists have been searching for ways to attain superconductivity at increasingly higher temperatures.

In summer 1993, Hans-Rudi Ott and colleagues at the Technical Institute of Zurich, Switzerland, reported achieving superconductivity at −140 °C (−220 °F). That broke the old record of −148 °C (−230 °F), which had stood since 1987. Ott and his team used a mercury-containing material called Mercury-1223.

In December, a group of French researchers announced that they had achieved an even higher temperature for a superconductor, −23 °C (−10 °F). More testing will be needed to verify the results, however. (See CHEMISTRY.)

Engineers say that higher-temperature superconductors hold great promise for energy savings. The elimination of resistance would reduce energy use in all electrical appliances, for example. If the French experiments prove valid, superconductivity may be built into many devices using cooling systems no more exotic than those available in commercial freezers.   [Pasquale M. Sforza]

In WORLD BOOK, see ENERGY SUPPLY; SOLAR ENERGY.

Engineering

A new device for locating victims of earthquakes and other disasters who are buried alive was reported in April 1994 by engineers at Michigan State University in East Lansing. The new system probes the ground using microwaves, a form of electromagnetic radiation.

Underground detection. Currently, rescue workers rely on trained dogs or sensitive microphones to detect people buried beneath rubble. But dogs cannot detect the scent of people who are buried deeply, and microphones are useful only if the victims are making noise.

The microwave system detects underground motion by sending microwave signals into the rubble and measuring changes in the signals that bounce back. Microwaves that have been reflected off a moving object undergo a recognizable change in the shape of their wave. The engineers based their system on microwave radiation because microwaves have very short wavelengths. The shorter the wavelength of radiation, the more easily it can pass through matter.

Electrical engineer Kun-Mu Chen said the system can detect the movement of an arm or leg, the rising and falling of a person's chest, or even the beating of a heart. According to the designers, the microwaves in the new detection system are not powerful enough to harm a person.

The engineers spent 10 years developing the microwave life-detection system. The major obstacle was that rubble and other matter reflect microwaves, producing unwanted signals. The engineers had to design electronic circuits that could detect those background signals and filter them out.

Chen said the microwave system has already been used elsewhere for similar purposes. For example, a version of the system has been developed for the military to allow soldiers to determine from a distance whether bodies on the battlefield are alive or dead. Another version for security systems at nuclear power plants detects human intruders hidden in boxes or trucks or behind walls.

Inflatable dams. When floods threaten electric power stations, water purification plants, and other facilities, the structures can be protected with inflat-

The *Sea Shadow,* a ship that employs the same technology as the F-117A Stealth fighter plane, was unveiled by the United States Navy in June 1993. Hidden exhaust vents and an angular shape help make the *Sea Shadow* virtually invisible to radar, sonar, and heat-seeking sensors. Engineers say the ship will be able to evade guided missiles more easily than conventional ships.

able dams, according to civil engineers at the Virginia Polytechnic Institute in Blacksburg. In March 1994, the engineers reported progress toward using "blowup" dams to protect buildings from floodwaters.

Inflatable dams have been used in many nations to divert streams and rivers, halt chemical spills, and create artificial lakes. The dams take the form of large cylinders whose walls are made of reinforced rubber about as thick as automobile tires. Many models are less than 3 meters (10 feet) high when inflated, though some reach as high as 6 meters (20 feet). A single dam can be more than 100 meters (330 feet) long. Engineers can connect a series of dams to form a barrier of any length.

The Virginia Tech researchers, led by civil engineer Raymond Plaut, showed that the dams could serve a role in flood control. The engineers used a miniature dam that was about 8 centimeters (3 inches) high and 2 meters (7 feet) long. They tested the dam by placing it around models of buildings and measuring its performance against

typical floodwater stresses. The researchers found that the inflatable dam could withstand waves and vibrations of the magnitude that normally accompany floods.

Plaut said uninflated dams could be buried in the ground around critical buildings in flood-prone regions. If floodwaters threatened the building, the dams could be inflated quickly with air or a combination of air and water to form an instant levee. According to Plaut, an inflatable dam 3 meters (10 feet) in height could have saved a water treatment plant in Des Moines, Iowa, that was severely damaged during the Midwest floods in 1993. Damage to that plant interrupted the city's drinking water supply for 12 days.

Smart concrete. A new kind of concrete that can sense tiny structural flaws before they become serious was reported in January 1994 by engineers at the University of Buffalo in New York. Materials engineer Deborah D. L. Chung, who headed the project, said the concrete could be very useful in structures whose failure could endanger many people, such as bridges and nuclear power plants.

The new concrete contains strong carbon fibers mixed in with the usual ingredients. The fibers, which are 5.1 millimeters (0.2 inches) long and only 10 micrometers thick, serve several purposes. They increase the strength of the concrete, making it able to withstand more stress before cracking. The fibers also help keep any cracks that do develop from spreading.

The biggest advantage of the fibers, though, is that they allow observers to detect weaknesses in a structure before cracks appear. The carbon fibers conduct electricity easily, so they boost the electrical conductivity of the concrete. When a fiber breaks as a result of stress, the conductivity of the concrete drops. Thus, engineers can check for flaws by running a current through the concrete and measuring the conductivity. A decrease in the conductivity indicates a growing stress. Engineers can then monitor small flaws to check that they do not grow to dangerous dimensions, or they can repair more serious flaws.

Other stress-sensitive concrete has been created using imbedded *optical fibers* (thin glass strands that carry light) or electronic sensors. But Chung said the new carbon-fiber concrete is easier to monitor. She noted that the concrete would be especially valuable in an earthquake-prone region. After a quake, engineers could measure conductivity in buildings made with the new concrete to uncover structural damage that may not be visible.

Communication solution. Equipment that lets people communicate clearly while wearing gas masks or other types of protective headgear was unveiled by engineers at the Battelle Memorial Institute in March 1994. Battelle is a nonprofit research and development group headquartered in Columbus, Ohio.

Many people wear protective headgear in the course of their jobs. Such workers include fire fighters, workers cleaning up toxic spills, and soldiers engaged in chemical warfare. The masks usually contain two-way radios to allow the people to talk to their co-workers without taking off their headgear. How-

The Cheetah bicycle held the world speed record for a human-powered vehicle in 1993. Pedaled by sprinter Chris Huber (seated), the Cheetah attained a speed of 111.61 kilometers per hour (68.73 miles per hour). To achieve that feat, the Cheetah's designers used lightweight materials and vibration-reducing glue to make the frame and the aerodynamic shell that fits over the rider.

Engineering Continued

ever, the mask itself can distort speech and make radio transmissions hard to understand.

The new equipment was designed by a team of Battelle researchers led by electrical engineer Kenneth Kimes. The device consists of a piece of clear plastic attached to the front of a cloth hood that fits over a person's face like a ski mask. The cloth, which is worn under conventional gas-filtering headgear, is thin enough to allow the wearer to hear nearby sounds. Embedded in the plastic to the left of the mouth is a pea-sized microphone. A cable connects the small microphone to a radio transmitter in a vest that is worn over the person's uniform.

The key component of the equipment is an amplification unit included in the vest. The unit has special electronic circuitry that detects and eliminates feedback from the microphone signal before it sends the message over the radio. According to Kimes, the new equipment allows clear-voice transmissions that can be understood more than 90 percent of the time.

Engineering award. Computer scientist John Backus, who wrote the computer programming language known as FORTRAN (for *for*mula *trans*lation), won the 1993 Charles Stark Draper Prize in October. The Draper Prize is the world's most prestigious engineering award.

The award is given every two years by the National Academy of Engineering (NAE), an organization of about 700 prominent engineers located in Washington, D.C. The award is named for Charles Stark Draper, an American aeronautical engineer who played an important role in improving the control, guidance, and navigation systems used in spacecraft.

Backus created FORTRAN in 1957, when he was the director of computer programming research for International Business Machines Corporation (IBM). The development of FORTRAN made computers much easier to use. The NAE awarded Backus a gold medal and $375,000. (See also AWARDS AND PRIZES.)
[Michael Woods]
In WORLD BOOK, see ENGINEERING.

Environment

Some 50,000 to 60,000 people in the United States may die prematurely each year as a result of breathing a form of air pollution called *fine particulates*—very small airborne particles and tiny droplets containing sulfuric acid. That was the finding of a December 1993 report by researchers at the Harvard School of Public Health in Cambridge, Mass. Fine particulates lodge deep within the lungs and can lead to premature death in certain individuals. Children with respiratory problems and elderly people with illnesses such as pneumonia, bronchitis, and emphysema are most commonly affected.

Deadly particulates. Epidemiologist Donald W. Dockery and his co-workers examined the link between a city's level of fine particulates and its death rate from 1974 through 1991. The study involved six U.S. cities: Harriman, Tenn.; Portage, Wisc.; Topeka, Kans.; Watertown, Mass.; St. Louis, Mo.; and Steubenville, Ohio.

After accounting for various other health risks, such as cigarette smoking, the researchers found that death rates were 26 percent higher in the most polluted city, Steubenville, than in the least polluted cities, Portage and Topeka. The researchers also found a higher rate of lung cancer and other respiratory illnesses in the most polluted cities.

U.S. law places limits on the amount of particulates allowable in a city's air, but the new study revealed that current air pollution laws may not be strict enough. None of the cities in the study had particulate concentrations that exceeded U.S. Environmental Protection Agency (EPA) guidelines. Partly as a result of this study, some scientists and health experts in late 1993 called for tighter controls on factories and other sources of pollution.

Cleaner gasoline. While evidence concerning the connection between urban air pollution and health problems grew, the Administration of U.S. President Bill Clinton introduced a proposal in December 1993 that would help U.S. cities reduce air pollution and meet the requirements of the Clean Air Act of 1990.

The Clean Air Act requires the nation's nine smoggiest cities to introduce cleaner-burning gasoline by 1995. The cities are New York; Los Angeles; Baltimore; Chicago; Hartford, Conn.; Houston; Milwaukee; Philadelphia; and San Diego. Twelve states and Washington, D.C., have notified the EPA that they will require gas stations to sell cleaner-burning fuels by 1995.

The Clinton proposal will require that ethanol, a fuel made from corn, make up at least 30 percent of the new gasoline formulations. Ethanol and other compounds can be added to gasoline to increase its oxygen content, making the fuel burn cleaner. The Clinton proposal would increase the amount of ethanol used in gasoline from 3.8 billion to 6.4 billion liters (1 billion to 1.6 billion gallons) per year. Boosting the use of ethanol will also reduce emissions of carbon dioxide, a gas linked to a potentially harmful projected warming of Earth's atmosphere. (In the Science You Can Use section, see also CHOOSING THE RIGHT GASOLINE.)

Pipeline dangers. The environmental safety of the Alyeska Trans-Alaska Pipeline was called into question in a November 1993 report by the United States Bureau of Land Management (BLM), a federal agency that oversees much of the nation's public lands. The BLM report noted that potentially serious problems in the design and operation of the pipeline could result in oil spills, fires, or the electrocution of workers.

The pipeline carries crude oil from oil wells near Prudhoe Bay in Alaska to the port of Valdez. Owned and operated by seven major oil companies, the 1,300-kilometer (800-mile) pipeline has functioned well since it opened in 1977. But the BLM noted that in hundreds of locations the pipeline rests directly on vertical supports rather than on saddlelike structures designed to protect the pipeline during earthquakes, which are not uncommon in Alaska. The saddles allow sections of the pipe to roll back and forth without falling off the supports.

Other safety deficiencies included a lack of safety inspections and electrical safety violations that could lead to fires and electrocution. In November 1993, the oil companies pledged to the U.S. Congress that they would fix the problems with the pipeline by 1997.

Pesticides and children's health. The amount of pesticide residue on food in the United States is generally small and within legal limits. But a report in late June 1993 suggested that exposure to pesticides may pose a greater-than-expected cancer risk for children. The report, presented by the Environmental Working Group (EWG), a Washington, D.C., environmental research organization, contained the results of a three-year study on pesticides found in common fruits and vegetables.

Although about 70 pesticides used on food can cause cancer, government scientists have determined that the risk of low levels of pesticides is so small that the chemicals can be considered safe to use. Previous studies to evaluate pesticide safety have focused solely on the risk to adults, however. According to the EWG report, the risk to children is greater because a child's tissues *metabolize* (chemically process) pesticides differently than an adult's.

The new study also considered the effect of having more than one pesticide in the same food. After examining 20,000 samples of fruits and vegetables, the researchers found that each sample contained at least two and as many as eight pesticides. Using EPA data on the cancer risk associated with each pesticide, the researchers calculated the amount of additional risk created by combining pesticides. According to Richard Wiles, director of the agricultural pollution prevention program at EWG, the researchers ultimately found that average pesticide levels in fruits and vegetables were high enough to increase a child's lifetime risk of developing cancer 12 times above the federal government's acceptable maximum risk of 1 in 1 million.

The National Academy of Sciences, an advisory group to Congress, also reported on the dangers to children of pesticides in food. In late June 1993, the academy issued a related report that concluded that pesticide regulations must be strengthened to protect children from potential harm.

In September 1993, the Clinton Administration announced it would adopt many of the suggestions in the two reports. The Administration's plan would allow the government to reject or restrict the use of pesticides without as much study of their harmful effects as currently needed. The plan also encourages U.S. farmers to cut pesticide use in half by the year 2000 and requires new standards for determining the acceptable levels of pesticide residues on foods.

Dioxin and cancer. Exposure to dioxin appears to be associated with several rare forms of cancer, according to a September 1993 report by Italian researchers. Scientists have long suspected that dioxin, a toxic chemical by-product of certain industrial processes, is a human *carcinogen* (cancer-causing agent). Research has failed to uncover a conclusive link between the two, however.

In the new study, epidemiologist Pier Alberto Bertazzi of the Institute of Occupational Health at the University of Milan in Italy studied the health records of 37,000 people exposed to dioxin in Seveso, Italy, in 1976 as a result of an accident at a chemical plant. The researchers compared the incidence of various types of cancer in this group to their occurrence in 180,000 individuals who were not exposed to dioxin.

The researchers found that men exposed to dioxin were six times more likely to develop a rare cancer of the lymphatic system known as non-Hodgkin's lymphoma than men not exposed to the chemical. In women with dioxin exposure, a rare *leukemia* (cancer of the white blood cells) known as multiple myeloma was five times more prevalent than in the group not exposed. In the exposed women, the incidence of another rare form of leukemia, called myeloid leukemia, was almost four times higher. The group of men and women exposed to dioxin also had more cases of other types of cancers, including those of the gall bladder and liver.

Bertazzi cautioned, however, that the number of people with cancer in the study was relatively small and that further investigation was needed to establish a definite link between dioxin exposure and cancer.   [Daniel D. Chiras]

See also ATMOSPHERIC SCIENCE; CONSERVATION; ECOLOGY. In the Special Reports section, see THE COST OF TAMING A RIVER. In WORLD BOOK, see ENVIRONMENTAL POLLUTION.

Fossil Studies

Life may have existed on land almost 1 billion years earlier than had been thought, according to a report in February 1994. Fossil specialist Robert J. Horodyski of Tulane University in New Orleans and geologist L. Paul Knauth of Arizona State University in Tempe made the announcement.

The researchers reported on their discovery of tube-shaped fossil microbes, possibly bacteria or fungi, at two sites in the American Southwest, the older one dating to about 1.2 billion years ago. The earliest land fossils known previously are about 500 million years old. Scientists cautioned, however, that the conclusion that the sites were on land when the fossils were formed remained to be confirmed.

Cambrian explosion. All the major body plans known in animals may have evolved within less than 10 million years, a dramatically brief span of time, according to research published in September 1993. Scientists have long regarded the appearance of those body plans as perhaps the most important event in the history of life. The event is

known as the *Cambrian explosion* because it occurred during the Cambrian Period of Earth's history.

The new estimate is based on a redating of the start of the period, which paleontologists had placed at about 570 million years ago. The 1993 research indicated that the Cambrian Period actually began nearly 30 million years later. In addition, the research suggests that the time of greatest diversification, during which soft-bodied creatures gave way to a wide variety of animals with shells and skeletons, did not begin until about 10 million years after that. The new research does not contradict earlier estimates that the Cambrian explosion ended about 525 million years ago, indicating that the explosion may have lasted only 5 million to 10 million years.

A team led by Samuel A. Bowring, a geologist at the Massachusetts Institute of Technology in Cambridge, arrived at the new dates by analyzing crystals in volcanic rocks from the Early Cambrian Period in Siberia. The scientists based their analysis on the fact that uranium in the crystals changes into lead at a

New fossil primate from Asia
Fossils of a previously unknown primate dating back 45 million years (inset) have been uncovered in eastern China, according to an April 1994 report by American and Chinese researchers. The primate, dubbed *Eosimias sinensis* ("dawn monkey"), *right,* is one of a variety of early primates, including five new species, found at the site. The finds suggest that Asia may have been a cradle of early primate development.

slow but measurable pace. By measuring the ratio of uranium to lead in the crystals, the researchers were able to determine the age of the rocks.

By dating rocks that were laid down next to examples of the oldest Cambrian fossils, Bowring and his colleagues determined that the Cambrian Period began no earlier than about 544 million years ago. Rocks from the beginning of the Cambrian's second stage, the time of the greatest evolutionary change, yielded dates of about 530 million years ago.

The appearance of most of the major animal body plans within 5 million to 10 million years, more than 3 billion years after life first appeared in the oceans, raises significant questions: What factors brought about such a burst of evolutionary activity? What caused the long delay before the explosion, and why has no similar event occurred since then? Some scientists speculate that an environmental change, such as an increase in the amount of oxygen in the oceans, set off the Cambrian explosion, while others suggest that genetic changes within living things were responsible. Scientists

are working to determine which of these or other theories may be correct.

New dinosaur. Fossils unearthed in Antarctica belong to a previously unknown species of dinosaur, researchers reported in May 1994. Paleontologists uncovered the fossils in 1991 at a site about 650 kilometers (400 miles) from the South Pole. The new species, *Cryolophosaurus ellioti* ("frozen crested reptile"), was one of a group of dinosaurs known as *theropods*—meat-eating dinosaurs that walked upright on two legs. It was about 8 meters (25 feet) long and had small forefeet, a long tail, large jaws, and a bony crest on its head.

C. ellioti lived about 200 million years ago, when Antarctica was closer to the equator and the climate was mild enough to support both meat-eating dinosaurs and the plant-eaters that would have been their prey. Bones from such a plant-eater, a dinosaur called a prosauropod, were mixed in with the *C. ellioti* fossils when they were found.

Dinosaurs and birds. Two studies published in December 1993 provided strong support for the theory that modern birds are the descendants of dinosaurs. Many paleontologists have long argued that birds evolved from theropods, a group of dinosaurs that first appeared about 220 million years ago. The best-known theropods are the allosaurs, which lived about 150 million years ago, and the tyrannosaurs, which lived about 70 million to 65 million years ago.

Supporters of the bird-dinosaur link point to similarities in the skeletal structures of birds and theropods. Other scientists believe those features developed in birds and theropods independently.

In one of the 1993 studies, paleontologist Peter Wellnhofer of the Munich Museum in Germany reported on an *Archaeopteryx* fossil discovered in 1992 in southern Germany. Scientists regard *Archaeopteryx*, which lived about 150 million years ago, as the earliest known bird. The new specimen is only the seventh *Archaeopteryx* fossil skeleton to be uncovered.

The new fossil displays a feature not seen in previous *Archaeopteryx* specimens: a row of small, triangular, bony plates between the teeth at the gum line of the bird's lower jaw. The only other animals, living or extinct, to possess such plates were the theropod dinosaurs. The presence of these plates in the *Archaeopteryx* jaw may thus represent a direct evolutionary link between this early bird and the theropods.

Also unlike the previous specimens, the new *Archaeopteryx* fossil displays a well-defined breastbone resembling the keel of a ship. In modern birds, such a breastbone serves to anchor the strong flight muscles that power the bird's wings. The breastbone thus provides the first strong evidence that *Archaeopteryx* could fly, rather than simply glide. Partly for this reason, Wellnhoffer designated the fossil as a new species, *Archaeopteryx bavarica*. The previous six fossils are classified as *Archaeopteryx lithographica*.

In the second 1993 study, researchers reported a new characteristic shared by modern birds and dinosaurs. Claudia Barreto, a graduate student at the University of Wisconsin School of Veterinary Medicine in Madison, and her colleagues studied microscopic structures in the leg bones of young birds and of

Fossil bones from an ancient seabed in Pakistan belong to an ancestor of modern whales that had usable hind legs, according to a January 1994 report by American and Pakistani scientists. The 52-million-year-old bones may help scientists reconstruct how whales evolved from land mammals beginning about 57 million years ago. The new specimen, *Ambulocetus natans,* had large but weak hind limbs and probably moved somewhat like a seal.

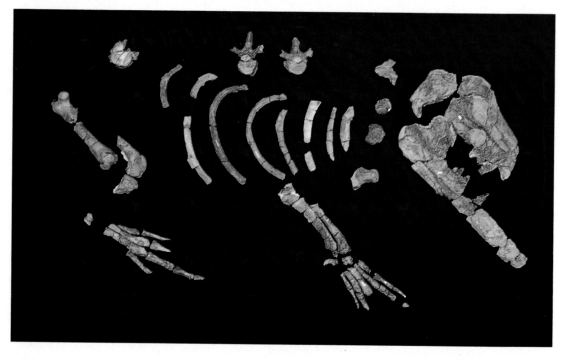

fossil maiasaurs, plant-eating dinosaurs that lived about 70 million years ago.

In all animals, the leg bones grow as soft connecting tissue is replaced by cartilage, which is then replaced by bone. Barreto found that young birds and juvenile maiasaurs shared a similar pattern of bone growth, marked by features such as wavy-shaped junctions between bone and cartilage. In modern reptiles and mammals, the borders of such junctions are straight.

Barreto said her research supports the theory that dinosaurs and birds are closely related. The research also provides evidence for another idea: that dinosaurs were fast-growing, active animals that more closely resembled birds than they did modern reptiles.

Insect evolution. Most insect groups may have evolved long before the appearance of *angiosperms* (flowering plants) about 125 million years ago, according to a report in July 1993. The report reverses scientists' long-held belief that the evolution of angiosperms triggered a burst of evolution in insects, leading to the rise of the more than 1 million insect species known today.

In the new research, paleontologists J. John Sepkoski, Jr., of the University of Chicago and Conrad C. Labandeira of the Smithsonian Institution in Washington, D.C., surveyed a mass of data on fossil insects from around the world, including much information from Russia, China, and other sources that had been neglected by Western scientists. The survey filled in major gaps in the fossil insect record, which begins about 400 million years ago.

The newly compiled data indicate that some 85 percent of insect mouth parts—including various types of mandibles, beaks, tongues, piercers, and siphons—had appeared more than 100 million years before angiosperms became common. Scientists had assumed that insects' wide variety of feeding mechanisms, most of them well suited to extracting food from flowering plants, must have evolved in response to the proliferation of these new food sources. In fact, the researchers found, the greatest diversification in insect mouth parts began after about 250 million years ago, presumably in response to a sharp rise in the variety of nonflowering plants such as ferns and conifers. Angiosperms

may then have evolved by taking advantage of the tools insects had developed for extracting food from seeds, stems, and leaves.

Sepkoski and Labandeira's work also challenged long-held assumptions about how insects came to make up such a large proportion—about two-thirds—of all living species. The scientists found that insects' evolutionary success may be due to resistance to extinction rather than to especially high rates of evolutionary change. Mass extinctions, in which large numbers of species die out, have occurred periodically in Earth's history. Only one of these mass extinctions, about 250 million years ago, seems to have had an impact on insects. Even then, only about 60 percent of insects died out, compared with much higher percentages in other animals.

Ice Age carnivores. Large *carnivorous* (meat-eating) mammals may have had trouble finding food toward the end of the Pleistocene Ice Age, a period in which many large mammals, including saber-toothed cats and mammoths, died out. Blaire Van Valkenburgh and Fritz Hertel, paleontologists at the University of California in Los Angeles, reported this finding in July 1993.

The researchers studied teeth from living carnivores and from carnivores that died when they were trapped in the La Brea tar pits, near present-day Los Angeles, from 36,000 to 10,000 years ago. They found that the Ice Age mammals, which included saber-toothed cats, lions, wolves, and other carnivores, had three times as many chipped and broken teeth as did living carnivores such as lions, wolves, and hyenas.

The researchers noted that when the food supply is limited, carnivores may eat more rapidly and crack and gnaw bones to obtain their marrow—activities that increase the risk of tooth breakage. The disproportionate number of broken teeth among the Ice Age carnivores thus suggests that the grazing mammals on which these predators depended for food were becoming scarce. That, in turn, may have resulted from changes in the climate or overhunting by prehistoric human beings.   [Carlton E. Brett]

See also OCEANOGRAPHY. In the Special Reports section, see UNEARTHING THE JURASSIC. In WORLD BOOK, see DINOSAUR; PALEONTOLOGY.

The discoveries of two genetic defects responsible for the most common form of inherited colon cancer were reported in December 1993 and March 1994. Because colon cancer is the second leading cancer killer in the United States, after lung cancer, the findings held significance for more people than any other genetic defect yet identified.

Colon cancer genes. Working separately, two groups of geneticists each discovered the same two genes. One group was led by Richard Fishel of the University of Vermont Medical School in Burlington and Richard D. Kolodner of the Dana-Farber Cancer Institute in Boston. The other group was led by Kenneth Kinzler and Bert Vogelstein, both of Johns Hopkins University Medical School in Baltimore.

The form of colon cancer caused by the defective genes is called hereditary nonpolyposis colon cancer (HNPCC). Experts believe that about 1 in every 200 people has one of the defective genes, and that the genes account for about 95 percent of all cases of hereditary colon cancer. Roughly 15 percent of all cases of colon cancer are of this type.

The two groups of scientists took different paths to the genes. In May 1993, Vogelstein's team and another group of scientists had reported locating a particular stretch of DNA (deoxyribonucleic acid, the molecule that genes are made of) in the cells of people known to be at a high risk of colon cancer. The scientists suspected that the DNA contained a flawed version of a gene critical for genetic repair, because cancer cells from these people contained numerous errors in their DNA. After the scientists announced their finding, they worked to isolate the gene.

Meanwhile, Fishel and Kolodner's group had been studying a gene in bacteria and yeast cells called MSH2, which helps repair damaged DNA. The scientists noticed that a defective version of the gene led to DNA errors similar to those Vogelstein and his colleagues had seen in colon cancer cells. Fishel and Kolodner theorized that Vogelstein's group had identified a human version of MSH2, and they began looking for the gene as well.

The two groups of scientists located the gene almost simultaneously. It was indeed a human MSH2 gene. The scientists also showed that all patients with HNPCC had defective versions of the gene. They announced their findings in December. Then in March 1994, the two groups identified a second colon cancer gene, this one called MLH1.

MSH2 and MLH1 work in the same way. In their normal form, the genes produce proteins that help correct DNA errors that arise when a cell divides. The defective versions create proteins that have lost their error-correcting ability. For that reason, cells with either defective gene are 100 times more likely to turn cancerous than ordinary cells.

Scientists said a DNA test to determine whether people have the genetic defects may be ready in 1994. Such a test will not identify everyone who may develop colon cancer, but it could save many lives, because doctors can cure colon cancer if it is caught early. People found to carry the genes could begin having regular colon examinations at a young age.

Osteoporosis gene. A gene that plays a major role in *osteoporosis* (the thinning of bones) was identified in January 1994 by geneticists at the Garvan Institute of Medical Research in Sydney, Australia. According to the scientists, the gene helps determine the strength of bones. Researchers had long known that osteoporosis had a genetic component because of the way the disease runs in families. Other factors already linked to the disease include having inadequate calcium in the diet, not exercising enough, and having low levels of the hormone estrogen.

The Garvan Institute scientists decided to study the influence of a gene known to direct the manufacture of a protein that binds to vitamin D. Vitamin D helps the body absorb calcium and phosphorus from the intestines and aids the *mineralization* (deposit of minerals) of bones. Both processes are important for maintaining bone density. The scientists theorized that a known altered version of the gene creates a protein that does not adequately bind to vitamin D and thus results in less dense bones.

The researchers measured the bone density of 250 pairs of twins and 311 unrelated women, and then tested the subjects to see which versions of the gene they had. (Every person has two copies of most genes, one inherited from the father and one inherited from the mother.)

The scientists discovered that much of the differences in bone density could be explained by the presence of different forms of the gene. People with two copies of the normal gene had the densest bones, whereas people with two copies of the altered version had the least dense bones. The scientists estimated that a woman with two copies of the altered version could get dangerously thin bones about 10 years before a woman with two copies of the normal gene.

Other researchers applauded the scientists' study but said more work needed to be done. For one thing, scientists do not yet know how the protein affects bone density. Also, bone formation is a complex process, so scientists think other genes must be involved. Finally, all the subjects in the study were white, so observers said the study must be performed on members of other ethnic groups to ensure that the results apply to the population as a whole.

Nevertheless, researchers said that the finding gave hope for developing a genetic test that could predict early in life whether a person is at high risk for osteoporosis. Such a person could then follow a program of diet, exercise, and hormone therapy to offset the bone weakness.

Human embryos cloned. The first attempt to *clone* (make genetically identical copies of) human embryos was announced in October 1993 by a group led by embryologists Jerry Hall and Robert Stillman of the George Washington University Medical Center in Washington, D.C. The embryos that were cloned were chosen because they had an abnormal number of chromosomes and so could not survive long enough to develop fully. (In the Special Reports section, see CLONING RESEARCH ON THE MARCH.)

Human genetic map. The most complete genetic map of the human chromosomes yet produced was unveiled in December 1993 by a group of French researchers led by molecular biologist Daniel Cohen of the Centre d'Étude du Polymorphisme Humain in Paris. Chromosomes are structures inside cells that carry genes. They consist of long chains

Colon cancer genetic defect

Scientists in 1993 announced that they had found a gene that can lead to colon cancer. The defective gene lets genetic mistakes accumulate in a cell.

When a cell divides, it must replicate its DNA (deoxyribonucleic acid, the molecule that genes are made of). Sometimes during replication, the wrong chemical subunit is put in place.

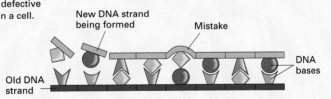

The normal version of the newly discovered gene is responsible for creating a protein that scans new DNA. When the protein finds a mistake, it cuts out the improper subunit so other proteins can add the right one.

The defective version of the gene makes a faulty DNA checker that cannot cut out the mistake. If the mistake occurs in a gene that regulates cell growth, the cell may begin dividing uncontrollably, leading to cancer.

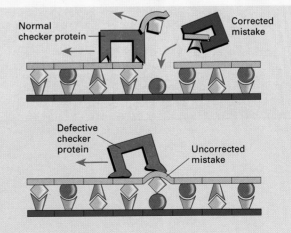

of DNA and associated proteins. Human beings have 23 pairs of chromosomes.

Cohen and his colleagues created what geneticists call a physical map—a map of chromosome fragments. The map does not give the location of any specific genes. However, it does give scientists a rough idea of where a gene may be located, and so it should help geneticists to track down the locations of the 100,000 or so human genes.

To create the map, the researchers used special DNA-slicing proteins to cut human chromosomes into 33,000 overlapping pieces. Then they used computers to analyze information from the pieces and figure out how the pieces had been grouped and ordered on the chromosomes. The researchers combined this data with results from previous mapping attempts to make a map that covers approximately 90 percent of the human genetic material.

To let other scientists examine their findings and update their information, the French researchers placed their map in a computerized database that could be accessed by scientists around the world. In addition, the researchers offered scientists copies of any of the 33,000 chromosome pieces. They made the copies using a common technique in which scientists splice each DNA fragment into a yeast cell and then grow the cells. When the yeast cells divide, they replicate the human DNA along with their own chromosomes. In this way, yeast cells created thousands of copies of each piece of chromosome.

Geneticists hoped a combined international effort would quickly improve the precision and accuracy of the map. The ultimate goal of the researchers was to determine the exact location and chemical makeup of all human genes. That is the aim of the Human Genome Project, a program underway at dozens of laboratories in the United States and abroad. Experts say the task will not be completed until after the year 2000.

Alzheimer's disease gene. A major breakthrough in the effort to establish a genetic link to Alzheimer's disease was announced in August 1993 by researchers at Duke University Medical Center in Durham, N.C. Alzheimer's disease leads to a progressive loss of memory and other mental functions. Although experts think the disease has both ge-

netic and nongenetic causes, the Duke researchers showed that one gene is a major factor in the most common form of the disease. This form is called late-onset Alzheimer's because it arises after age 65. It accounts for more than 75 percent of all Alzheimer's cases.

The Duke researchers studied a gene that was known to produce a protein called ApoE, which carries cholesterol in the blood. ApoE also binds to beta amyloid, a protein that builds up in the brains of Alzheimer's patients.

The researchers, who knew the site of the ApoE gene from previous studies, tested 234 people from 42 families in which late-onset Alzheimer's disease seemed to run. The scientists discovered that almost all the subjects who had two copies of an altered form of the ApoE gene, called Apo-E4, developed Alzheimer's disease by age 80. Overall, a person with two copies of the Apo-E4 gene was eight times more likely to get the disease than a person with two copies of the normal form of the gene.

The finding generated tremendous excitement among Alzheimer's investigators. Two other genes had previously been linked to Alzheimer's, but they involved rarer forms of the disease. However, critics pointed out that the Apo-E4 gene might not be directly associated with the illness. Instead, the gene may be only a *marker*, a gene that just happens to lie close to the gene that is truly responsible.

Most experts believed the ApoE protein was involved, however. The Apo-E4 version of the protein binds to beta amyloid better than other versions do, so some researchers theorized that Apo-E4 helps anchor beta amyloid in the brain.

Researchers still do not know how Alzheimer's harms brain cells or how the damage may be prevented. Nevertheless, scientists said the new finding provides a direction for future work. (See also MEDICAL RESEARCH.)

Human gene therapy success. The first effort to use *gene therapy* to permanently reverse a disease in a human patient seems to be working, said scientists at the University of Pennsylvania Medical Center in Philadelphia in April 1994. Gene therapy is a technique for fighting diseases in which defective or missing genes are replaced with normal ones.

The patient had *familial hypercholester-*

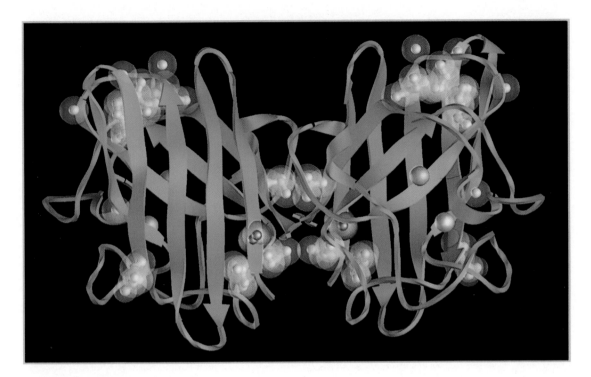

The protein associated with the genetic disease amyotrophic lateral sclerosis (shown as green strips in the computer image) contains flaws that weaken its structure, researchers reported in August 1993. Scientists had already known that certain sites along the protein (blue and orange spots) carry out important chemical reactions. The new report said the genetic abnormalities of amyotrophic lateral sclerosis produce flaws at other sites (red and yellow spots) that normally hold the protein together. As a result, the protein falls apart more readily, leading to the symptoms of the disease.

olemia, a disease in which the arteries become clogged with cholesterol because the liver cannot remove cholesterol from the blood. People with familial hypercholesterolemia lack a gene for a protein that binds to cholesterol.

The scientists treated the woman in 1992 by using a harmless virus to transfer the missing gene to some of her liver cells. The cells that received the gene began producing the desired protein. In 1994, the scientists reported that the woman's cholesterol levels had fallen 20 percent since the gene therapy.

Tuberculosis genes. Two key genes of the bacterium responsible for tuberculosis (TB) were identified in September 1993 by scientists at Cornell University Medical College in New York City. Tuberculosis is an infectious disease that breaks down cells of the body, usually lung cells. The cause of the disease is a bacterium called *Mycobacterium tuberculosis.* One of the newly discovered genes lets the bacterium invade human cells. The other gene helps the bacterium survive attack by the immune system.

To find the genes, the Cornell scientists first cut the DNA from *Mycobacterium tuberculosis* into small pieces. Then they inserted each piece into another bacterium called *Escherichia coli,* which can multiply inside human beings but normally lacks the ability to invade human cells. However, when given a particular piece of DNA from the TB bacterium, *E. coli* acquired the ability. The researchers concluded that the piece of DNA contained the TB invasion gene, and they identified the gene on the fragment.

Using a similar approach, the scientists found a second piece of DNA from *M. tuberculosis* that allowed *E. coli* to live inside a type of human cell called a macrophage. Normally, the macrophages help protect the human body against infection by digesting disease-causing agents. But *M. tuberculosis* can resist digestion and even multiply inside macrophages.

With this pair of TB genes in hand, scientists said they could start experiments to reveal exactly how the TB bacterium operates.   [David S. Haymer]

In WORLD BOOK, see CELL; GENETICS.

Geology

Changes in the motions of the plates that form Earth's *crust* (outer shell) caused ancient massive volcanic eruptions in certain areas of the globe. That was the conclusion of geophysicist Don L. Anderson of the Seismological Laboratory at the California Institute of Technology in Pasadena, Calif., in January 1994. Anderson's work helps explain why some eruptions occur at the middle rather than the edges of plates. Such eruptions included the massive outpourings of lava in the western Pacific Ocean about 120 million years ago. A series of eruptions there formed plateaus that have a combined area larger than the 48 contiguous states in the United States.

Mid-plate volcanoes. According to the widely accepted theory of plate tectonics, Earth's crust is made up of about 30 rigid pieces called tectonic plates. The plates slide or drift continuously upon a layer of partly melted rock. The plates once formed a single land mass called Pangaea, but they began to separate about 200 million years ago. As the plates move, they collide, separate, or slide past one another. Where plates move away from one another, they form *rifts* (spaces). Volcanoes form at rifts as *magma* (molten rock) rises to the surface.

Plate tectonics explains why there are many volcanoes at the boundaries of plates. A commonly accepted theory for the eruptions that occur away from plate edges concerns *mantle plumes*—columns of magma that rise from the *mantle* (the area between Earth's inner core and the crust). This theory holds that ancient massive eruptions in the middle of plates were the result of giant mantle plumes that broke through Earth's crust.

Anderson theorized that something else caused these eruptions. He suspected that they occurred because the paths of the plates had changed, causing them to smash into one another and break into smaller pieces. Such collisions would have produced rifts in the middle of plates. Because of the openings, the pressure on rocks in the upper mantle was reduced, which allowed those rocks to melt. The resulting magma erupted through the openings to the surface.

Anderson tested this theory by analyzing the speed of *seismic waves,* waves that travel through the ground during earthquakes. He found that seismic waves traveling through the middle of plates where massive volcanic eruptions occurred moved more slowly than seismic waves in other regions. Because seismic waves move more slowly through hot rock than through cooler rock, Anderson concluded that leftover heat from rising magma warmed the rock and slowed the waves.

According to Anderson, a major reorganization of tectonic plates occurred about 147 million years ago, when South America began to separate from Africa. The separation forced changes in the motions of all the plates, changes that were most marked in the South Pacific and Indian Ocean regions, where India, Australia and Borneo broke away from Pangaea. Anderson calculated that the plate reorganization started vast outpourings of lava not only in the western Pacific Ocean but in southern Brazil and along the boundary where India was beginning to separate from Antarctica.

Yellowstone mantle plume. In January 1994, geophysicists described the mantle plume beneath Yellowstone National Park in the Western United States. According to Tom Parsons of the U.S. Geological Survey in Menlo Park, Calif., and George Thompson and Norman Sleep of the Department of Geophysics at Stanford University in Stanford, Calif., the plume first appeared beneath northern Nevada 17 million years ago. As the North American plate moved over the plume, it affected the geology of what is now Utah, Idaho, Wyoming, and other Western states. The plume is responsible for Yellowstone's past volcanic activity and the park's present geysers.

The scientists suggested that after the Yellowstone plume first reached the base of the *lithosphere* (lower portion of the crust) under northern Nevada, it spread out like the cap of a mushroom to form a pool 800 kilometers (480 miles) in diameter. The upward pressure of the molten rock causes Earth's surface to arch and crack. The scientists attributed the geologic formations in Nevada and Utah's Basin and Range area to such a stretching of the crust. In the Basin and Range region, mountain ranges alternate with basins such as Death Valley.

The team also said that cracks in Earth's crust caused by the stretching allowed lava to flow onto the surface. The lava flows produced the extensive Columbia River Plateau in Washington,

Oregon, and Idaho. As the continent moved further over the plume, the lava formed Idaho's Snake River Plain.

Vesuvius danger. Volcanologists reported in February 1994 that as many as 1 million people living near Mount Vesuvius in Italy could be killed in as little as five minutes if a large eruption occurred. Vesuvius is one of the world's best-known volcanoes. Its eruption in A.D. 79 buried the Roman towns of Pompeii and Herculaneum. It erupted explosively again in 1631.

The authors of the new study were Flavio Debran of the Department of Earth System Science at New York University in New York City and two colleagues in Italy. The team reported that the chief danger of a Vesuvius eruption would be an avalanche of deadly pyroclastic material from the volcano. Pyroclastic material consists of extremely hot dust, sand, and pebble-sized fragments that form a concentrated volcanic ash. The ash is heavier than air, and it can race down the slopes of a volcano at high speeds.

Volcanologists can classify eruptions according to the amount of pyroclastic material they emit. An eruption is called Plinian if it produces more than 1 cubic kilometer (0.24 cubic mile) of pyroclastic material. The 79 A.D. eruption was the last Plinian eruption of Vesuvius, but the geologic record indicates that such large eruptions occur every few hundred to every few thousand years.

Debran and his co-workers used a computer model to analyze the likely effects of a Vesuvius eruption. The model showed that about 20 seconds after a Plinian eruption, Vesuvius would blow a column of ash 3 kilometers (1.9 miles) into the air. The column would then collapse, and the pyroclastic flow would rush down the volcano at up to 120 kilometers (75 miles) per hour. Temperatures in the flow could exceed 800 °C (1,500 °F).

The team reported that the flow could reach an area with a population of 1 million in five minutes. They recommended that officials develop effective evacuation plans and build better roads but concluded that the only real protection is for people to move away from the volcano.

Submarine canyons. Certain undersea canyons may be the result of groundwater flowing out of the ocean bottom, according to a California marine geologist. In February 1994, Daniel L. Orange of the Monterey Bay Aquarium Research Institute in Monterey, Calif., and his colleagues reported that so-called headless submarine canyons may form this way.

Undersea canyons are found at the edge of many continents. Some appear to be the underwater extensions of rivers. The canyons stretch across the continental shelf (the nearly horizontal extension of a coastal plain) before it descends into the continental slope. On the continental slope, however, are another type of submarine canyon. These canyons are called headless because they are not associated with rivers, they cannot be traced back to the continental shelf, and they end abruptly at the upper part of the continental slope.

Using detailed underwater maps made by bouncing sound waves off the sea floor, Orange and his co-workers examined the shapes of 59 headless submarine canyons and measured the spacing between them. The group gathered data from the Pacific Ocean off the coast of Oregon, the Gulf of Mexico off Florida, and the northern coast of Hispaniola in the Caribbean Sea.

The researchers found that all the headless submarine canyons had steep walls and closed, oval-shaped ends. The formations resembled canyons in Utah and western Colorado. Those canyons formed where groundwater seeped out of the Earth. The water had collected underground when rain soaked the soil and entered underground layers of rocks, such as sandstone, that contains tiny pores. The groundwater flowed sideways through the rock until it came to an opening where it could seep out. There, freezing and thawing of the water in the exposed rock caused the rock above it to break away, forming cliffs.

Orange and his colleagues concluded that a similar process occurs in the upper part of the continental slopes. There, water left in the sediment as it was deposited is squeezed out by the weight of new sediment layers. The water does not freeze and thaw, but as it seeps out, it weakens the slope above it. That causes the sediment to slide down and leave a steep canyon wall behind.

[William W. Hay]

In the Special Reports section, see THE BIGGEST ERUPTIONS ON EARTH. In WORLD BOOK, see GEOLOGY.

The Quake of '94

At 4:31 a.m. on Jan. 17, 1994, an earthquake measuring 6.7 on the Richter scale struck the Los Angeles area. The quake's *epicenter* (the location on Earth's surface directly above the point where the break in the rock occurred) was in the town of Northridge, about 40 kilometers (25 miles) north of downtown Los Angeles. Sixty-one people died in the disaster.

The quake was similar in magnitude to an earthquake that hit the San Fernando Valley in 1971, but the 1994 quake caused far more property damage. Estimates of the damage ranged up to more than $20 billion, making it the costliest earthquake in United States history.

A few hours after the quake, seismologist Kerry Sieh of the California Institute of Technology in Pasadena flew over the area in a helicopter, looking for the crack or rupture in the ground that would help seismologists identify the *fault* (break in the rock layer) that had caused the earthquake. Although he saw damaged buildings, fires, landslides, and huge dust clouds, Sieh detected no evidence of a rupture at the surface.

Realizing that it might be difficult to identify the fault that caused the quake, seismologists set out several portable *seismometers* (devices that measure the direction, intensity, and duration of earthquakes) to measure aftershocks in the area. The scientists monitored thousands of aftershocks, including three strong ones on January 29, one of which measured 5.0 on the Richter scale. (The Richter scale indicates the magnitude of earthquakes. Earthquakes measuring 4.5 or higher are considered potentially destructive.)

After analyzing seismometer tracings from the earthquake and the aftershocks, seismologists concluded that the quake took place along a previously unknown fault. They described the fault as a "blind reverse" fault. It is called *blind* because it occurs below the surface of the ground and the break in the rock layer is not visible. The fault is called *reverse* because rocks on one side of the fault move over those on the other. Seismologists estimated that the fault that caused the Northridge earthquake occurred 11 kilometers (6.8 miles) below the surface.

The scientists also measured the "dip," or slope, of the fault plane. The dip of the plain affects the motion felt at the surface of the ground. The reverse fault that moved in 1971 dipped from the San Fernando Valley toward the San Gabriel Mountains to the north. The fault that caused the 1994 Northridge earthquake, by contrast, dipped south.

The Northridge quake produced only a slight side-to-side movement of the surface. Most of its force was in a sudden vertical motion that lifted the land by about 1 meter (3.3 feet), causing objects to rise off the ground and slam back down again.

The greatest damage occurred to a Northridge apartment building where the vertical movement thrust the building off its foundation, and the quake's slight horizontal movement slid the foundation away. When the building fell fractions of a second later, the upper floors collapsed onto the ground floor, causing many deaths.

The Northridge quake caused so much damage in part simply because it occurred in a heavily populated area. The vertical motion of the fault added to the damage toll, according to seismologists. Even if the ground had not moved horizontally, the vertical movement would have caused extensive damage as buildings collapsed back onto the ground. Because of such collapses, faults that cause vertical movement do more damage than faults that cause horizontal movement—even if the vertical motion results from quakes of lesser magnitude.

The fault that caused the Northridge quake developed because of motion along California's San Andreas Fault. The San Andreas marks the boundary between the North American and Pacific plates, 2 of the 30 tectonic plates that make up Earth's outer shell. The huge, rigid tectonic plates float about on the partially melted rock in Earth's *mantle* (the area between the core and the crust). As the plates move, they bump into and sometimes fold under one another. Earthquakes occur most frequently along the boundaries of plates.

The San Andreas Fault extends about 970 kilometers (600 miles) from the southeastern part of California to an area off the state's northwestern coast. In southern California, the fault extends southeast to northwest, from the Gulf of California to east of Los Angeles. The fault heads to the west in the Los Angeles area, forming a large bend, before reverting to its southeast-northwest course north of Santa Barbara.

The Pacific Plate, which includes southwestern California, is sliding to the northwest past the North American Plate. But the fault's westward bend acts like a brake to the motion of the Pacific Plate, compressing the plates and creating a complex pattern of faults. Since 1971, all the earthquakes in southern California have occurred along reverse faults, with rock layers being thrust on top of each other as the area becomes more compressed. Seismologists believe that increasing

Destructive force

An earthquake with a magnitude of 6.7 struck the Los Angeles area on Jan. 17, 1994, creating more damage than any other earthquake in United States history. A section of freeway, *below*, was one of many structures destroyed when the earthquake caused the ground to heave up, *bottom*.

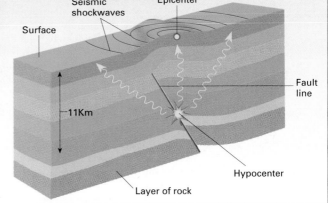

Geologists believe the *fault* (break in Earth's crust) that caused the earthquake lies completely hidden below Earth's surface. Geologists call such faults blind faults. The earthquake occurred when one layer of rock thrust itself over another, sending shock waves in all directions. The epicenter of the earthquake was on the surface about 11 kilometers (6.8 miles) above the *hypocenter*—the point at which the fault slipped.

tension along the San Andreas Fault may cause more of those quakes.

Scientists believe that the San Andreas Fault could produce southern California's "Big One," an earthquake with a magnitude of 8 or higher. Such a quake would be more than 10 times as powerful as the Northridge earthquake, but experts say the damage toll is likely to be less. Much of the San Andreas Fault extends through sparsely populated areas. That fact, combined with the fact that rock layers move horizontally, not vertically, along the fault, reduces the likely severity of the projected San Andreas quake.

The last great quake along the San Andreas Fault in southern California was in 1857. Since then, the bend in the San Andreas near Los Angeles has become more compressed. As that has happened, the geologic tensions that will lead to another large quake have been building up. Los Angeles suffered only minor earthquakes from 1857 until 1971, but since then, southern California earthquakes have become more frequent. Seismologists believe that quakes will continue along other reverse faults or along the San Andreas until the stress that has been building since 1857 is released.   [William W. Hay]

Medical Research

The virus responsible for an outbreak of a deadly flulike disease centered in the Southwestern United States was isolated in November 1993 by researchers with the U.S. Centers for Disease Control and Prevention (CDC) in Atlanta, Ga., and the U.S. Army Medical Research Institute of Infectious Diseases in Frederick, Md. The researchers found that the respiratory ailment was caused by a hantavirus. Other members of the hantavirus family are known to cause disease in Asia and Europe.

Hantavirus outbreak. Health officials first became aware of the outbreak in the American Southwest in May 1993, when a New Mexico doctor alerted them to the deaths of young, previously healthy patients. All had been suddenly stricken with flulike symptoms, including fever, chills, muscle aches, and coughing. But in this illness, the patients' lungs rapidly filled with fluid, leading to respiratory failure and, in most cases, death.

The first clue to the cause of the disease came from blood samples taken from stricken patients. Their blood contained *antibodies* (disease-fighting proteins made by the immune system) that reacted with a type of hantavirus found in Europe. Based on this information, CDC researchers theorized that the disease agent was a previously unknown hantavirus.

Researchers made that discovery only one month after the death of the first patient, but it took several months to isolate the virus and grow it in laboratory dishes. Using a variety of laboratory techniques, the researchers discovered that the disease-causing agent was indeed an unknown form of hantavirus, one that appeared to target the cells lining the lungs.

Investigations also showed that the virus was primarily carried by deer mice, which are found throughout most of North America. Health experts believe that people were infected through airborne particles from the urine and feces of deer mice and other rodents that carry the virus.

A scientific team led by University of New Mexico mammalogist Robert Parmenter provided a clue to why the outbreak occurred when it did. Parmenter discovered that unusually wet weather in the Southwest had produced an abundant food supply—pine nuts and insects—for the deer mice. With so much food, the deer mice population temporarily exploded, leading to the presence of more virus-laden feces and urine in the environment.

As of June 1994, 75 cases of the hantavirus infection had been identified, causing death in about 60 percent of those stricken with the disease. Cases occurred in 17 states, but most of the patients lived in the Four Corners region, where New Mexico, Utah, Arizona, and Colorado meet.

Human embryos cloned. The first cloning of human *embryos* (organisms in the earliest stage of development) was reported in October 1993 by fertility researchers from the George Washington University Medical Center in Washington, D.C. Cloning is the creation of organisms with identical sets of *genes* (the components of cells that contain the blueprint for an organism's characteristics and functions).

The researchers used abnormal embryos incapable of growing into fetuses, and the resulting clones lived for only a few days. Reports of the study nonetheless touched off a passionate debate concerning the ethics and possible misuse of human cloning. (In the Special Reports section, see CLONING RESEARCH ON THE MARCH.)

Rheumatoid arthritis treatment. A treatment called oral tolerization may offer help to patients suffering from rheumatoid arthritis, according to a September 1993 report by a team of researchers led by rheumatologist David E. Trentham of Harvard Medical School in Boston. In rheumatoid arthritis, the body's disease-fighting immune system mistakenly attacks the tissue that lines the joints, causing pain and swelling. In many cases, the disease spreads throughout the body, damaging organs and connective tissue. In the new treatment, patients swallow a protein similar to those in the tissue being attacked by the immune system.

Previous laboratory research had suggested that feeding animals collagen, a protein found in the rubbery cartilage that cushions the joints, could prevent or alleviate the symptoms of arthritis. In addition, the Harvard researchers had found in a pilot study with 10 patients that the treatment helped relieve arthri-

Sinus congestion and the common cold

Scans of the sinuses of people with colds revealed in 1994 that sinus problems are a typical symptom of the common cold. Scientists at the University of Virginia Health Center in Charlottesville conducted the research, which overturned a previously held notion that colds lead to sinus problems only because of a secondary infection caused by bacteria.

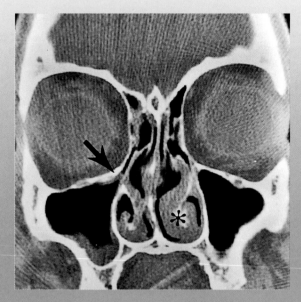

Congestion in the early stages of a cold is visible in the sinus (arrow) and the nose (asterisk).

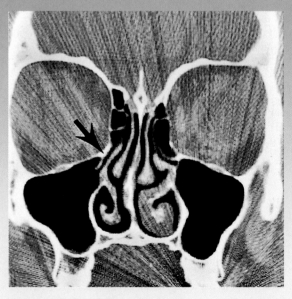

The same patient shows a cleared nose and sinus passages three weeks later.

tis symptoms in human beings.

Based on these promising results, the researchers decided to test the approach in a larger group of patients. They prepared a liquid formulation of a protein called type II collagen, which they extracted from chicken breastbones. One group of 28 patients drank daily doses of the type II collagen in orange juice for 90 days, while a group of 31 patients was given a *placebo* (inactive substance) in orange juice for the same period. None of the patients knew whether they were taking the collagen or the placebo.

At the end of 90 days, the researchers found that the patients who had taken the type II collagen showed improvement, including a decline in the number of swollen and tender joints, compared with patients taking the placebo. Four of the patients experienced a complete *remission* (absence of symptoms).

Just why collagen taken by mouth would dampen the immune system's attack on the joints is unknown. One hypothesis is that the body may be able to suppress immune reactions to substances encountered in the digestive tract, thus preventing allergic reactions to foods. Although health experts described the study as encouraging, they cautioned that long-term studies with large numbers of patients will be needed to assess whether oral tolerization is truly a useful treatment.

A landmark diabetes study showed that people with Type I diabetes can prevent or delay serious complications, such as blindness and kidney failure, by tightly controlling blood sugar levels, researchers announced at the American Diabetes Association annual scientific sessions in June 1993. The study, called the Diabetes Control and Complications Trial (DCCT), involved researchers at 27 medical centers in the United States and Canada, who monitored 1,441 diabetics aged 13 to 39.

The approximately 1.5 million Americans who have Type I diabetes cannot produce the hormone insulin, which plays a key role in regulating the body's use of glucose, a sugar that is the main source of energy for cells. People with Type I diabetes typically take one or two daily injections of insulin. The DCCT examined whether a closer control of blood glucose levels could help reduce the complications of diabetes.

Half of the subjects followed the standard regimen of checking their glucose levels once a day and taking one or two daily insulin injections. The other patients took three or more insulin injections a day or received continuous doses through a pump implanted under the skin. These patients also tested their blood sugar levels four to seven times daily and adjusted their insulin intake accordingly. After nine years, patients in the intensive-therapy group experienced fewer serious complications of diabetes than those in the standard-treatment group. (See DRUGS.)

Diabetes blocked in mice. Research conducted using diabetic mice may show a way to stop diabetes in human beings at its beginning. That was the November 1993 finding of researchers at the University of California at Los Angeles and the Stanford University Medical Center in Stanford, Calif. The scientists reported that they had blocked in mice a form of diabetes that resembles Type I diabetes in human beings.

Previous studies had suggested that a crucial step in the development of Type I diabetes occurs when *T cells* (disease-fighting white blood cells) attack an enzyme called glutamic acid decarboxylase (GAD), found in the cells of the pancreas, the gland that produces insulin. Although it is not clear what triggers the attack, scientists believe that a part of the GAD molecule that resembles a virus may cause T cells to attack.

The California researchers injected diabetes-prone mice with GAD when the rodents were three weeks old, before the body's T cells had begun attacking the pancreas. After treatment, most of the mice did not develop the disease. As a possible explanation for that outcome, the researchers suggested that early exposure to GAD helped "teach" the immune systems of the young mice that the enzyme is a normal chemical in their bodies rather than part of an invading microbe that must be attacked.

Alzheimer's disease explained? A new theory that a protein that carries cholesterol through the body could play a role in the most common form of Alzheimer's disease caused a stir among scientists who study the disease. In November 1993, neurologists Allen D. Roses and Warren Strittmatter of Duke

University in Durham, N.C., presented evidence for the theory at the annual meeting of the Society for Neuroscience. Alzheimer's disease afflicts an estimated 4 million people in the United States. It rarely occurs before age 40, and the risk of the disease increases with age. The disorder involves a gradual destruction of brain cells that leads to profound mental deterioration.

The Duke researchers said that these symptoms may be unleashed by one type of cholesterol-carrying protein called apolipoprotein-E (ApoE). There are three variants of this protein: Apo-E2, Apo-E3, and Apo-E4. Because everyone inherits two copies of the gene that directs the body's manufacture of ApoE, each person has either one or two forms of the cholesterol carrier. In August 1993, the Duke researchers had shown that people who inherit two genes for Apo-E4 are more likely than those with two genes for Apo-E3 to develop late-onset Alzheimer's, the most common form of the disease. (See GENETICS.)

The Duke researchers then analyzed the differences between Apo-E3 and Apo-E4. They found that in the test tube, Apo-E3 bound easily and firmly to a protein that plays a key role in stabilizing tiny structures called microtubules in nerve cells. The structures are vital to nerve cell functioning. Apo-E4, on the other hand, failed to become firmly bound to the protein.

The researchers thus theorized that Apo-E4 increases the risk of Alzheimer's disease because it fails to stabilize microtubules. They also suggested that a drug that mimics Apo-E3 could be used to prevent Alzheimer's disease in people with one or two genes for Apo-E4, or to treat the disease in its early stages.

However, critics cautioned that the Duke team's test-tube experiments might not paint an accurate picture of what actually occurs in the brain and said that any suggestions for prevention or treatment were highly speculative. Furthermore, factors other than Apo-E4 must play a role in the development of Alzheimer's disease, because the new theory does not account for every case. Many people with Apo-E4 do not have Alzheimer's, and not all Alzheimer's patients have inherited a gene for Apo-E4.

AIDS and pregnancy. Pregnant women infected with the human immunodeficiency virus (HIV) can reduce the risk of passing the virus to their babies by taking the drug zidovudine (AZT) after the 14th week of pregnancy, health officials announced in February 1994. HIV is the virus that causes AIDS.

Officials based the announcement on the results of a study conducted from 1991 to 1993 by American and French health agencies. The study showed that giving AZT to an HIV-infected pregnant woman reduced her baby's risk of infection from about 26 percent to about 8 percent. The dramatic reduction prompted officials to end the study and to alert doctors to consider the drug for HIV-infected pregnant patients.

The study involved 477 HIV-infected women who were still healthy. Half of them received AZT and half received doses of a placebo during pregnancy, labor, and delivery. Then, for six weeks after delivery, the babies were given the same substance (AZT or placebo) the mother had been taking. Preliminary findings showed that 53 out of 364 babies became HIV-infected. Only 13 of them were in the AZT-treatment group,

as opposed to 40 in the group that had received the placebo.

There were no serious short-term side effects among the mothers or babies taking the drug. Experts said that determining whether the treatment causes any long-term side effects will take further study, and federal officials stopped short of making a formal recommendation that all pregnant HIV-infected women take AZT. However, the National Institute of Allergy and Infectious Diseases in Bethesda, Md., co-sponsor of the study, sent out a letter to physicians to urge them to consider the potential benefits of AZT for their HIV-infected pregnant patients.

AZT disappointment. In a study reported in April 1994, British and French researchers said that AZT does not prevent or delay the onset of full-blown AIDS in people who are infected with the virus but have not yet developed symptoms. In this study, more than 1,700 HIV-infected patients with no symptoms had been given either AZT or a placebo. Some of those who had been taking a placebo were later given AZT

States reporting cases of Hantavirus

Ore. 1 case
Mont. 2 cases
N. Dak. 2 cases
Minn. 2 cases
Ida. 5 cases
S. Dak. 3 cases
R.I. 1 case
Nev. 3 cases
Colo. 5 cases
Kans. 4 cases
Ind. 1 case
Calif. 5 cases
Ariz. 17 cases
N. Mex. 20 cases
Texas 2 cases
La. 1 case
Florida 1 case

Source: U.S. Centers for Disease Control and Prevention.

Tracking down a deadly virus
Cases of a mysterious respiratory disease centered in the Southwestern United States demanded the attention of researchers in 1993 and 1994. Scientists at the Centers for Disease Control and Prevention in Atlanta, Ga., *below,* isolated the virus that causes the disease in November 1993. The virus, of a type called hantavirus, is carried mainly by deer mice. By mid-1994, 75 cases of hantavirus infection had been reported, *left.*

Medical Research Continued

when they started showing symptoms.

The researchers found that both groups were equally likely to develop full-blown AIDS, and that during the three year study, the disease progressed equally quickly in both groups. The scientists cautioned that because of the drug's side effects and the fact that HIV can develop resistance to AZT, doctors should think carefully before prescribing AZT for HIV-infected patients.

AIDS-linked cancer. HIV appears to directly cause cancer in some infected patients, researchers with the University of California at San Francisco reported in April 1994. The virus does this by inserting genetic material into the genes of human cells, in the process activating a dormant cancer-causing gene.

Although scientists have long known that patients with AIDS often develop certain cancers, most thought that those malignancies arose only because the patient's HIV-weakened immune system was unable to suppress them. However, the California researchers found that the virus appeared to play a more direct role in seven HIV-infected patients who developed a rare type of *lymphoma* (cancer of immune system cells).

The researchers examined the genes in the patients' cancerous cells and found that the virus had inserted its genetic material in almost exactly the same spot in all seven patients. The virus material had lodged near an existing *oncogene,* a gene with cancer-causing potential. Such genes often have normal roles in cell growth and division. Various agents can trigger a change in an oncogene's function, causing the uncontrolled growth of a cancer cell.

Cancer experts said that the findings could stimulate more research into the possible role of other viruses in human cancers. Some experts warned, though, that the study raises concerns about the safety of using a form of HIV in creating an AIDS vaccine, because of the virus's apparent ability to trigger cancer-causing genes. [Joan Stephenson]

In the Special Reports section, see EXPLORING THE MYSTERIES OF THE RETROVIRUS. In WORLD BOOK, see AIDS; ALZHEIMER'S DISEASE; ARTHRITIS; CLONE; DIABETES.

Meteorology

See Atmospheric Science

Neuroscience

See Biology; Medical Research

Nutrition

Contrary to popular belief, eating refined sugar does not cause hyperactivity or other behavioral problems in children, according to evidence published in February 1994 by pediatrician Mark L. Wolraich and a team of scientists at the University of Iowa in Iowa City. Wolraich and his co-workers studied how diets high in sucrose (table sugar) and the artificial sweetener aspartame affect children's behavior and *cognition* (awareness and judgment).

The study included two groups of subjects: 25 normal preschoolers and 23 grammar-school children. The parents of the grammar-school children had described their children as being sensitive to sugar.

During the study, the children and their families ate three different diets. They followed one diet for three weeks, then followed the second diet for three weeks, and then the third. One diet was high in sucrose and contained no artificial sweeteners. Another diet was low in sucrose but contained aspartame. The third was low in sucrose and had saccharin as the sweetener. The first two diets contained greater amounts of sweetener than normal diets do.

Each week, the investigators gauged the children's behavior and cognition, which was measured in terms of the children's attention span, impulsiveness, memory, learning, and performance in school. The children's parents and teachers also rated the behavior and cognition of the children.

For the normal preschool children, only 4 of 31 measurements of behavior and cognition differed significantly according to the diets the children ate. The investigators could find no consistent pattern in the differences. For the children considered sensitive to sugar, there were no significant differences among the three diets in any of 39 measures of behavior or cognition. The researchers concluded that sugar and aspartame do not influence the behavior of children, even if the sweeteners are eaten in larger than normal amounts.

Fat linked to prostate cancer. Men who consume large amounts of fat, particularly from red meat, have an almost 80 percent greater risk of developing advanced prostate cancer than do men who eat a lower-fat diet, according to a study published in October 1993 and directed by Edward Giovannucci of Harvard Medical School in Boston.

The prostate is a walnut-sized gland located under a man's bladder. As a man ages, the gland becomes more prone to developing cancer cells. Prostate cancer is one of the most common types of cancer in men in the United States, killing about 35,000 American men a year.

The researchers examined the health records of more than 51,000 men who had provided detailed reports of their eating habits in 1986. By 1990, 300 of the men who started the study in good health had developed prostate cancer. Of that number, 126 were suffering from advanced cases in which the cancer had spread to other parts of the body.

The researchers found that among the men with prostate cancer, those who had lower fat intake had more slowly spreading cancers. There were 80 percent more cases of advanced prostate cancer among the men with the highest fat intake (averaging 89 grams daily) than among the men with the lowest fat intake (averaging 53 grams daily).

Different sources of fat in the diet had different effects. The men eating the most red meat had 2.6 times more cases of advanced cancer than did the men eating the least amount of red meat. High intakes of a fatty acid called alpha-linolenic acid, found in soybean and rapeseed oils and red meats, were also associated with advanced prostate cancer. Men eating the highest amount of alpha-linolenic acid (about 1.5 grams daily) had nearly 3.5 times more cases of advanced cancer than those eating the lowest amount (0.8 grams daily). Eating fats from fish, vegetables, and most dairy products was not associated with the risk of advanced prostate cancer.

The researchers did not know why an increased intake of red meat should increase the risk of prostate cancer. However, they proposed that this type of dietary fat may raise the level of sex hormones in the blood, which may be related to the risk of prostate cancer. Another possible explanation is that cancer-causing compounds formed during the cooking of meat may be responsible for the increased risk of prostate cancer.

Flavonoids and heart disease. Consuming compounds called flavonoids may reduce the risk of coronary heart disease, according to an October 1993 study by Michael G. L. Hertog and his colleagues at the National Institute of Public Health and Environmental Protection in the Netherlands. Flavonoids are water-soluble compounds that occur naturally in vegetables, fruits, and beverages such as tea and wine. They are *antioxidants*, chemicals thought to protect body compounds by preventing them from combining with oxygen.

Although flavonoids are not nutrients, they are important to the color and flavor of foods. Nutritionists have suspected that flavonoids may also be important to maintaining health. Red wine is a significant source of flavonoids, for example, and some researchers have found a reduced risk of coronary heart disease among wine drinkers. The antioxidant properties of flavonoids may explain this reduced risk.

To examine the link between flavonoids and health, the Dutch researchers determined the flavonoid content of the vegetables, fruits, and beverages consumed by 805 men aged 65 to 84. The main contributors to the flavonoid intake for the men were black tea, onions, and apples.

The scientists also asked the men about their history of cardiovascular disease. They measured the subjects' levels of future risk for cardiovascular disease by weighing such factors as age, smoking history, weight in proportion to height, physical activity level, blood pressure, nutrient intake, and amount of fat and cholesterol in the blood.

Five years later, the researchers found that 185 of the subjects had died, 43 of them due to coronary heart disease. The researchers discovered that the risk of dying of coronary heart disease and the risk of having a first heart attack were about 50 percent lower in the men with the highest flavonoid intake (greater than 30 milligrams daily) than in the men with the lowest intake (0 to 19 milligrams daily). Experts said that those findings suggest that flavonoids may have important implications for health.

[Phylis B. Moser-Veillon]

In WORLD BOOK, see NUTRITION.

Human activities have contributed to a rise in sea level since the 1990's. That was the conclusion of a January 1994 report by geologists Dork L. Sahagian and Frank W. Schwartz of Ohio State University in Columbus and oceanographer David K. Jacobs of the American Museum of Natural History in New York City.

Records of tide levels around the world indicate that sea level has risen about 11.8 millimeters (0.46 inch) during the 1900's. The 1994 report estimates that human activities may account for about 30 percent of that rise. Warm weather that melts sea ice is thought to be responsible for the rest. Scientists had believed that melting ice was responsible for nearly all of the rise in sea level.

According to the new report, human activities that remove water from the land have directly and indirectly increased the amount of fresh water entering the oceans. Such activities include destroying forests and wetlands, draining water from underground reservoirs faster than rain water can replenish it, taking water for irrigation from lakes and rivers, and using farming and grazing practices that turn semiarid land into desert. For each of these activities, the water removed from underground or surface areas eventually reaches the sea via streams, rivers, or runoff, or through evaporation and rainfall.

The loss of forests and wetlands contributes more to rising sea levels than any other human activity, according to the researchers. Forests and wetlands retain water in several ways. Plants contain water in their tissues, for example, and wetland soils hold standing water. The roots of plants also help retain water in soils.

The researchers based their estimates on calculations of the amount of water withdrawn from *aquifers* (underground layers of rock that hold water) in North America, North Africa, and certain areas in the Middle East and southwest Asia. The scientists also calculated the increasing amount of fresh water lost from lakes and aquifers in areas around the Caspian Sea and the Aral Sea. In addition, they estimated moisture losses in soil resulting from the destruction of forests and wetlands and from desert fluctuations in the Sahel region south of the Sahara in northern Africa.

Ancient whales with feet. In January 1994, *paleobiologists* (scientists who study ancient life by examining fossils) announced the first discovery of fossil bones of a whale with working hind legs. J. G. M. Thewissen of Northeastern Ohio University College of Medicine in Rootstown led a team of scientists that found the 52-million-year-old fossil in Pakistan.

The finding is significant because it enables scientists to reconstruct how whales may have evolved from land animals. Whales belong to a group of aquatic mammals called cetaceans whose ancient ancestors were four-legged, hoofed mammals similar to large wolves. Scientists believe that this family of animals began to adapt to life in the oceans around 57 million years ago. Fossils from that time show that cetaceans had begun to lose the legs and pelvis characteristic of land mammals and had begun to develop a specialized tail for swimming.

In 1990, paleontologist Philip Gingerich reported finding in Egypt a 40-million-year-old whale fossil with evidence of hind legs. However, Gingerich said that the legs were too small to propel the animal on land.

According to Thewissen, the bone fragments his team found are those of a new member of the ancient cetacean family. He named the species *Ambulocetus natans.* The animal was about 3 meters (10 feet) long and weighed about 300 kilograms (660 pounds), making it the size of a modern sea lion.

The shape of the bones suggests that *Ambulocetus* had well-developed but weak hind limbs that could help it move on land and in water. On land, it may have walked by dragging its body as sea lions do. It swam by moving its back up and down, propelling itself through the water with its large feet. Although it had a long tail, it probably lacked the flattened appendages called flukes that modern whales use for propulsion. The recovered fossils did not include a pelvis, so it was not possible to determine just how *Ambulocetus'* legs were attached to the rest of the skeleton. (See also FOSSIL STUDIES.)

Tough bugs. Microorganisms live in oil reservoirs nearly 3 kilometers (1.9 miles) below the bed of the North Sea and in the far north of Alaska, German

Video beach mapping
Gradual changes in the shape of sand bars (light-colored bands) along an Oregon beach are visible in pictures made using a new video imaging technique. Oceanographer Rob Holman of Oregon State University in Corvallis developed the technique as an alternative to using equipment that is difficult to install and maintain. After analyzing the images, Holman noted more frequent and complex changes in the beach's shape than expected, a finding that may influence efforts to restore and protect beaches.

October

November

December

microbiologists reported in October 1993. K. O. Stetter of the University of Regensburg in Germany and his colleagues examined oil recovered from four deep wells in the East Shetland basin in the North Sea and in northern Alaska. They found high concentrations of a type of microorganism called a hyperthermophile.

Temperatures above water's boiling point of 100 °C (212 °F) kill most microorganisms, but hyperthermophiles thrive in temperatures up to 110 °C (230 °F). During the 1980's, scientists found hyperthermophiles in many hot springs, active volcanic craters, and hot vents on the ocean floor. Most hyperthermophiles are archaebacteria, which are chemically different from bacteria and may be Earth's oldest organisms. Stetter's team found archaebacteria and bacteria in the hot oil.

These hyperthermophiles survived in temperatures as high as 102 °C (216 °F) and were identical to those discovered living in deep ocean vents. That may indicate that the microorganisms normally live in environments of high temperature and high pressure. The possibility that such organisms live at such depths and pressures has caused scientists to speculate about the possibility of a "deep biosphere," in which specialized organisms thrive throughout the upper few miles of Earth's crust.

The German scientists were not sure where the organisms in the oil wells came from. Stetter said it is likely that the hyperthermophiles found in the oil had come from someplace else. He suggested that the microorganisms may have entered the deep reservoirs via the seawater that engineers commonly use to flush out wells to gather more oil. Drills used to form the reservoirs may also have carried the organisms below the surface, the scientists said.

Regardless of their origin, the ability of hyperthermophiles to tolerate such extreme pressures and temperatures caused some researchers to wonder whether the organisms are responsible for breaking down crude oil in deep reservoirs into hydrogen sulfide. That compound is troublesome to well operators because it corrodes pipes and reduces oil production and quality.

[Lauriston R. King]
In WORLD BOOK, see OCEAN; WHALE.

Physics

A key missing piece in the puzzle of elementary particles may have been found, physicists working at the Fermi National Accelerator Laboratory (Fermilab) in Batavia, Ill., reported in April 1994. The researchers announced finding strong evidence for the existence of the long-sought "top quark."

Top quark. For decades, physicists have believed that all matter is made from 12 subatomic building blocks—6 particles called quarks and 6 other particles called leptons. Ordinary matter on Earth contains mainly one kind of lepton—electrons—and two kinds of quarks, which are designated up and down. The up and down quarks are the building blocks for protons and neutrons, the particles that make up the nucleus of an atom.

The other quarks and leptons can play important roles elsewhere in the universe. They were particularly important in the earliest moments of the big bang, the explosion of matter and energy that scientists think gave birth to the universe about 15 billion years ago.

Of the 12 building blocks of matter, 11 had been found by the end of the 1970's, but physicists had hunted in vain for the top quark. One reason the top quark was so hard to find was that it is a very massive particle. (The mass of any object is the amount of matter it contains.) The top quark's mass is somewhere between 130 and 220 times the mass of the proton, making it by far the heaviest subatomic particle. The top quark's next heaviest relative, the bottom quark, has just five times the mass of the proton.

Because the top quark is not present in the everyday world, physicists had to create it by turning energy into matter. They do that by causing speeding particles to collide in a huge machine called a particle accelerator. When particles moving at extremely high speeds in opposite directions slam into one another, they create a violent burst of energy. A moment later, the energy "condenses" to form new particles. The paths taken by the particles, which can be discerned with the aid of large electronic detectors, give physicists clues to the particles' identities.

The more massive a particle is, the more energy is required to create it in this way. Only one particle accelerator in the world—Fermilab's Tevatron— had enough energy to make a particle as heavy as the top quark. The Tevatron accelerates two narrow beams of particles—a beam of protons in one direction and, in the other direction, a beam of their antimatter opposites, antiprotons. Antimatter particles are identical to particles of regular matter except that they have the opposite electric charge.

In addition to being heavy, the top quark and its antimatter counterpart are too unstable to be observed directly. In less than a trillionth of a trillionth of a second they break up into lighter particles, which are themselves unstable and break apart. At that point, physicists are dealing with a crazy-quilt pattern of dozens of particles that must be traced back to the original pair.

Despite that difficulty, the Fermilab scientists found 12 collisions, out of billions, that strongly suggested the presence of the top quark. Measurements of the collision debris allowed them to estimate the top quark's mass—about 185 times the mass of the proton.

Further collisions pointing to the presence of the top quark will have to be found before physicists can be absolutely certain they have discovered the elusive particle. But the odds look favorable that the top quark has indeed been found.

Supercollider gets thumbs down. In October 1993, the U.S. Congress voted to end construction of the Tevatron's successor, the Superconducting Super Collider (SSC). At the time, an 87-kilometer (54-mile) tunnel was being excavated for the accelerator near Waxahachie, Tex. The legislators considered the SSC's estimated cost of $11 billion too high in an era of continuing federal budget deficits.

The decision to kill the SSC, which would have been about 10 times as powerful as the Tevatron, left the future of U.S. particle physics research in doubt. About 200 physicists were directly employed on the supercollider project, and at least as many more were working at universities and other institutions in the United States to design and construct the SSC's particle detectors. In all, more than 2,000 U.S. scientists had been expected to carry out research at the SSC laboratory when it went into service early in the next century.

The Administrations of U.S. Presidents Ronald Reagan, George Bush, and Bill Clinton had all backed the construction of the SSC as a way to restore American leadership in high-energy physics. Since 1980, most of the major discoveries in particle physics have been made in Europe.

Congress, while terminating the SSC, approved some modest improvements in existing particle-physics laboratories in the United States. The jobs created at those facilities, however, will not be sufficient to absorb more than a small fraction of the scientists displaced by the SSC closeout.

With the SSC out of the picture, it seemed almost a certainty that the next major particle accelerator would be built in Europe. The European Organization for Nuclear Research (CERN), a multinational organization that operates a large accelerator near Geneva, Switzerland, has proposed constructing a machine called the Large Hadron Collider (LHC) in an existing 27-kilometer (17-mile) tunnel. The CERN accelerator would essentially be a scaled-down ver-

sion of the SSC and would achieve energy levels less than half as great.

Powerful magnets in the LHC would steer and focus two beams of protons moving in opposite directions inside two vacuum pipes. At several points around the machine, the proton beams would cross and particle collisions occur.

The primary scientific goal of the SSC was to find out why the particles that are the basic building blocks of matter have mass. Current theory suggests that mass is generated by a force transmitted by a particle called the Higgs boson. The particle is named for physicist Peter Higgs of Edinburgh, Scotland, who first proposed the idea.

As yet, no accelerator has verified the theory by producing Higgs bosons. Most physicists believe the reason for this failure has simply been that existing accelerators do not produce particle collisions with sufficient energy to create the Higgs boson.

Theorists had expected the SSC to produce plenty of Higgs bosons. There is some doubt, on the other hand, that the LHC would generate high enough

The excavation of an 87-kilometer (54-mile) oval tunnel in Texas for the Superconducting Super Collider (SSC) ceased in October 1993 when the U.S. Congress terminated funding for the $11-billion project. The SSC was to have been the world's largest *particle accelerator*, a device that smashes speeding particles into one another, allowing physicists to study the particles created in the collision.

energies to produce the Higgs particle, and so approval of the LHC has been on hold. But with the SSC defunct, many physicists now think it probable that the LHC will be built.

CERN has agreed to take in some of the American physicists who were gearing up to work at the SSC, though it is asking the U.S. government to make a substantial contribution to the cost of building the LHC or the particle detectors. But even if the LHC is constructed, it will probably be able to accommodate only a few hundred American physicists. Thus, it seems likely that the particle-physics community in the United States, in addition to losing the world's most powerful accelerator, will be forced to thin its research ranks over the next few years.

A "corral" for electrons. A striking new picture that is likely to find a place in physics textbooks for years to come was published in September 1993 by three International Business Machines Corporation (IBM) scientists. The image, produced at IBM's Almaden Research Center in San Jose, clearly illustrates the wave nature of electrons, the negatively charged particles that orbit the atomic nucleus. The picture also provides a vivid demonstration of the power of the device that produced it, the scanning tunneling microscope (STM).

Electrons are governed by the laws of quantum mechanics, which describe the behavior of matter at the subatomic level. Quantum mechanics holds that while electrons may behave like particles when they interact with other objects, their motions can be fully understood only by regarding them as waves.

The STM, which made it possible for scientists to visually confirm that notion, is so precise that it can reveal details of the atoms on a solid surface. At the heart of an STM is a needlelike probe. A tracking mechanism keeps the probe very close to the surface being studied. Electrons in the tip of the probe are attracted to the surface, and a quantum-mechanical effect called tunneling allows some electrons to jump the gap to the surface. As the needle scans the surface, it moves up and down. A computer translates the motion into a picture of the surface.

Skilled operators can also use an STM to move atoms and position them exactly where they want them. The IBM researchers did just that, placing 48 iron atoms in a circle 14 nanometers (14 billionths of a meter) in diameter on a copper crystal.

On a flat surface of copper or other metals, electrons can normally roam freely. But when the scientists scanned the ring of iron atoms with the microscope, they found that a "herd" of electrons from the tip of the STM had become confined within the circle. The electrons took the form of concentric *standing* (stationary) waves that looked much like a pattern of motionless ripples on a pond. The researchers announced that they had built a "corral" for electrons.

The electrons were not permanently trapped in the corral—they could escape through the tunneling effect. But while inside the ring, the electrons were forced into wave patterns dictated by quantum mechanics. The quantum corral opened the possibility of constructing other kinds of structures for confining electrons or other particles to study quantum-mechanical effects.

A fusion milestone. A new record for the controlled release of energy from nuclear fusion, the process that powers the sun and other stars, was achieved in December 1993 by researchers at the Tokamak Fusion Test Reactor (TFTR) in Princeton, N.J. The experimental reactor momentarily reached a peak power level of 6.2 megawatts. If converted to electricity, that output could provide power for a community of several thousand residents. In May 1994, the Princeton scientists set still another fusion-power record, 9 megawatts. (See also ENERGY.)

In fusion, two kinds of atomic nuclei join together to form a new, heavier atomic nucleus. In most cases, two hydrogen nuclei fuse to form a nucleus of helium. When the nuclei fuse, they release energy.

A sustained fusion reaction is hard to start or to maintain because it requires a temperature of tens or hundreds of millions of degrees. At temperatures that high, every known substance is not only vaporized but also stripped of its electrons. The result is an electrically charged gas called a plasma.

Because of its extreme heat, a plasma

Electrons surrounded by a "corral" of iron atoms form *standing* (stationary) waves, much like frozen ripples on a pond. Researchers made the image with an instrument called the scanning tunneling microscope, which they also used to position the atoms. The picture provides a visual confirmation of physicists' theories about the wave nature of electrons.

is very difficult to confine. In the central region of a star, a plasma is kept in place by the immense weight of all of the matter pressing in on it. Machines such as the TFTR try to hold the plasma with strong magnetic fields inside a large doughnut-shaped container. Like nearly all modern fusion reactors, the TFTR is a variant on the "Tokamak" design pioneered in the 1950's by the Russian physicist Andrei Sakharov.

The TFTR uses a plasma consisting of nuclei of two *isotopes* (forms) of hydrogen, called deuterium and tritium. Deuterium is fairly common—about 1 of every 6,500 hydrogen atoms in nature is deuterium. With every molecule of water containing two hydrogen atoms, there is enough deuterium in Earth's oceans to provide a virtually inexhaustible source of fuel for fusion reactors. Tritium, a highly radioactive isotope, is not present in nature in any significant amount, so obtaining it in usable quantities is difficult.

In the December test, the Princeton scientists generated fusion in a mixture of half deuterium and half tritium. A 50-50 mixture of the two isotopes is the richest possible fuel for a fusion reactor because it ignites at the lowest temperature and delivers the highest energy release of any fusion reaction.

In such a plasma, deuterium nuclei also fuse, with each two deuterium nuclei producing a tritium nucleus and a proton. A fusion reactor with the right initial mix of deuterium and tritium could in principle generate its own supply of tritium through deuterium-deuterium fusions.

But there are problems to be solved before fusion can become a commercial reality. Because a plasma is constantly moving, it is unstable and hard to control. Scientists thus find it difficult to keep hydrogen nuclei from leaking out of the magnetic "bottle."

Even harder to control, because they move faster than hydrogen nuclei, are alpha particles. These particles, one of two end products of deuterium-tritium fusion, are the nuclei of helium atoms. It is essential to keep alpha particles in the plasma because they provide much of the energy that keeps it hot.

Physics Continued

The experimenters monitoring the Princeton reactor were encouraged to find that no serious instabilities arose in the plasma and that the alpha particles remained confined. The result gave researchers good reason to hope that the next generation of fusion reactors may be able to produce more energy from fusion than is required to get the fusion reaction going.

But even if the break-even point is achieved, major engineering problems must be overcome before a practical power plant can be built. For one thing, the searing heat of a plasma can damage the walls of its container even though it never actually touches them. Neutrons, the other end product of deuterium-tritium fusion, also present a challenge. Neutrons damage all known metals by knocking their atoms out of position, making the metals brittle after a few years.

Neutrons can also make metals and other materials radioactive, leading to a waste disposal problem when the plant goes out of service. However, this problem would be less severe than that posed by present nuclear reactors, which generate energy through the *fission* (splitting) of heavy atoms such as uranium, a process that produces huge amounts of highly radioactive waste. The end products of fusion are two nonradioactive isotopes of helium.

The Princeton physicists hoped to reach power levels in excess of 10 megawatts by the end of 1994. After that, the researchers intended to shut down the reactor, which would be too radioactive to permit its overhaul or modification for new experiments.

The scientists were already working on the design for the successor to the TFTR, the Tokamak Physics Experiment (TPX). The TPX will serve as a test reactor for the next-generation fusion machine, the International Thermonuclear Experimental Reactor. That reactor is to be a joint effort of the United States, Russia, Europe, and Japan.

[Robert H. March]

In the Special Reports section, see Conversation with a Particle Smasher. In World Book, see Particle physics; Physics; Quark.

Pollution

See Environment

Psychology

The auditory hallucinations that occur in people with schizophrenia stem from a malfunction in the part of the brain responsible for speech, according to a September 1993 report by researchers at King's College Hospital, London. The researchers made this finding by using an imaging technique to examine brain activity in 12 schizophrenic men.

Mapping "voices" in schizophrenia. Schizophrenia is a severe mental disorder in which the patient's thoughts and perceptions are extremely inconsistent with reality. People with schizophrenia often have *delusions*, unrealistic thoughts that they believe despite evidence to the contrary. Delusions that occur frequently in schizophrenia include the belief that other people are taking away the schizophrenic's ideas, are putting ideas into his or her mind, or are aware of the patient's thoughts.

Other very disturbing symptoms of schizophrenia are false sensory perceptions called hallucinations. Hearing "voices" is an auditory hallucination, and seeing things that are not present is a visual hallucination.

To learn what area of the brain was most active during schizophrenic auditory hallucinations, the King's College researchers used a technique called single photon emission tomography (SPET). In brain imaging, this technique takes advantage of the fact that blood flow to the brain is increased in more active regions. A SPET system includes a scanner that creates X-ray images. To make the active regions of the brain show up on the X-ray images, technicians inject a harmless radioactive chemical into the patient's bloodstream.

In the King's College studies, patients with schizophrenia were connected to the imaging device. When an auditory hallucination began, the subject raised a finger, and the researchers released the chemical into the bloodstream. The patients lowered their fingers when the voices became softer and stopped.

The research team repeated the scans at an average of 19 weeks after the first test. In the second scan, the blood-marking chemical was released only when the subject had his finger down, signaling that he was having no

Imitation starts early

Children can learn from their peers at a very young age, researchers reported in July 1993. In one part of the new study, a 14-month-old, *below,* succeeds in taking apart a toy while another toddler watches. Later, the second baby is able to repeat the process.

hallucination. The two different scans gave the scientists a comparison between the blood flow measurements during auditory hallucinations and in the absence of them.

The resulting images showed that brain activity was increased in the part of the brain known to be active when a person is talking. This region, called *Broca's area,* is also active when people talk to themselves silently. The fact that the schizophrenia patients had greater activity in this area when they were hearing voices suggests that schizophrenics somehow misinterpret their own internal thoughts as external voices.

Babies imitate babies and remember what they learn, according to a study published in July 1993 by developmental psychologist Andrew N. Meltzoff of the University of Washington in Seattle. Meltzoff studied 128 toddlers and found that they could learn simple motor tasks from other toddlers before knowing how to talk.

For their study, Meltzoff and a graduate student assistant created five new toys that the babies could never have seen before. One toy was a box with a hidden button that rang a bell when pressed. Another toy was a plastic cup made of rings of increasing size. The baby could collapse the cup by pushing it down with a flat, open hand.

The experimenters first trained a group of "expert" babies, whose average age was 14 months. The researchers showed the babies how the toys worked and then praised the babies when they performed the task correctly.

Next, researchers placed "student" babies of the same age with the expert babies and allowed them to watch as the trained babies played. The observing babies received the toys immediately after the lesson. Meltzoff found that the student babies had learned how to work the toys 64 percent of the time.

To test the babies' ability to remember what they learned, Meltzoff tested them again at about 20 months of age. The researchers brought the expert babies to a day care center, where the babies played with the other toddlers for a few minutes. Then, the researchers seated the expert babies at a table and allowed them to show how each of the five toys worked. The other toddlers observed without being allowed to touch

The Repressed-Memory Controversy

The May 1994 ruling of a Napa County, Calif., jury electrified mental health professionals. The plaintiff, Gary Ramona, had sued two therapists and a medical center for encouraging his daughter to believe that Ramona had abused her when she was a child. While undergoing mental health treatment, the daughter came to believe she had recovered long-repressed memories of abuse. Ramona charged that the abuse had never happened and that his life was ruined by the accusation. The jury ordered the therapists and medical center to pay Ramona $475,000 in damages.

The case spotlighted a debate raging among mental health professionals concerning the validity of repressed memories of childhood abuse or other traumatic events. In psychological terms, repression is a process in which a person forces unpleasant feelings or painful experiences from the conscious mind into the unconscious. A now-famous murder trial in San Mateo County, Calif., brought the topic to public attention in 1990. George Franklin, Sr., stood accused of killing a young girl in the presence of his 8-year-old daughter, Eileen, some two decades before. Eileen Franklin Lipsker, the eyewitness in the case, claimed to have repressed the memory for 20 years. She said she retrieved the memory after looking down at her own daughter's face and spotting a resemblance to the dead girl. On the basis of his daughter's testimony, Franklin was convicted of first-degree murder.

Since the Franklin case, many more people have come to believe that they suffered, and then repressed the memory of, a traumatic event in childhood. But while all mental health professionals are aware that child abuse is widespread, and that therapists must be alert to the signs and symptoms of abuse, they do not agree on whether memories of abuse are commonly repressed. At one extreme are therapists who use hypnosis or the hypnotic drug sodium amytal to help patients recover repressed memories. At the other extreme are those who believe that recovered memories are almost always false.

Resolving the issue is difficult because of the lack of extensive research on childhood trauma and on memories formed in childhood. Nevertheless, the findings of the handful of studies on the topic can begin to answer some crucial questions.

One such question is whether it is common for children to "block out" the painful memories of a traumatic event. To try to find an answer, a 1988 study evaluated the memories of 20 children who had been traumatized before age 5 in events that could be verified. The children younger than 28 to 36 months were too young to form memories expressed clearly in words. But even though the children seemed to have amnesia, they showed by their behaviors that memories of the trauma had not been repressed. The children played in ways that mimicked the traumatic event, for example, and were afraid of things related to it.

A study begun in the late 1970's sought to discover how accurate were children's memories of traumatic events. The study involved 26 children who had been kidnapped from their Chowchilla, Calif., school bus, driven around for 11 hours in vans, and then buried underground in a truck trailer for 16 hours. The study found that none of the children suffered amnesia or blocked memory within the first year of the kidnapping and for four years afterward. However, eight victims incorrectly described a kidnapper within the first year. After four years, eight more children made similar mistakes in recall. Although three young, slim, white men were convicted of the crime, individual children recalled a "fat" man, a "peg-legged mastermind," a "girl with pigtails," and a "black" man.

A new study by developmental psychologist Steven Ceci of Cornell University in Ithaca, N.Y., considered whether children can be encouraged to remember things that never happened. Ceci arranged for an associate, whom he called Sam Stone, to visit a group of 3- to 6-year-old children at a nursery school. Before and after the visit, Ceci told the children that Sam Stone was a very messy person. During the visit, the man did nothing more than pat a few heads. Later, however, the children recalled that the man had made a mess at their nursery school. Although the false memories were not related to traumatic episodes, they demonstrated that children's memories can be influenced, especially by adults suggesting misinformation.

How then do we assess the memories of people who say that they suddenly remember something terrible that happened in childhood? Many legal and mental health professionals say the answer is to look for internal and external confirmation. Internal confirmation is a cluster of behaviors that indicate a person had been traumatized even if he or she had not yet recalled it. For example, the Chowchilla victims feared buses and had nightmares about being kidnapped. External confirmations are news or police reports, eyewitness accounts, photos, and other evidence that a recovered memory has a basis in fact. Until more research is done, experts say, these confirmations provide the best way to assess whether a disturbing memory is true or false.   [Lenore C. Terr] the toys. Afterward, all the babies played with other toys. Two days later, the psychologists brought the five toys to the homes of the student babies. The babies correctly worked the toys 72 percent of the time.

Family moves cause problems. Frequent family moves increase a child's risk of failing in school and having behavior problems, according to a group of public health scientists from California who reported the results of their study in September 1993. In their study, the researchers used information that had been gathered in a 1988 questionnaire of families in the United States. The scientists examined data on almost 10,000 children aged 6 to 17 years, in 1st grade through 12th.

Previous studies of the effects of family moves often looked only at those relocations associated with improved jobs and social status for the parents. The 1993 study looked at moves resulting from lost jobs, divorce, inability to pay the rent, or evictions as well as moves resulting from work transfers or other positive factors.

The scientists divided the children into two groups that they called "never moved/infrequent relocation" and "frequent relocation." The researchers adjusted the data to account for other factors that may affect a child's well-being, such as the family's economic level. This was an important step because poor families move 50 to 100 percent more often than more well-to-do families.

The researchers found that children in the frequent relocation group had more of the emotional and academic problems that were measured. About 23 percent of the frequently relocated children repeated a school grade, compared with only 12 percent of the other children. About 18 percent of the often moved children had four or more behavioral problems, compared with 7 percent in the other group.

The researchers reported that the frequently moved children did not suffer delays in growth or development, nor were they more prone to learning disorders. The researchers nonetheless concluded that parents and people who work with children should be aware of the stresses of frequent moves, which may upset a child's school performance, emotional health, or behavior.

Depression costs the United States about $43.7 billion per year, economists at the Massachusetts Institute of Technology in Cambridge estimated in a study published in November 1993. The estimate was based on costs resulting from the lost work days, treatment, and lowered productivity of the estimated 11 million working Americans who suffer from depression. That number included people with *manic-depressive disorder* (alternating high and low moods), *major depression* (severe depression), and *dysthymia* (chronic mild depression).

The researchers estimated that depressed workers lose 20 percent of their productivity, at a total annual cost for the United States of $12.1 billion. The economists said that lost work days cost $11.7 billion, and the lifetime earnings lost due to depression-related suicides amounted to $7.5 billion. The study put the cost of hospitalization at $8.3 billion, the cost of outpatient care at $2.9 billion, and that of medicines at $1.2 billion.

The report set off debate among health-care providers and others. Some welcomed the figures as support for the idea that public health policy should make treatment for depression more available. Others pointed out the difficulty in arriving at accurate numbers for such estimates as lost work productivity.

Mental disorders common. Fourteen percent of people in the United States have suffered from three or more mental disorders at the same time, sociologist Ronald Kessler of the University of Michigan, Ann Arbor, reported in January 1994. According to Kessler, this group of people accounts for 60 percent of all psychiatric disorders and 90 percent of the most severe disorders.

In his three-year study of more than 8,000 men and women from 15 to 54 years of age, Kessler also found that 48 percent of Americans have had at least a minor mental disorder at some point in their lives. The most common disorder was major depression and the next most common was alcohol dependence.

The study also found that 12 percent of women had experienced a psychiatric disorder as a result of a traumatic event, such as an auto accident or rape, and 6 percent of men had suffered such a disorder. [Leah Blumberg Lapidus]

In WORLD BOOK, see MENTAL ILLNESS; PSYCHOLOGY; SCHIZOPHRENIA.

If current trends continue, deaths caused by firearms will outnumber deaths from motor vehicles in the United States by the year 2003. That finding was reported in January 1994 by the Centers for Disease Control and Prevention (CDC) in Atlanta, Ga.

Between 1968 and 1991, the number of deaths caused by firearms increased 60 percent nationwide, according to the report. In contrast, deaths due to motor vehicles declined by 21 percent. In Virginia, California, Louisiana, Maryland, Nevada, New York, Texas, and Washington, D.C., the number of gun-related deaths already equals or exceeds the number of deaths due to motor vehicles.

Guns in the home. Firearms are used in half of all homicides that occur inside the home, according to a study reported in October 1993. The study was conducted by researchers at the University of Tennessee in Memphis, the University of Washington in Seattle, the Harborview Injury Prevention and Research Center in Seattle, and Case Western Reserve University in Cleveland.

The scientists found that the presence of a loaded gun in a home tripled the odds that a person would be killed there.

In addition, researchers at Children's Memorial Hospital in Chicago reported in March 1994 that 37 percent of all homes with children in them also have firearms present. Thirteen percent of those handguns were loaded and not locked away.

Alcohol and tobacco ads appear to exert a powerful influence over young people, according to two studies reported in February 1994. In the same month, U.S. Surgeon General Joycelyn Elders advocated a ban on tobacco advertising that is aimed at young people.

In a study by the National Institute of Alcohol Abuse and Alcoholism in Bethesda, Md., researchers found that among fifth- and sixth-grade students, those who were most familiar with beer brands, slogans, and advertisements held more positive attitudes about drinking. These young people were also more likely to say that they intended

While motor vehicle deaths decreased over two decades, deaths by firearms increased. If the trend continues, firearm deaths will outnumber motor vehicle deaths by the year 2003.

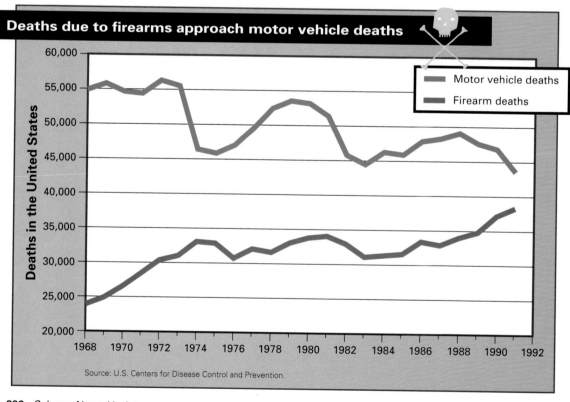

Deaths due to firearms approach motor vehicle deaths

Motor vehicle deaths

Firearm deaths

Deaths in the United States

Source: U.S. Centers for Disease Control and Prevention.

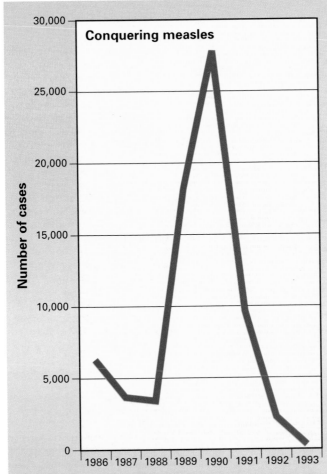

Conquering measles

Number of cases

30,000
25,000
20,000
15,000
10,000
5,000
0

1986 1987 1988 1989 1990 1991 1992 1993

Source: U.S. Centers for Disease Control and Prevention.

Public health workers claimed victory in October 1993 over a United States measles epidemic that had peaked at nearly 28,000 cases in 1990. By the end of 1993, only about 300 cases had been reported for the year, the lowest number of cases since the measles vaccine was introduced in 1963. According to public health workers, the 1990 epidemic occurred because many children had not been vaccinated. A major campaign to vaccinate children quickly brought the rates down.

to drink alcohol when they were older.

A research project at the University of California San Diego Cancer Center in La Jolla, Calif., used historical records to examine the effect of tobacco ads on the smoking habits of young women. The researchers found that after 1967, when tobacco companies began advertising cigarette brands for women, smoking rates among girls age 17 and younger grew rapidly. The rates peaked in 1973, when the total sales of women's brands peaked.

In the Surgeon General's 23rd Report on Smoking and Health, Elders strongly criticized the tobacco industry. The report, "Preventing Tobacco Use Among Young People," blamed tobacco advertising for making youngsters believe smoking will help them join what Elders called the "Five-S Club": slim, sexy, sociable, sophisticated, and successful.

Hantavirus epidemic. By June 1994, 75 people from 17 states had become ill with a severe respiratory illness that mysteriously appeared in the Southwestern United States in the spring of 1993. At first baffled by the disease, CDC medical investigators soon found the cause of the illness to be a form of *hantavirus*, a strain of viruses found in various other parts of the world. (See MEDICAL RESEARCH.)

Health toll of Midwestern floods. Heavy rains caused disastrous flooding in June and July 1993 throughout nine Midwestern states, mainly along the Mississippi and Missouri rivers. At least 48 people died in the floods, mainly from drowning.

Health department officials in Missouri, where 36 people drowned, reported that 27 of those deaths were motor-vehicle related. Authorities said that although many people believe being in a motor vehicle will protect them from rising waters, just 0.6 meters (2 feet) of water can carry away most automobiles.

As a result of heavy rainfall, cities in western Iowa reported extremely high numbers of mosquitoes known to carry a virus that causes a type of *encephalitis* (inflammation of the brain). Health officials saw no cases of the disease in 1993, but they prepared for the possibility that summer 1994 could bring even more mosquitoes and a potential encephalitis outbreak.

California earthquake aftermath.
Weeks after an earthquake shook southern California on Jan. 17, 1994, an outbreak of *acute coccidioidomycosis,* often called valley fever, sickened dozens of people living in Ventura County, near the earthquake's center. Patients suffered a range of health problems, from flulike symptoms to more serious illnesses, including *meningitis,* an inflammation of the membranes covering the brain and spinal cord. Laboratory tests confirmed 170 cases of the disease by March 15.

Acute coccidioidomycosis is caused by inhaling spores of a fungus called *Coccidioides immitis,* which grows in soil in the Southwest. The spores became airborne as the earthquake, aftershocks, and cleanup work increased the amount of dust in the air, according to officials from the California Department of Health Services and the CDC.

AIDS toll. Infection with the human immunodeficiency virus (HIV) is the leading cause of death among U.S. men aged 25 to 44, the CDC reported in November 1993. (HIV is the virus that causes AIDS.) HIV infection was the second leading cause of death for black women in the United States and the sixth leading cause of death among white women.

HIV-related deaths increased steadily during the 1980's and early 1990's. From 1982 to 1992, the death rate from HIV infection among men increased from less than 1 per 100,000 people to about 53. Among women it increased from 0.1 per 100,000 people to about 8.

Heterosexual transmission of HIV—passing the virus between males and females through sexual contact—is increasing, according to CDC statistics. From 1985 through 1993, the percentage of HIV-infected people who reported acquiring the virus through heterosexual contact increased from less than 2 percent to 9 percent. In contrast, the proportion of cases resulting from male-to-male sexual contact decreased from about 67 percent to 47 percent.

[Richard A. Goodman
and Deborah Kowal]
In WORLD BOOK, see AIDS; PUBLIC HEALTH; IMMUNIZATION.

Science and Society

Ethical issues associated with scientific research continued to attract the attention of American scientists, policymakers, and members of the press in 1993 and 1994. Much concern centered on revelations that the United States government had conducted secret experiments, beginning in the 1940's, in which human beings were intentionally exposed to radiation. (See Close-Up.)

No patents for gene fragments. The U.S. government's controversial attempt to control the rights to findings from federally funded genetics research ended in February 1994. At that time, the National Institutes of Health (NIH) in Bethesda, Md., said it would not appeal the rejection of its patent application on thousands of gene fragments. An NIH researcher had isolated the fragments as part of the Human Genome Project, an international effort to decipher the complete human genetic code.

The application, filed in June 1991, covered some 7,000 fragments whose chemical makeup had been determined but whose function was not known. The United States Patent and Trademark Office had previously granted patents only on complete genes whose functions were understood.

NIH officials had argued that patenting the gene fragments would protect the public interest by preventing private firms from filing their own patent applications and then withholding the genes' use from researchers. Critics charged that granting patents on unidentified fragments would keep scientists, institutions, and nations from sharing the results of their work, hindering the free exchange of information on which scientific progress depends.

The patent office first rejected the NIH's application in August 1992. After the NIH appealed the decision, the office rejected the application again in August 1993.

Science in the courts. The U.S. Supreme Court on June 28, 1993, made federal judges responsible for deciding whether scientific evidence presented in the courtroom is scientifically valid. Many scientists and legal scholars have charged that in the absence of clear guidelines for judges and juries, who generally lack technical expertise, the courts were being flooded by questionable experts and "junk science," scientific testimony with little foundation in scientific methods and principles.

Before the high court's ruling, lawyers could argue for or against the admissibility of scientific evidence according to two conflicting standards. The so-called Frye rule, based on a 1923 federal court decision, required judges to accept evidence only if it is based on principles that hold "general acceptance" in their field. Under that standard, judges could exclude evidence that had not been reviewed by other qualified scientists and published in a respected scientific journal. Under a rule enacted by Congress in 1975, judges were not required to apply the "general acceptance" standard to testimony, though they still had to limit scientific witnesses to those qualified by training or expertise.

The June 1993 case concerned a lawsuit involving the drug Bendectin, widely prescribed in the 1970's to reduce morning sickness in pregnant women. (The drug was removed from the market in 1983.) Two California families had sued the Paris-based Merrell Dow Pharmaceuticals, the maker of Bendectin, on the grounds that the drug had caused birth defects in their children. Merrell Dow denied the claim. Two lower courts dismissed the suit, ruling that the scientific evidence brought by the families was inadmissible because it had not been published or reviewed by other scientists and because it contradicted the results of 30 published studies.

The Supreme Court's decision struck down the Frye rule in favor of a broader standard. Voting 7 to 2, the justices held that federal judges are capable of deciding "whether the reasoning or methodology underlying the testimony is scientifically valid . . . and can be applied to the facts in issue." Under the new standard, publication in a respected journal is just one of several factors that judges may consider in determining whether to admit evidence in a trial. More important, according to the justices, is that the evidence have been derived by scientific methods and be testable by other scientists.

Science and Technology Council. Federal officials announced in November 1993 the formation of a National Science and Technology Council (NSTC) to coordinate the federal government's science and technology programs. The council is the highest-level science policy body ever created in the United States.

The NSTC's creation was the latest in a series of actions on science and technology by the Administration of President Bill Clinton. The Administration's technology initiatives also found support in the U.S. Congress. In autumn 1993, lawmakers voted to expand federal funding of research and development in industry and to fund programs to help small and medium-sized defense contractors develop technologies for commercial markets.

Nuclear test ban extended. In July 1993, Clinton announced that the United States would extend a ban on the testing of nuclear weapons until at least October 1994. The announcement intensified a debate on the future of the nation's large nuclear weapons laboratories, including Los Alamos National Laboratory in New Mexico and Lawrence Livermore National Laboratory in California. As of mid-1994, the question of what to do with the institutions—to close one or more, to consolidate them, or to convert them to civilian use—remained unresolved.

Funding cuts. Several science programs fell victim to a congressional drive to reduce the federal budget deficit in 1993. Most prominent was the Superconducting Super Collider, an $11-billion particle accelerator being built near Dallas. Congress cut off funding for the project in October. (See PHYSICS.)

Breast cancer data flawed. U.S. investigators disclosed in March 1994 that a Canadian physician had falsified research data more than a decade earlier. The news forced medical researchers to reconsider the findings of a 1985 study that helped change the way doctors treat breast cancer.

Before the study, which was coordinated by researchers at the University of Pittsburgh in Pennsylvania, doctors treated most breast cancer cases with a *full mastectomy,* a procedure in which surgeons remove the entire breast. The Pittsburgh study found that for many women whose cancer is detected early, an equally effective option was radiation

Radiation Experiments Revealed

The disturbing revelations appeared in November 1993. New Mexico's *Albuquerque Tribune* broke a story about a group of people who had been injected with high doses of a radioactive material in the mid-1940's. The people were subjects of a secret experiment conducted by the United States Army. Apparently, they had never been told exactly what was being done to them.

This was not the first time that government-sponsored radiation experiments were made public. A Washington, D.C., based newsletter had published a story on the subject in 1976. A magazine article about radiation experiments appeared in 1981 and prompted hearings by a congressional subcommittee. A second subcommittee held hearings in 1986.

None of those events attracted much public attention. But in late 1993, federal officials, led by Secretary of Energy Hazel O'Leary, approached the subject with what observers described as a new attitude of openness. If past abuses had occurred, O'Leary said, she wanted the government to acknowledge them. She promised a full investigation and stated a willingness to consider compensation for those who may have been harmed.

Over the following weeks, Americans learned of more than 30 radiation studies conducted between the 1940's and the 1970's. Observers said it was likely that more would come to light. The news touched off deep concerns about the treatment of human beings in scientific experiments, especially those involving radiation.

To understand why scientists undertook the experiments, historians say, it is important to realize that attitudes were different in the 1940's, when the studies began. The awesome power of the nuclear bomb was just becoming known. After World War II (1939-1945), Americans felt a growing suspicion that the Soviet Union would threaten the hard-won peace. When the Soviets tested a nuclear bomb in 1949, tensions rose. The Cold War had begun, and the need to fully understand radiation dangers seemed more urgent.

In those unstable times, the radiation experiments began. Some were conducted under the government's nuclear weapons research program to learn more about the effects of radiation on people in order to make weapons more effective. Other experiments were conducted to learn how to treat people exposed to radiation due to enemy attack, an accident at a nuclear reactor, or the handling of radioactive materials. These studies involved large doses of radiation and carried a risk of significant harm to the subjects.

Other experiments involved minute amounts of radioactive material and posed slight risk to the subjects. Most of the experiments were done for medical purposes unrelated to the Cold War, national security, or any aspect of nuclear power. Radioactive substances were used to study how certain chemical elements—for example, calcium and iron—are absorbed in the body.

The common factor in all the experiments is that they involved radiation. Although the experiments are often discussed as a group, there are many differences in the ethical issues they raise and in the degree to which people today might judge them to be appropriately conducted.

The experiment reported in *The Albuquerque Tribune* involved the injection of high doses of plutonium into human subjects. Plutonium, discovered in 1940, is the highly toxic, radioactive material that was used in one of the nuclear bombs dropped on Japan. Although thousands of people may have been exposed to plutonium as they worked in the United States to produce the deadly bombs, physicians in the 1940's knew very little about how the element affected the human body. They did not know whether it was excreted quickly or whether it accumulated in tissues and organs, causing harm years later. Studies using animals had not produced clear results. Therefore, government scientists proposed a plan to inject plutonium into 18 terminally ill volunteers and then monitor its passage through their bodies. The experiments occurred between April 1945 and July 1947.

Today, the pressure to learn more about plutonium is perhaps understandable. And the experiment, while not well designed, did in fact yield important results that are still useful today. Nevertheless, even when judged by the less-strict standards of its time, experts say the study was ethically unacceptable. The most serious problem with the experiment was the violation of the principle of "informed consent." According to this principle, subjects must be made aware of the risks of the study and should agree to participate without any form of coercion. But in the plutonium experiment, gaining informed consent was impossible, because the U.S. military had imposed strict rules to ensure that the nature of plutonium was kept secret. Another ethical problem with the study was that it brought no expected benefit to the subjects but it did carry considerable risk of harm. Observers say it is unlikely that the subjects knew those facts. Finally, it appears that the subjects were not carefully chosen. At least six of the subjects were not close to death, and one woman lived until 1983.

Troops with the United States Army 11th Airborne Division watch a nuclear bomb explosion from 11 kilometers (7 miles) away at Yucca Flats, Nev., on Nov. 1, 1951. The U.S. military began conducting radiation experiments in the 1940's to find out how to make more effective nuclear weapons and how exposure to radiation affected people.

In a different ethical category were certain experiments conducted by scientists at the Massachusetts Institute of Technology (MIT) in Cambridge. In the 1950's, MIT scientists laced milk with a tiny amount of radioactive calcium and fed it to a group of mentally retarded children at the Fernald School in Waltham, Mass. These studies were designed to determine whether oat cereals, which naturally contain compounds that bind to calcium, interfere with the body's absorption of calcium. Such a problem could affect bone growth. The radioactive material was placed in the milk to serve as a tracer, allowing the scientists to monitor how much calcium remained in each child's body.

The Fernald School was a residential facility, so researchers could easily monitor their subjects' diet and collect their bodily wastes. Thus, the experiments were very reliable. In addition, the amount of radiation was not thought to be harmful. It was just barely above the background radiation that people are exposed to constantly from cosmic rays and radioactive substances that exist in nature. The use of similar radioactive tracers is common in current medical research and diagnostic procedures.

Still, the Fernald School experiments raise troubling ethical issues. First, gaining informed consent from mentally impaired individuals is difficult. In fact, the researchers apparently recruited their subjects by making the experiment part of joining a "science club." Furthermore, the consent forms sent to the students' parents failed to mention radioactivity, describing the study simply as a nutritional experiment. While there is no evidence that the experiments caused any physical harm to the children, experts say that the use of such methods to gain participation violates scientific ethics and current government regulations.

Could such an experiment receive government funding today? Modern regulations make that unlikely. In 1966, the Public Health Service began requiring the institutions whose research it funds to establish boards that oversee research involving human subjects. Scientists are required to weigh a study's risks and benefits to its subjects, to consider subjects' welfare and human rights, and to provide for their informed consent. In 1991, those regulations were extended to cover all federal agencies that support research.

In January 1994, U.S. President Bill Clinton instructed federal departments and agencies to review their policies on the protection of human subjects in research and to strictly enforce them. He also announced the creation of an Advisory Committee on Human Radiation Experiments to review the radiation studies' ethical and scientific standards. The committee, chaired by an expert in medical ethics, is to present a report in 1995.

In coming to terms with the revelations about the experiments, experts say, it is important not to condemn studies simply because they involved radiation. Instead, we must distinguish among experiments by considering whether the subjects' rights were respected, whether informed consent was properly obtained, and whether the study inflicted harm.   [Albert H. Teich] therapy combined with a *partial mastectomy,* also called *lumpectomy,* in which only the tumor and a small amount of healthy surrounding tissue is removed.

Roger Poisson, a surgeon at St.-Luc Hospital in Montreal, headed one of nearly 500 teams of doctors who supplied data to the study. Poisson, whose patients represented 16 percent of the study population, admitted to investigators from the NIH and other federal agencies in May 1991 that he had falsified the dates patients were diagnosed; obtained patients' consent after, rather than before, they were enrolled in the study; and in other ways enrolled patients who were ineligible under the study's rules. Poisson said he had falsified the patients' data because he believed they would receive better treatment if they were part of the study than they would otherwise.

University of Pittsburgh researchers said they had reanalyzed the study, excluding Poisson's data, after detecting flaws in his records in February 1991. They reported that the study's conclusions were not affected. The NIH accepted the reappraisal but said in late March that it would also examine data from the study in an effort to ensure the accuracy of the research. In April, another group of researchers, led by doctors from the University of California at Irvine, published a smaller study that supported the Pittsburgh results.

The Pittsburgh study came under more fire in June 1994 after federal officials uncovered a second case of falsification from another Montreal hospital, this one involving data on a potential drug treatment for breast cancer. The officials charged the Pittsburgh researchers with failing to identify and correct problems in the study data.

Gallo cleared. One of the most heavily publicized cases of alleged scientific misconduct in the 1990's was resolved in November 1993, when federal investigators dropped charges against Robert C. Gallo, an NIH virologist. The case centered around Gallo's 1984 announcement that he had isolated the human immunodeficiency virus (HIV), the virus that causes AIDS (acquired immunodeficiency syndrome). Charges against Gallo arose after a 1989 *Chicago Tribune* article suggested that Gallo had stolen credit for the discovery from scientists

led by Luc Montagnier at the Pasteur Institute in Paris.

The article provoked investigations by the NIH and, later, by the Office of Research Integrity (ORI) of the U.S. Department of Health and Human Services (HHS). The ORI soon dropped its most serious charge, that Gallo had knowingly used samples of HIV from the French laboratory when he claimed to have identified the virus.

But in December 1992, the ORI concluded that Gallo had made false statements in his 1984 report on isolating HIV and that he had claimed credit for discoveries belonging to the French group. Gallo denied the ORI's findings and took his case to an HHS appeals board. On Nov. 3, 1993, the board rejected misconduct charges against cell biologist Mikulas Popovic, an associate of Gallo's and coauthor of the 1984 paper. The ORI dropped its case against Gallo on Nov. 12, 1993.

Surveying misconduct. Controversy erupted in November 1993, when a group of researchers published the results of a survey designed to assess the prevalence of scientific misconduct. The team was led by social scientist Judith P. Swazey of the Acadia Institute in Bar Harbor, Me. The institute is an independent organization that studies issues in science, medicine, and education.

Swazey and her colleagues polled 2,000 graduate students and 2,000 faculty members from nearly 100 American graduate departments about their perception of various abuses, ranging from misuse of university resources to outright fraud. Between 6 and 9 percent of both students and faculty said they had "direct knowledge of faculty who had plagiarized or falsified data."

According to Swazey, the findings indicated that misconduct is not as rare as scientists had thought. Critics noted, however, that the study measured perceptions of misconduct and not the behavior itself. In addition, critics said, the survey could not reveal how many respondents might have been reporting knowledge of the same incidents, thus making scientific misconduct seem more prevalent than it actually was.

[Albert H. Teich]

See also ENVIRONMENT. In the Special Reports section, see Is IT WORTH THE RISK?

Science Student Awards

See Awards and Prizes

One of the space age's greatest victories over failure occurred in December 1993 when seven astronauts on the United States space shuttle Endeavour installed new optics on the flawed Hubble Space Telescope. The Hubble repairs were carried out during five consecutive days of spacewalks, a record for a single U.S. space flight.

The Hubble repairs resulted in a dramatic reversal of fortune for the Hubble, one of the world's most important scientific instruments, and for the National Aeronautics and Space Administration (NASA), which operates the shuttle program. Astronomers were ecstatic when tests of the repaired telescope produced images of unprecedented detail and clarity.

When the Hubble was put into orbit in April 1990, astronomers had been dreaming for decades of a telescope in space. Even on a clear night, Earth's atmosphere obscures the details of stars and galaxies. An orbiting telescope offered the best hope of obtaining perfectly sharp images of celestial objects.

But astronomers soon discovered that the telescope's 2.4-meter (94.5-inch) primary mirror had been incorrectly ground. Scientists were able to use computers to manipulate the data from the telescope to compensate for most of the defect, called spherical aberration. But the orbiting observatory's performance still fell short when it came to producing images of very dim and closely spaced celestial objects.

The mission to fix the Hubble was the most extensively rehearsed of any flight in the history of the shuttle program. And the equipment the astronauts installed on the telescope, as well as the tools they used for the job, were perhaps the most thoroughly tested cargo ever sent into space.

The astronauts made several changes to the telescope, including giving it a new camera, new gyroscopes, and new solar panels. The biggest alteration, however, was the installation of a set of small mirrors to correct the fuzzy vision of the primary mirror. The new mirrors were contained in a special telephone-booth-sized unit called COSTAR.

The corrective optics worked beyond

Mars Observer lost in space
The Mars Observer spacecraft is launched in September 1992, *left,* beginning its mission as the first U.S. probe to study Mars since the 1970's. But in August 1993, as the spacecraft was nearing Mars, all contact with the vessel was lost. An investigation concluded that a rupture in the probe's fuel lines was probably at fault. An artist's conception, *below,* shows the spacecraft in an uncontrolled spin from such a rupture.

The Hubble Gets 20/20 Vision

In December 1993, astronauts aboard the United States space shuttle Endeavour installed new equipment on the Hubble Space Telescope to fix the telescope's faulty optics. The repair work, accomplished during a record-setting five spacewalks, was a resounding success. Images made with the Hubble after the shuttle mission contained a level of detail never before obtained with an astronomical telescope.

With the repairs finished on December 9, the Hubble separates from Endeavour and goes back into its own orbit around the Earth.

Anchored to the end of the shuttle's remote manipulator arm, astronaut Kathryn C. Thornton moves a device called COSTAR from the shuttle's cargo bay to the Hubble before astronauts installed the device in the telescope. COSTAR contains a system of mirrors designed to compensate for a defect in the telescope's primary mirror that caused it to produce fuzzy images.

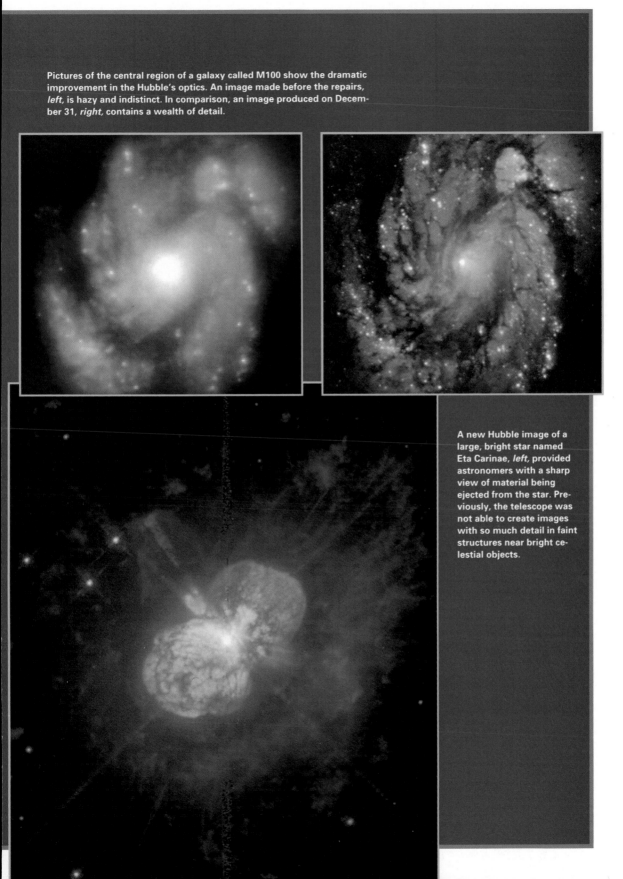

Pictures of the central region of a galaxy called M100 show the dramatic improvement in the Hubble's optics. An image made before the repairs, *left,* is hazy and indistinct. In comparison, an image produced on December 31, *right,* contains a wealth of detail.

A new Hubble image of a large, bright star named Eta Carinae, *left,* provided astronomers with a sharp view of material being ejected from the star. Previously, the telescope was not able to create images with so much detail in faint structures near bright celestial objects.

scientists' hopes. Among the findings after the repairs was the first conclusive evidence of a black hole. (See Close-Up. In the Special Reports section, see THE SEARCH FOR BLACK HOLES.)

Endeavour carried a crew of six into orbit in June 1993. In the highlight of that mission, the astronauts retrieved a European Space Agency satellite called EURECA, which had been placed in orbit by the shuttle Atlantis in August 1992. The crew also conducted experiments in a commercial facility called Spacehab, a module that connects to the shuttle cabin to provide extra room for experiments.

Endeavour went into space again in April 1994. The six-member crew tested an advanced radar system designed to produce *digital* (computer language) images that could be transformed into three-dimensional pictures of the Earth. The radar is expected to be useful for environmental studies of the planet and even for discovering possible archaeological sites.

Other shuttle flights in 1993. In September 1993, the space shuttle Discovery placed in orbit the Advanced Communications Technology Satellite (ACTS), designed to relay large quantities of information to ground receivers. Researchers at a number of universities and companies planned to use ACTS to develop new techniques for transmitting information by satellite.

Seven astronauts on the space shuttle Columbia flew the longest shuttle mission to date—14 days—in October 1993. During the mission, the crew studied the effects of weightlessness on themselves and several dozen laboratory rats.

Discovery and Columbia flew again in early 1994. In February, Discovery went into space with a crew of six, including Sergei K. Krikalev, the first Russian cosmonaut to fly aboard a U.S. spacecraft. The mission failed to successfully carry out one of its primary objectives, the deployment of a satellite—which was to be retrieved later by the shuttle—designed to grow semiconductor crystals in space. The crystals were to be used in computers and other electronic systems.

Columbia carried a crew of five into

In a composite photograph made from multiple exposures, an experimental single-stage rocket called the DC-X passes its first big test at a White Sands, N.M., launching site in August 1993. After leaving the launching pad (far right), the rocket soars into the air, hovers, moves sideways, and then returns to the ground. The DC-X, developed by the Department of Defense, may lead to economical, reusable rockets that could replace the space shuttle fleet.

orbit in March. During that lengthy mission—just 56 minutes shorter than Columbia's record flight a few months earlier—the astronauts conducted several experiments, including a study of how molten metals solidify in space.

Mars space probe lost. One of the biggest disappointments in the history of the U.S. space program occurred in August 1993 with the loss of NASA's Mars Observer space probe. The probe was supposed to orbit the Red Planet and study it for a Martian year, or 687 Earthdays. It was the first U.S. spacecraft sent to Mars since the two Viking landers arrived there in 1976.

The trouble began on Aug. 21, 1993, just as the Mars Observer was finishing its 11-month voyage. The probe was about to use its propulsion system to begin a braking maneuver that would put it into Mars orbit. Before the maneuver began, controllers at the Jet Propulsion Laboratory in Pasadena, Calif., signaled the spacecraft to turn off its transmitter, a standard procedure aimed at protecting delicate electronic circuitry.

When the controllers later commanded the spacecraft to switch the transmitter back on, there was no response. For several days, they tried in vain to contact the probe.

There was a chance the probe would "phone home" on its own. The spacecraft had been programmed with instructions to do just that if it did not hear from Earth for five days in a row. But the craft did not make contact.

Investigators subsequently tried to figure out what went wrong with the Mars Observer. When scientists and engineers have no physical evidence to examine, they often can deduce the cause of an accident from secondary information. But since there was no data from the probe to work with in this case, investigators had nothing to go on. They could only speculate about what was the most probable cause of the probe's failure to complete its mission.

They started by listing every possible breakdown they could think of. Then they evaluated each one, looking at test data of Mars Observer components and sometimes conducting new tests of duplicate components.

Most explanations for the loss of contact with the probe would have required multiple random failures of the spacecraft's systems, coincidences that were deemed unlikely. Moreover, a set of coincidental breakdowns occurring just as the propulsion system was being turned on was considered an even more remote possibility.

In the end, the investigators reasoned that the most likely failure was some event brought on by activating the propulsion system. They reported in January 1994 that the most probable occurrence was a rupture in the spacecraft's fuel lines. Such a rupture would have caused fuel to spew out of the lines, destroying vital electronics or simply putting the spacecraft into an uncontrollable spin.

The loss of the Mars Observer ruined a project costing nearly $1 billion. It was the first total failure of a successfully launched U.S. interplanetary spacecraft since 1967. Early in 1994, NASA announced plans to send two more spacecraft to Mars to recover from the Mars Observer loss.

A bad month in space. August 1993 was a trying month for the U.S. space program. On the same day that the Mars Observer space probe went dead, a weather satellite of the U.S. National Oceanic and Atmospheric Administration (NOAA) lost its electrical power. And earlier in the month, on August 2, a Titan IV rocket being launched by the Air Force exploded shortly after liftoff.

Investigators looking into the power failure of the satellite, called NOAA-13, blamed the problem on a flaw in the wiring connecting the satellite's array of solar power cells with the rest of its electrical system. The satellite remains in orbit, but it is useless and, because it is above the reach of the space shuttles, cannot be repaired.

The Titan IV, the largest rocket in the U.S. inventory, exploded 101 seconds after it roared off its launching pad at Vandenberg Air Force Base in California. The rocket was carrying a secret military payload, possibly three satellites designed to spy on ships at sea. An investigation of the accident determined that the cause was an imperfection in one of the Titan's booster rockets. The loss of the Titan and its military cargo cost U.S. taxpayers $1 billion.

Reusable rockets. In 1993, the United States moved closer to the dream of a fully reusable launch vehicle that could be operated much like an airplane. Beginning in September, the Department of Defense conducted the first tests of a lightweight one-stage rocket called the Delta Clipper-Experimental, or DC-X.

Looking like something out of science fiction, the cone-shaped, liquid-fuel rocket made several short test flights at the White Sands Missile Range in New Mexico. The rocket was able to reach a height of about 100 meters (330 feet), move sideways, and then settle back to the ground on a pillar of flame.

The DC-X is a scaled-down prototype for a possible new generation of economical spacecraft. The Defense Department envisions developing a fleet of rockets that would lift off vertically and fly into orbit without the use of boosters or other external aids. The rockets would return from orbit with enough fuel to use their engines to slow themselves down for a vertical landing.

The rockets are seen as a potentially great improvement on the space shuttle fleet. Although a shuttle can be used many times, a shuttle flight requires a huge support staff on the ground. A shuttle must also undergo extensive inspection and refurbishing and be fitted with a new fuel tank before it can be launched again.

In contrast, although much of its technology must still be developed, the DC-X promises a new era of space flight in which rockets will need minimal ground support and will be ready to return to space after just a quick reservicing. If that hope is fulfilled, it will greatly reduce the cost of putting cargo into Earth orbit.

New Japanese rocket. Japan flew a new, larger rocket for the first time on Feb. 1, 1994. Called the H-2, the rocket is the first major launch vehicle that Japan has developed without U.S. help, and it assures Japan of an independent means of putting large payloads into space. The debut of the H-2 was a sign that Japan intends to become a major spacefaring nation.

Back to the moon. On January 25, 1994, the United States launched its first spacecraft to the moon since 1972. Named Clementine 1, the small and relatively inexpensive space probe was lofted into space from Vandenberg Air Force Base aboard a Titan 2 rocket.

The spacecraft was developed by the military to test sensors in space for antimissile defense systems and to measure the effects of radiation in space on microelectronic systems. At the request of scientists, the Defense Department agreed to expand the mission to also obtain new information about the moon.

Clementine reached the moon on February 19 and went into an orbit that took it over the lunar poles. The probe photographed the surface of the moon in different wavelengths of light. Scientists hoped the photographic data would add to their knowledge of the moon's chemical composition.

Aerobraking. In June 1993, controllers of the Magellan space probe, which has been in orbit around Venus since 1990, completed tests of a novel braking method for spacecraft. The technique, known as aerobraking, uses atmospheric drag to slow the vehicle instead of firing a spacecraft's thrusters.

Aerobraking had been tested with spacecraft in Earth orbit but had never been tried with a craft circling another planet. It was tested with Magellan because the probe had completed its radar mapping of Venus.

NASA officials said they were encouraged by the demonstration. They said aerobraking could prove valuable for putting space probes into orbit around other planets. Fuel that ordinarily would be used to slow a probe when it reaches its destination could be conserved for other maneuvers.

Satellite navigation. In 1993, the United States completed a network of 24 navigation satellites known as the Global Positioning System (GPS). In September, the Federal Aviation Administration successfully tested the system for landing airplanes.

With a GPS receiver, which picks up simultaneous signals from at least four of the satellites, a person can determine his or her location anywhere on Earth within 100 meters or less. The receiver can also give the user's altitude.

The GPS was developed by the Defense Department for military uses. But the government has authorized civilian applications of the GPS, and observers expect that commercial airlines and individuals will make extensive use of the system.   [James R. Asker]

In WORLD BOOK, see SPACE EXPLORATION; SPACE TRAVEL.

Zoology

See Biology

Science You Can Use

In areas selected for their current interest, *Science Year* presents information that the reader as a consumer can use in understanding everyday technology or in making decisions—from buying products to caring for personal health and well-being.

Preserving Your Family's Keepsakes

One hundred years ago, families preserved the history of their everyday lives in letters, diaries, and the occasional black-and-white photograph. Today, we are just as likely to use audio- and videotapes, color photographs, and home movies to chronicle our life and times.

Since the 1980's, automatic cameras that focus and adjust for light levels and colors have become more affordable, and annual sales of 35-millimeter cameras in the United States have more than doubled to 10 million. The number of pictures taken and printed has increased by 50 percent since 1984 to more than 16 billion. The widespread use of video cameras has turned many a parent into a would-be movie director, and home videos are even featured on television news shows and popular entertainment programs.

These newer technologies capture events with such vividness and detail that the recordings may seem permanent. Unfortunately, they are not.

Without the right care, the color snapshots of prom night and the video of the school play may fade faster than your memories of the event. Even the paper documents that you save today are likely to yellow and fade much faster than those your ancestors stored generations ago.

All these types of personal memorabilia are faced with the same enemies that vex professional archivists who preserve important records for libraries and institutions. Heat, humidity, sunlight, and other villains make paper crumble, color photos fade, and film and videotape

snap. Fortunately, once you understand how your records are affected by the elements, you can take simple precautions to ensure that they last as long as possible.

Photographs. Like all objects, photographs undergo chemical changes over time that cause them to disintegrate. But certain conditions can speed up such reactions, in some cases altering a photo within as little time as a few months.

Each component of a color photograph is vulnerable to changes. Photos consist of three parts: dyes, a binder or emulsion, and a substrate, the paper backing for the image. The dyes are compounds (colored magenta, cyan, and yellow) that together create the color image on the print. The binder is a gelatinlike material. The dyes and binder are layered thinly on the substrate, which is typically a piece of heavy paper.

The chief menaces to color photos are sunlight and heat, which foster the breakdown of dyes. The most dramatic change occurs in color pictures left in the sun. Magenta dyes are particularly vulnerable to light, and as these dyes are destroyed, the pictures take on a greenish cast.

Heat also damages photographs. Cyan dyes are the most sensitive to heat, and magenta dyes are the least heat-sensitive. As a result, if you keep your photographs boxed up in a hot attic, the pictures will take on a reddish cast over the years.

Heat and humidity work together to speed up chemical reactions that cause binders and substrates to break down. As these substances degrade, the photos become brittle, split, and ultimately disintegrate.

Because dyes are not used in black-and-white photographs, these pictures are much more stable than color prints. But black-and-white photos don't last forever, either, because their binders and substrates are as vulnerable to aging as those of color pictures.

Photographic negatives and slides, which contain dyes and binders just as prints do, are threatened by the same forces that attack photographs. Since the 1980's, however, the dyes used on color film have been greatly improved, giving negatives and slides increased resistance to deterioration. Differences exist among brands, however.

If you do not save negatives, you need not be too concerned about the stability of the print film you purchase. Instead, choose a film that provides the color reproduction you like best—and then select a long-lasting color-print paper. Even on display, a high-quality print may look good for more than 20 years, about the maximum length of time a print made today can be displayed before showing changes.

How you handle raw film can also affect the life span of negatives, slides, and prints. Unprocessed photographic film is vulnerable to heat and humidity and should be stored in a cool, dry place. A plastic bag in the refrigerator is a good spot for film, but it must be allowed to warm to room temperature before being used.

Once exposed, film begins to undergo chemical changes and can start to deteriorate within just a few days. So it's not a good idea to keep a partially exposed roll of film in your camera. Shoot a whole roll of film at one time and take it to be processed quickly, preferably within a few days.

The way film is processed can also make a significant difference in the longevity of the resulting negatives and prints. Negatives and prints need to be carefully rinsed of the chemicals used to develop them. Chemicals left on the objects may lead to rapid deterioration.

Professional archivists face the challenge of preserving photographs that have been processed hurriedly and not thoroughly rinsed. Newspaper photos processed to meet publication deadlines and put into storage the same day are an example of this problem.

Fortunately, complete rinsing is a routine step at any competent commercial film processor. From the standpoint of preservation, there is no significant difference between photographs developed by professional photographers and those processed at one-hour shops.

The negatives and prints made with instant color films, typically used in Polaroid cameras, tend to degrade very rapidly, in part because the chemicals that develop the print remain on it. Thus, photography experts caution against keeping instant prints as archival copies. Instead, have a professional make standard copies of your instant prints for both storage and display.

Use care when handling prints of any type, as well as negatives and slides. Always touch them by the edges so that you don't transfer oils, dirt, or chemicals onto the image. Avoid bending prints or putting things on top of them that could mar them.

Properly stored, most color photographs can remain in good condition for 100 years. The ideal storage place in the home is cool, dark, and dry, such as a shelf in a bedroom closet. Be sure to keep photos out of attics, basements, and garages, which may undergo extreme temperature changes or have high concentrations of fumes from cars and stored chemicals.

One of the worst storage containers for photos is a shoebox. The cardboard in these boxes is likely to contain acids that can break the molecular bonds in the paper that the photo is printed on. As that happens, the paper begins to disintegrate.

A good quality album is generally acceptable for storing photos, but avoid "magnetic" types, which have gluey pages. The chemicals in these glues leak into the photos and, over time, destroy them. For the same reason, never use glue or tape to affix photos to a page. Instead, buy inexpensive self-sticking corners that hold photos in place.

If you prefer to use albums that contain plastic pages with sleeves for holding prints, steer clear of pages containing polyvinyl chloride (PVC), a type of plastic that has a strong smell and contains chemicals that can react with photos and cause deterioration in dyes and binders. Instead, ask for pages made of polyethylene or polypropylene, which are considered safe.

Special bags, envelopes, and boxes are available for storing slides, photos, and negatives. Materials made of uncoated polyester, also called Mylar, are an excellent choice.

When displaying photographs, remember that direct sunlight is deadly to them. Also keep them away from heat sources and air conditioners. Picture frames having nonpaper or rag-board backs are less risky options than those backed with cardboard, which contains acids that can harm the print paper.

Finally, for extra insurance, take advantage of second-set options offered by film processors. Display one set of prints and keep the other in storage. Having a duplicate photo of professional photographs, such as wedding and school pictures, is particularly important. Generally, the studio retains the negatives for a few years, but it will eventually destroy them.

Videotape and film. Motion-picture film and videotape face the same enemies as photographs, though they are less likely to be exposed to sunlight. Home movies and tapes are also at risk of being damaged by the machines that play them. But of the two technologies, the newer—videotape—is the more vulnerable to deterioration over time.

Videotape consists of three main components: a long plastic strip, particles of iron oxide or other magnetic materials, and a binder to hold the particles on the strip. The particles' magnetic charges are arranged on the tape in patterns that encode sounds and images. When exposed to heat and humidity, the particles break away from the binder. Then, when the tape is played, the particles may be stripped off the plastic strip, damaging or destroying the recording.

The iron oxide particles are easily magnetized, and a strong magnet or an electromagnetic field can also destroy the information on the tape. Electromagnetic fields surround electric appliances, such as televisions, stereos, computers, and refrigerators, whenever they are turned on. Videotapes should not be stored in direct contact with such devices.

Why documents deteriorate:

- Heat, humidity, or sunlight can cause paper to yellow, become brittle, and disintegrate.
- Acids and glues used in cardboard storage boxes or other types of paper can cause documents to disintegrate.

How to protect them:

- Display or store documents in a cool, dry place away from direct sunlight.
- Do not keep documents on display for long periods of time.
- Store documents in storage items made of rag paper, which is derived from cotton and is acid-free, rather than paper made from wood pulp.
- Store documents individually to prevent acid build-up among the papers.
- Never bend, fold, or roll documents.

The rapid changes in video technology also impact the longevity of today's tapes by threatening to make them obsolete. Tapes recorded in an out-of-date format may eventually be unplayable simply because the necessary machines are no longer being manufactured. The only way you can be sure of retrieving your memories in the future is to copy your tapes into new formats as they become available.

The technology behind motion pictures, on the other hand, has persisted with little change for a century. In addition, electromagnetic fields do not harm motion-picture film. If reels are stored with the same care as photographic slides and negatives, movies can survive 100 years. By comparison, videotape has a lifetime of only a few decades.

Film is vulnerable to mechanical damage, however, because projectors are apt to cause stretching or tears. But by copying your film onto videotape, you can preserve the original film as an archival

Why videotapes deteriorate:

- Heat or humidity causes magnetic particles that encode information to break away from the tape when it is played.
- Poorly maintained videotape players can crinkle and break tape.
- Magnetic fields produced by appliances can erase sound and images if tapes are stored nearby.

How to protect them:

- Store in a cool, dry place away from televisions, stereo equipment, computers, and other appliances or electronic devices that produce magnetic fields.
- Keep videotape players in good working order.
- To maintain proper tension on tapes, periodically play and rewind them, and store them flat rather than on their sides.
- Copy tapes into new formats as they become available.

copy, untouched by sprockets, gears, and gummy fingers. Then, when you wish to view old home movies, you can simply load a tape into the videocassette recorder rather than hauling out a film projector and screen. To avoid unnecessary wear and tear on the film during the transfer process to videotape, have it copied in its entirety rather than editing it in segments.

Videotapes are even more vulnerable than film to mechanical damage, and faulty players can do irreparable harm. As tapes are played, they are forced through a 90-degree turn, which puts extra stress on them, and they can be permanently damaged by crinkling and folding. Before putting a precious videotape into a little-used machine, test the player using a replaceable tape. If trouble develops, stop the machine immediately and investigate the cause of the problem.

Like photographs, videotapes and films should be stored in a cool, dry place. Storage in a freezer isn't a good idea, however, because unstable humidity levels and dramatic changes in temperature are likely to cause damage.

Videotape needs extra care during storage because too much or too little tension on the tape can cause problems over time. Every six months, fast-forward and then rewind the stored tape to even out the tension. Use a separate rewind machine, which applies a more consistent tension than does a video player. Storing the tape flat rather than on end also avoids uneven stress on the tape.

Finally, it's always a good idea to knock out the tape's safety lug, the plastic tab near the label, to avoid accidental erasure or overtaping. And, to document especially precious moments, remember to take along a camera as well as a video recorder.

Audiotape. Audiotapes have the same basic composition as videotape and suffer the same types of deterioration. The main difference is that audiotape players are mobile, so that tapes end up at the beach or in hot cars rather than stored in a cool, dry place. In addition, because audiotapes are smaller and thinner than videotapes, and because a portion of the tape is exposed, they are especially vulnerable to unfavorable environments and the mechanical failures of tape players. Never-

theless, if you handle your audiotape with the same care as videotape, it will have a similar life expectancy.

Paper documents. The single greatest threat to old letters, clippings, and other paper artifacts is acid, which causes paper to turn yellow and eventually to disintegrate. Ironically, newer documents are at greater risk than old. Before the 1800's, most paper was of a type called *rag*, which has low acid content and is made of cotton fibers. Since then, rag paper has increasingly been replaced by pulp paper, a high-acid form that is made from wood.

Today, certain documents, such as marriage and birth certificates, diplomas, and many legal papers, are still apt to be printed on rag paper. But day-to-day artifacts, such as letters, diaries, children's drawings, newspaper clippings, and comic books are likely to be produced on high-acid pulp paper.

Although it is possible to extract acid from paper, the chemicals involved in the process are highly toxic and suitable for use only by professional archivists. However, amateurs can take a few simpler precautions.

Once again, protection from heat and humidity is of greatest importance because those factors encourage the chemical reactions that cause ink to fade and paper to yellow and crumble. Keep all your papers in a cool, dry place, but do not store letters, cards, and comic books in stacks, because the acid in some papers may affect others in the stack. For best protection, enclose each item in a Mylar bag, keeping the bags open so that acidic vapors can escape. Photographic supply stores and some art stores often sell quality storage materials. However, mail-order purchases may be less costly alternatives, and catalogs often offer useful storage tips.

Keep colored items out of sunlight, which will fade them, and avoid displaying them on a continual basis. Finally, never roll or fold paper documents, because these actions weaken the paper.

The keys to preserving documents and all other types of family memorabilia are storing them properly, making copies, and keeping up with technological changes. Taking such pains can help ensure that the images of today last long enough for your grandchildren to admire. [Peter J. Andrews]

A Scientific Look at Sports Drinks

As millions of Americans have embarked upon the quest for strong and healthy bodies, manufacturers have jumped to develop products to satisfy almost every fitness need. While lacy leotards and neon-bright athletic shoes cannot promote better bodies, other products may directly impact performance and health. Among them are sports drinks, which are beverages designed to replenish fluids and nutrients lost during exercise.

The granddaddy of sports drinks is Gatorade. Researchers at the University of Florida in Gainesville introduced this beverage in 1965 to help prevent *dehydration* (the excessive loss of water from the body) in athletes. The new drink was tested on the university's football team, the Gators, and dubbed Gatorade. It has since become the leading sports drink in the United States.

Beverage makers introduced many other sports drinks since the mid-1980's, including All Sport (made by Pepsico Incorporated of Purchase, N.Y.), Power-Ade (made by Coca-Cola Company Incorporated of Atlanta, Ga.), and 10-K (made by Suntory Water Group, Incorporated, of Atlanta). Market analysts expect sports drinks to generate more than $1 billion in sales by 1995. But few consumers know how the products affect the body, what they are made of, or how to choose among them.

All sports drinks are designed primarily to combat dehydration. Dehydration can occur during exercise if the water lost through sweating is not quickly replaced. At first, the volume of water in the blood drops. Then, if sweating is profuse, water is pulled from skin and muscle tissue. Without adequate blood volume, the heart pumps faster, the muscles may begin to cramp, and the body begins to have difficulty shedding excess heat. If the weather is hot and the person continues to exercise, the body may eventually become overheated to the point of collapse.

Of course, plain water can combat dehydration, and exercise physiologists say that sports drinks are probably not necessary for healthy people who exercise moderately—engaging in aerobic dance, for example—for no more than one hour. The fluids lost through sweating can be replaced simply by drinking water when thirsty.

But if you exercise vigorously for more than an hour at a time, you may find that a sports beverage provides other benefits. In addition to water, the commercial drink contains ingredients that enable the body to absorb fluids efficiently, that supply energy for working muscles, and that make the beverage taste good enough to encourage you to drink plenty of it.

How effective your fluid intake will be is determined by how quickly fluids empty from the stomach and are absorbed through the small intestine and into the bloodstream. Because *carbohydrates* (compounds, such as sugars and starches, that are composed of carbon, oxygen, and hydrogen) encourage rapid fluid absorption, they are an important ingredient in sports drinks. Carbohydrates also impart an appealing taste and supply energy for muscles.

The main types of carbohydrates used in sports drinks are simple sugars called glucose, fructose, and sucrose. Glucose is found naturally in honey, and fructose is responsible for the sweet taste of fruit. Sucrose is ordinary table sugar.

Research has shown that glucose and sucrose are very effective at stimulating fluid absorption and providing energy to working muscles. Fructose, added in small amounts, helps sweeten beverages but is absorbed very slowly and can cause *gastrointestinal* (stomach and intestinal) distress and diarrhea if it is the only carbohydrate in the beverage. Fructose also is not absorbed rapidly enough to be a good source of energy for working muscles.

Manufacturers of sports beverages have been tinkering with the amount of carbohydrates in their products for years. In the 1970's, research showed

that if carbohydrates compose more than about 2.5 percent of the beverage's volume, the drink empties relatively slowly from the stomach. By the mid-1980's, however, studies concluded that higher amounts of carbohydrates would not necessarily cause stomach upset and were much better at promoting fluid absorption through the intestines. In addition, sports drink manufacturers began adding small chains of glucose, called *glucose polymers,* to drinks. These were initially thought to promote fluid emptying from the stomach but have since been shown to be no more advantageous than ordinary glucose.

Fitness experts now say carbohydrates should make up between 5 percent and 10 percent of a sports drink's volume. Drinks containing less than 5 percent carbohydrate won't provide enough energy to promote muscle performance.

Most drinks on the market are between 5 percent and 8 percent carbohydrate. Beverages that exceed 10 percent carbohydrate, such as soft drinks and fruit juices, take so long to be absorbed that they may fail to replace fluid losses as rapidly as needed. And drinking them while exercising may cause intestinal cramping, nausea, and diarrhea.

The carbonation and caffeine content of some soft drinks can pose problems as well. When warmed in the stomach, carbonated drinks may release carbon dioxide gas, which may cause gastrointestinal upset. And the caffeine that many soft drinks contain actually increases fluid loss by stimulating urine production. Alcohol also increases urination and should be avoided as well.

How does plain water stack up for fluid replacement during extended periods of exercise? Researchers at the University of South Carolina in Columbia in the mid-1980's tried to answer this question by comparing the performance of three groups of people performing 10,800 pedal revolutions as fast as possible on stationary bicycles. The exercise took place in an air temperature of 27 °C (80 °F) with 67 percent humidity. One group of subjects replenished lost fluids by drinking plain water. A second group consumed water that contained 2.5 percent glucose. A third group drank a 6-percent glucose solution.

The researchers found that all three drinks helped regulate body temperature and helped maintain a healthy heart rate, but only the 6 percent solution provided enough energy to improve performance, as indicated by how long and how fast the participants cycled. Other studies with similar results have led researchers to conclude that sports drinks can offer benefits when used under the appropriate conditions.

In addition to fluid and carbohydrates, many sports drinks also contain sodium. Sodium, along with potassium, chloride, and other chemicals, are known as *electrolytes,* substances that conduct electricity when dissolved. Adequate levels of electrolytes in the body are necessary for many vital functions, including the contraction of muscle fibers, the transmission of nerve impulses, and the maintenance of proper fluid levels in cells.

Sweat contains sodium along with other dissolved substances—which accounts for its salty taste. But exercise physiologists say that most people do not need to be concerned about losing electrolytes due to exercise. Stores of sodium and other electrolytes typically risk becoming depleted only during an extremely long period of sustained exercise, such as a triathlon or marathon. In these cases, sodium replenishment is important to prevent a condition called *hyponatremia* (low blood sodium). The symptoms of hyponatremia start with confusion and headache and can progress to unconsciousness and coma. The condition occurs infrequently but, if untreated, can be fatal.

The sodium contained in sports drinks has less dramatic benefits for recreational exercisers. An elevated sodium level in the blood is the mechanism that triggers thirst. If you drink plain water during prolonged exercise, you may satisfy your thirst before your body's true rehydration needs have been met. But by consuming sodium along with the water, you may continue to feel thirsty longer, and thus will drink more.

The sodium content of most sports drinks is much lower than the sodium content in the bloodstream. So drinking the beverages carries virtually no risk of an electrolyte overload.

The sodium provides an additional benefit by enhancing fluid absorption in the small intestine. Small amounts of sodium also improve a drink's taste, leading to greater consumption.

The amount of fluid a body will need to have replaced during a workout varies from person to person, depending on how much he or she sweats. Most people will fare well by consuming 0.2 to 0.5 liter (1 to 2 cups) of their preferred drink about 15 minutes before exercising. During exercise, you should drink about half that amount every 15 to 20 minutes in warm weather and every 30 minutes in cool conditions.

Weighing yourself before and after exercise can provide a more exact indication of your body's fluid needs. For every 0.5 kilogram (1 pound) you sweat away during exercise, your body will require 0.5 liter (2 cups) of fluid to replace it.

If you have determined that your level of exercise requires something more than water to keep you going, you will probably wonder which sport drink is best. That decision is mostly a matter of personal preference. Fitness experts suggest experimenting with drinks that contain between 5 percent and 10 percent carbohydrate along with some sodium. Avoid drinks high in fructose. The drink you choose may cause some gastrointestinal upset at first, but that should disappear within a few days. If it does not, try switching to a brand with a different concentration of carbohydrates. Also keep in mind that the beverage should taste good, so that you will be inclined to drink adequate amounts of it.

Despite the benefits of sports drinks, physiologists say it's wise to ignore advertising that portrays these products as able to boost a person's strength, skill, or overall athletic ability. Every body has its limit, and while sports drinks can support your athletic performance, no magic elixir can make everyone a star. [Ellen Coleman]

Choosing the Right Gasoline

Drive into a filling station in any major city in the United States and you may find that some changes have taken place at the gasoline pump. Since 1992, the federal government has required that 41 U.S. cities with the worst winter-time concentrations of carbon monoxide, a poisonous gas, ensure the availability of new, less-polluting fuels. By Jan. 1, 1995, gas stations in the nine metropolitan areas with the highest amounts of ground-level *ozone* (a lung and eye irritant created by the action of sunlight on pollutants such as automobile exhaust) must also start selling the new fuels. Other parts of the country may be seeing the new fuels soon afterward.

These new products, whose introduction was mandated by the Clean Air Act of 1990, are expected to ease smog in many urban areas. But they may add to the fog of confusion that motorists have often experienced when choosing a gasoline.

Drivers already face a bewildering array of fuels with different ingredients, octane ratings, prices, and performance claims. To select the one that is best for your car, your wallet, and the environment requires an understanding of the basic components of various fuels and how they work in your car engine.

The gasoline you fill your car's tank with is not a single substance but a mixture of more than 100 *hydrocarbons* (compounds consisting of carbon and hydrogen atoms) extracted from petroleum, or crude oil, at refineries. In addition, most gasolines contain detergents, which prevent dirt from clogging the car's fuel lines. Compounds called corrosion inhibitors, which prevent rust, are another ingredient in many gasolines.

Your car derives power from gasoline by vaporizing it, mixing it with air, and igniting it with a spark in the engine's cylinders. A miniature explosion follows in which the gasoline burns, producing hot, expanding gases. These gases push down a metal rod in the cylinder called a piston. The piston's movements turn a crankshaft, creating the primary motion that makes the car go.

Ideally, the spark would ignite the fuel-air mixture at perfectly timed intervals, and the mixture would burn completely. But even in the most efficient automobile engines, this never happens. Imperfections in the timing of the spark, the ratio of fuel to air, and many other variables cause incomplete *combustion* (burning) of the fuel. This results not only in decreased engine performance but also in the creation of *emissions,* by-products and pollutants that are released into the air.

A typical symptom of a problem in the combustion process is *engine knock,* a repetitive banging noise that occurs when the explosions in the cylinders take place too rapidly. Over an extended period, the problem can severely damage an engine.

Leaded gas was designed to prevent engine knock, because lead slows the rate of explosions in the cylinder. In the 1960's, however, lead-containing auto emissions were linked to cancer and found to cause brain and nervous-system damage in children. Since 1975, most cars have been designed to run only on unleaded fuel. Sales of leaded gasoline have steadily declined, and many service stations no longer sell it.

The choice between unleaded and leaded gas is the simplest one drivers face. Drivers of cars made before 1975 should choose leaded gas. Although these models will run on unleaded gas, their engine valves may be damaged by it, particularly if the car is driven at high speeds.

Conversely, models made after 1975 and designed to run on unleaded gas should never be filled with leaded fuel. Leaded gas will not improve the car's performance, and it can damage the catalytic converter, a device in the exhaust system that changes polluting emissions into less harmful compounds.

Refiners have compensated for the loss of lead's antiknock qualities by increasing the amount of knock-resistant hydrocarbons in unleaded gasoline. Like lead, certain hydrocarbons help promote steady combustion. A gasoline's ability to resist knocking is called its octane rating. The octane rating is expressed as a number, usually between 80 and 100. The higher the octane value of a gasoline, the less likely it is to cause knocking. "Regular" unleaded gasoline usually has an octane rating of 87. "Premium" gasolines generally have ratings of 92 or 93. Many gas stations also offer a midrange gasoline with an octane rating somewhere between those of regular and premium fuels.

Different oil companies use different names—for example, "Super Premium," "Gold," or "Ultimate"—to denote their grades of gasoline, and the inconsistency may make it difficult for drivers to select and compare high-octane and low-octane fuels. However, federal law requires that a gasoline's octane rating be posted at the pump. Checking those ratings is the best way to compare the grades of fuel.

High-octane gasolines cost more than their low-octane counterparts, but do they actually improve engine performance? Although many people seem to think so, this is not necessarily the case.

A quick check of your car owner's manual should tell you whether your car's engine was designed to run on high-octane fuel. The engines of some cars—typically high-performance luxury cars and sports cars—do not burn low-octane fuel thoroughly, and they must be given high-octane fuel to avoid reducing engine performance and increasing polluting emissions.

If your car's engine was not designed for high-octane fuel, and if the engine does not knock when burning low-octane gas, the car probably does not need high-octane fuel. And, according to automotive engineers, occasionally or regularly using a high-octane gas in such a car provides no benefit.

However, a vehicle that today purrs like a kitten on regular unleaded fuel may, in a few years, require a premium gasoline to keep it running smoothly.

As a car ages, deposits build up in the engine that reduce its efficiency, and high-octane fuels may be required to keep the engine from knocking.

It's also important to note that even though one brand of gasoline may have the same octane rating as another, the two may perform quite differently in your car engine. Different refiners use varying types and amounts of hydrocarbons in their gasoline recipes, and they alter their formulas based on the seasons and the region in which they will be sold. (Gasoline sold in wintertime in northern states, for example, contains a relatively large number of hydrocarbons that combust easily—a formulation that helps engines start in cold weather.) The amounts of detergents, corrosion inhibitors, and other additives in the fuel also vary from brand to brand.

Generally, the way to find the best

Comparing fuels

Type of gasoline	Leaded gasoline	Unleaded gasoline with octane rating of 87 (also called "regular")	Unleaded gasoline with octane rating of 92 or above (also called "premium" or "super premium")	Reformulated fuel (sometimes referred to as "reduced-emissions gasoline")
Derived from	Petroleum (crude oil)	Petroleum (crude oil)	Petroleum (crude oil)	Gasoline made from petroleum combined with either MTBE (methyl-tert-butyl ether), a compound made from natural gas; ethanol, an alcohol made from corn; or methanol, an alcohol derived mainly from natural gas or coal.
Engine performance	Eliminates engine knock in cars made before 1975. Inappropriate for use in most newer models.	Fine for most cars, but low octane rating may cause engine knock or run-on as the car ages.	Usually eliminates engine knock and run-on.	Reduces mileage per gallon by 1 percent to 3 percent but increases resistance to engine knock. Ethanol formulas may accelerate corrosion in fuel tanks and lines.
Pollutants released	Tailpipe emissions contain lead, hydrocarbons, nitrogen oxides, carbon monoxide, carbon dioxide.	Tailpipe emissions contain hydrocarbons, nitrogen oxides, carbon monoxide, and carbon dioxide. Quantities tend to be greater in older cars.	Tailpipe emissions contain hydrocarbons, nitrogen oxides, carbon monoxide, and carbon dioxide. Quantities tend to be greater in older cars.	Tailpipe emissions contain carbon dioxide but have lower levels of hydrocarbons, nitrogen oxides, and carbon monoxide than those produced by other gasolines.
Availability	Limited	Widespread	Widespread	Most major cities, but not all service stations.
Average cost	About 10 cents per gallon lower than regular unleaded.	About $1.00 per gallon (as of early 1994).	From 15 to 40 cents more per gallon than regular unleaded.	From 15 to 40 cents more per gallon than regular unleaded.

formula for your car is to try different brands, compare prices, and determine whether your car's performance is affected. Several telltale signs indicate a need to switch fuels. Knocking is one of them. So is engine run-on, in which the engine keeps firing for a few seconds after the ignition is turned off. Like knocking, engine run-on can be cured by changing to a higher-octane fuel. And if your well-tuned car starts delivering disappointing gas mileage, you may be able to remedy the problem by switching to a different brand of gaso-

line that has the same octane rating.

Soon, consumers may have another option to consider—the gasoline's effect on the environment. By 1995, gas stations in many U.S. communities will offer gasolines reformulated to be less polluting. These fuels contain oxygenates, compounds that contain oxygen. Oxygenates include the alcohols methanol, ethanol, and isopropanol, as well as compounds called ethers. These chemicals make up between 10 percent and 15 percent of the total volume of the fuel. Some reformulated gasolines

Which fuel is right for you?

- **Leaded fuel**
  Necessary for cars made prior to 1975 and for cars made between 1975 and 1980 and designed to use leaded fuels.

- **Regular unleaded fuel**
  Suitable for cars that do not exhibit engine knock or run-on, and for situations requiring optimal gas mileage at the lowest cost per gallon.

- **High-octane unleaded fuel**
  Appropriate for cars designed to run primarily on this fuel, such as high-performance sedans or sports cars, and for cars showing signs of engine knock or run-on.

- **Reformulated fuel**
  Suitable for cars exhibiting engine knock or run-on and for cars whose owners want to help reduce air pollution.

also contain reduced levels of olefins and aromatics, the hydrocarbons that are the main culprits in ozone formation.

Oxygenates reduce engine knock by increasing the octane rating of gasoline. They also promote more complete gasoline combustion and help reduce harmful emissions. During combustion, oxygenates release oxygen atoms that attach to molecules of carbon monoxide and form carbon dioxide and water. In a similar fashion, the oxygen atoms combine with unburned hydrocarbons, yielding carbon dioxide and fewer ozone-forming compounds.

Most reformulated gasolines on the market contain one of two types of oxygenates: methyl-tert-butyl ether (MTBE) or ethanol. Scientists obtain MTBE by converting a component of gasoline called butane into isobutylene, which is then combined with methanol. Ethanol, or grain alcohol, can be derived from corn.

Service stations that sell reformulated gasoline post at the pump the type and amount of oxygenate in the fuel. For example, one of these new gasolines might be identified by a sign saying: "Formulated with 10 percent ethanol." The fuel's ability to reduce emissions is often advertised as well.

How does reformulated gasoline stack up against ordinary gasoline in cost and performance? On a pound-per-pound basis, MTBE and ethanol are more expensive to produce than gasoline, so adding them to a formula raises the price of the fuel. In 1994, retailers were selling reformulated fuels for about the same price as unleaded premium gasolines. When MTBE and ethanol are burned, they release less energy than hydrocarbons do. Consequently, reformulated fuels cause a 1- to 3-percent reduction in gas mileage and a slight increase in the frequency of trips to the gas pump. On the other hand, MTBE and ethanol significantly enhance a fuel's octane rating.

The reformulated fuels' major benefit is their relative kindness to the environment. The new fuels can reduce carbon monoxide emissions by up to 20 percent in vehicles built before the mid-1980's. They also reduce emissions produced by newer cars, though not as dramatically.

Before using a reformulated gasoline, check your car owner's manual for the maximum levels and types of oxygenates your engine will tolerate. Some vehicles, for example, can be damaged by even small amounts of methanol. If you do not have an owner's manual, or if your manual does not provide this information, ask the car's manufacturer for advice.

In a few decades, reformulated gasoline may be as outdated as leaded fuels are today. Hydrogen, natural gas, and electricity all hold promise for powering the car of the future. But until a new breed of car takes over the highway, most consumers will have to settle for a choice among regular, premium, and reformulated.   [Gordon Graff]

Snuffing Out the Sniffles

When it comes to physical ailments, nothing is more common than a cold, which strikes people more frequently than all other diseases combined. Each year, the disruption and discomfort of colds send millions of people groping in their medicine cabinets for relief.

Despite the popularity of over-the-counter cold medications, medical researchers caution that the drugs' possible usefulness must be carefully balanced against their potential for side effects. For cold sufferers who don't want to "tough it out," physicians recommend selecting cold medications designed to precisely target symptoms. By avoiding products with ingredients you don't need, you also avoid unnecessary side effects.

The sheer number of over-the-counter cold medications can make label reading a chore, however. Fortunately, the *active ingredients* (those compounds designed to relieve symptoms) in cold medications are few in number. Various brands tend to use similar ingredients but in differing strengths, proportions, and combinations.

What none of the medications do is cure or shorten the illness. Colds—which may also be called *upper respiratory infections*—are caused by at least 100 different types of viruses. But it takes only a single virus infecting a single cell, usually in the nose or throat, to bring on a cold. Within a matter of hours, the virus has used the cell to reproduce itself several hundred times over. These newly formed viruses then break out of the cell and infect other cells in the nose, the throat, and, sometimes, the lungs.

In an attempt to defend themselves against invading viruses, the infected cells are responsible for many of the unpleasant symptoms of the cold. The cells may trigger the release of compounds such as histamine, which *dilates* (widens) nearby blood vessels, allowing blood and its infection-fighting components to enter the area. The increased volume of blood causes congestion, stuffiness, and inflammation—which leads to further discomfort by stimulating nerve endings. The chemicals released by the cells also stimulate increased production of *mucus,* a clear, slimy fluid that is produced to wash out foreign bodies.

Scientists have been unable to develop drugs that kill cold viruses without harming the body. Antibiotics, which can kill bacteria, are useless against viruses and should not be taken to fight a cold. However, your doctor may prescribe an antibiotic if, along with your cold, you develop a bacterial infection, such as an ear infection or strep throat.

Although no medications cure colds, the hundreds of preparations on the market do attack cold symptoms. The active ingredients in these drugs fall into five major categories: analgesics, antihistamines, decongestants, cough suppressants, and expectorants. Choosing among the products is less confusing and frustrating if you understand what each of these ingredients do.

Analgesics. Analgesics relieve pain and fever associated with colds and many other illnesses. These compounds include aspirin, acetaminophen (such as Tylenol), ibuprofen (found in Advil, Nuprin, and Motrin), and a newcomer in 1994, naproxen (Aleve).

Although analgesics have been available for years, either by prescription or over the counter, scientists still do not know precisely how they work. A leading theory suggests that aspirin, ibuprofen, and naproxen lessen fever and pain primarily by slowing production of *prostaglandins,* chemical messengers that help regulate a number of functions, including body temperature. As prostaglandin levels drop, fever and inflammation—and their resultant aches and pains—subside.

These analgesics' effect on prostaglandins explains the drugs' typical side effects as well. Prostaglandins control the production of acid in the stomach, and inhibiting prostaglandin production can cause excess stomach acid, leading to irritation or even stomach bleeding or ulcers. Physicians generally recommend that people who have ulcers or who have experienced stomach irritation with aspirin in the past should not use it or ibuprofen or naproxen.

Aspirin poses a more serious problem for children and teen-agers. The drug is thought to trigger *Reye's syndrome,* a rare but life-threatening *neurological* (brain and nervous system) condition that can develop when a child has a mild viral infection such as chickenpox or influenza.

Acetaminophen's method of action is different from that of aspirin, but scientists are still uncertain about the details of how it works. Acetaminophen does not cause stomach irritation, but it is not as effective as other analgesics in reducing inflammation. If taken in large doses over an extended period, it may cause kidney or liver damage. Thus, you should not take more than eight 5-milligram tablets of acetaminophen per day for more than 10 days unless you are taking it under a doctor's supervision.

Antihistamines. After fever, aches, and pains, the most annoying cold symptoms may be a runny nose and sneezing. Drugs called antihistamines target these problems. The antihistamines most often included in cold preparations are chlorpheniramine (found in Chlor-Trimeton, Dristan, and Allerest), brompheniramine (in Dimetapp and Dimetane), diphenhydramine (in Benadryl), and tripolidine (in Actidil).

Antihistamines do not directly block histamine, but they do prevent the biochemical from stimulating nerves in mucous membranes. As a result, the flow of mucus from the nose declines or stops. Antihistamines probably foil histamine by blocking the transmission of *acetylcholine,* a type of chemical that relays information between nerve cells.

A side effect of most antihistamines is drowsiness. In fact, diphenhydramine is used in sedatives, drugs that have a relaxing effect or promote sleep. Avoid such antihistamines when you must

Treating cold symptoms

Symptom: Sore throat

Treatments: Topical anesthetics (benzocaine).

How they work: Topical anesthetics numb the throat by inhibiting nerve impulses.

Side effects: Usually none.

Symptom: Cough

Treatments: Cough suppressants (dextromethorphan) and expectorants (guiafenesin).

How they work: Cough suppressants inhibit the coughing reflex. Expectorants are thought to thin mucus secretions in lungs.

Side effects: Usually none.

Symptom: Stuffy nose

Treatments: Topical decongestants (oxymetazoline, phenylephrine) or oral decongestants (pseudoephedrine).

How they work: Both types of decongestants reduce nasal swelling by causing blood vessels to constrict.

Side effects: Topical forms (nose sprays or drops) used for more than three days lose their effectiveness and may cause a rebound congestion that actually increases nasal congestion. Oral forms may increase heart rate and blood pressure.

Symptoms: Sneezing and runny nose

Treatments: Antihistamines (chlorpheniramine, brompheniramine, diphenhydramine, tripolidine).

How they work: Antihistamines prevent *histamine,* a chemical in body tissues, from stimulating nerves in nasal membranes that produce mucus.

Side effects: Drowsiness and excessively dry mouth and nose.

Symptoms: Fever, aches, and pains

Treatments: Analgesics (aspirin, acetaminophen, ibuprofen, naproxen)

How they work: Aspirin, ibuprofen, and naproxen reduce inflammation by blocking the production of prostaglandins, compounds involved in pain perception and body temperature regulation. Acetaminophen's method of action is unknown.

Side effects: Stomach upset or irritation with aspirin, ibuprofen, or naproxen. Excessive amounts of acetaminophen can damage the kidneys and liver. In children and teenagers, aspirin may bring on Reye's syndrome, a life-threatening disorder affecting the nervous system.

drive or engage in other activities that demand alertness. Finally, by stopping the flow of mucus, antihistamines may also cause another side effect—an excessively dry nose and mouth.

Decongestants. If that stuffed-up feeling is what bothers you most during a cold, a decongestant may help. Decongestants cause the blood vessels in the nose to constrict and the membranes to shrink, thus reducing nasal swelling, inflammation, and mucus production.

Decongestants are most effective when taken in topical forms—that is, as nose drops or sprays, which tend to stay in the nasal passage in greater concentrations than can be provided by oral forms. However, after a few days' use, topical decongestants can actually bring about the very problem they are supposed to alleviate. This happens as the body senses the reduced blood flow to the nose and tries to counteract it by redoubling its efforts to widen the blood vessels. This so-called rebound congestion can result in symptoms even more severe than those of the original cold. Thus, physicians generally recommend that cold sufferers not use over-the-counter nose sprays or drops for more than a few days in a row. Common topical decongestants include oxymetazoline (contained in Afrin) and phenylephrine (in Neo-Synephrine).

Oral decongestants do not cause rebound congestion because they do not affect as great an area in the nasal passages in as high a concentration as do drops or sprays. But oral forms may constrict other blood vessels, causing an increased heart rate and elevated blood pressure. The most widely used oral decongestant is pseudoephedrine (found in Actifed and Sudafed).

If you are taking other medications, check with your doctor before using a decongestant. The remedy may adversely interact with other drugs, such as those prescribed for high blood pressure or depression.

Cough formulas. If a cold sets up camp in your lungs, you may have a cough that is hard to squelch. Two different remedies treat this symptom: cough suppressants and expectorants.

Most cough suppressants rely on dextromethorphan (found in Robitussin DM, Vicks Formula 44, Triaminic, and Comtrex). Scientists do not know exactly how this drug works but they think it acts on the area of the brain responsible for the cough reflex. Because coughing helps keep airways clear, experts recommend using a suppressant only for a nonproductive cough—one that does not produce mucus—unless your doctor advises otherwise.

Expectorants, the most common of which is guiafenesin (found in Robitussin products and Naldecon), are a better choice for productive coughs. Expectorants cause secretions to become watery and more easily coughed up. How this occurs is not well understood. The side effects of both suppressants and expectorants appear to be minimal, if any, in most people.

The two different remedies for coughs illustrate the importance of reading ingredient labels in order to precisely match your symptoms with a treatment. To simply stop a runny nose, for example, experts recommend you use a product that contains only an antihistamine. For nasal congestion, a decongestant may be all that is necessary to bring relief. You may be able to bring a cough to a tolerable level with only a suppressant or an expectorant.

Also consider a drug's strength. Generally, drugs advertised as long-acting do not put more medicine to work in the body at any one instant. Instead, they are simply digested more slowly than other pills. Long-acting formulas cost more than a comparable supply of single doses, with the trade-off being convenience for price.

Cold preparations are also sold in various forms, ranging from tablets to capsules to liquids. Except for the case of oral and topical decongestants, one form of medication is no more likely to ease symptoms than another. Be aware, however, that many liquid cold medications contain about 10 percent alcohol, which can increase drowsiness caused by antihistamines. Also take note of other additives, such as caffeine, that can adversely affect how you feel.

Finally, no matter how bad you feel when you reach for a cold medicine, use the same care as when taking any other drug. Read and follow the package instructions carefully, and if you experience questionable side effects, discontinue using the drug and call your physician.   [Peter Radetsky]

Paper or Plastic: Which Bag Is Better for the Environment?

The scene occurs millions of times each day at supermarket checkout counters across the United States. A clerk holds up two bags—one made of thin plastic, the other of brown paper—and asks the shopper to choose between them.

The choice is more difficult than it may seem. Some shoppers concerned about the environment believe that paper bags are a more "natural" product and must be kinder to the environment. But other equally concerned shoppers say plastic bags are the best to use.

The ideal solution would be to use fewer of both types of bags. By reducing the number of bags we use, we reduce the amount of raw materials used to create them as well as the pollutants released in manufacturing and shipping them. But on those occasions when we must choose between paper or plastic bags, knowing something about the products' environmental impact at each stage of their lives—from manufacture to disposal—can help.

To begin with, the creation of both paper and plastic bags involves the use of natural resources and the release of pollutants. The main resources used in paper manufacturing are wood, water, and petroleum.

The wood comes from trees, which are considered a renewable resource—that is, nature, often aided by human beings, can renew the supply of the material. More than half of the trees used in papermaking are grown on tree farms that replace the trees they cut with new seedlings. According to the American Forest and Paper Association in Washington, D.C., nearly 2 million new trees are planted in the United States every day to replace and increase the supply of wood for paper products. The remainder of new wood comes from trees cut down in forests.

The sturdy brown paper, called *kraft paper*, that grocery bags are made of is created in paper mills. First, the mills reduce wood to small pieces in a chipper (a machine that breaks wood into chips), and those pieces are cooked in a solution of chemicals. This process separates the wood's fibers from its *lignin* (a group of compounds that hold the fibers together), producing wood pulp. Then the lignin is washed out of the pulp with water. The mushy fibers are passed through screens, which drain off most of the water and strain away undesirable materials. As rollers and heat get rid

of the remaining water, chemical bonds form between the fibers, holding the fibers together to make a continuous sheet.

Papermaking requires lots of water—about 64,300 liters (17,000 gallons) per ton of paper. Most of this water is recovered, cleaned up, and reused, but some is unavoidably lost, mainly through evaporation.

A great deal of energy is needed to run the machinery in a paper mill and heat the pulp mixture. About 44 percent comes from oil and other fossil fuels. The remainder is produced by burning wood waste, paper scrap, and lignin.

Even though paper bags are made of natural ingredients, the papermaking process can give off toxic substances. According to a 1992 report prepared for the Council of State Governments and the United States Environmental Protection Agency, kraft paper production releases 11 types of pollutants into the atmosphere. These chemicals include foul-smelling sulfur compounds, nitrogen oxides (lung irritants and components of acid rain), carbon monoxide (a poisonous gas), and lead (a metal known to cause brain and nervous system damage in children).

In addition, more than 20 pollutants from papermaking may end up in lakes, rivers, and other waterways. Some of these chemicals may combine with the oxygen in the water, a process that can deplete the oxygen needed for use by living inhabitants. Other water-borne pollutants created in the papermaking process include heavy metals, such as lead and mercury.

At most of the mills that produce significant amounts of paper, however, water-borne waste is directed into artificial ponds, and the resulting muddy sludge is periodically dug out. The sludge then can be trucked to landfills, dried and burned as fuel, or spread on the land to add organic matter to the soil.

For plastic bags, the major raw materials used are petroleum (crude oil) and in some cases natural gas. Neither are renewable resources.

Most plastic bags are made of low-density polyethylene (LDPE). To produce this substance from petroleum, the liquid is "cracked"—broken down into various *hydrocarbons*, molecules consist-ing of hydrogen and carbon. Chemists subject one of these hydrocarbons, ethylene, to high temperatures and pressures, which forces the molecules into long chains called polymers. The end product is LDPE. The cracking process also yields other hydrocarbons, some of which are combined to produce gasoline.

Once the LDPE is created, it is made into thin sheets called film, cut to size, and formed into bags. The amount of oil needed for the entire operation—including the petroleum used for the bag's raw material and for energy to power the manufacturing plant—is roughly 2,000 liters (530 gallons) per ton of bags.

This is about 85 percent more oil per ton than is used for making paper bags. But because plastic bags are lighter than paper, there are many more of them in a ton.

The first step in the manufacture of a plastic bag—cracking petroleum to produce ethylene—can release into the atmosphere toxic compounds, including some thought to cause cancer. In addition, some 55 types of pollutants may enter the waterways, mainly via municipal sewer systems or water filtration plants, but also through direct discharge into lakes and streams and through airborne emissions that settle onto bodies of water.

The second step—turning ethylene into polyethylene—can create more air and water pollutants. Furthermore, before petroleum can be cracked, the salt in it must be removed. (The oil comes out of the ground mixed with salt

The pros and cons of paper bags

- **Natural resources used:** Paper is made from wood harvested from trees, which are a renewable resource. To produce 1 ton of paper, manufacturers use about 64 metric tons (70 short tons) of water, most of which is reused, and 620 liters (164 gallons) of oil.

- **Recycling potential:** Paper grocery bags may be recycled up to five times.

- **Disposal:** Paper bags may be burned or deposited in landfills. Because a paper bag is heavier and bulkier than a plastic one, paper bags take up more landfill space and require more fuel to transport than the same number of plastic bags.

- **Biodegradability:** Paper bags decompose relatively easily in open areas but not in most landfills.

Logs being readied for shipment, *left*. Paper refuse in a landfill, *below*.

A petroleum refinery.

A plastic-bag recycling center.

water.) The salt-removal process consumes a good deal of water, and the salt that has been removed must also be disposed of to prevent it from leaching into underground water supplies.

All told, most of the emissions created by the manufacture of paper bags are also given off during plastic-bag manufacturing. Plastics manufacturing also releases additional types of pollutants whose environmental impact is difficult to gauge precisely.

The disposal of paper and plastic bags raises another set of questions. Because plastic bags are made of much thinner material than paper bags, they take up much less space in landfills, bag for bag and pound for pound. According to plastics industry statistics, 1,000 paper bags would make a stack 117 centimeters (46 inches) high, weighing 64 kilograms (140 pounds). The same number of plastic bags would make a stack only 9 centimeters (3.5 inches) high, weighing 7 kilograms (15 pounds).

Obviously, plastic bags take up less space in landfills. And their lighter weight means that less fuel is needed to transport them. On the other hand, because plastic bags tear so easily, supermarket clerks usually use at least two plastic bags for every paper bag. But even at that rate, plastic bags would still take up only about 23 percent of the space that paper would occupy.

One of paper's seeming advantages is that it is *biodegradable* (able to be broken down by microbes) under the right conditions. Such conditions include plenty of moisture, optimal temperatures, and the presence of oxygen. But modern landfills are designed to be dry and airtight, and paper does not decompose readily there. In fact, researchers have dug up old landfills and found newspapers more than 30 years old that were still readable. In addition, some experts view biodegradability as a negative feature because it can result in harmful compounds seeping into soil and ground water and can produce harmful methane gas. On the other hand, other experts say, the methane could be captured and used as an energy source.

Plastic bags in landfills raise other questions. Researchers surmise that a plastic bag will need decades to break down when exposed to air and moisture, and that in a landfill a plastic bag might last indefinitely. But because plastic bags have not existed for very long, scientists cannot say with certainty how long they will last.

Some companies have experimented with adding starch, a powdery substance derived from plants, to the plastic mix to make a bag that will disintegrate when the starch decomposes. Because starch weakens plastic bags, it can make up no more than 15 percent of the bag. When the starch decomposes, the 85 percent that is polyethylene remains in the landfill as a fine dust.

A second alternative for disposing of used grocery bags and other solid wastes is *incineration* (burning at extremely high temperatures). In some communities, the heat from incineration helps to generate electric power. However, in 1993, only about 16 percent of solid municipal waste was burned in waste-to-energy incinerators, according to the National Solid Waste Management Association, an industry group in Washington, D.C.

According to a report commissioned by the American Plastics Council in Washington, D.C., plastic bags release almost 2.75 times as much heat energy as do paper bags, pound for pound. And plastic produces almost no residual ash, whereas paper bags leave ash equal to about 1 percent of their weight. However, incineration can release a number of pollutants into the air.

Environmental researchers say that recycling is part, though by no means all, of the solution to our environmental problems, and both paper and plastic bags can be recycled. Here again, the two types have their own sets of advantages and disadvantages.

When paper is recycled, it is shredded, mixed with water, and passed through a hydropulper, a machine that mashes it into pulp again. Each time paper is recycled, its fibers become thinner and more brittle. Eventually, they become too small to be caught by the filter that traps them for reuse. The fibers in a grocery bag can probably be recycled up to five times before they are unusable, according to the paper industry.

Recycling saves trees, uses much less energy than making new paper, and reduces pollution by eliminating some production steps, such as wood chipping. However, the process does create sludge and some air pollutants.

Plastic bags are recycled by washing and shredding them, melting them, and recasting them into film or other forms. The process creates little or no air pollution and uses only about half as much energy per bag as recycled paper needs, according to industry reports. However, like paper fibers, plastic resins also degrade each time they are reused, and plastic bags have not been recycled enough to accurately predict LDPE's longevity.

Experts say there is little demand from recyclers for used polyethylene grocery bags. One reason is that the bags are often contaminated with things like bits of vegetables or smears of ice cream, and washing the bags thoroughly is expensive. Another problem for the plastics industry is that the film the bags are made of is so thin that huge quantities of bags must be available to make recycling the material profitable.

Industry experts also say it isn't clear how many of the plastic bags customers turn in for recycling are actually recycled. Some apparently still end up in landfills or incinerators. According to an estimate by the Plastics Institute of America in Fairfield, N.J., only about 2 percent of the plastic bags used in the United States in 1992 were recycled. Many of them were used to make products that are not themselves recycled, rather than for grocery bags or other products whose plastic could be reused.

Obviously, neither paper bags nor plastic bags emerge as a clear environmental villain or angel. The manufacture of both paper and plastic can release harmful pollutants into the air and water. While paper bags are recycled in greater quantities, plastic's true recycling potential remains largely unknown. Other factors—such as the air pollutants released by the trucks used to haul bags to stores and landfills—can make the issue even more complicated.

In the end, choosing between paper or plastic may depend most on the type of recycling programs available in your community as well as your own commitment to reducing the number of bags you use.

One option is to do your own "recycling" by reusing grocery bags of either type until they wear out. Or use them to hold trash and kitchen scraps. Tear up paper bags and compost them with your lawn clippings and other biodegradable waste. Or use paper bags as a garden *mulch* (a ground covering that helps prevent weed formation and the evaporation of water from soil). Better yet, you can forego using paper or plastic bags altogether by taking reusable cloth shopping bags with you to the market.   [Peter R. Limburg]

World Book Supplement

Twelve new or revised articles reprinted from the 1994 edition of *The World Book Encyclopedia.*

Lasers create an image in a light show.

Chuck O'Rear, West Light

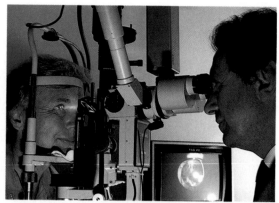

Hank Morgan, Rainbow

A physician uses a laser to perform eye surgery.

Chuck O'Rear, West Light

A laser beam scans a bar code in a supermarket.

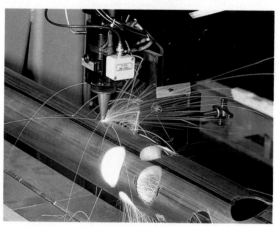

Coherent General, Inc.

A powerful laser beam cuts steel tubing.

Laser beams have special properties that enable them to perform a variety of functions. They are narrow, they spread little, and they can be focused very precisely. The photographs above illustrate some of the many uses of lasers.

Laser

Laser, *LAY zuhr,* is a device that produces a very narrow, powerful beam of light. Some beams are thin enough to drill 200 holes on a spot as tiny as the head of a pin. The ability to focus laser light so precisely makes it extremely powerful. For example, some beams can pierce a diamond, the hardest natural substance. Others can trigger a small nuclear reaction. A laser beam also can be transmitted over long distances with no loss of power. Some beams have reached the moon.

The special qualities of laser light make it ideal for a variety of applications. Some types of lasers, for example, are used to play music, read price codes, cut and weld metal, and transmit information. Lasers can also guide a missile to a target, repair damaged eyes, and produce spectacular displays of light. Still other lasers are used to align walls and ceilings in a building or to print documents. Some lasers even can detect the slightest movement of a continent.

Lasers vary greatly in size. One is almost as long as a football field. Another type is as small as a grain of salt.

A typical laser has three main parts. These parts are (1) an *energy source,* (2) a substance called an *active medium,* and (3) a structure enclosing the active medium known as an *optical cavity.* The energy source supplies an electric current, light, or other form of energy. The atoms of the active medium can absorb the energy, store it for a while, and release the energy as light. Some of this light triggers other atoms to release their energy. More light is added to the triggering light. Mirrors at the ends of the optical cavity reflect the light back into the active medium. The reflected light causes more atoms to give off light. The light grows stronger, and part of it emerges from the laser as a narrow beam. Some beams are visible. Others consist of invisible forms of radiation.

There are four main kinds of lasers. They are solid-

Lasers vary greatly in size. Lasers used to concentrate power in nuclear energy research, *left,* fill a huge room. Tiny lasers, like the one shown in the center among magnified grains of salt, *below,* are built to transmit messages as flashes of light.

Lawrence Livermore National Laboratory

state lasers, semiconductor lasers, gas lasers, and dye lasers.

In 1960, the American physicist Theodore H. Maiman built the first laser. At first, lasers had few uses, and scientists often thought of them as "a solution looking for a problem." Today, however, lasers rank among the most versatile and important tools in modern life.

How lasers are used

Lasers can do a number of incredible things. Their special qualities make them particularly useful in recording, storing, and transmitting many kinds of information. Lasers also are valuable in such activities as scanning, heating, measuring, and guiding. As a result of their wide use, lasers can be found in equipment used in homes, factories, offices, hospitals, and libraries.

Recording, storing, and transmitting information. The most common uses of lasers include the recording of music, motion pictures, computer data, and other material on special discs. Bursts of laser light record such material on the discs in patterns of tiny pits. The discs with recorded music and computer data are called *compact discs* (CD's).

A laser beam's tight focus allows much more information to be stored on a CD than on a phonograph record, making CD's good for holding data as well as music. Some CD's even can hold an entire encyclopedia. A disc used for storing data is usually called a *CD-ROM* (Compact Disc Read-Only Memory). Such discs store *databases* (large files of information held in computers) and are used widely by businesses, libraries, and government agencies.

Lasers can also read and play back the information recorded on discs. In a CD player, a laser beam reflects off the pattern of pits as the compact disc spins. Other devices in the player change the reflections into electrical signals and decode them as music. More lasers are used in CD players than in any other product.

Lasers are used to record movies on large platters

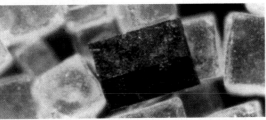

AT&T Bell Laboratories

called *videodiscs.* In addition, laser beams can produce three-dimensional images in a photographic process called *holography.* The images, recorded on a photographic plate, are known as *holograms.* They appear in advertising displays, artwork, and jewelry, and some are placed on credit cards to prevent counterfeiting.

One of the laser's greatest uses is in the field of *fiber-optics communication.* This technology changes electrical signals of telephone calls and television pictures into *pulses* (bursts) of laser light. Strands of glass called *optical fibers* conduct the light. An optical fiber is about as thin as a human hair. But one fiber can carry as much information as several thousand copper telephone wires. Laser light is ideal for this technology because it can be focused precisely and because all its energy can be introduced into the fiber. Fiber-optic transmission of laser light allows enormous amounts of telephone, TV, and other data to be communicated relatively cheaply.

Scanning involves the movement of a laser beam across a surface. Scanning beams are often used to read information. Many people have become familiar with laser scanners used at supermarket checkout counters. What looks like a line of light is actually a rapidly moving laser beam scanning a *bar code.* A bar code consists of a pattern of lines and spaces on packages that identifies the product. The scanner reads the pattern and sends the information to a computer in the store. The computer identifies the item's price and sends the information to the register.

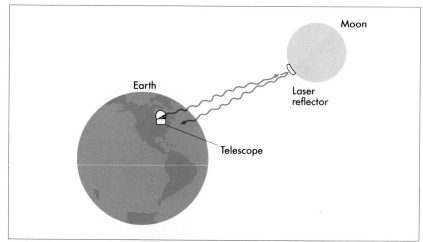

NASA

The distance to the moon is measured to an accuracy of 5 centimeters by a laser beam sent from the earth, *left.* The beam bounces off a laser reflector, *above,* placed on the moon by astronauts, and returns to the earth.

WORLD BOOK diagram by Bensen Studios

Many other kinds of stores use bar code scanners. In addition, such scanners keep track of books in libraries, sort mail in post offices, and read account numbers on checks in banks. Laser printers use a scanning laser beam to produce copies of documents. Other scanners make printing plates for newspapers.

In entertainment, laser light shows are created with scanning laser beams. These beams can "draw" spectacular patterns of red, yellow, green, and blue light on buildings or other outdoor surfaces. The beams move so rapidly they produce what looks like a stationary picture. Laser scanners also produce colorful visual effects that create excitement at rock concerts.

Heating. A laser beam's highly focused energy can produce a great amount of heat. Industrial lasers, for example, produce beams of thousands of watts of power. They cut and weld metals, drill holes, and strengthen materials by heating them. Industrial lasers also cut ceramics, cloth, and plastics.

In medicine, the heating power of lasers is often used in eye surgery. Highly focused beams can close off broken blood vessels on the *retina,* a tissue in the back of the eyeball. Lasers also can reattach a loose retina. Laser beams pass through the *cornea* (front surface of the eye) but cause no pain or damage because the cornea is transparent and does not absorb light.

Doctors also use lasers to treat skin disorders, remove birthmarks, and shatter gallstones. Laser beams can replace the standard surgical knife, or scalpel, in some operations. The use of lasers permits extraordinary control and precision in cutting tissue and sealing off cuts. Thus, lasers reduce bleeding and damage to nearby healthy tissues.

In nuclear energy research, scientists use lasers to produce controlled, miniature hydrogen bomb explosions. They focus many powerful laser beams onto a pellet of frozen forms of hydrogen. The intense beams *compress* (pack down) the pellet and heat it to millions of degrees. These actions cause the pellet's atoms to *fuse* (unite) and release energy. This process, called *nuclear fusion,* may produce enough energy to solve the world's energy problems. Lasers have produced the tremendous heat needed to create fusion but have not yet produced usable amounts of energy.

Measuring. People also use lasers to measure distance. An object's distance can be determined by measuring the time a pulse of laser light takes to reach and reflect back from the object.

In 1969 and 1971, United States astronauts placed mirrored devices called *laser reflectors* on the moon. Using a high-powered laser, scientists measured the distance between the earth and the moon—more than 238,000 miles (383,000 kilometers)—to within 2 inches (5 centimeters). They made the measurement by shining laser light from a telescope on the earth to the reflectors on the moon.

Laser beams directed over long distances also can detect small movements of the ground. Such measurements help geologists involved in earthquake warning systems.

Laser devices used to measure shorter distances are called *range finders.* Surveyors use the devices to get information needed to make maps. Military personnel use them to calculate the distance to an enemy target.

Guiding. A laser's strong, straight beam makes it a valuable tool for guidance. For example, construction workers use laser beams as "weightless strings" to align the walls and ceilings of a building and to lay straight sewer and water pipes.

Instruments called *laser gyroscopes* use laser beams to detect changes in direction. These devices help ships, airplanes, and guided missiles stay on course. Another military use of lasers is in a guidance device called a *target designator.* A person using the device aims a laser beam at an enemy target. Missiles, artillery shells, and bombs equipped with laser beam detectors seek the reflected beam and adjust their flight to hit the spot where the beam is aimed.

How a laser works

Parts of a laser. A typical laser has three main parts. These parts are an active medium, an energy source, and an optical cavity.

An active medium is a material that can be made to create laser light. Gases, liquids, or solid materials can be used.

An energy source is any type of device that supplies energy to the active medium in a process called *pump-*

ing. Lasers often use electricity, another laser, or a *flash lamp* as an energy pump. A flash lamp produces a bright flash of light, just as a camera flash does.

An optical cavity, also called a *resonator,* is a structure that encloses the active medium. A typical cavity has a mirror at each end. One mirror has a fully reflecting surface, and the other one has a partly reflecting surface. The laser beam exits the laser through the mirror with the partly reflecting surface.

The nature of atoms. Laser light results from changes in the amount of energy stored by the atoms in an active medium. The atoms of a substance normally exist in a state of lowest energy, called a *ground state.* Atoms also can exist in higher energy states, called *excited states.* Atoms can change from a ground state to an excited state by absorbing various forms of energy. This process is called *absorption.* In many lasers, atoms absorb packets of light energy called *photons.* In most instances, the excited atom can hold the extra energy for only a fraction of a second before the atom releases its energy as another photon and falls back to its ground state. This process is called *spontaneous emission.*

Some atoms have excited states that can store energy for a relatively long time. These long-lived states can last as long as $\frac{1}{1,000}$ of a second—much longer than the duration of most excited states. When a photon of just the right amount of energy shines on an atom in a long-lived excited state, it can stimulate the atom to *emit* (give off) an identical photon. This second photon has an equal amount of energy and moves in the same direction as the original photon. This process is called *stimulated emission.*

Producing laser light. Stimulated emission is the central process of a laser. One photon—the stimulating photon—produces another photon. It doubles the amount of light energy present, a process called *amplification.* The word *laser* comes from the first letters of the words that describe the key processes in the creation of laser light. These words are *l*ight *a*mplification by *s*timulated *e*mission of *r*adiation.

Stimulated emission only occurs if there are atoms in the excited state. However, atoms in the ground state generally greatly outnumber those in excited states. For amplification to take place, more atoms of a substance must exist in excited states than in ground states. This condition is called a *population inversion.* In a laser, the energy source helps create a population inversion by pumping energy into the active medium. This energy places atoms in long-lived excited states and enables stimulated emission to occur. The mirrors in the optical cavity reflect the photons back and forth in the active medium.

Each interaction of a photon and an excited atom produces a chain reaction of stimulated emissions. This chain reaction causes the number of stimulated emissions to increase rapidly and produce a flood of light. The light becomes so intense that a part of it exits through the partly reflecting mirror as a very strong beam.

Characteristics of laser light. Laser light differs from ordinary light in two major ways. (1) It has low *divergence* (spreading). (2) It is *monochromatic* (single-colored). Light with these two characteristics is known as *coherent light.*

Parts of a typical laser

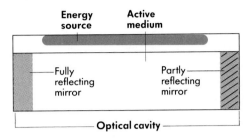

A typical laser has three main parts: an *energy source,* a substance called the *active medium,* and an *optical cavity* enclosing the active medium and two mirrors. One mirror reflects only part of the light striking it.

How a typical laser works

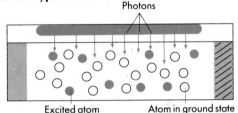

When the laser is turned on, the energy source gives off packets of light energy known as *photons.* Atoms absorb this energy, going from their *ground state* (state of lowest energy) to an *excited state.*

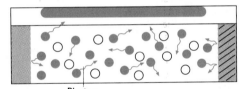

Excited atoms then give off photons. Some of this light reflects off the mirrors and remains in the cavity.

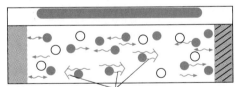

Some photons cause *stimulated emission:* A photon shining on an excited atom causes this atom to give off an identical photon that travels in the same direction.

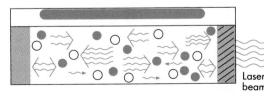

Stimulated emission increases rapidly. The light becomes so strong that a small part of it exits through the partly reflecting mirror as an intense beam.

WORLD BOOK diagrams by Bensen Studios

Most sources of light diverge rapidly. Light from a flashlight, for example, fans out quickly and fades after a short distance. But laser light travels in an extremely narrow beam. It spreads little, even over long distances. For example, a typical laser beam expands to a diameter of only 1 meter after traveling 1,000 meters, or only 64 inches per mile.

Light consists of waves, and the color of light is determined by its *wavelength* (distance from one peak of a wave to the next). Ordinary light consists of waves of many wavelengths—and colors. When all these waves are seen together at the same time, their colors appear white—like those from a light bulb. But light produced by most lasers consists of waves with a very narrow range of wavelengths. Because this range is so narrow, laser light appears to consist of a single color. Some lasers can produce beams with several different colors, but each color band will be narrow. Some lasers produce an invisible beam. These beams consist of such forms of radiation as ultraviolet or infrared rays.

Its coherence makes laser light highly organized. The waves of a laser beam move *in phase*—that is, all the peaks move in step with one another. These waves travel in a narrow path and move in one direction. Thus, coherent light is like a line of marchers in a parade moving with the same strides in the same direction. The waves of ordinary light, on the other hand, spread rapidly and travel in different directions. Ordinary light is known as *incoherent light.* Incoherent light acts much like the way people usually travel along a street—with different strides and in many directions. A laser beam's coherence allows it to travel long distances without losing its intensity.

Kinds of lasers

Most lasers can produce light either in a continuous beam or in pulses. The lasers that generate pulses, called *pulsed lasers,* supply all their energy in only a fraction of a second. As a result, they generally produce much greater peak power than lasers that produce a continuous beam, called *continuous-wave lasers.* Most continuous-wave lasers range in power from less than $\frac{1}{1,000}$ of a watt to more than 10,000 watts. But some pulsed lasers can produce beams of several trillion watts for a billionth of a second.

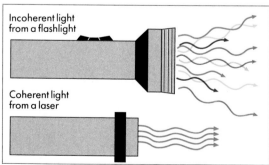

Incoherent light
from a flashlight

Coherent light
from a laser

WORLD BOOK diagram by Bensen Studios

Lasers produce coherent light. Waves of coherent light, unlike waves of incoherent light, move "in step" with one another. As a result, they spread only slightly—even over great distances.

There are four main types of lasers. These types are (1) solid-state lasers, (2) semiconductor lasers, (3) gas lasers, and (4) dye lasers.

Solid-state lasers use a rod made of a solid material as the active medium. Substances made of crystals or glass are widely used. The most common crystal laser contains a small amount of the element neodymium (chemical symbol Nd) enclosed in an yttrium aluminum garnet (YAG) crystal. It is called an Nd:YAG laser. In some lasers, the neodymium is enclosed in glass. Flash lamps are generally used to pump the active mediums of solid-state lasers.

The world's largest and most powerful laser is an Nd:glass laser at Lawrence Livermore National Laboratory in Livermore, Calif. This laser, called Nova, is about as long as a football field. It produces laser light in pulses and is used for nuclear energy research. Its light is split into 10 beams, which are amplified to focus more than 100 trillion watts of power on a target for a billionth of a second.

Nd:YAG and Nd:glass lasers are used widely in industry to drill and weld metals. They are also found in range finders and target designators.

Semiconductor lasers, also called *diode lasers,* use semiconductors, which are materials that conduct electricity but do not conduct it as well as copper, iron, or other true conductors. Semiconductors used in lasers include compounds of metals such as gallium, indium, and arsenic. The semiconductor in a laser consists of two layers that differ in their electric properties. The junction between the layers serves as the active medium. When current flows across the junction, a population inversion is produced. Flat ends of the semiconductor materials serve as mirrors and reflect the photons. Stimulated emission occurs in the junction region.

Semiconductor lasers are the smallest type of laser. One kind is as tiny as a grain of salt. Another type is even smaller and can be seen only with a microscope. Semiconductor lasers are the most commonly used type of laser because they are smaller and lighter and use less power than the other kinds. Their size makes them ideal for use in CD and videodisc players and for fiber-optic communications.

Gas lasers use a gas or mixture of gases in a tube as the active medium. The most common active mediums in gas lasers include carbon dioxide, argon, krypton, and a mixture of helium and neon. The atoms in gas lasers are excited by an electrical current in the same way that neon signs are made to light. Gas lasers are commonly used in communications, eye surgery, entertainment, holography, printing, and scanning.

Many gas lasers produce infrared beams. The most important one is the carbon dioxide laser. It ranks among the most efficient and powerful lasers. Carbon dioxide lasers convert 5 to 30 percent of the energy from their energy source into laser light. Many other lasers convert only about 1 percent of the energy they get. Carbon dioxide lasers can produce beams ranging from less than 1 watt to more than 1 million watts. They are often used to weld and cut metals. They also are used as laser scalpels and in range finders.

Dye lasers use a dye as the active medium. Many kinds of dyes can be used. The dye is dissolved in a liquid, often alcohol. A second laser is generally used to

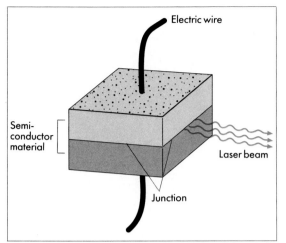

Electric wire

Semi-
conductor
material

Junction

Laser beam

WORLD BOOK diagram by Bensen Studios

A semiconductor laser consists of two layers of material that differ electrically. Electric current passing through the layers produces laser light in the area of their junction.

pump the atoms of the dye. The most important property of dye lasers is that they are *tunable*—that is, a single laser can be adjusted to produce monochromatic beams over a range of wavelengths, or colors. Tunable lasers are valuable to researchers who investigate how materials absorb different colors of light.

History

Lasers were not invented before the 1900's chiefly because scientists did not know about stimulated emission. The process was first described in 1917 by the German-born physicist Albert Einstein. The next major advance in laser development came in 1954. That year, the American physicist Charles H. Townes created a population inversion in a device that amplified microwaves, an invisible form of radiation. The device was called a *maser* because it demonstrated *m*icrowave *a*mplification by *s*timulated *e*mission of *r*adiation.

During the late 1950's, researchers proposed designs for a device that would use stimulated emission to am-

plify light. Several people have received credit for developing the laser's basic design. They include Townes, American physicist Arthur L. Schawlow, the Russian physicists Alexander M. Prokhorov and Nikolai G. Basov, and the American inventor Gordon Gould.

Theodore H. Maiman of the United States constructed the first laser in 1960. His laser used a ruby rod as its active medium. Later that year, the American physicist Ali Javan constructed the first gas laser. In 1962, three separate teams of U.S. scientists operated the first semiconductor lasers. In 1966, the American physicist Peter Sorokin built the first dye laser.

Advances in laser technology and uses have soared since the early 1970's. Today, the enormous information-carrying capacity of optical fibers is opening a new era in home entertainment, communication, and computer technology. Even so, researchers remain convinced that the most exciting and revolutionary uses of lasers still lie ahead.   Donald C. O'Shea

Related articles in *World Book* include:

Bar coding	Glass (Specialty
Bomb (Guided bombs)	glasses)
Communication (Communi-	Gyroscope (Laser gyroscopes)
cation of the future)	Holography
Compact disc	Maser
Crime laboratory (picture: A	Optical disc
laser beam)	Range finder
Fiber optics	Videodisc

Outline

I. How lasers are used
 A. Recording, storing, and transmitting information
 B. Scanning
 C. Heating
 D. Measuring
 E. Guiding
II. How a laser works
 A. Parts of a laser
 B. The nature of atoms
 C. Producing laser light
 D. Characteristics of laser light
III. Kinds of lasers
 A. Solid-state lasers
 B. Semiconductor lasers
 C. Gas lasers
 D. Dye lasers
IV. History

Questions

What is the most important property of dye lasers?
What occurs in the process called *stimulated emission*?
Who built the first laser? When?
Why are semiconductor lasers the most commonly used lasers?
How are lasers used in medicine?
Why is laser light known as *coherent light*?
What are the main parts of a typical laser?
What is a *population inversion*?
What is the origin of the word *laser*?
What is the world's largest and most powerful laser?

Additional resources

Anderberg, Bengt, and Wolbarsht, M. L. *Laser Weapons.* Plenum, 1992.
Asimov, Isaac. *How Did We Find Out About Lasers?* Walker, 1990. For younger readers.
Billings, Charlene W. *Lasers: The New Technology of Light.* Facts on File, 1992.
Bromberg, Joan L. *The Laser in America, 1950-1970.* MIT Pr., 1991.
Encyclopedia of Lasers and Optical Technology. Ed. by Robert A. Meyers. Academic Pr., 1991.
Hecht, Jeff. *The Laser Guidebook.* 2nd ed. McGraw, 1991.

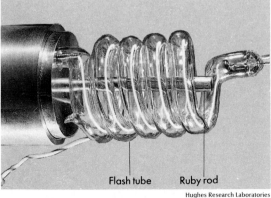

Flash tube   Ruby rod

Hughes Research Laboratories

The first type of laser, *above,* used a ruby rod as an active medium and a coiled flash tube as an energy source.

© Richard Hutchings

© Peter Pearson, Tony Stone Images

Fermi National Accelerator Laboratory

Magnetism causes a horseshoe magnet to attract paper clips, *top left,* and enables industrial magnets to lift heavy loads of scrap metal, *top right.* Magnets are also used in scientific devices. Physicists use magnets to boost atomic particles to high speeds in a particle accelerator, *above.*

Magnetism

Magnetism is the force that electric currents exert on other electric currents. Magnetism may be created by the motion of electrons in the atoms of certain materials, which are called magnets. Magnetic force may also be produced by ordinary electric current flowing through a coil of wire, called an *electromagnet.* The magnetic force may cause *attraction* or *repulsion*—that is, it may pull magnets together or push them apart.

The contributors of this article are Richard B. Frankel, Professor of Physics at California Polytechnic State University; and Brian B. Schwartz, Professor of Physics at Brooklyn College and Associate Executive Secretary and Education Officer of the American Physical Society.

Magnets have many different shapes. The most common are bars and thick disks, squares, or rectangles. A horseshoe magnet is a bar magnet bent into a U shape.

Magnets have a wide variety of uses. Magnets stick to certain metals, which makes them useful as fasteners and latches. Electric tools, appliances, and trains require magnets to run because all electric motors basically consist of a rotating electrical conductor situated between the poles of a stationary magnet. Huge magnets move iron and steel scrap. Tiny magnets on audiotape and videotape store sound and images. Magnets in telephones, radios, and TV sets help change electrical impulses into sounds. Scientists use powerful magnets to hold extremely hot gases in nuclear energy research.

Some rocks, minerals, and meteorites are natural magnets. The earth itself is a giant magnet, and so are the sun and other stars and most of the planets. Some insects, birds, and fish have extremely small magnets in their bodies. Biologists think these magnets may help animals find their way when migrating.

People in ancient Greece and China independently discovered magnetism when they found that the mineral magnetite attracted iron. Scientists could not explain what caused magnetism, however, until the mid-1800's.

What magnets do

Magnetic poles. A magnet with two poles, such as a bar magnet, is called a *magnetic dipole.* (The prefix *di-* means *two.*) If a bar magnet is hung by a string tied around its middle, it rotates until one end points north and the other end points south. The end that points north is called the *north pole,* and the south-pointing end is the *south pole.* In a disk or other flat magnet, the flat surfaces are the poles. If a magnet is broken or cut in half, each piece has a north and south magnetic pole.

Attraction and repulsion. Magnetism causes unlike magnetic poles to attract each other but like poles to *repel* (push away from) each other. If the north pole of a magnet is brought near the south pole of another magnet, the magnetic force pulls the magnets together. But two north poles or two south poles repel each other. If a bar magnet is suspended between the ends of a horseshoe magnet, it will move so that its north pole faces away from the horseshoe magnet's north pole.

Magnetic fields. The region around a magnet where the force of magnetism can be felt is said to contain a *magnetic field.* A magnetic field is invisible. You can picture the magnetic field of a bar magnet, however, if you place a piece of paper over the magnet and sprinkle iron filings on the paper. The filings bunch together near the poles and form a pattern around the magnet that corresponds to its magnetic field. A magnetic field can also be thought of as a set of imaginary lines called *field lines, flux lines,* or *lines of force.* We think of these lines going out from the north pole of a magnet, looping around, and returning to the magnet at its south pole. The lines lie closest to each other near the poles, where the magnetic field is strongest.

A magnetic field exerts a force on nearby magnets to make them align along its field lines. The needle of a magnetic compass, for example, is actually a slender bar magnet. It normally points north along one of the earth's magnetic field lines. But a strong bar magnet placed next to the compass will cause the needle to point along one of the bar magnet's field lines.

The strength of a magnetic field is measured in units called *gauss* or *tesla.* One tesla equals 10,000 gauss. The earth's magnetic field at its surface is about $\frac{1}{2}$ gauss. The field near the poles of a small horseshoe magnet may be several hundred gauss. Fields of magnets used in industry may measure more than 20,000 gauss (2 tesla).

Magnetization. A magnet attracts iron, steel, nickel, and certain other materials. The attracted materials then become magnets themselves in a process called *magnetization.* A steel nail placed near a magnet, for example, becomes magnetized and can attract a second nail. Magnetization occurs because the magnet causes spinning particles called *electrons* in the atoms of the nail to align along the magnet's field lines. The atoms with aligned electrons then act like tiny bar magnets.

Kinds of magnets

Most objects made of aluminum, concrete, copper, cotton, glass, gold, paper, plastic, rubber, silver, and wood are *nonmagnetic materials.* Magnets neither repel nor attract these substances, and magnetic fields pass through them without weakening. But other materials, called *magnetic materials,* become magnetized when exposed to a magnetic field. Magnetic materials are used in making temporary and permanent magnets. An electromagnet is produced by an electric current.

Temporary magnets are made of such materials as iron and nickel. These materials are known as *soft magnetic materials* because they usually do not retain their magnetism outside a strong magnetic field. A magnetized iron nail, for example, loses its magnetism if it is removed from a magnetic field.

Permanent magnets keep their magnetism after they have been magnetized. For this reason, they are

WORLD BOOK diagram by J. Harlan Hunt

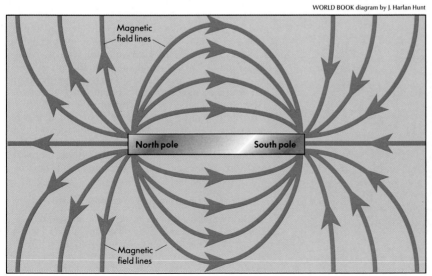

Magnetic field lines

North pole   South pole

Magnetic field lines

A magnetic field can be shown as imaginary lines that flow out of the north pole and into the south pole of a magnet. The magnetic field of a bar magnet, *left,* is strongest near the magnet's poles, where the lines lie closest to each other.

known as *hard magnetic materials.* Many strong permanent magnets are *alloys* (mixtures) of iron, nickel, or cobalt with other elements. These magnetic alloys include Alnico, a group of alloys usually containing a mixture of aluminum, nickel, cobalt, iron, and copper; and an alloy of cobalt and chromium called cobalt-chromium. Alloys containing metallic elements called *rare-earth elements* have produced some of the strongest permanent magnets. These alloys include samarium-cobalt, a mixture of cobalt and the rare-earth element samarium; and a combination of boron, iron, and the rare-earth element neodymium. Another important group of magnetic alloys, called *ferrites,* consist of iron, oxygen, and other elements. The best-known natural permanent magnet is a ferrite known as *magnetite* or *lodestone* (also spelled *loadstone*).

Some soft magnetic materials can be made into weak permanent magnets. An iron needle for a compass, for example, can be permanently magnetized by stroking it in one direction with a magnet.

Electromagnets are temporary magnets produced by electric currents. The simplest electromagnets consist of electric current flowing through a cylindrical coil of wire called a *solenoid.* One end of the solenoid becomes the north pole of the electromagnet, while the other end becomes the south pole. The poles switch position if the direction of the current is reversed. If the current is shut off, the solenoid loses its magnetism.

Many electromagnets have a cylinder of soft magnetic material, such as iron, within a coil of wire to strengthen the magnetic field the electromagnet produces. When current passes through the coil, the cylinder becomes strongly magnetized. The cylinder loses its magnetism, however, when the current is shut off. This characteristic of electromagnets makes them useful as switches in electric doorbells and telegraphs.

The strength of an electromagnet depends on the number of windings in the coil and the strength of the electric current. More windings and stronger current

Francis Bitter National Magnet Laboratory, M.I.T.

Technicians assemble a hybrid magnet by lowering an electromagnet into a superconducting magnet. Hybrid magnets can produce extremely strong fields of about 350,000 gauss.

produce more intense magnetic fields. Fields of about 250,000 gauss (25 tesla) have been produced by passing extremely strong electric current through a coil made of copper plates. These magnets require cooling systems that pump water past the coils, however, to prevent the heat produced by the current from melting the copper plates. Some electromagnets, called *superconducting magnets,* use coils that conduct current with no loss of energy and, thus, do not heat up. The strongest electromagnets, called *hybrid magnets,* consist of a water-cooled electromagnet within a superconducting magnet. These devices can produce magnetic fields of about 350,000 gauss (35 tesla).

Uses of magnets and magnetism

In homes, the attractive force between magnets makes them useful as latches on cabinet doors, as knife racks, and as fasteners for holding papers on refrigerators. The most important use of magnets in the home, however, is in electric motors. All electric motors use

Artstreet

Magnetite, also called *lodestone,* is a natural magnet that attracts iron nails and certain other metals. It belongs to an important group of magnetic materials called *ferrites.*

electromagnets or a combination of electromagnets and permanent magnets. These motors run refrigerators, vacuum cleaners, washing machines, compact disc players, blenders, hedge trimmers, drills, sanders, and such toys as electric trains, race cars, and robots.

Audiotape and videotape players have electromagnets called *heads* that record and read information on tapes covered with many tiny magnetic particles. The magnetic field of a recording head makes the magnetic particles on the tape form patterns that another type of head can read. The second head transforms the magnetic patterns into an electric signal. Magnets in speakers transform the signal into sound by making the speakers vibrate. An electromagnet called a *deflection yoke* in TV picture tubes helps form images on a screen.

In industry and business, magnets in electric motors help run almost any machine that makes something move or rotate. These devices include cranes, cutters, electric typewriters, fax machines, machine tools, photocopiers, and printing presses. Magnets in computers store information on magnetic tapes and disks. Powerful electromagnets attached to cranes move scrap iron and steel and separate metals for recycling.

One of the most important uses of magnets is electric power production. Generators in power plants rely on magnets similar to those in electric motors to produce electricity. Devices called *transformers* use electromagnets to change the high-voltage electricity carried by power lines to the lower voltage needed in homes and businesses.

In transportation. All electrified transportation systems depend on magnets in electric motors. These systems include trains, subways, trolleys, monorails, cable cars, escalators, elevators, and moving sidewalks. Electric motors operate windshield wipers, electric windows and doors, door locks, and other devices in automobiles, buses, and airplanes. Electromagnets also produce radio waves in radar systems, an important navigation aid for ships and airplanes.

Scientists and engineers have developed trains that use electromagnets to *levitate* (float) above a track without touching it. These trains, called *magnetic levitation* or *maglev* trains, eliminate the friction of wheels on the track and thus can move at much higher speeds than ordinary trains do.

In science and medicine. Magnets and magnetic fields are widely used in scientific research. Electromagnets in electron microscopes focus a beam of electrons on a sample to be studied. Powerful magnets called *bending magnets* help control beams of atomic particles that have been boosted to high speed in devices called *particle accelerators.* In nuclear energy research, physicists make the nuclei of atoms *fuse* (unite) in extremely hot gases called *plasmas.* The plasmas are so hot they would melt the walls of any container made of ordinary materials. Therefore, physicists hold the plasmas away from the container's walls in a strong magnetic field that functions as a "magnetic bottle."

In medicine, many devices for diagnosing diseases use magnets. In a technique known as *magnetic resonance imaging* (MRI), the patient lies inside a large cylindrical magnet. MRI uses magnetic fields and radio waves to produce images of the head, spine, internal organs, and other body parts. Other diagnostic devices enable physicians to observe magnetic fields generated by the brain, heart, and other internal organs.

How magnetism works

Magnetism and electricity are closely related. Together, they make a force called *electromagnetism,* one of the basic forces in the universe. A moving magnet near a coil of copper wire, for example, can *induce* (produce) an electric current in the coil. Similarly, an electric current flowing through a wire creates a magnetic field around the wire.

The direction of the magnetic field around a straight wire can be determined according to the *right-hand rule.* If the thumb of the right hand points along the flow

WORLD BOOK illustrations by Richard Lo

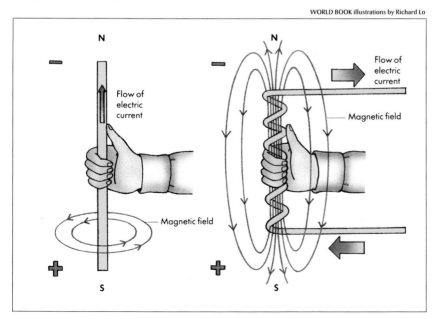

The right-hand rule shows the direction of the magnetic field around a wire that carries an electric current. If the thumb of the right hand points along the flow of current in a straight wire, *far left,* the fingers curl around the wire in the direction of the field. If a wire carrying current is wound into a coil, the magnetic field is strengthened. Such a coil is called a *solenoid.* The direction of the magnetic field surrounding a solenoid, *left,* can be found by wrapping the fingers around the coil in the direction of the current. The thumb then points to the solenoid's north pole and shows the direction of the field.

of current, the fingers curl around the wire in the direction of the magnetic field.

The right-hand rule also applies to the magnetic field produced by a coil or solenoid. Magnetic field lines flow through the length of a coil. If the fingers of the right hand curl around the coil in the direction of the current, the right thumb points to the coil's north pole and shows the direction of the magnetic field lines.

The right-hand rule is used when the current is thought of as a flow of positive electric charges. In a simple electric circuit connected to a battery, for example, the current is defined as flowing from the battery's positive terminal to its negative terminal.

Magnetism in atoms. Atoms have a small, dense center called a *nucleus* surrounded by one or more lighter, negatively charged electrons. Nuclei consist of *protons,* which have positive charges, and *neutrons,* which have no charge. Under most conditions, the atoms of each element contain an equal number of protons and electrons, and so the atoms are electrically neutral.

The relationship between magnetism and electricity also operates in the atom. The motion of negatively charged electrons around a nucleus makes an electric current, which produces a magnetic field. However, the effect of the electrons moving in one direction equals the effect of the electrons moving in the opposite direction. As a result, the magnetic fields of the moving electrons cancel each other out, and the atom has no magnetic field.

In addition to circling the nucleus, an electron spins on its axis like a top. This motion also produces an electric current and a magnetic field. But in most atoms, one electron spins in one direction for each electron that spins in the opposite direction. The magnetic fields caused by the spinning motion of the paired electrons cancel each other out.

The orbiting motions of paired electrons change slightly when an atom is placed in a magnetic field. The magnetic fields of the electrons then no longer cancel each other out, and their motions produce a weak magnetic field opposite to the external field. This effect is known as *diamagnetism* (opposite magnetism). The atoms making up most chemical compounds are held together by chemical links called *bonds* that consist of paired electrons. As a result, most compounds—including water, salt, and sugar—are diamagnetic. Diamagnetic materials are weakly repelled by magnets.

In some atoms, including those of cobalt, iron, nickel, oxygen, and the rare-earth element gadolinium, the spins of some electrons are not paired. As a result, each atom has a magnetic field and acts like a tiny magnet. Such an atom is called an *atomic dipole.* These atoms, like other magnets, tend to align themselves parallel to the lines of an external magnetic field. This alignment is called *paramagnetism* (same magnetism) and causes the individual atoms to be weakly attracted to magnets.

Magnetism of materials. In some paramagnetic materials, the atomic dipoles arrange themselves in certain patterns in relation to each other. These arrangements include *ferromagnetic, antiferromagnetic,* and *ferrimagnetic* ordering. In ferromagnetic materials, such as iron, an atomic dipole points in the same direction as neighboring dipoles. The ferromagnetic arrangement produces the most strongly magnetic substances. An atomic dipole in an antiferromagnetic material, how-

The magnetism of materials   Certain materials have magnetic properties because of the arrangement of their *atomic dipoles,* atoms that act like tiny magnets because they have unpaired electron spins. These arrangements include ferromagnetic, antiferromagnetic, and ferrimagnetic ordering.

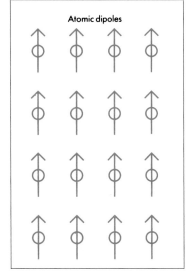

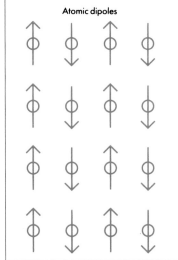

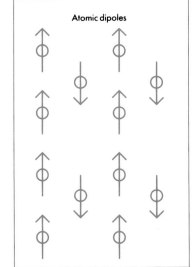

WORLD BOOK illustrations by Linda Kinnaman

Ferromagnetic materials have atomic dipoles that align in the same direction as neighboring dipoles. Such materials are strongly magnetic.

Antiferromagnetic materials, which are weakly magnetic, have atomic dipoles that align opposite to neighboring dipoles.

Ferrimagnetic materials have more atomic dipoles pointing in one direction than in the other and are strongly magnetic.

ever, points opposite to its neighbors. Antiferromagnetic materials are weakly magnetic. Ferrimagnetic ordering occurs in materials with several kinds of atoms, including magnetite and ferrite alloys. These materials have more dipoles pointing in one direction than in the other and are strongly magnetic.

Atomic dipoles of ferromagnetic and ferrimagnetic materials settle into an ordered arrangement when the material's temperature falls below its *magnetic ordering temperature* or *Curie point.* For antiferromagnetic materials, this temperature is called the *Néel temperature.* Iron, for example, has a magnetic ordering temperature of 1418 °F (770 °C); nickel, 676 °F (358 °C); and cobalt, 2050 °F (1121 °C). Above this temperature, stronger atomic vibrations prevent the atomic dipoles from arranging themselves in relation to each other. As a result, the materials then show only the weak magnetic attraction of paramagnetism.

In ferromagnetic and ferrimagnetic materials, the atomic dipoles usually align to form larger dipoles called *magnetic domains.* Domains combine the strength of the individual atomic dipoles. A piece of magnetic material may contain many magnetic domains. The domains often point in different directions, however, and tend to cancel each other out.

Ferromagnetic or ferrimagnetic materials become magnetized when exposed to a strong magnetic field. The domains parallel to the field grow as more atomic dipoles line up with it. If the magnetic field is extremely strong, all the atomic dipoles may align and the entire piece of material may become a single magnetic domain. The domains of a hard magnetic material remain aligned when removed from a magnetic field. Thus, the material becomes a permanent magnet. Soft magnetic materials, however, become *demagnetized* when removed from the field—that is, their original magnetic domains re-form and cancel each other out.

The magnetism of astronomical bodies

The magnetism of the earth. The earth is a giant magnet with poles called the *north magnetic pole* and the *south magnetic pole.* These poles are near the geographic North and South poles, respectively. The north magnetic pole attracts the north pole of a compass needle, so it is actually the south pole of the earth magnet. Similarly, the south magnetic pole is the north pole of the earth magnet because it repels the north pole of a compass needle.

The magnetic field at the surface of the earth, known as the *geomagnetic field,* has a strength of about $\frac{1}{2}$ gauss. The earth's inner structure creates the geomagnetic field. The earth's *crust* is the outermost portion on which we live. A rocky *mantle* lies beneath the crust. Under the mantle is a dense *core,* which has a solid inner part and a liquid outer part. Scientists believe the motion of electric charges in the liquid outer core produces the geomagnetic field.

Scientists who study the lava of ancient volcanoes have found that the geomagnetic field periodically reverses direction—that is, the earth's north and south magnetic poles switch places. Lava contains small particles of hard magnetic material. When the lava was hot, these magnetic particles were paramagnetic and, thus, were only weakly influenced by the earth's magnetic field. But once the lava cooled below the magnetic ordering temperature, the particles aligned themselves with the geomagnetic field like tiny compass needles. Thus, lava leaves a record of the geomagnetic field at the time when the lava cooled.

The earth's magnetic field also extends into space beyond the atmosphere. There, it is called the *magnetosphere.* The magnetosphere interacts with a flow of charged particles from the sun called the *solar wind.* This interaction produces displays of light called *auroras* and a zone of charged particles around the earth known as the *Van Allen belts.*

The magnetism of the sun. The sun has an overall magnetic field of about 1 to 2 gauss. But it also has stronger magnetic fields concentrated in relatively cooler areas of its surface called *sunspots.* These regions have magnetic fields of 250 to 5,000 gauss. Other solar features associated with strong magnetic fields include bright bursts of light called *flares* and huge arches of gas known as *prominences.*

The magnetism of other astronomical bodies. The moon has virtually no magnetic field because it does not have a liquid core. But moon rocks brought to the earth by astronauts show that the moon at one time had a stronger magnetic field. This evidence suggests that it once probably had a liquid core. Mercury, Venus, and Mars all have weaker fields than the earth's. But Saturn, Jupiter, Neptune, and Uranus have relatively strong magnetic fields and magnetospheres.

Some types of stars have magnetic fields much stronger than the sun's. These stars include *white dwarfs,* which can have magnetic fields of more than 1 million gauss. A type of collapsed star called a *neutron star* can have a field as strong as 10 trillion gauss.

Magnets in living things

Scientists have discovered that many animals—including pigeons, honey bees, salmon, tuna, dolphins, and turtles—are able to detect the earth's magnetic field and may use it to help find their way. Scientists have found particles of magnetite in the body tissues of some of these animals. They suspect that the particles form part of a system that senses the geomagnetic field.

Scientists have also found that some bacteria in water use the geomagnetic field to find their preferred habitat. Each of the bacteria, called *magnetotactic bacteria,* contains one or more chains of magnetite particles. The

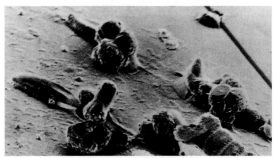

AP/Wide World

Magnetic bacteria contain extremely small chains of magnetite particles. These particles cause the bacteria, shown greatly magnified above, to align with the field lines of a bar magnet.

A *World Book* science project

Experimenting with magnetism

The purpose of this project is to demonstrate magnetic fields from permanent magnets and the magnetic effects of an electric current. The materials needed for this project are shown below. They can be purchased at most hardware or hobby stores.

Materials needed

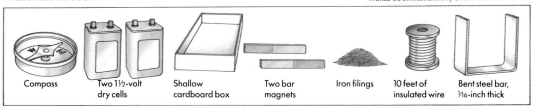

| Compass | Two 1½-volt dry cells | Shallow cardboard box | Two bar magnets | Iron filings | 10 feet of insulated wire | Bent steel bar, ¹⁄₁₆-inch thick |

Mapping magnetic fields

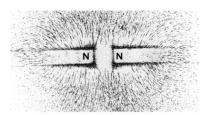

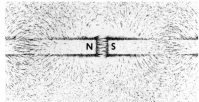

WORLD BOOK photos

To map the field of a bar magnet, place the magnet under a sheet of white paper. Sprinkle iron filings on the paper and tap the paper gently. The filings will line up as shown. The field between two magnetic poles curves outward from the gap between the poles if they are alike, *left*. If opposite poles are used, the field extends across the gap from one pole to the other, *right.*

Other experiments include mapping the field when one of the magnets is turned to a different position or when several magnets are placed under the paper. You can also study the effect of placing a steel coat hanger, coins, or other metal objects in contact with one or more magnets.

Magnetism and electricity

To see the magnetic effects of electricity, wrap about 10 turns of wire around a small box. Place a compass inside the box and turn the box so that the compass needle lines up with the wire. Strip the insulation from the ends of the wire, and connect the wire to the terminals of a dry cell. Then observe how the compass needle moves.

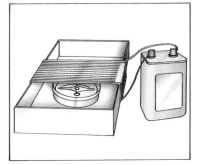

To experiment further, try switching the wires from one terminal to the other to see how the needle changes direction. By switching the wires at the proper rate, you may be able to make the needle spin completely around. Try changing the number of turns of wire to see the effect this has on the compass.

Experimenting with an electromagnet

To make an electromagnet, wind two layers of wire around a flat iron bar that is bent into the shape shown here. Strip the insulation from the ends of the wire and connect the wire to two dry cells. When you hold the compass between the poles of the electromagnet, the needle will pick up iron objects when the current is on.

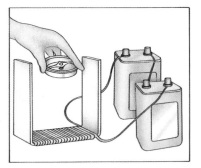

Electromagnet experiments. Try mapping the field of your magnet. You can also change the number of turns of wire and the number of dry cells to increase the lifting power of the magnet. The more turns of wire you add or the more dry cells you connect, the stronger your magnet will be.

bacteria use the particles as tiny compass needles to guide them along geomagnetic field lines.

The study of magnetism

Early discoveries. People in ancient Greece and China independently discovered that natural lodestone magnets attracted iron. The Chinese also found that a piece of lodestone would point in a north-south direction if it was allowed to rotate freely. They used this characteristic of lodestone to tell fortunes and as a guide for building. By A.D. 1200, Chinese and European sailors used magnetic compasses to steer their ships.

In 1269, a French soldier named Pierre de Maricourt (also known as Petrus Peregrinus) mapped the magnetic field around a lodestone sphere with a compass. He discovered that the sphere had two magnetic poles. William Gilbert, a physician of Queen Elizabeth I of England, concluded in 1600 that the earth itself is a giant magnet with north and south poles.

Electricity and magnetism. In 1820, Hans Christian Oersted, a Danish physicist and chemist, observed that an electric current flowing in a wire caused the needle of a magnetic compass to rotate. His discovery proved that electricity and magnetism were related. The French physicist André Marie Ampère worked out the mathematical relationship between current and the strength of the magnetic field during the 1820's. He also proposed that electric current in atoms caused magnetism. In the early 1830's, the English scientist Michael Faraday and the American physicist Joseph Henry independently discovered that a changing magnetic field induced a current in a coil of wire. In 1864, James Clerk Maxwell, a Scottish scientist, developed the mathematical theory that described the laws of electricity and magnetism.

The magnetic properties of materials became a focus of research in the late 1800's. The French physicist Pierre Curie found that ferromagnetic materials lose their ferromagnetism above a certain temperature, which became known as the Curie point.

In the early 1900's, a number of physicists developed the theory of quantum mechanics, which describes the behavior of electrons and other particles. The pioneers of quantum theory included Niels Bohr of Denmark, Wolfgang Pauli of Austria, and the German physicists Albert Einstein, Werner Heisenberg, Max Planck, and Erwin Schrödinger. Richard P. Feynman and Julian S. Schwinger of the United States and Sin-itiro Tomonaga of Japan later developed an improved theory of quantum electrodynamics. Their work led to a better understanding of the interaction between charged particles and an electromagnetic field. John H. Van Vleck of the United States and Louis E. F. Néel of France applied quantum mechanics to understand the magnetic properties of atoms and molecules.

Modern research in magnetism. In the 1940's, the American physicists Edward M. Purcell and Felix Bloch independently developed a way to measure the magnetic field of nuclei. They placed a substance in a strong magnetic field and exposed it to radio waves. They discovered that the waves interacted with the nuclei of the substance's atoms. This discovery, known as *nuclear magnetic resonance,* led to magnetic resonance imaging and other methods for studying the structure of living tissues.

The American physicist Francis Bitter pioneered in developing stronger magnets for research. In the 1930's, he developed electromagnets made of water-cooled copper plates that generated powerful magnetic fields. In the 1960's and 1970's, scientists developed superconducting materials. When cooled to near *absolute zero* (-459.67 °F or -273.15 °C), these materials could be used in magnets to generate fields as high as 200,000 gauss. Superconducting magnets are used in maglev trains and in nuclear research. In the 1980's and 1990's, researchers discovered materials that become superconducting at higher, though still extremely cold, temperatures—about -280 °F (-173 °C). These new superconductors will enable scientists to generate even stronger fields.   Richard B. Frankel and Brian B. Schwartz

Outline

I. **What magnets do**
   A. Magnetic poles
   B. Attraction and repulsion
   C. Magnetic fields
   D. Magnetization
II. **Kinds of magnets**
   A. Temporary magnets
   B. Permanent magnets
   C. Electromagnets
III. **Uses of magnetism**
   A. In homes
   B. In industry and business
   C. In transportation
   D. In science and medicine
IV. **How magnetism works**
   A. Magnetism and electricity
   B. Magnetism in atoms
   C. Magnetism of materials
V. **The magnetism of astronomical bodies**
   A. The magnetism of the earth
   B. The magnetism of the sun
   C. The magnetism of other astronomical bodies
VI. **Magnets in living things**
VII. **The study of magnetism**
   A. Early discoveries
   B. Electricity and magnetism
   C. The magnetic properties of materials
   D. Modern research in magnetism

Questions

How do hard magnetic materials and soft magnetic materials differ?

What do scientists think causes the earth's magnetic field?

What is a magnetic dipole?

How are atomic dipoles arranged in ferromagnetic materials?

Who developed the mathematical theory that describes the relationship between magnetism and electricity?

What is the right-hand rule?

Why are ferromagnetic and ferrimagnetic materials useful in making permanent magnets?

Who discovered magnetism?

What is the magnetic ordering temperature or Curie point?

How is a "magnetic bottle" used in nuclear energy research?

Additional resources

Catherall, Ed. *Exploring Magnets.* Steck-Vaughn, 1990. For younger readers.

Dobbs, E. Roland. *Electricity and Magnetism.* Routledge, 1984.

Lafferty, Peter. *Magnets to Generators.* Gloucester Pr., 1989. For younger readers.

Vogt, Gregory. *Electricity and Magnetism.* Watts, 1985. For younger readers.

Computer chip is a tiny piece of material, usually silicon, that contains a complex electronic circuit. These chips are essential in modern computers and a variety of other electronic devices. The circuit on a computer chip, sometimes called an *integrated circuit,* is made up of electronic components built into the chip. Most chips are no larger than a fingernail.

There are two main kinds of computer chips: (1) *microprocessors,* which carry out the instructions that make up computer programs, and (2) *memory chips,* which hold computer programs and other data. Memory chips are used primarily in computers. Microprocessors are used in computers and hundreds of other products. A microprocessor serves as the "heart" of every personal computer. Larger computers have more than one such chip. Other products controlled by microprocessors include video games, digital watches, microwave ovens, and some telephones.

Structure. The body of most chips is made of silicon. This material is used because it is a *semiconductor.* In its pure form, silicon does not conduct electricity at room temperature. But if certain impurities are added to silicon, it can carry an electric current. Manufacturers "dope" silicon chips with such impurities as boron and phosphorus. The doped regions form the chip's electronic components, which control the electric signals carried on the chip. The kind and arrangement of the impurities determine how each component controls signals. Most components serve as switches called *transistors.* Others serve mainly as *capacitors,* which store an electric charge; *diodes,* which prevent current from flowing in one direction but not the other; and *resistors,* which control voltage.

Some chips contain millions of components. Certain parts of these components measure less than 1 *micrometer* (0.001 millimeter) across. Manufacturers create thin lines of metal—usually aluminum—on the chip to connect these tiny components.

External connections. Most chips connect with other devices by means of a container called a *package.* One common type of container is a *dual in-line package* (DIP), an oblong box about 2 inches (5 centimeters) in length. Two rows of metal pins extend downward from the box, one from each long side. Each pin is connected by a wire to an electric terminal on the chip.

In a computer, the packaged chip is mounted on a circuit board. Printed circuits on the board connect the package—and thus the chip—with other devices.

Characteristics of microprocessors. Microprocessors perform essential computer operations. A microprocessor obtains instructions and data from an external memory device; performs arithmetic and logic operations with these data and data contained in its own memory circuits; and, after obtaining a result, moves the calculated data back to the external memory device.

Word length. Instructions and other data handled by computers are in the form of "words." A word is a group of *bits.* A bit is a *binary digit*—a 0 or a 1. Computers operate on the basis of bits. For example, the presence of an electric charge in a capacitor can represent a "1" and the absence of a charge can represent a "0."

The maximum word length that a microprocessor can handle helps determine how rapidly it can operate. The earliest microprocessors used 4-bit words. As micro-

Tom Way, International Business Machines Corporation

A microprocessor is a chip that performs computer operations and holds some memory. This microprocessor measures 12.7 millimeters ($\frac{1}{2}$ inch) on a side.

processors advanced, they were able to handle longer words—usually made up of 8, 16, 32, or 64 bits.

Clock speed is another important characteristic of a microprocessor. Bits travel through a computer in pulses of electric current that occur at regular intervals called *clock cycles.* Today's microprocessors run at speeds of more than one million cycles per second, or 1 megahertz (MHz).

Instruction sets. There are two basic types of microprocessors: (1) complex instruction set computer (CISC), and (2) reduced instruction set computer (RISC). The microprocessors used in the first computers were the kind now known as CISC. Since about 1986, RISC chips have appeared in certain computers called workstations.

Tom Way, International Business Machines Corporation

Chips for the main control board of a personal computer are mounted inside square and oblong packages. Each chip is wired to metal pins that electrically connect its package to the main control board.

A CISC chip has a very large instruction set—that is, it has many ways to carry out each instruction. For example, it may be able to add two numbers by following any one of 10 procedures. These procedures take various numbers of clock cycles. The number of cycles depends on such factors as the size of the numbers to be added and the location of the numbers in the computer system. A RISC chip uses instructions that are always the same length and can be executed in one clock cycle. By using its special circuits, a RISC chip can execute many times more instructions per second than can a comparable CISC chip.

Memory chips. Most computers use two types of memory chips: (1) read-only memory (ROM), and (2) random access memory (RAM). A ROM chip retains its stored memory even when the computer is turned off, but the computer user cannot change the stored memory. In contrast, the user can change the memory stored in a RAM chip, but the chip holds its memory only as long as power is on.

There are two main kinds of RAM: static RAM (SRAM) and dynamic RAM (DRAM). SRAM holds its memory until the microprocessor changes it, but DRAM can only hold its memory for a few thousandths of a second. Therefore, a DRAM chip must be *refreshed* at least 100 times per second, or it will lose its data. To refresh a DRAM, the computer removes the information from each group of *cells* (memory storage units) in the chip, then puts the *same* information back. This may seem wasteful. But the time and expense involved are more than made up for by the amount of memory that can be fit into a small space on a DRAM and the cost of these devices. Most personal computers use DRAM's because they are inexpensive to make and can store much memory.

Researchers have developed memory chips with useful features of both ROM and RAM chips. These *erasable ROM* chips can be erased and reprogrammed, yet they do not lose their memory when the computer is turned off.

One successful design is the electrically, selectively erasable, programmable ROM (EEPROM) chip. A pulse of electric current can erase all the memory in a selected area of the chip. The user can then reprogram this area as if it were part of a RAM chip.

Chip manufacture. The manufacture of a computer chip begins with a wafer of doped silicon. The wafer measures from 1 to 8 inches (2.5 to 20 centimeters) in diameter. A photographic process reduces a large master design for the integrated circuit to microscopic size. Technicians use these microscopic designs, called *masks,* as stencils to make hundreds of chips on one wafer. After the wafer has been processed, it is divided into individual chips.

History. The first chips were patented in 1959 by two Americans—Jack Kilby, an engineer, and Robert Noyce, a physicist—who worked independently. During the 1960's, scientists developed chips for guided missiles and satellites. Engineers soon began to build smaller and faster computers by using chips in place of conventional circuits. The first microprocessors were produced in 1971 for use in desktop calculators.   Charles Melear

Materials are solid substances of which manufactured products are made. Materials belong to two groups: (1)

natural materials and (2) extracted materials. Natural materials, which include stone, wood, and wool, are used much as they occur in nature. Extracted materials, such as plastics, *alloys* (metal mixtures), and ceramics, are created through the processing of various natural substances.

Manufacturers determine which material to use for a given product by evaluating *properties* (qualities) of materials. For example, wood is used for boats because of its low *density* (weight per unit of volume). Stainless steel, an alloy, serves as a material for pots and pans largely because of its resistance to heat and *corrosion* (chemical attack by the environment).

Some properties can be linked with a material's *macrostructure* (structure visible to the unaided eye). For example, the long, parallel fibers of wood give this material relatively strong resistance to a force applied along the *grain* (the direction of the fibers), but relatively weak resistance to a force applied at a right angle to the grain.

Other properties are explained by a material's *microstructure* (structure that can be seen only through a microscope). The low density of wood is due to the open structure of its cells, which are visible only when viewed through a microscope. At the most basic level, properties of materials are determined by *chemical bonds,* forces that attract atoms to one another and hold them together.

Materials scientists study how the structure of materials relates to their properties. A large part of their work involves experimentation. For example, they alter the microstructure of a material, then determine how the changes affect the properties. *Materials engineers,* who work in much the same way, develop new materials for use in commercial products.

Materials scientists and engineers have developed a wide variety of engineered materials in recent years. These include strong but lightweight alloys of titanium used for aircraft parts. An important new class of substances called *composite materials* are produced by combining other substances. For example, some tennis rackets are made of a composite of carbon fibers and plastic.

Properties of materials

Scientists group the properties of materials according to various functions that must be performed by the objects that are made of the materials. For example, *mechanical properties* are critical in a material for a part such as a beam of a bridge that must resist strong mechanical forces.

Most properties of materials fall into six groups: (1) mechanical, (2) chemical, (3) electrical, (4) magnetic, (5) thermal, and (6) optical.

Mechanical properties are critical in a wide variety of structures and objects—from bridges, houses, and space vehicles to chairs and even food trays. Some of the most important mechanical properties are (1) stiffness, (2) yield stress, (3) toughness, (4) strength, (5) creep, and (6) fatigue resistance.

Stiffness measures how much a material bends when first subjected to a mechanical force. For example, the degree to which a shelf first bends when a book is put on it depends on the shelf's stiffness.

Uses of materials   **A variety of materials** are used in different products. Basic types of materials range from wood, which has been used for thousands of years, to composite materials, which are still under development. The photos below show products made of several materials.

Superstock

Iron beams

Broyhill Furniture, Inc.

Wooden desk

Corning Incorporated

Ceramic cookware

Goodyear

Rubber tire

Comstock

Semiconducting solar cells

Dunlop Slazenger Corporation

Composite tennis racket body

Yield stress measures how much force per unit area must be exerted on a material for that material to permanently *deform* (change its shape). Materials that deform easily—that is, those that have a low yield stress—are generally not desirable.

Toughness measures a material's resistance to cracking. The tougher a material, the greater the stress necessary to break that material near a crack.

Strength measures the greatest force a material can withstand without breaking. A material's strength depends on many factors, including its toughness and its shape.

Creep is a measure of a material's resistance to gradual deformation under a constant force. At room temperature, creep is almost nonexistent in many metals, including aluminum and steel. However, manufacturers of metal parts such as jet engine turbine blades that operate at high temperatures must consider creep.

Fatigue resistance measures the resistance of a material to repeated applications and withdrawals of force. Metal that is used for gears must have a high resistance to fatigue because, as a gear rotates, force is repeatedly applied to, and withdrawn from, the individual gear teeth.

Chemical properties include *catalytic properties* and *resistance to corrosion.* Catalytic properties measure the ability of a material to function as a *catalyst*—that is, its ability to provide a favorable site for a certain chemical reaction to occur. Automobile pollution-controlling devices called *catalytic converters* are made partly of metals such as platinum that reduce pollution by causing certain chemical reactions.

Resistance to corrosion measures how well a material holds up to chemical attack by the environment. For example, iron has low resistance to corrosion by oxygen. It reacts with oxygen in the air to form rust.

Electrical properties are important in products designed either to *conduct* (carry) or block the flow of electric current. *Electrical resistance* is a measure of the energy lost when a current passes through a given material. The lower the resistance, the lower the loss of energy. Copper and other materials that have low resistance are good conductors.

Dielectric strength describes a material's response to an electric field. It is used to evaluate how well a material can act as an *insulator* (an object that blocks current). A material's dielectric strength is the highest voltage difference a given thickness of the material can withstand before a current passes through it.

Magnetic properties indicate a material's response to a *magnetic field*—the region around a magnet or a conductor where the force of magnetism can be felt. *Magnetic susceptibility* is a measure of how well a material can be magnetized by an external magnetic field. A material is *ferromagnetic* if a magnetic field remains inside the material after the external magnetic field has been removed. The object composed of this material then becomes a permanent magnet.

Thermal properties reflect a material's response to heat. *Thermal conductivity* is a measure of how well a material conducts heat. Pots and pans are best made of materials that have a high thermal conductivity so they can efficiently and evenly transfer heat to food. *Heat capacity* measures a material's ability to contain heat. This property can be important in insulation materials.

Coefficient of thermal expansion indicates the increase in length of materials as they heat up. This is an important property to consider, for example, when building a telescope to orbit the earth. There is no air in outer space to equalize temperatures. Therefore, a spot on a telescope that is exposed to direct sunlight becomes much hotter than one not so exposed. If the telescope were made of material with a high coefficient of thermal expansion, its hot parts would expand much more than its cold parts, causing the telescope to warp.

Optical properties indicate how a material responds to light. The *refraction index* of a material indicates the degree to which the material changes the direction of a beam of light going through it. Manufacturers of eyeglasses use materials with a high refraction index because the higher the index is, the thinner the lenses can be made. These manufacturers must also consider *optical absorption,* a measure of how much light a material absorbs. The lower the optical absorption, the more transparent the material.

Natural materials

Natural materials generally are used as they are found, except for being cleaned, cut, or processed in a simple way that does not use much energy. Natural materials include stone and biological materials.

Stone. Certain types of rock are extremely strong and hard, and are therefore used as building stone. There are two types of building stone—*crushed stone* and *dimension stone.* Crushed stone is mixed with tarlike substances such as asphalt to make paving material. It is also mixed with portland cement and sand to make concrete. Common crushed stone includes limestone and granite. Dimension stone is used for finishing and decorating buildings. Common building stones include granite, limestone, marble, sandstone, and slate.

Biological materials are substances that develop as part of a plant or animal. Common plant materials include wood and various fibers such as cotton. Animal materials include leather and fibers such as wool.

Wood is a valuable biological material because of its strength, toughness, and low density. These properties make wood an excellent material for thousands of products, including houses, sailboats, furniture, baseball bats, and railroad ties. In addition, wood serves as a raw material for a wide variety of products, including paper, rayon, and charcoal.

Plant fibers used in their natural state include cotton, flax, and jute. Many plant fibers are flexible and can be spun into yarn. Cotton cloth is soft, absorbs moisture well, and is comfortable to wear. Flax is a strong fiber made from the stems of flax plants. It is made into linen fabric and other products, including thread and rope. Jute is a long, soft fiber that can be spun into coarse, strong threads. Jute products include cloth for wrapping bales of raw cotton.

Leather is a tough, flexible material made from the skin of animals. It is strong and durable. Leather can be made as flexible as cloth or as stiff as wood. Leather products range from shoes, belts, and gloves to baseballs, basketballs, and footballs. A soft leather known as *suede* serves as a clothing material.

Animal fibers include fur, wool, and silk. Fur and wool consist of animal hair. Because these materials can trap air, they are excellent insulators and are therefore used for clothing. Silk is the strongest natural fiber. Manufacturers unwind strands of silk from silkworm cocoons and make yarn for fabrics.

Extracted materials

An extracted material is created through processes that expend a great deal of energy or alter the microstructure of the substances used to make the material. Extracted materials include ceramics, metals and their alloys, plastics, rubber, composite materials, and semiconductors.

Ceramics include such everyday materials as brick, cement, glass, and porcelain. These materials are made from mineral compounds called *silicates,* including clay, feldspar, silica, and talc.

The properties of ceramics make them useful in a number of ways. Exposure to acids, gases, salts, and water generally does not corrode ceramics. Their freedom from corrosion makes ceramics an excellent material for dinnerware and for bathroom fixtures. Such ceramics as bricks and concrete are used in construction because of their low price and their resistance to crushing. The high dielectric strength of ceramics suits them for use as insulators for electric power lines. Their high melting points make them useful as materials for cookware. The transparency and strength of glass make it an obvious choice for applications ranging from windows to precision lenses for microscopes.

Certain advanced ceramics have an unusual property known as *superconductivity.* At extremely low temperatures, these materials conduct electric current with no resistance. Like other ceramics, however, these materials are brittle. Materials engineers are working to make them into commercially useful products.

Metals and alloys. People have used such metals as copper, gold, iron, and silver for thousands of years to make various practical and decorative objects. Today, metals are important in all aspects of construction and manufacturing. Metals are strong and are good conductors of heat and electric current. They are also easy to hammer into thin sheets and can be drawn out into wires.

Most metals are not used in their pure form because they are soft. Instead, they are used as ingredients in alloys.

One exception is copper, which is used in its pure form in electric wiring. Copper is an excellent conductor of electricity. The only better conductor is silver, but silver is too expensive for common use.

Iron and steel are the chief metals used in construction. Steel is an alloy of iron and carbon, as are the materials called *cast iron* and *wrought iron.*

The addition of other elements gives various kinds of steel different properties. For example, stainless steel, which contains at least 12 percent chromium, resists corrosion better than any other kind of steel. Nickel increases the hardness of steel. Tungsten makes steel more resistant to heat.

Plastics are synthetic materials made up primarily of long chains of molecules called *polymers.* There are two basic types of plastics: (1) *thermosetting plastics* (usually called *thermosets*) and (2) *thermoplastics.*

Thermosets can be heated and set only once; they cannot be remelted or reshaped. Because they are highly resistant to heat, thermosets are used for electrical parts, insulation foam, oven gaskets, and appliance handles. Other objects made of thermosets include luggage and parts for automobile bodies.

Thermoplastics can be melted and reshaped. Thermoplastics are used much more widely than thermosets because they are easier to process and require less time to set. Common thermoplastic products include telephone bodies, packaging, and bottles.

Rubber is made up of *elastomers,* polymers that stretch easily to several times their length and then return to their original shape. This property is known as *elasticity.* Rubber's elasticity, its ability to hold air and keep out water, and its toughness make it an important material.

About three-fifths of the rubber used in the United States goes into tires and tubes. Other uses include mechanical products such as gaskets, and waterproof clothing such as boots and raincoats. *Natural rubber* comes from the juice of a tree. *Synthetic rubber* is made from petroleum.

Composite materials. Engineers may artificially combine various materials to create a new *composite material.* Many composite materials contain a large amount of one substance to which fibers, flakes, or layers of another substance are added. Fiberglass, for example, consists of glass fibers and a polymer such as epoxy. This composite, in turn, can be used as an ingredient in another composite called a *fiberglass-reinforced plastic.* This is made up of cloth, mats, or individual strands of fiberglass added to a plastic. Fiberglass-reinforced plastics are used for such products as automobile bodies, fishing rods, and aircraft parts. Other common composites include carbon-reinforced plastics, which are used for such products as tennis rackets and golf clubs.

Composite materials usually have the favorable qualities of their ingredient materials. For example, fiberglass-reinforced plastics have the stiffness of glass but, like plastic, weigh less than glass.

Semiconductors are materials that conduct electricity better than insulators, but not as well as conductors, at room temperature. Extremely pure crystals of semiconductor material *doped* (combined) with small, precisely controlled amounts of other substances can perform many electronic functions. Such crystals, usually of silicon, are the building blocks of computer chips. In addition, *photovoltaic cells,* also called *solar cells,* consist of thin slices of doped semiconductor materials. When the sun shines on a photovoltaic cell, electric current flows from one side of the cell to the other. Photovoltaic cells power most artificial satellites.

The role of bonds

Wide differences in the properties of certain kinds of materials are a result of differences in *bonds*—forces that attract atoms and molecules to one another and hold them together.

Chemical bonds hold atoms together through the transfer or sharing of *electrons,* the negatively charged particles that whirl about the positively charged nucleus of an atom (see **Atom**). Weaker forces called *physical bonds* hold molecules together in a group.

Chemical bonds are *ionic, covalent,* or *metallic.* Ionic bonds are created by the transfer of electrons from one atom to one or more other atoms. In covalent bonding, two or more atoms share pairs of electrons. A shared pair consists of one electron from each of two atoms. In metallic bonding, all the atoms in a metal crystal share electrons. The shared electrons are free to move throughout the crystal. This movement creates a "sea" of negative electrons that surrounds and holds together the metal nuclei.

Physical bonds, also called *van der Waals forces,* hold molecules together in a group. Van der Waals forces are electrical forces caused by an interaction between charges of neighboring molecules. They are much weaker than chemical bonds because no transfer or sharing of electrons occurs.

One example of how bonding determines properties occurs in the area of electrical resistance. Ordinary ceramics are held together chiefly by covalent and ionic bonds. In these bonds, electrons are positioned near individual atoms. Much energy is therefore needed to make these electrons flow as electric current. Ceramics thus have a high resistance. By contrast, metals are held together by metallic bonds. Because many atoms share electrons, the electrons can circulate easily within the material. Metals therefore conduct current and have a low electrical resistance.

Bonding also determines important properties of polymers. These materials are made of long molecules featuring chainlike structures of carbon atoms linked by covalent bonds. In some polymers, covalent bonds also join chains to one another. These polymers are said to be *cross-linked.*

When a thermoset is heated for the first time, its chains cross-link. When the material is heated again, the cross-links do not break, so the material does not melt. A thermoplastic, however, does not form crosslinks. When it is heated, its physical bonds become so weak that the chains can slide past one another. The material therefore melts.   Andreas Mortensen

Related articles in *World Book* include:

Materials

World Book has hundreds of separate articles on materials. See **Ceramics; Composite materials; Metal; Plastics; Rock; Semiconductor; Textile; Wood;** and their lists of related articles.

Properties of materials

Absorption and adsorption	Dynamics	Light (How light behaves)
Acoustics	Elasticity	Magnetism
Aerodynamics	Electricity (Conduction of electric current)	(Magnetism of materials)
Catalysis		
Corrosion	Heat (How heat travels)	Melting point
Density		Refraction
Ductility	Hydraulics	Reflection
		Thermodynamics
		Viscosity

Other related articles

Atom	Cell	Molecule
Bond	Crystal	

Transplant, in medicine, is the transfer of any tissue or organ from one person to another. Transplanted tissues and organs replace diseased, damaged, or destroyed body parts. They can help restore the health of a person who might otherwise have died or been seriously disabled.

Transfers of tissue from one part of a person's own body to another part are also called transplants. Such procedures include skin grafts and hair transplants. This article discusses person-to-person transplants.

Doctors often divide transplants into two major types—organ transplants and tissue transplants. Organs, such as the heart and kidney, are complex structures that require a blood supply and oxygen to survive. Some organs, such as the heart and lungs, cannot be preserved for more than a few hours outside of the body. Doctors must transplant these organs very quickly. Tissues are also complex, but those that are commonly transplanted—bone, corneas, and skin—can be stored for much longer periods of time. Transplant tissues can be preserved in refrigerators or freezers at special tissue banks.

Another major difference between organ and tissue transplants involves the body's disease-fighting immune system. The immune system reacts differently to transplanted organs than it does to certain transplanted tissues. The immune system often attacks transplanted organs. Doctors use special techniques and drugs to protect the new organs. Transplants of certain tissues, however, do not usually require these procedures.

Tissue transplants

The most commonly transplanted tissues include corneas, skin, and bone. Doctors may use corneal transplants to improve the vision of patients with corneas that are scarred by injury or clouded over by infection. Corneal transplants have a success rate of more than 90 percent. Skin transplants may be used to temporarily cover areas of the body that have been badly burned and thus reduce the risk of infection. These transplants can last until skin from another part of the patient's body can be used for a permanent transplant.

Bone transplants may be used to replace bones that contain malignant tumors. The success rate of bone transplants varies from 70 to 95 percent, depending on the type of bone transplanted. A bone transplant differs from a bone marrow transplant, which is a more complex procedure used to treat patients with leukemia and other blood diseases. In a bone marrow transplant, surgeons remove bone marrow from the donor's hipbone and inject it into the patient's bloodstream.

Organ transplants

Organ transplants have become an established form of treatment for a variety of diseases and injuries. The most commonly transplanted organs are the heart, kidney, and liver. Other types of transplants, including lung and pancreas transplants, are less common.

Qualifying for a transplant. Once doctors have suggested transplantation as a possible form of treatment, patients undergo additional testing to determine whether they qualify. The most obvious qualification for a transplant is that patients must have badly damaged organs that do not respond to other forms of treatment.

These damaged body parts must either greatly reduce the quality of patients' lives or significantly shorten their life expectancy.

Waiting for a donor. After patients are accepted as transplant candidates, they must wait until suitable donors are found. The United Network for Organ Sharing (UNOS), headquartered in Richmond, Va., keeps lists of patients who are waiting for an organ transplant. In 1992, more than 30,000 patients in the United States waited for organ transplants. However, many of them did not receive a transplant because fewer than 5,000 donors provided organs that year.

There are three main types of donors—living people, people whose brain function has totally and irreversibly stopped, and *cadavers* (dead bodies). Living people can provide only those organs that they can live without. For example, a person can live with only one kidney and donate the other. Sometimes people can donate part of an organ without suffering harm. If someone donates part of the liver, the liver will grow back and replace the lost part. In most cases, however, transplant organs come from brain-dead or cadaver donors—because the organ is vital to life or because no living donor is available.

Cadaver organs are usually taken from someone who was involved in an accident injuring the head. After the accident, the brain dies, but the rest of the body is kept alive with a respirator or with other artificial means. Once all brain activity stops, hospital staff or a representative of a local Organ Procurement Organization (OPO) may ask the family about organ donation. If the family agrees, the OPO begins to search for appropriate recipients. After a recipient has been chosen, donor organs are removed by physicians and transported to recipients' hospitals. Meanwhile, the recipient is prepared for surgery.

Many patients die while awaiting an organ transplant

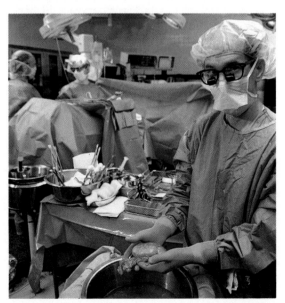

© Eric Sander, Gamma/Liaison

A kidney transplant is one of the most successful types of transplant surgery. In 90 percent or more of all cases, the transplanted kidney is still functioning after one year.

Commonly transplanted body parts

Transplants can be divided into two chief types: organ transplants and tissue transplants. The most commonly transplanted organs include the heart, kidney, liver, and lung. Corneas and bones are frequently transplanted tissues.

WORLD BOOK illustration by Barbara Cousins

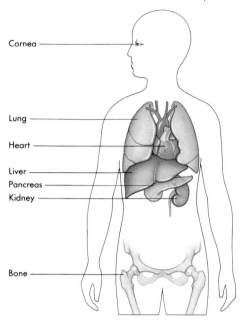

Cornea

Lung

Heart

Liver

Pancreas

Kidney

Bone

because the number of donors falls far short of the number needed. To save lives, health care professionals encourage more people to consider organ donation. People can express their desire to donate organs at the time of their death by signing and carrying a donor card or by marking the space on their driver's license.

Most organ transplant operations last several hours, and most patients survive the operation. Patients must remain in the hospital for a period of one to four weeks, depending on the particular organ.

Preventing rejection. A transplant succeeds only if doctors can prevent *rejection* of the transplant. Rejection occurs when the body's immune system attacks the

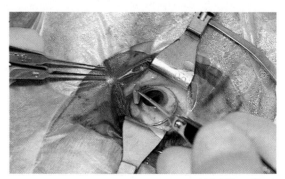

Medical College of Georgia

A transplant of the cornea, the clear tissue covering the eye, can restore sight lost because of injury or illness. Doctors have transplanted more corneas than any other body part.

new organ. The immune system fights disease by finding and destroying foreign materials in the body. The immune system does not distinguish between disease-causing foreign materials, such as viruses, and harmless ones, such as a transplanted liver. As a result, the body's defense system will try to destroy any transplant that it recognizes as foreign. Doctors try to prevent rejection by choosing the best donor. They also use special medication to protect the transplant.

Matching donors and recipients. To reduce the risk of immediate rejection of the transplant, doctors must find a donor who has the same blood type as the patient. For some organs—such as the lung, heart, and liver—it is also important that the donor's organ be similar in size to that of the recipient.

In addition to matching for blood type, physicians also try to match certain inherited proteins of the donor and the patient. These proteins, called *HLA antigens,* are found on the surface of cells. Scientists have identified many HLA antigens, and each person has a unique combination. Doctors try to match six different HLA antigens from the donor and recipient. A transplant is more likely to succeed if the donor's and recipient's HLA antigens match. HLA matching is used mainly in kidney and bone marrow transplantation.

The best possible organ donor would be the patient's identical twin. All their proteins would match perfectly, and the patient's immune system would not identify the transplant as different or foreign. As a result, rejection would not occur. In most cases, however, people waiting for organ transplants do not have identical twins. Relatives of the patient are the next best possible organ donors because they are most likely to have similar HLA antigens. In fact, there is a 25 percent chance of a complete HLA match between brothers and sisters.

Using immunosuppressive drugs. Because most transplants come from unrelated individuals, the patient receiving a transplant must take *immunosuppressive drugs.* These drugs prevent the body from rejecting the transplant by interfering with the immune system. Unfortunately, the drugs also prevent the body from defending itself against infections. As a result, patients can easily become infected while they are taking immunosuppressive drugs.

Immunosuppressive drugs that are commonly used to prevent organ rejection include azathioprine, cyclosporine, and prednisone. These drugs inhibit the action of cells of the immune system that are directly responsible for the rejection of the organ. Cyclosporine has proved especially useful because it interferes less than other immunosuppressive drugs with the immune system's ability to fight infection. Most transplant patients require a combination of cyclosporine and other immunosuppressives.

Survival rates. Kidney transplants are the most successful type of organ transplant. Ninety percent or more of these transplants are still functioning after one year. About 80 percent of heart transplant patients and about 75 percent of liver transplant patients survive for at least one year, and 60 to 70 percent of these patients live for five years or longer. But survival requires continued medical care, including close supervision, and patients must take immunosuppressive drugs for the rest of their lives. William A. Baumgartner

The reconstructed skeleton of an *Apatosaurus* makes a stunning exhibit in a museum. Scientists rebuild dinosaur skeletons by fitting together fossilized dinosaur bones and teeth. These skeletons help people visualize how dinosaurs may have looked.

Allosaurus, *AL uh SAWR uhs,* was a large, meat-eating dinosaur that lived about 150 million years ago. *Allosaurus* lived in what is now the western United States, including Colorado, Utah, and Wyoming. It grew about 36 feet (11 meters) long, stood about 7 feet (2 meters) high at the hips, and weighed about 2 short tons (1.8 metric tons).

The head of *Allosaurus* was 3 feet (0.9 meter) long. Its jaws had about 70 teeth, each 3 inches (8 centimeters) long with jagged edges for slicing flesh. Holes in the skull lightened the weight of the dinosaur's large head. A pair of distinctive low, bony bumps rose in front of the eyes. The short front legs had three strong, curved claws on each hand. The hind feet were birdlike, with three toes pointing forward and a small inner toe pointing backward. *Allosaurus* walked on two legs with its body parallel to the ground and held its long tail out behind for balance. The animal could rear up to a height of 12 feet (3.7 meters) or more.

Allosaurus preyed on other dinosaurs. Many dinosaurs, including *Apatosaurus* and *Diplodocus,* were much larger, and so *Allosaurus* may have eaten mostly smaller dinosaurs. When *Allosaurus* did eat larger dinosaurs, it may have attacked only the weaker ones, such as the young or the sick. It may also have eaten dinosaurs that had already died.   Peter Dodson

Ankylosaurus, *ANG kuh luh SAWR uhs,* was a large, armored dinosaur that lived between 68 million years and 65 million years ago in what is now western North America. The name *Ankylosaurus* means *fused lizard* and describes the dinosaur's armor, which consisted of bony pieces that had *fused,* or grown together. This heavy armor protected all the exposed parts of the body, including the head, back, and tail.

Ankylosaurus was one of the largest of the armored dinosaurs. It was about 30 feet (9 meters) long and weighed about 4 to 5 short tons (3.6 to 4.5 metric tons). *Ankylosaurus* was a plant-eater with small teeth. The dinosaur's triangular skull was 30 inches (76 centimeters) long and equally wide. A spike stuck out from each cheek, and two more stuck out from the back of the head. Short, thick legs supported the weight of the dinosaur's low, broad body. The tail ended in a big, heavy ball of bone.

When attacked, *Ankylosaurus* may have crouched down and pressed itself to the ground. In this position, the attacker could only bite or claw at the thick, hard armor. *Ankylosaurus* also may have defended itself by swinging its tail and hitting an attacker with the bony club at the end.   Peter Dodson

Apatosaurus, *uh PAT oh SAWR uhs* or *AP uh toh SAWR uhs,* was a giant, plant-eating dinosaur that lived about 150 million years ago in what is now the Western United States. It belonged to a group of huge, long-necked, long-tailed dinosaurs called *sauropods.*

Apatosaurus was about 70 feet (21 meters) long, stood about 15 feet (4.6 meters) high at the hips, and weighed about 33 short tons (30 metric tons). It had long, thin teeth and may have eaten tree leaves and ferns. Its nostrils were on top of its relatively small, slender head. The neck was about 20 feet (6 meters) long. The animal's straight, thick legs ended in broad feet, and the inner toe of each foot had a blunt claw. The front legs were shorter than the hind legs, and so the body sloped down from the hips to the neck. The tail extended about 30 feet (9 meters) and ended in a slender point.

Apatosaurus is the official name for this dinosaur, but it is also known as *Brontosaurus*. The American scientist Othniel C. Marsh, a pioneer in *paleontology* (the study of prehistoric life), first discovered an incomplete skeleton of this dinosaur in 1877. He named it *Apatosaurus.* Two years later, scientists found a more complete skeleton, which Marsh mistakenly believed to be a new type of dinosaur. He named it *Brontosaurus,* meaning *thunder lizard,* because of the noise that such a large animal must have made when it walked. But scientists soon realized that these two dinosaurs were the same, and so the first name, *Apatosaurus,* became the formally accepted name.　　Peter Dodson

Brachiosaurus, BRAK ee uh SAWR uhs or BRAY kee uh SAWR uhs, was a gigantic, plant-eating dinosaur that lived about 150 million years ago in what are now Africa and North America. The name *Brachiosaurus* means *arm lizard.* Unlike most dinosaurs, *Brachiosaurus* had arm bones that were longer than its leg bones. These long arm bones placed the shoulders higher than the hips, and so the body sloped down from the base of the neck to the tail.

Brachiosaurus was about 75 feet (23 meters) long, stood about 40 feet (12 meters) tall, and weighed at least 40 short tons (36 metric tons). For many years, *Brachiosaurus* was thought to be the largest and heaviest dinosaur. But scientists have discovered even larger ones, including *Ultrasauros* (also spelled *Ultrasaurus*), a dinosaur that stood about 55 feet (17 meters) tall.

Brachiosaurus was a *sauropod,* a large dinosaur with a small head and a long neck and tail. But compared to other sauropods, such as *Apatosaurus*, *Brachiosaurus* had a longer neck and a shorter, thicker tail. The animal's head featured a broad, flat snout and a large, dome-shaped ridge above the eyes. The nostrils opened from the ridge at the very top of the head.

Brachiosaurus bones found in western North America indicate that the dinosaur lived entirely on dry land. It probably ate leaves from the tops of trees, as giraffes do. Bones were also found near the sea in Tanzania in eastern Africa, where *Brachiosaurus* apparently lived in lowlands near the shore.　　Peter Dodson

Diplodocus, duh PLAHD uh kuhs, was an extremely long, slender, plant-eating dinosaur that lived about 150 million years ago in what is now the Western United States. It belonged to a group of giant, plant-eating dinosaurs known as *sauropods.* The first *Diplodocus* bones were found in 1877 near Morrison, Colo. The name *Diplodocus* means *double beam* and describes the beams of bone in the underside of the animal's tail.

Diplodocus grew to about 90 feet (27 meters) long and weighed about 11 tons (10 metric tons). The neck was about 26 feet (8 meters) long and had 15 vertebrae. The skull was relatively small, only about 2 feet (61 centimeters) long, with slender peglike teeth in the front of the mouth. The tail had more than 70 vertebrae and stretched about 45 feet (14 meters), tapering to a whiplike end. The animal could have swung the tail to defend itself against enemies. *Diplodocus* stood about 13 feet (4 meters) high from the ground to the hips. The front legs were much shorter than the hind legs. The dinosaur might have been able to stand on its hind legs, using its tail for support. *Diplodocus* ate large amounts of cycad, fern, and ginkgo leaves.　　Peter Dodson

Stegosaurus, STEHG uh SAWR uhs, was a large, plant-eating dinosaur that lived about 150 million years ago in what is now the western United States. *Stegosaurus* had two rows of bony plates shaped like huge arrowheads sticking out of its back and tail. Scientists are not certain how these rows of plates were positioned on the animal's back.

Stegosaurus grew up to 30 feet (9 meters) long and had a heavy, bulky body. The dinosaur's small, narrow head had a beak at the front and teeth farther back. The front legs were less than half as long as the back legs, and so the body sloped down from the hips. At the end of the tail, the animal had a pair of bony spikes, each about 3 feet (0.9 meter) long. *Stegosaurus* could have defended itself by swinging its heavy tail and hitting an attacker with its sharp spikes.

No one really knows why *Stegosaurus* had its bony plates. They may have discouraged attackers or attracted mates. The plates may also have helped *Stegosaurus* warm up and cool down. It could warm up by turning the broad, flat sides of the plates toward the sun to soak up heat. If it became too warm, air moving along its back could have cooled blood flowing through the thin plates.　　Peter Dodson

Tyrannosaurus, tih RAN uh SAWR uhs or ty RAN uh SAWR uhs, was a large, meat-eating dinosaur that lived about 68 million to 65 million years ago in what is now western North America. The name *Tyrannosaurus* means *tyrant lizard.* A tyrant is a cruel, powerful ruler. *Tyrannosaurus* got its name because scientists thought that such a huge beast must have ruled over all other animals, killing whatever and whenever it chose. The scientific name for this species of dinosaur is *Tyrannosaurus rex.*

Tyrannosaurus was the largest meat-eating dinosaur. It was about 40 feet (12 meters) long, stood about 12 feet (3.7 meters) high at the hips, and weighed about 7 short tons (6.3 metric tons). *Tyrannosaurus* could rear up to a height of 18 feet (5.5 meters). However, the animal usually walked with its body parallel to the ground, holding its heavy, muscular tail out behind for balance.

Tyrannosaurus had a huge skull that grew as long as $4\frac{1}{2}$ feet (135 centimeters). The strong jaws had sharp teeth that were about 6 inches (15 centimeters) long. The animal's short, flexible neck and powerful body allowed *Tyrannosaurus* to use its monstrous jaws to rip off large chunks of flesh. The dinosaur's other deadly weapons were the sharp claws on its feet. *Tyrannosaurus* could hold an animal in its jaws and slash and tear at the body with its large claws.

Unlike the rest of the dinosaur's body, its arms were tiny, and its hands had only two fingers tipped with little claws. Although the arms were small, they were strong. *Tyrannosaurus* may have used the arms to push itself up after it had been lying down.

Some scientists have suggested that the huge *Tyrannosaurus* would have moved too slowly to hunt live animals and instead fed on dead animals. But most scientists think *Tyrannosaurus* was an active hunter that could run for short distances. *Tyrannosaurus* may have waited in hiding for a plant-eating dinosaur, such as the duck-billed dinosaur, to get close. *Tyrannosaurus* could then make a quick rush and attack the animal with its sharp teeth and strong jaws.　　Peter Dodson

Index

How to use the index

This index covers the contents of the 1993, 1994, and 1995 editions of *Science Year,* The World Book Science Annual.

Each index entry gives the last two digits of the edition year, followed by a colon and the page number or numbers. For example, this entry means that information on the Sloan Digital Sky Survey may be found on pages 185 and 197 of the 1994 *Science Year.*

When there are many references to a topic, they are grouped alphabetically by clue words under the main topic. For example, the clue words under **Smoking** group the references to that topic under three subtopics.

An entry in all capital letters indicates that there is a Science News Update article with that name in at least one of the three volumes covered in this index. References to the topic in other articles may also be listed in the entry.

The "see" and "see also" cross references indicate that references to the topic are listed under another entry in the index.

An entry that only begins with a capital letter indicates that there are no Science News Update articles with that title but that information on this topic may be found in the editions and on the pages listed.

The indication (il.) after a page number means that the reference is to an illustration only.

An index entry followed by *WBE* refers to a new or revised *World Book Encyclopedia* article in the *Science Year* supplement section. This entry means that there is a *World Book Encyclopedia* article on *Stegosaurus* on page 352 of the 1995 *Science Year.*

Index

A

A8 (automobile), **95:** 262-263
Absolute zero, **93:** 161-173
Absorption lines, **94:** 218-219
Acanthostega (animal), **93:** 285
Accelerators, Particle. See **Particle accelerators**
Accidents. See **Risk assessment**
Accretion disks, **95:** 22 (il.), 24, 26-27, **94:** 226-227, **93:** 243
ACE gene, **93:** 291
Acetaminophen, **95:** 322-323
Acetylcholine, **94:** 277
Achondrites, **93:** 37
Acid rain, **95:** 181, 261, **93:** 211
Acquired immune deficiency syndrome. See **AIDS**
Acrophobia, **95:** 39-40
Actuators (engineering), **94:** 162
Addiction. See **Alcoholism; Drug abuse**
Adenomas, **93:** 313
Adenosine deaminase (ADA) deficiency, **95:** 133-135, **93:** 200-202
Adenosine triphosphate, **94:** 278
Adolescents, **95:** 291, **93:** 326-327
Advanced Communications Technology Satellite (ACTS), **95:** 306
Advertising, **95:** 296-297
Aegean Sea (tanker), **94:** 250
Aerobraking, **95:** 308
Aerodynamics, **94:** 67
Aerosol sprays, **93:** 215, 260-261
Africa
  AIDS, **93:** 101
  cats, **93:** 78, 80 (il.), 90-91
  cheetahs, **95:** 47, 59
  human origins, **95:** 208-209, 211, 220, **93:** 118, 232-233
  Sahel drought, **93:** 121-133
African Burial Ground, **94:** 117-131
Aging, **95:** 238
AGRICULTURE, **95:** 206-208, **94:** 202-205, **93:** 228-231
  ancient, **95:** 218, **93:** 48, 54
  biotic impoverishment, **93:** 222
  cloning, **95:** 93
  global warming, **93:** 219
  population growth, **93:** 208
  Sahel, **93:** 130
  songbird population, **94:** 38-39, 42
  wetlands loss, **93:** 26
  see also **Botany; Food; Pesticides**
AIDS
  cancer link, **95:** 284
  cats, **95:** 81-84
  deaths, **95:** 298
  drugs, **95:** 282-284, **94:** 243, **93:** 271-273
  fullerene HIV block, **95:** 246-247
  Gallo case, **95:** 302
  official definition, **94:** 293
  Osborn interview, **93:** 93-105
  pregnancy, **95:** 282-283
  retrovirus, **95:** 123-124, 131-132, 137
  vaccine, **93:** 105
AIDS-like illness, **94:** 271-272, 294 (il.)
Air cleaners, **94:** 317-320
Air conditioners, **94:** 248, **93:** 358-360
Air pollution, **93:** 209-213
  air cleaners, **94:** 317-320
  automobile emissions, **95:** 318,
  320-321, **93:** 63-75
  biomass energy, **95:** 189, 192
  fine particulates, **95:** 266
  fossil fuels, **95:** 180-181, **93:** 211
  indoor, **93:** 285
  Persian Gulf War, **93:** 282, 306
  risks, **95:** 161, 163
  see also **Acid rain; Ozone pollution; Smog**
Air pressure. See **Barometric pressure**
Airbags, **93:** 342-345
Airborne Arctic Stratospheric Expedition II, **93:** 306-307
Aircraft. See **Aviation**
Akbar the Great, **95:** 47, 49-50
Akkadian empire, **95:** 211-213
Alaskan wolves, **95:** 254-255
Alcohol advertising, **95:** 296-297
Alcoholism, **93:** 325
Alkali builders, **93:** 351-352
Allende meteor, **93:** 38
Allergy, **93:** 89
Allosaurus (dinosaur), *WBE,* **95:** 351
Alpha AXP (microprocessor), **94:** 236
Altai Mountains, **94:** 265
Aluminum, **95:** 262-263
Alyeska Trans-Alaska Pipeline, **95:** 267
Alzheimer's disease, **95:** 274, 282, **94:** 277, **93:** 310
Amber, **94:** 260 (il.)
Ambulocetus natans (animal), **95:** 270 (il.), 286
America Online (computer network), **95:** 252
Amino acids, **93:** 194
Ammonites, **95:** 78-81
Amorphous cells, **95:** 262
Amphibians, **95:** 63, 70, 94-101, 252-254, 261, **93:** 285
Amur tigers, **95:** 254
Amylase (enzyme), **95:** 136
Amyloid precursor protein, **94:** 277, **93:** 310
Amyotrophic lateral sclerosis (ALS), **95:** 275 (il.), **94:** 256-266
Analgesics, **95:** 322-323
Analog signals, **95:** 166-167
Analogy, and risk, **95:** 157-158
Andean civilization, **93:** 45-61
Anderson, Forrest N., **95:** 235
Andrews, Rodney D., Jr., **95:** 256
Andromeda galaxy, **95:** 24, 227 (il.)
Anemia, **94:** 270
Anencephaly, **94:** 284
Angiosperms, **95:** 271
Animals
  cloning, **95:** 93-94
  exotic invaders, **94:** 133-145
  ocean crust formation, **94:** 264
  pollution, **93:** 209-213
  risk assessment studies, **95:** 159
  river ecosystem, **95:** 63-66, 70-71
  wetlands, **93:** 22-24
  see also **Biology; Endangered species; Zoology;** and specific animals
Ankylosaurus (dinosaur), *WBE,* **95:** 351
Anning, Mary, **95:** 81-84
Antarctica
  dinosaurs, **95:** 269
  meteorites, **93:** 39
  ozone hole, **95:** 233, **94:** 253, 276,
  93: 215-216, 283-284, 307
  space photos, **93:** 331 (il.)
ANTHROPOLOGY, **95:** 208-211, **94:** 205-208, **93:** 231-233
  books, **95:** 242, **94:** 228
Antibiotics, **95:** 322
Antihistamines, **95:** 323-324
Antimatter, **95:** 288, **94:** 187, 188, 191-192, 198, 218 (il.), 233
Antioxidants, **95:** 285
Antiparticles. See **Antimatter**
Anxiety, **94:** 292-293
Apatosaurus (dinosaur), **95:** 87 (il.), 89
  WBE, **95:** 351-352
Apolipoprotein-E (ApoE), **95:** 274, 282
Apple Computer, Inc., **95:** 247-249, **94:** 235 (il.), 236-237, **93:** 264, 267
Apple maggots, **94:** 204
Appliances, Home, **94:** 248, **93:** 358-360
ARCHAEOLOGY, **95:** 211-220
ARCHAEOLOGY, NEW WORLD, **94:** 208-211, **93:** 234-237
  African Burial Ground, **94:** 117-131
  Andean civilization, **93:** 45-61
  book, **93:** 254
  Moche civilization, **94:** 45-57
  see also **Native Americans**
ARCHAEOLOGY, OLD WORLD, **94:** 212-216, **93:** 237-241
  Sahara region, **93:** 125-128
Archaeopteryx, **95:** 270, **94:** 256
Arctic
  ancient Indians, **95:** 215-218
  ozone layer depletion, **94:** 253, **93:** 216, 284, 306-307
Arecibo telescope, **94:** 110-111
Arenal volcano, **93:** 235-237
Argon-argon dating, **95:** 109
Armenia, **94:** 295
Army radiation experiments, **95:** 300
ARPAnet (computer network), **95:** 172
Arthritis, Rheumatoid. See **Rheumatoid arthritis**
Asbestos, **94:** 318
Asexual reproduction, **95:** 92-93
Aspartame, **95:** 284, **93:** 141, 146
Aspen trees, **94:** 231 (il.)
Aspero (site), **93:** 50-54
Aspirin, **95:** 322-323, **93:** 298-299
Asteroids
  collision danger to Earth, **94:** 221, **93:** 30, 32-33 (il.), 35-36
  extinction theories, **95:** 119, **93:** 287, 292
  moons of, **95:** 228-229
  space probe studies, **94:** 220-221, **93:** 247-249
Asthma, **93:** 284
Astrometry, **94:** 112-113
ASTRONOMY, **95:** 221-229
  books, **95:** 242, **94:** 228, **93:** 254
ASTRONOMY, MILKY WAY, **94:** 216-219, **93:** 241-246
  see also **Milky Way Galaxy; Stars**
ASTRONOMY, SOLAR SYSTEM, **94:** 219-222, **93:** 246-249
  see also **Solar system**
ASTRONOMY, UNIVERSE, **94:** 222-227, **93:** 250-253
  see also **Black holes; Galaxies; Universe**
Asymmetric digital subscriber line

Index

Index

Index

Index

Peanut plant, 94: 202-203
Peas, 95: 207-208
Peat, 94: 252, 93: 18
Pecking orders, 94: 306
Pectin, 93: 143
Pen computers, 93: 263 (il.), 265
Penguins, 94: 213
Pentium (microprocessor), 95: 248, 249, 94: 235-236
Peptic ulcers, 94: 243
Peptides, 95: 245-246
Peregrine falcons, 95: 254
Periodontal disease, 94: 242, 93: 270
Permian Period, 93: 285-286
Persian Gulf War, 94: 294-295, 93: 239, 282-283, 306
Personal digital assistants, 95: 249, 94: 235 (il.), 236-237
Peru, 94: 47, 82-83, 85
Peru Current, 94: 75
Pesticides, 95: 159-162, 267-268, 94: 321-324, 93: 209, 211, 258
PET scans. See Positron emission tomography
Petroleum
  formation, 95: 118
  plastic bags, 95: 326-327
  renewable alternatives, 95: 180-181, 184, 201, 202
  see also Gasoline; Oil spills; Oil wells
pH level, 94: 233-234
Pharmacology. See Drugs
Phase change (engineering), 94: 166-168
Phenylketonuria (PKU), 93: 193
Pheromones, 93: 209
Phosphates, 93: 352-353
Photo-CD player, 93: 277
Photocatalysts, 93: 262
Photochemical smog, 93: 67
Photographs, Preservation of, 95: 310-312
Photolyase, 95: 253
Photoreceptors, 95: 241
Photosynthesis, 94: 264, 93: 211, 219, 220
Photovoltaic cells, 95: 195-197, 262
Physical fitness. See Exercise
PHYSICS, 95: 288-292, 94: 287-291, 93: 318-323
  books, 95: 243, 94: 229
  Lederman interview, 95: 138-149
  Nobel Prizes, 95: 234, 94: 280-281, 93: 311-312
  science student awards, 95: 237, 94: 298, 93: 329
Phytoplankton, 95: 259, 94: 82, 138-139, 286, 93: 277
Piezoelectric materials, 94: 164-166
Pigs, 95: 218, 94: 140 (il.), 93: 228-229
Pinatubo, Mount. See Mount Pinatubo
Pitohui (bird), 94: 302-303
Plague, 93: 101-102
Planetesimals, 94: 104-108
Planets, 95: 221, 94: 103-115, 180, 93: 244-245
  see also Astronomy and individual planets
Plants
  chaotic growth, 93: 275
  cloning, 95: 93

electrical signals, 94: 230
exotic invaders, 94: 133-145
genetic engineering, 93: 258
global warming, 94: 252, 93: 219-220
insect evolution, 95: 271
Jurassic Period, 95: 81
light detection, 95: 240-241
ocean crust formation, 94: 264
pollution effects, 93: 209-213
river ecosystem, 95: 63-67, 70-71
self-pollination, 95: 240
see also Agriculture; Biology; Botany; Endangered species; Forests; Wetlands; and specific plants
Plaque, Dental, 94: 314, 93: 270
Plasma (physics), 95: 22 (il.), 27, 197, 290-292, 93: 279, 318-320
Plasmids, 93: 195-197
Plastics, 95: 325-328, 93: 258, 261-262
Plate tectonics
  computer model, 94: 264
  earthquakes, 95: 278-279, 94: 262-263
  geothermal energy, 95: 191
  ocean crust formation, 94: 261-264
  satellite research, 94: 300
  volcanoes, 95: 276
  WBE, 93: 368-371
Pleiades (star cluster), 94: 181 (il.)
Pleistocene Epoch, 95: 271
Plesiosaurs, 95: 83
Plinian column, 95: 113 (il.), 115
Plunkett, Roy J., 95: 257
Pluto, 95: 229, 94: 18 (il.), 21
Plutonium, 95: 300, 93: 323
Point bars, 95: 62, 65 (il.)
Poisson, Roger, 95: 302
Pollination, 95: 240
Polls. See Public opinion polls
Pollution, 93: 209-213, 222-224
  see also Air pollution; Environment; Water pollution
Polyacrylamide, 95: 206 (il.)
Polychlorinated biphenyls (PCB's), 93: 213
Polycyclic aromatic hydrocarbons (PAH's), 94: 219
Polyethylene, 95: 326
Polymerase chain reaction (PCR), 95: 234
Polymers, 94: 267, 93: 260-261
Pompeii, 93: 240 (il.)
Pools, 95: 63, 65 (il.), 71, 75
Population bottlenecks, 95: 54
Population growth, 94: 91, 93: 206-208
Positron emission tomography (PET), 94: 147-148, 158, 159, 93: 308-309
Positronium, 94: 233
Positrons, 93: 181, 182 (il.)
Possum, Brushtail, 94: 136 (il.)
Pottery, 94: 49-50, 93: 54-55, 234
Poverty, 94: 98, 93: 206
  see also Developing nations
PowerBook Duo (computer), 94: 237
PowerPC microprocessor, 95: 247-249
Prairie dogs, 93: 275-276
Precipitation, 93: 354
Predators, 95: 78, 260-261, 94: 34-35, 136-139, 93: 90-91

Pregnancy, 95: 282-283
Prehistoric animals, 95: 268-271, 94: 205-208, 93: 285-287
  Jurassic Period, 95: 77-89
  see also Dinosaurs; Fossil studies
Prehistoric people, 95: 208-211, 94: 205-208, 93: 231-233
  WBE, 94: 337-348
  see also Anthropology; Archaeology; Fossil studies; Native Americans; Neanderthals
Premature infants, 93: 302
Preservation of documents, 95: 310-314
Primate, Fossil, 95: 269 (il.)
Privacy, 95: 175-177
Probability, 95: 152
Progesterone, 93: 340
Programs. See Computer software; Computers and electronics
Pronghorns, 93: 334
Prostaglandins, 95: 322-323
Prostate cancer, 95: 284-285
Protective headgear, 95: 265-266
Proteins, 95: 124-125, 93: 136, 194, 197-198
Proterozoic Eon, 93: 296
Protogalaxies, 94: 195
Protons, 94: 186-187, 93: 321, 323
Protoplanets, 93: 38, 43
Proxima Centauri (star), 94: 65, 109, 112
Pseudoryx (animal), 95: 241 (il.)
PSR 1257+12 (pulsar), 94: 103-104, 115
PSYCHOLOGY, 95: 292-295, 94: 291-293, 93: 324-325
  virtual reality systems, 95: 39-40
  see also Brain
Pterodactyls, 95: 84, 89 (il.)
Ptolemy, 95: 176-177
PUBLIC HEALTH, 95: 296-298, 94: 293-295, 93: 325-327
  book, 95: 243
Public opinion polls, 93: 346-349
Pulsars
  binary, 95: 234
  gamma rays, 93: 181, 185, 186 (il.)
  Geminga, 94: 216-217
  high-speed, 94: 217-218
  planets around, 95: 221, 94: 103-104, 114-115, 93: 244-245
  radio image, 93: 243 (il.)
Pumice, 95: 110
Purring, 93: 78-79
Pyroclastic flows, 95: 113 (il.), 115, 120, 277

Q

Quaggas, 93: 340
Quantum mechanics, 95: 24-25, 290
Quarks, 95: 141-144, 288, 94: 187, 188, 288-289
Quartz, Shocked, 93: 286
Quasars, 95: 24, 26, 94: 224-225, 93: 176, 184-187, 252

R

Rabbits, 94: 306
Radar, 94: 32

Index

Index

Acknowledgments

The publishers of *Science Year* gratefully acknowledge the courtesy of the following artists, photographers, publishers, institutions, agencies, and corporations for the illustrations in this volume. Credits should read from top to bottom, left to right on their respective pages. All entries marked with an asterisk (*) denote illustrations created exclusively for *Science Year*. All maps, charts, and diagrams were prepared by the *Science Year* staff unless otherwise noted.

2	David Hiser, Photographers/Aspen; EOSAT
3	Institute of Human Origins; Reuters/Bettmann; NASA; Bettmann
4	Allosaurus model by Stephen Czerkas © 1986; Roger Ressmeyer, Starlight
5	Chuck O'Rear, West Light; Ken Abbott
10	Julian Baum, <u>New Scientist</u> (Science Photo Library from Photo Researchers); NASA
11	Richard L. Coleman; Bruce Davidson, Animals Animals
12	Julian Baum, <u>New Scientist</u> (Science Photo Library from Photo Researchers)
16-19	Roberta Polfus*
22-23	Roberta Polfus*
25	Holland Ford, Richard J. Harms, Johns Hopkins University/NASA
28	Computer Graphics by VPL Research (Peter Menzel); NASA
31	Microsoft Corporation; Lockheed; NASA
32	Virtual Presence Ltd.; Joe Rogers*;
34	Andy Freeberg; Intel Corporation; Andy Freeberg
37	Matsushita
38	Peter Menzel; © Stan Leary, Georgia Tech Research Corporation
40	Peter Menzel
41	NASA
42	Peter Menzel
44	Joe McDonald, Animals Animals
48	Erwin and Peggy Bauer, Bruce Coleman Ltd.; Anup & Manoj Shah, Animals Animals
53	NOAHS Center
54	Bruce Davidson, Animals Animals
56	Cheetah Conservation Fund
57	Cheetah Conservation Fund; Fossil Rim Wildlife Center
60	Robert I. Selby
64-65	Robin Dewitt*
68	Robin Dewitt*; Tennessee Valley Authority
69	Robin Dewitt*
72	Robin Dewitt*
73	Joel Robine, AFP; Carr Clifton
74	Richard L. Coleman
76	Allosaurus model by Stephan Czerkas © 1986; "Extinct animals that once lived where Dorsetshire now is," a scene from the <u>Wonders of the Earth Sea and Sky</u> (1837) by Peter Parley (Samuel Goodrich).
79	Bruce Coleman Ltd.; The Natural History Museum, London
80	The Natural History Museum, London; "The Oolitic [Jurassic] Period," from Franz Unger's <u>Primitive World</u> (1851).
82	Heather Angel, Biofotos; By permission of the Trustees of the British Museum of Natural History; © Douglas Henderson
87	© Douglas Henderson; Courtesy Department of Library Services American Museum of Natural History; Bruce Selyem, Museum of the Rockies
89	"Como Bluff Jurassic." Drawn by R. T. Bakker. Painted by Patrick Redman.
94	Carol Brozman*
96	Dept. of Biological Sciences University of Minnesota; Granada Biosciences
99-100	Carol Brozman*
103	©1993 Universal Studios/ Amblin Productions from Industrial Light and Magic
106	Robin Dewitt*
111-112	Robin Dewitt*
117	EOSAT; Chris Judson, Bandelier National Monument
120	Air Logistics (New Zealand) Ltd.
122	CNRI/Science Photo Library from Photo Researchers
125	Roberta Polfus*
128-129	Roberta Polfus*
130	Roberta Polfus*
133	Lennart Nilsson, Boehringer Ingelheim International, GMBH
134	Roberta Polfus*
135	John T. Crawford, National Institutes of Health
139	Ralph Brunke*
141	Ralph Brunke*
142-143	Fermilab Visual Media Services
144	Ralph Brunke*
147	Ralph Brunke*
149	Fermilab Visual Media Services; Ralph Brunke*
150-151	Johnston Clark*
153	Johnston Clark*
154-157	Johnston Clark*
159-161	Johnston Clark*
165	Dave Joly*
168	WORLD BOOK photo; Dave Joly*; Philips Consumer Electronics Company
170	Dave Joly*
174	Rob Crandall; Time Warner Cable; Rob Crandall
178	Jeff Blanton, Tony Stone Images; Tony Craddock, Tony Stone Images; Kenetech Corporation
179	Pacific Gas and Electric Company
181	Len Ebert*
182	Peter Lamberti, Tony Stone Images; Chris Jones, Arch Mineral Company; Tony Craddock, Tony Stone Images
183	Jim Pickerell, Tony Stone Images
186	Len Ebert*; Pacific Gas and Electric Company
188	National Renewable Energy Laboratory
189	Len Ebert*
192	Len Ebert*; National Renewable Energy Laboratory
195	Len Ebert*; National Renewable Energy Laboratory
196	Lajet Energy Company; Len Ebert*; National Renewable Energy Laboratory
198	Greek National Tourist Office
199	Kenetech Corporation; Len Ebert*
204	David Hiser, Photographers/Aspen
205	NASA; Lockheed; NASA
206	U.S. Dept. of Agriculture
207	Max Glaskin
209	AP/Wide World
210	Institute of Human Origins
212	David Hiser, Photographers/Aspen
213	Zev Radovan, Tel Dan Excavations
214	Randall White
215	University of Chicago
217	Maya Mountains Archeological Project; Jeanne Randall; Linda Schele
218	Jeffrey Newbury © The Walt Disney Co. Reprinted with permission of <u>Discover</u> Magazine.
219	Oriental Institute, University of Chicago
220	Ancient Biblical Manuscript Center/ Jet Propulsion Laboratory
223	David Sprayberry, University of Arizona
225	Lawrence Livermore National Laboratory
226	David Malin, Anglo-Australian Observatory
227	NASA
229	Janet Luu, Stanford University; Joseph Harrington, Massachusetts Institute of Technology
231	EOSAT
232	Ken Abbott, University of Colorado
235	Chet Gordon, Gamma/Liaison
237	Westinghouse Electric Corporation
239	Ivan Sazima, <u>Discover</u> Magazine
241	Asian Bureau of Conservation
245	M. Reza Ghadiri, Juan R. Granja, Ronald A. Milligan, Duncan E. McRee and Nina Khazanovich, The Scripps Research Institute
246	Sandia National Laboratories

World Book Encyclopedia, Inc., provides high-quality educational and reference products for the family and school. They include THE WORLD BOOK~RUSH-PRESBYTER-IAN-ST. LUKE'S MEDICAL CENTER~MEDICAL ENCYCLOPEDIA, a 1,072-page fully illustrated family health reference; THE WORLD BOOK OF MATH POWER, a two-volume set that helps students and adults build math skills; THE WORLD BOOK OF WORD POWER, a two-volume set that is designed to help your entire family write and speak more success-fully; and the HOW TO STUDY video, a presentation of key study skills with information students need to succeed in school. For further information, write World Book Ency-clopedia, Inc.; 2515 E. 43rd St.; P.O. Box 182265; Chattanooga TN 37422-7265.